KENJI TSURUBUCHI

3

Touge Oni

PRIMAL GODS IN ANCIENT TIMES

Like Hitokoto-Nushi's stone bridge, I fear the
night's vows will never come to fruition.

I too cannot bear the thought of being
seen in the morning's light.
—Kodai-no-Kimi, from the imperial poetry
anthology *Shuui Wakashuu*—

Contents

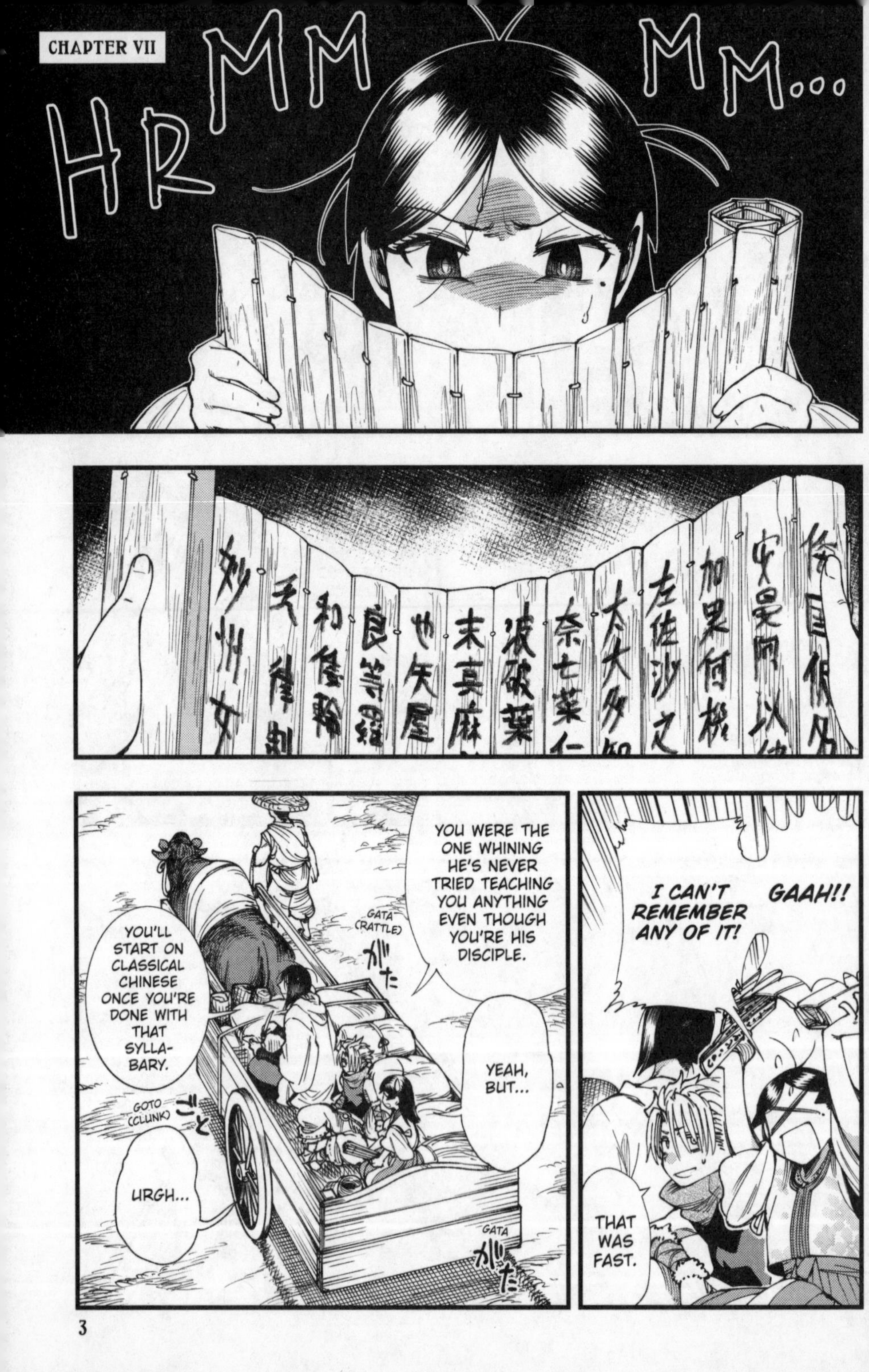
CHAPTER VII
HRMMMM...
GAAH!!
I CAN'T REMEMBER ANY OF IT!
THAT WAS FAST.
YOU WERE THE ONE WHINING HE'S NEVER TRIED TEACHING YOU ANYTHING EVEN THOUGH YOU'RE HIS DISCIPLE.
GATA (RATTLE) がた
YOU'LL START ON CLASSICAL CHINESE ONCE YOU'RE DONE WITH THAT SYLLABARY.
YEAH, BUT...
GOTO (CLUNK) ごと
URGH...
GATA がた

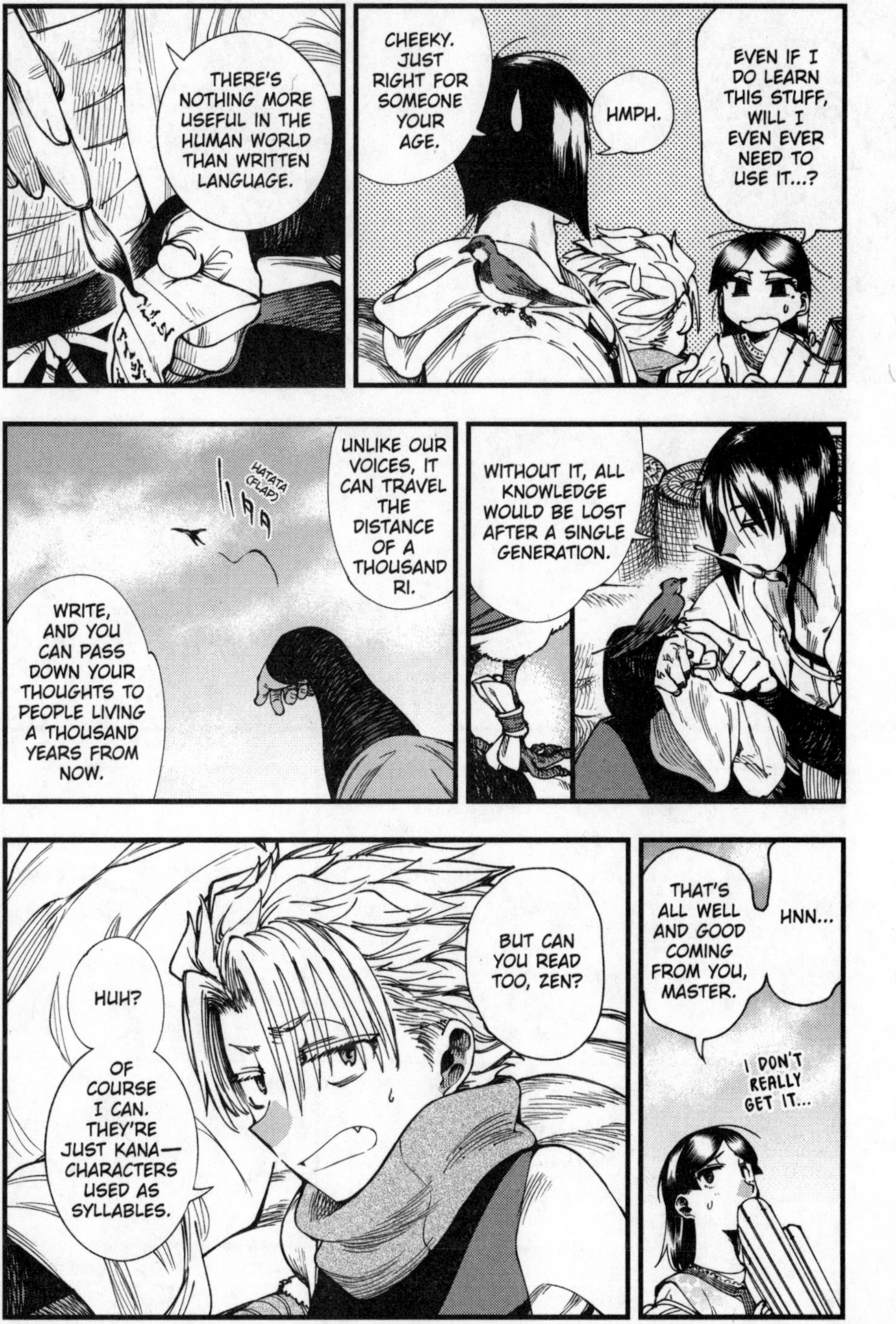
EVEN IF I DO LEARN THIS STUFF, WILL I EVEN EVER NEED TO USE IT...?
HMPH.
CHEEKY. JUST RIGHT FOR SOMEONE YOUR AGE.
THERE'S NOTHING MORE USEFUL IN THE HUMAN WORLD THAN WRITTEN LANGUAGE.
WITHOUT IT, ALL KNOWLEDGE WOULD BE LOST AFTER A SINGLE GENERATION.
UNLIKE OUR VOICES, IT CAN TRAVEL THE DISTANCE OF A THOUSAND RI.
HATATA (FLAP)
WRITE, AND YOU CAN PASS DOWN YOUR THOUGHTS TO PEOPLE LIVING A THOUSAND YEARS FROM NOW.
HNN...
THAT'S ALL WELL AND GOOD COMING FROM YOU, MASTER.
I DON'T REALLY GET IT...
BUT CAN YOU READ TOO, ZEN?
HUH?
OF COURSE I CAN. THEY'RE JUST KANA—CHARACTERS USED AS SYLLABLES.

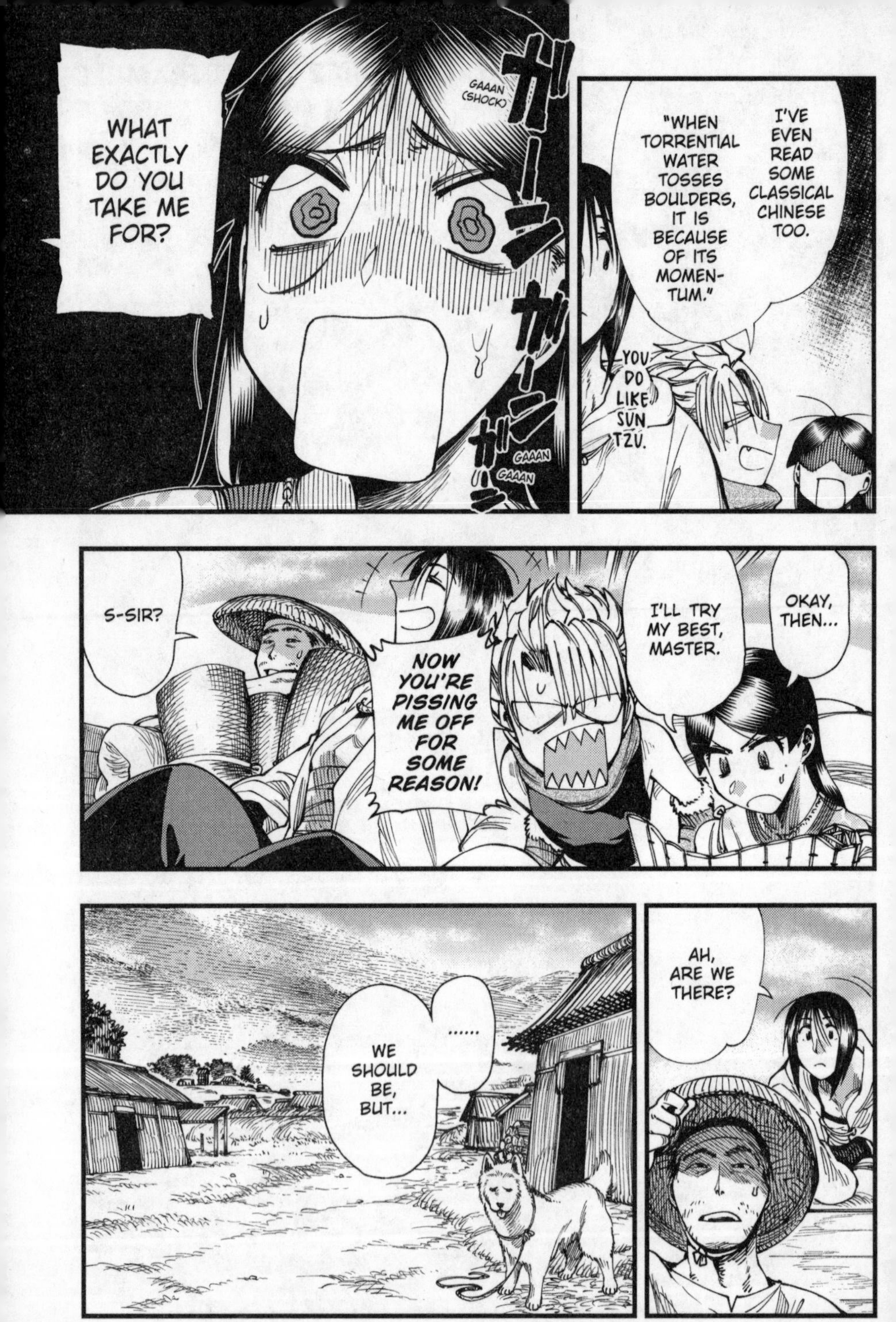
I'VE EVEN READ SOME CLASSICAL CHINESE TOO.
"WHEN TORRENTIAL WATER TOSSES BOULDERS, IT IS BECAUSE OF ITS MOMENTUM."
YOU DO LIKE SUN TZU.
GAAAN (SHOCK)
WHAT EXACTLY DO YOU TAKE ME FOR?
GAAAN
GAAAN
OKAY, THEN...
I'LL TRY MY BEST, MASTER.
NOW YOU'RE PISSING ME OFF FOR SOME REASON!
S-SIR?
AH, ARE WE THERE?
......
WE SHOULD BE, BUT...

CHAPTER VII TENDER BEAT SCRAMBLE

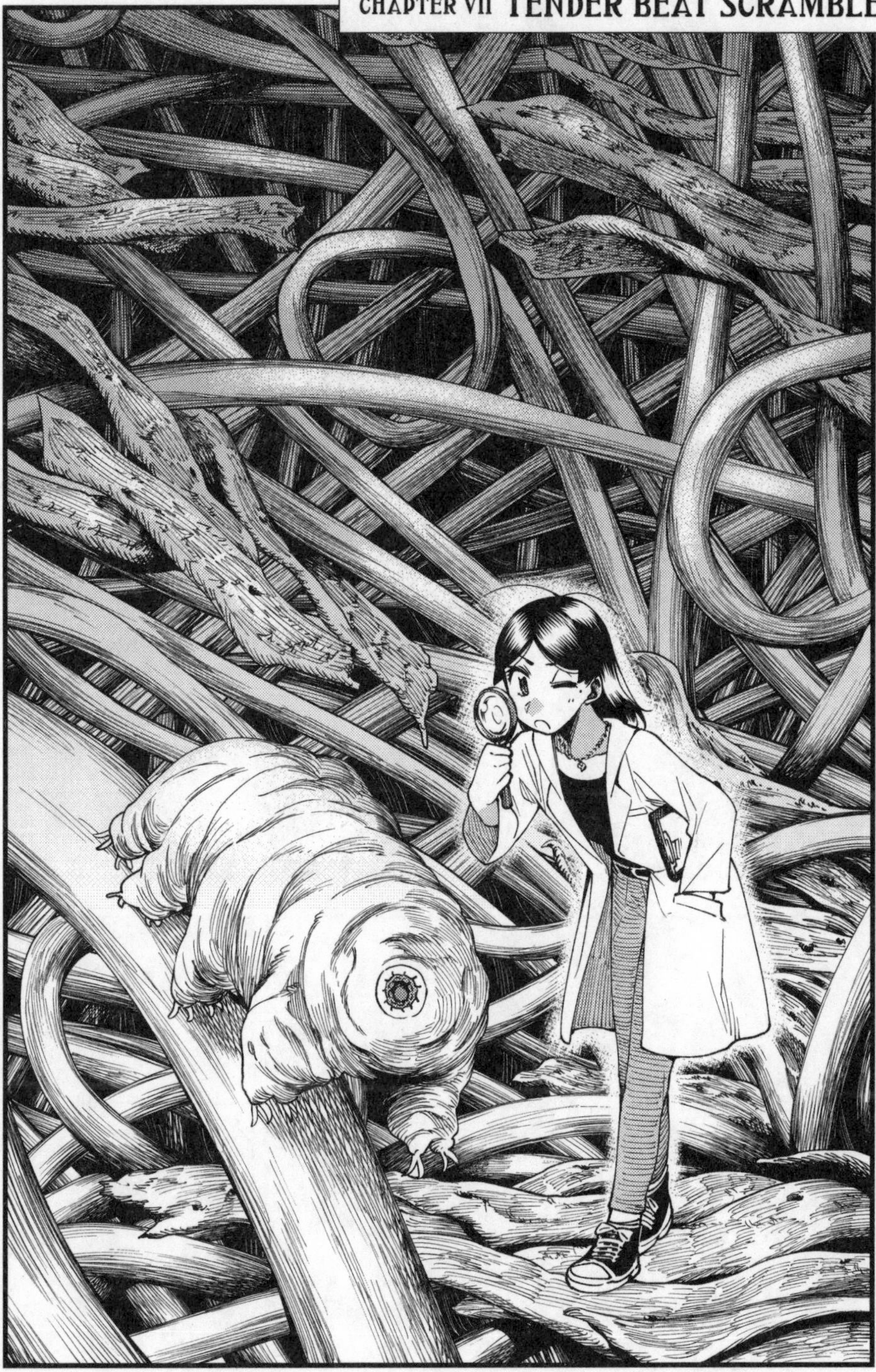

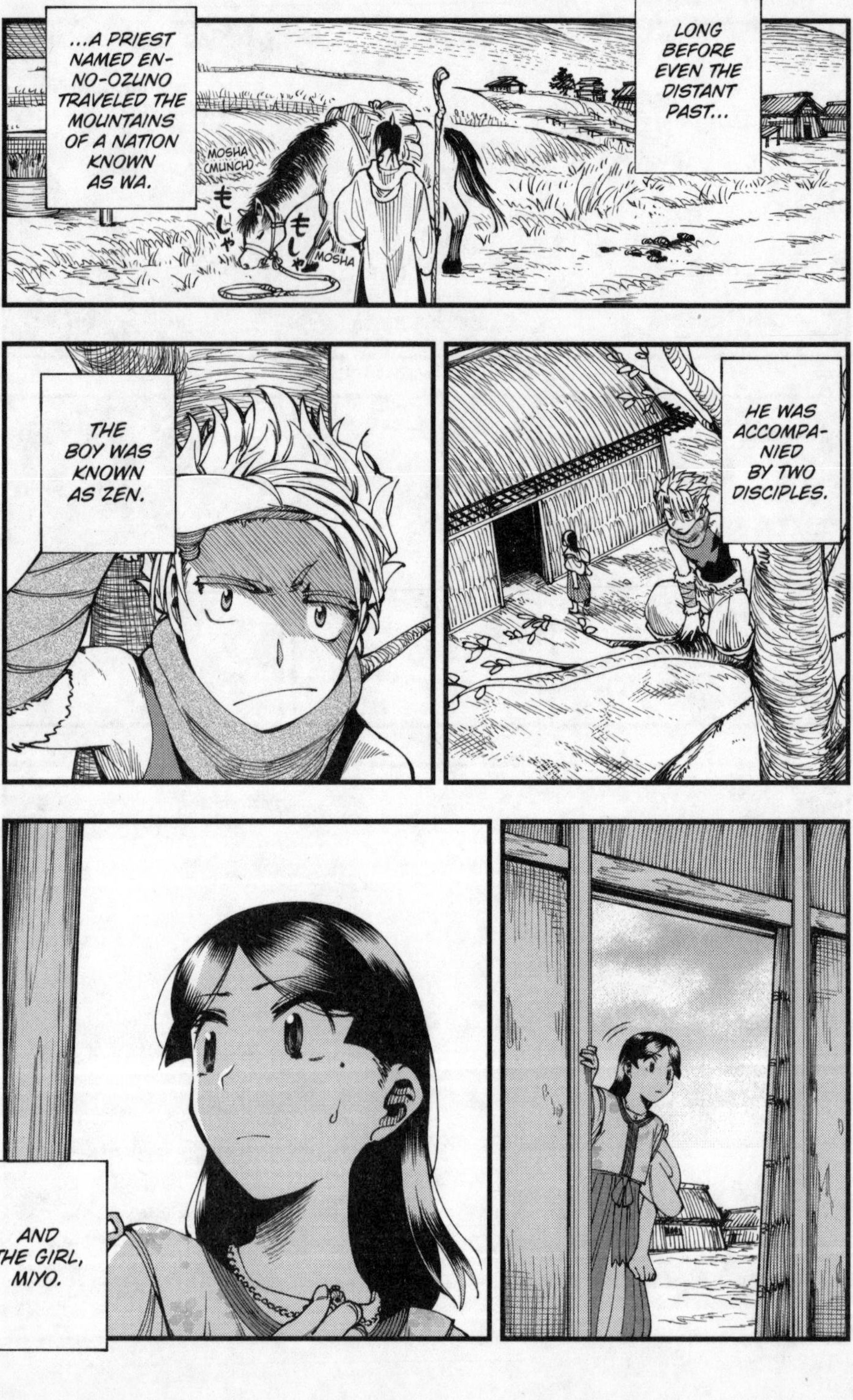
LONG BEFORE EVEN THE DISTANT PAST...
...A PRIEST NAMED EN-NO-OZUNO TRAVELED THE MOUNTAINS OF A NATION KNOWN AS WA.
もしゃ
MOSHA
もしゃ
MOSHA (MUNCH)
HE WAS ACCOMPA-NIED BY TWO DISCIPLES.
THE BOY WAS KNOWN AS ZEN.
AND THE GIRL, MIYO.

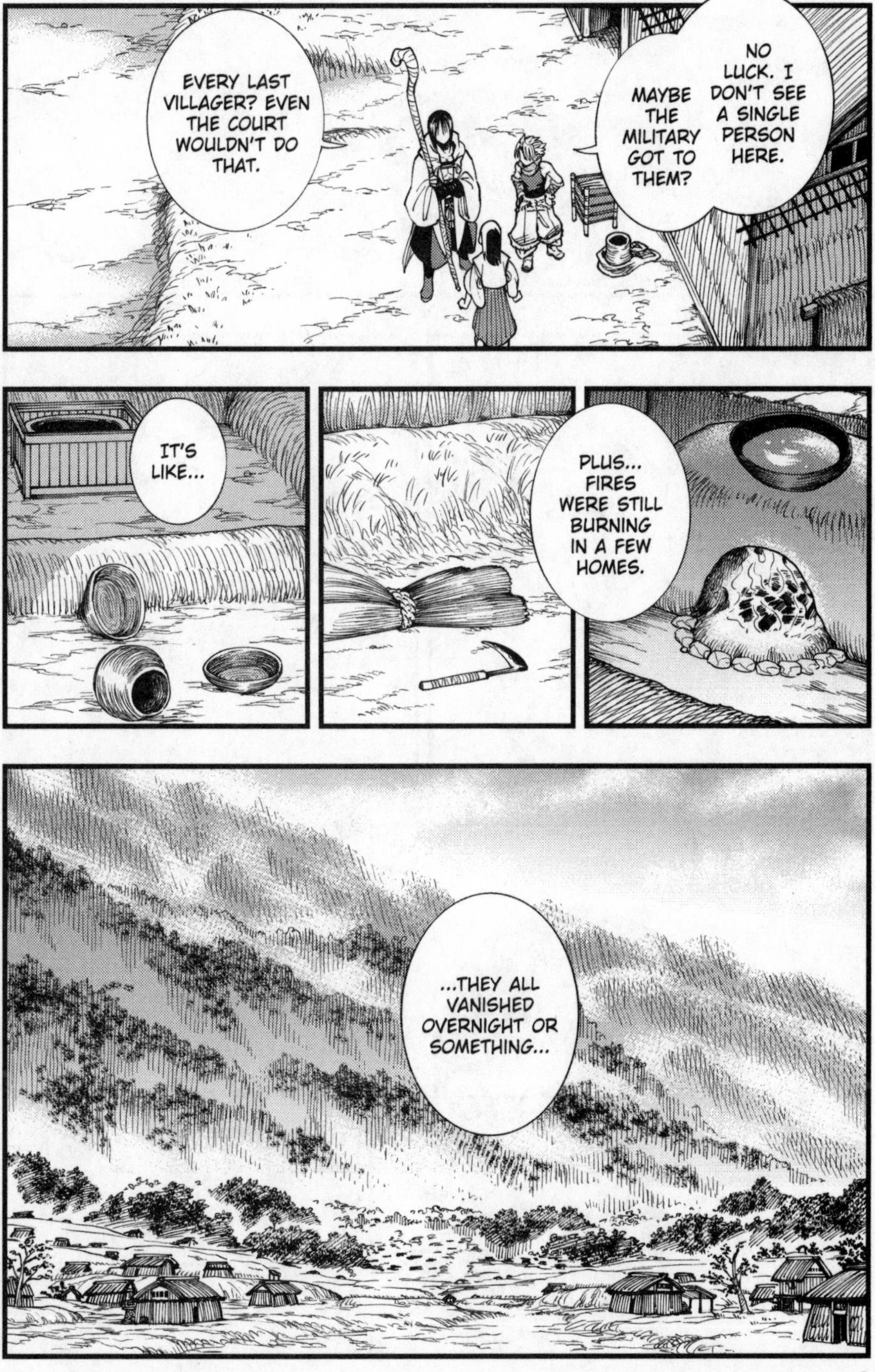
NO LUCK. I DON'T SEE A SINGLE PERSON HERE.
MAYBE THE MILITARY GOT TO THEM?
EVERY LAST VILLAGER? EVEN THE COURT WOULDN'T DO THAT.
PLUS... FIRES WERE STILL BURNING IN A FEW HOMES.
IT'S LIKE...
...THEY ALL VANISHED OVERNIGHT OR SOMETHING...

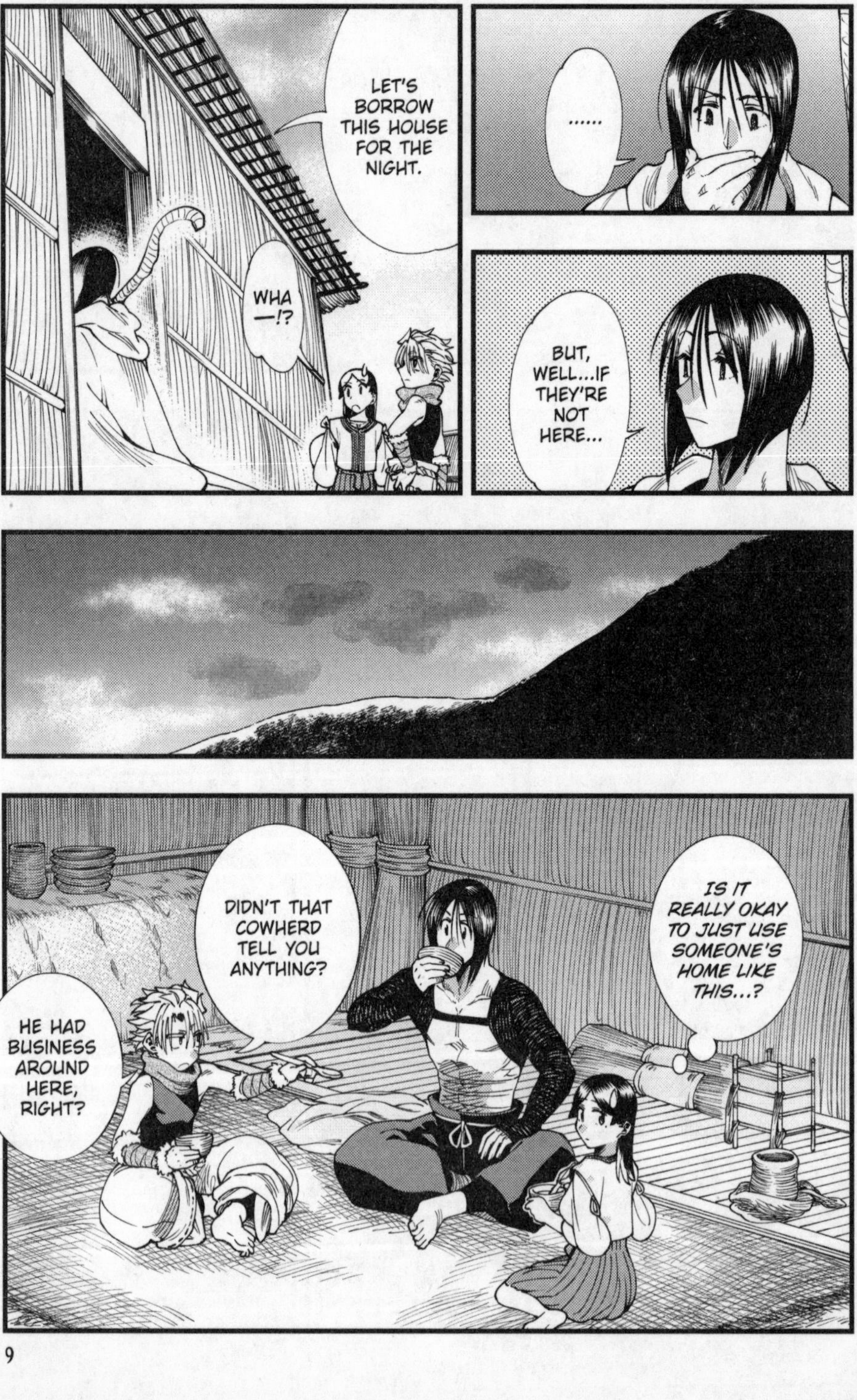
......
BUT, WELL...IF THEY'RE NOT HERE...
LET'S BORROW THIS HOUSE FOR THE NIGHT.
WHA—!?
IS IT REALLY OKAY TO JUST USE SOMEONE'S HOME LIKE THIS...?
DIDN'T THAT COWHERD TELL YOU ANYTHING?
HE HAD BUSINESS AROUND HERE, RIGHT?

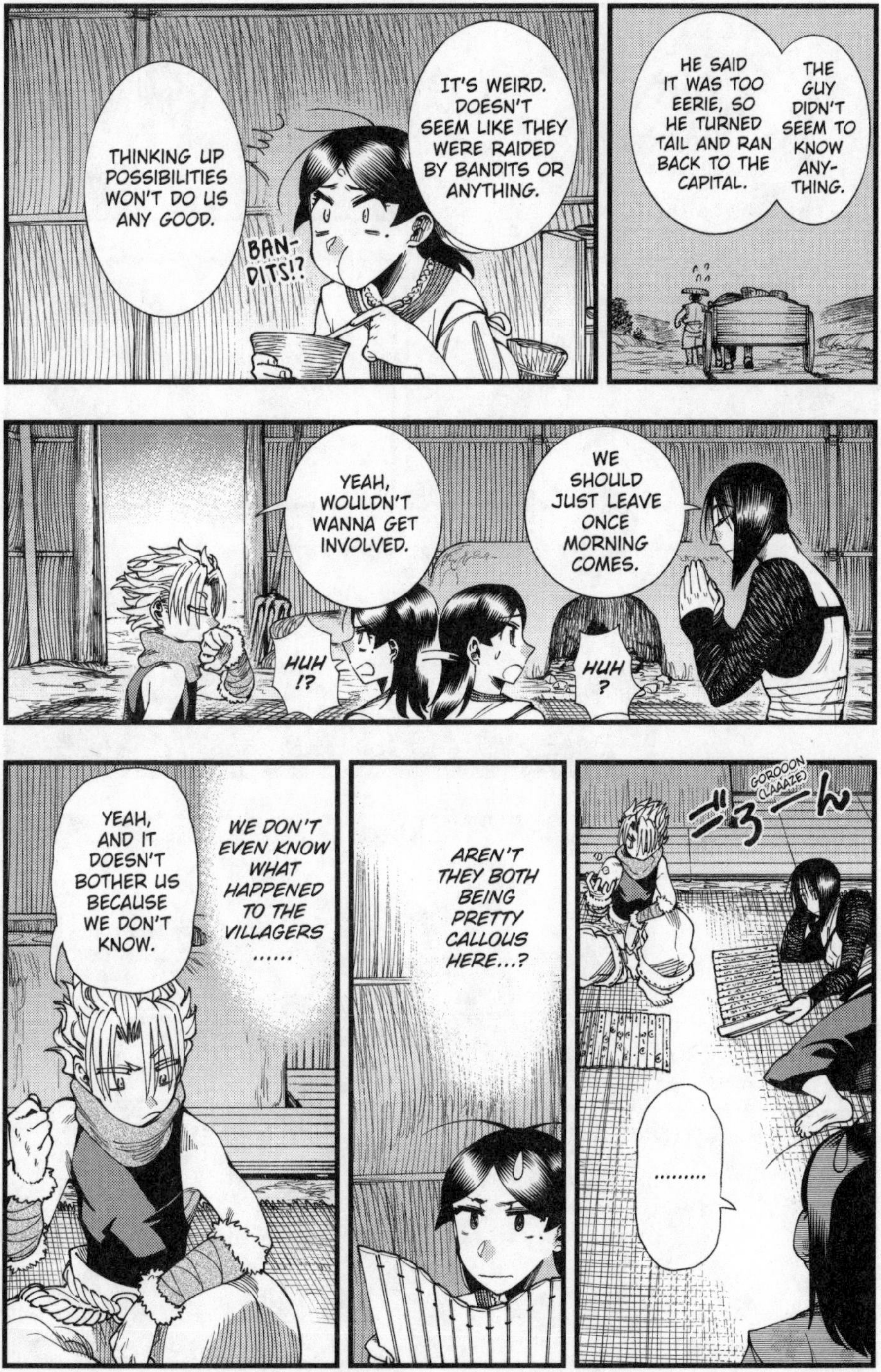
THE GUY DIDN'T SEEM TO KNOW ANY-THING.
HE SAID IT WAS TOO EERIE, SO HE TURNED TAIL AND RAN BACK TO THE CAPITAL.
IT'S WEIRD. DOESN'T SEEM LIKE THEY WERE RAIDED BY BANDITS OR ANYTHING.
BAN-DITS!?
THINKING UP POSSIBILITIES WON'T DO US ANY GOOD.
WE SHOULD JUST LEAVE ONCE MORNING COMES.
HUH ?
YEAH, WOULDN'T WANNA GET INVOLVED.
HUH !?
ごろーん
GOROOON (LAAAZE)
....
AREN'T THEY BOTH BEING PRETTY CALLOUS HERE...?
WE DON'T EVEN KNOW WHAT HAPPENED TO THE VILLAGERS ......
YEAH, AND IT DOESN'T BOTHER US BECAUSE WE DON'T KNOW.

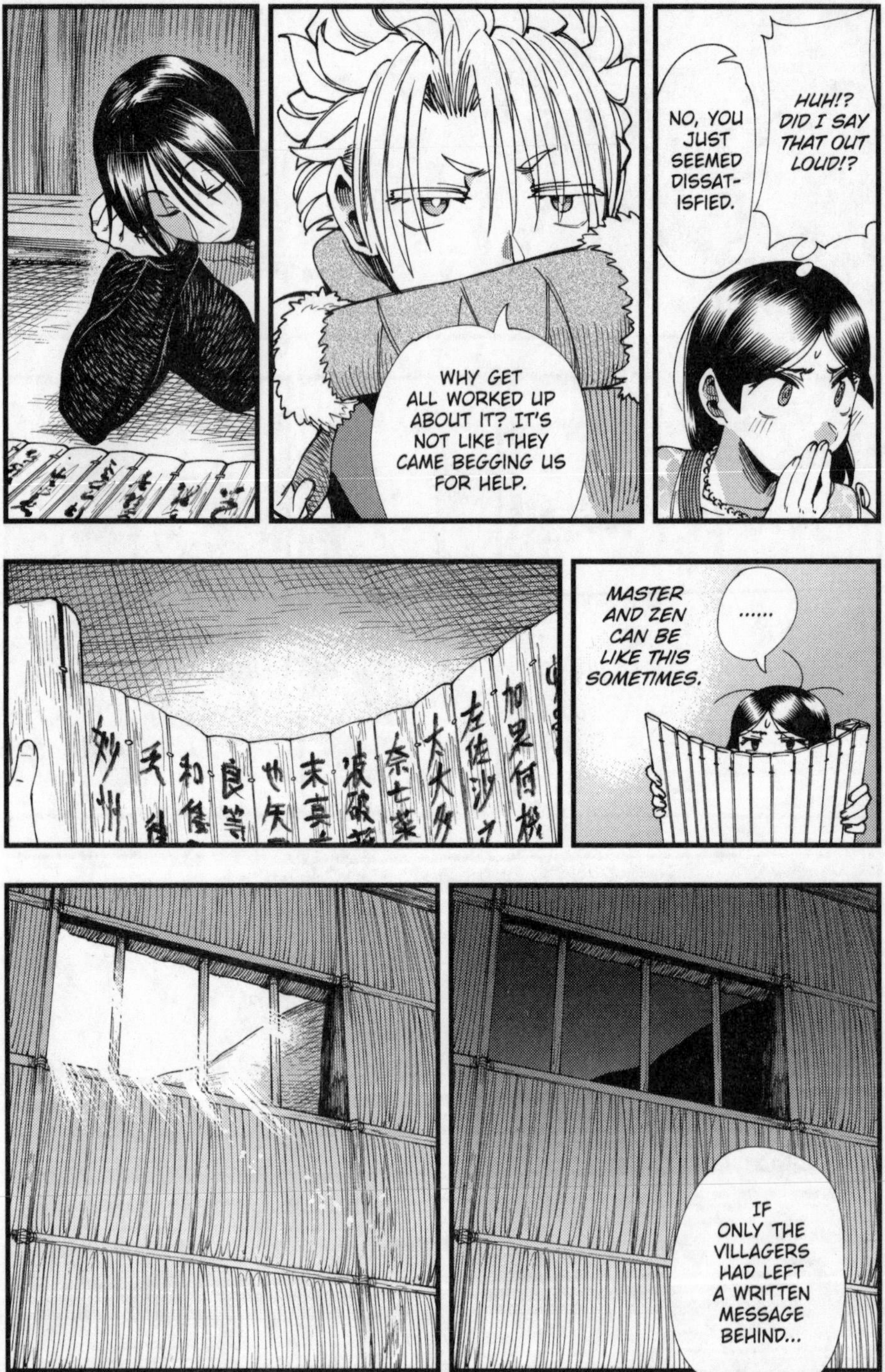
HUH!? DID I SAY THAT OUT LOUD!?
NO, YOU JUST SEEMED DISSAT-ISFIED.
WHY GET ALL WORKED UP ABOUT IT? IT'S NOT LIKE THEY CAME BEGGING US FOR HELP.
......
MASTER AND ZEN CAN BE LIKE THIS SOMETIMES.
IF ONLY THE VILLAGERS HAD LEFT A WRITTEN MESSAGE BEHIND...

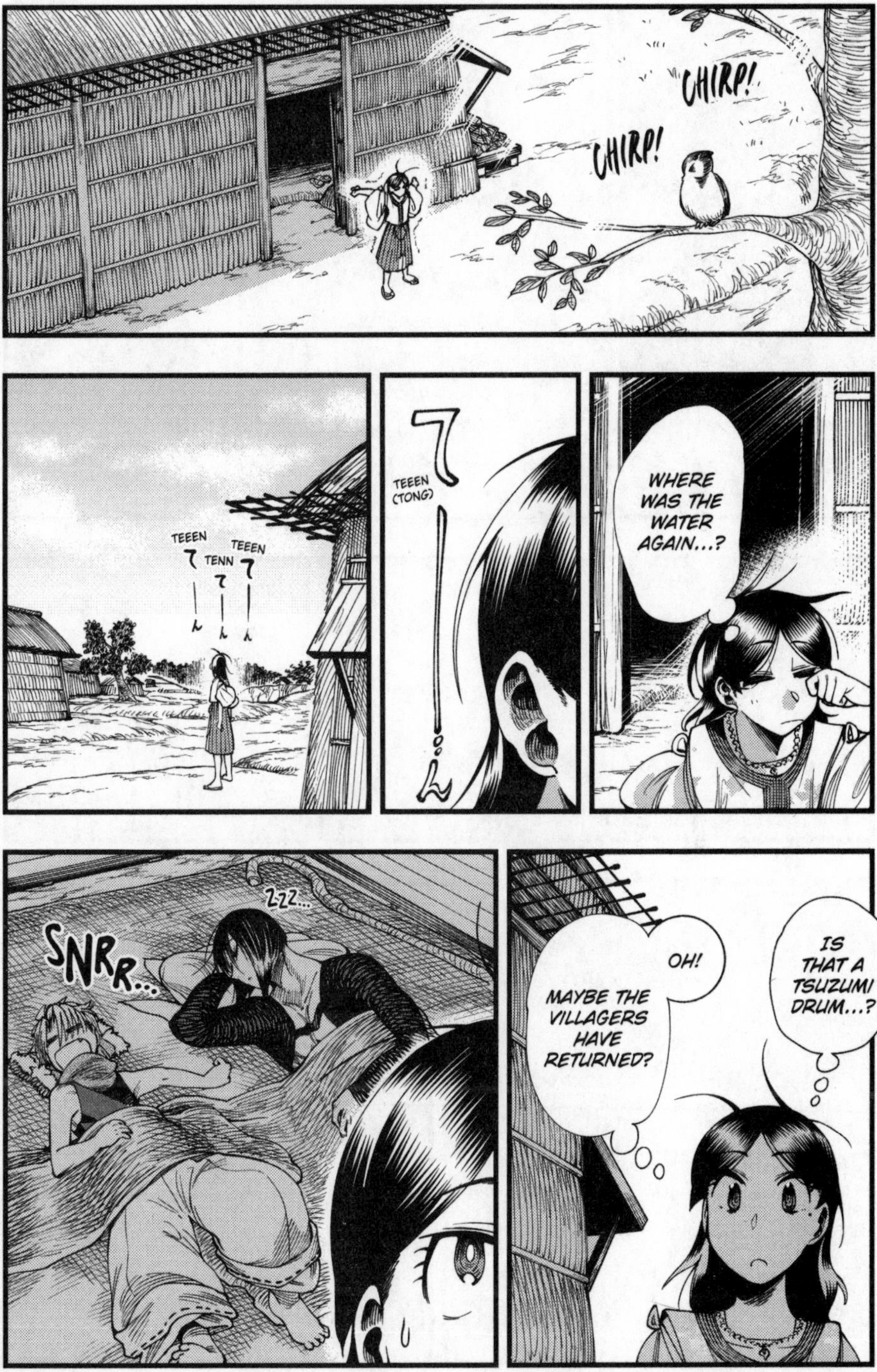
CHIRP!
CHIRP!
WHERE WAS THE WATER AGAIN...?
TEEEN (TONG)
TEEEN
TENN
TEEEN
IS THAT A TSUZUMI DRUM...?
OH! MAYBE THE VILLAGERS HAVE RETURNED?
Zzz...
SNRR...

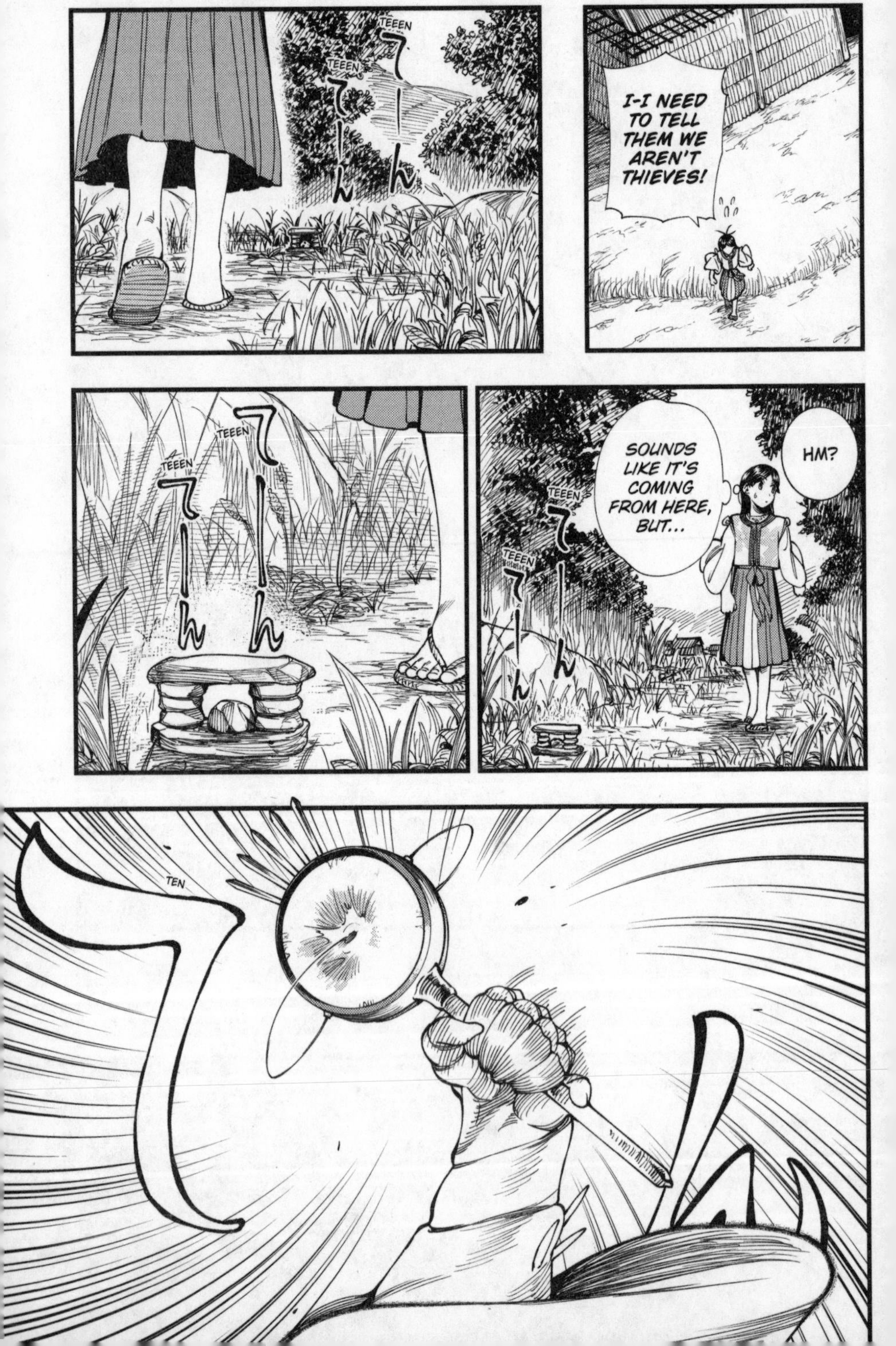
I-I NEED TO TELL THEM WE AREN'T THIEVES!
TEEEN
てーーん
TEEEN
てーーん
HM?
SOUNDS LIKE IT'S COMING FROM HERE, BUT...
TEEEN
てーーん
TEEEN
てーーん
TEEEN
てーーん
TEEEN
てーーん
TEN
て

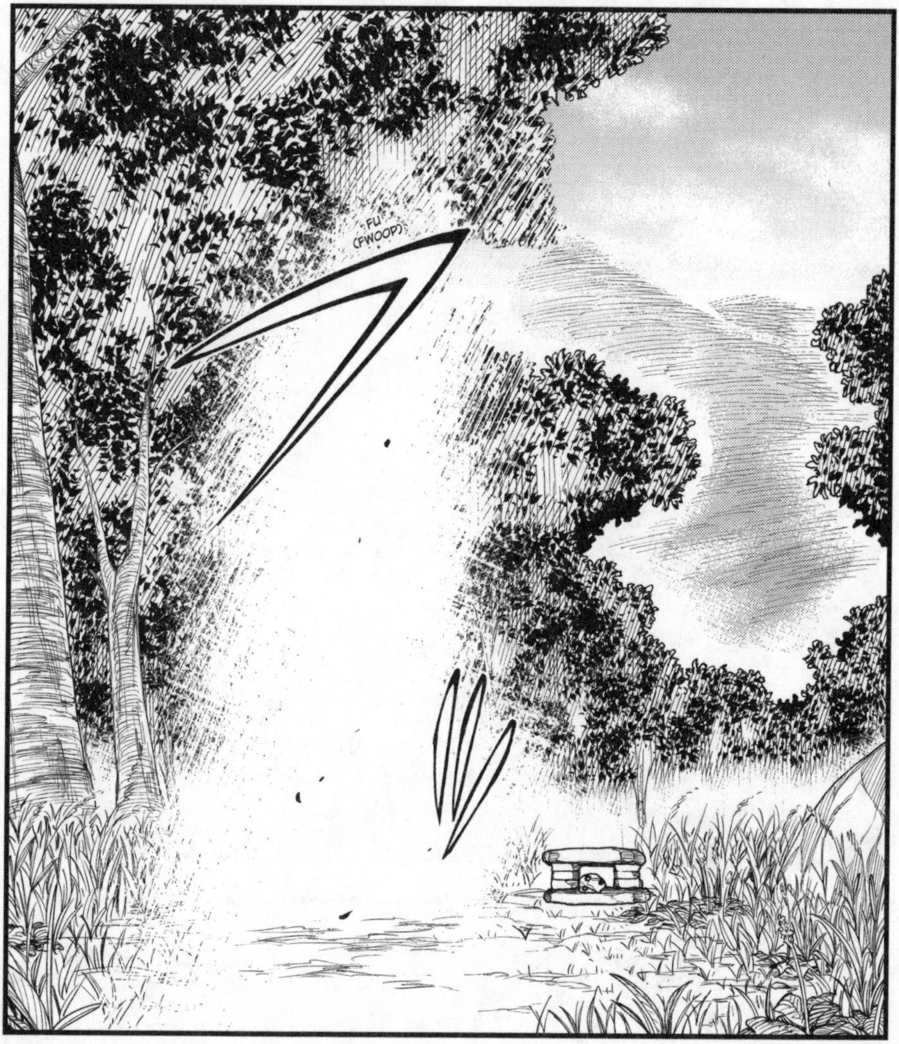
FU
(FWOOP)
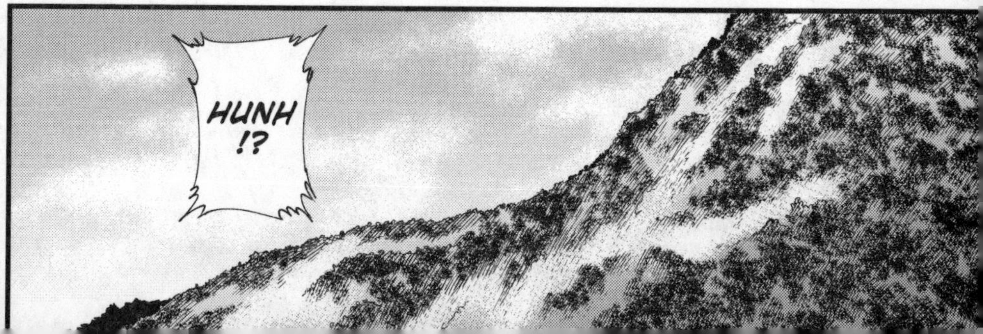
HUNH !?

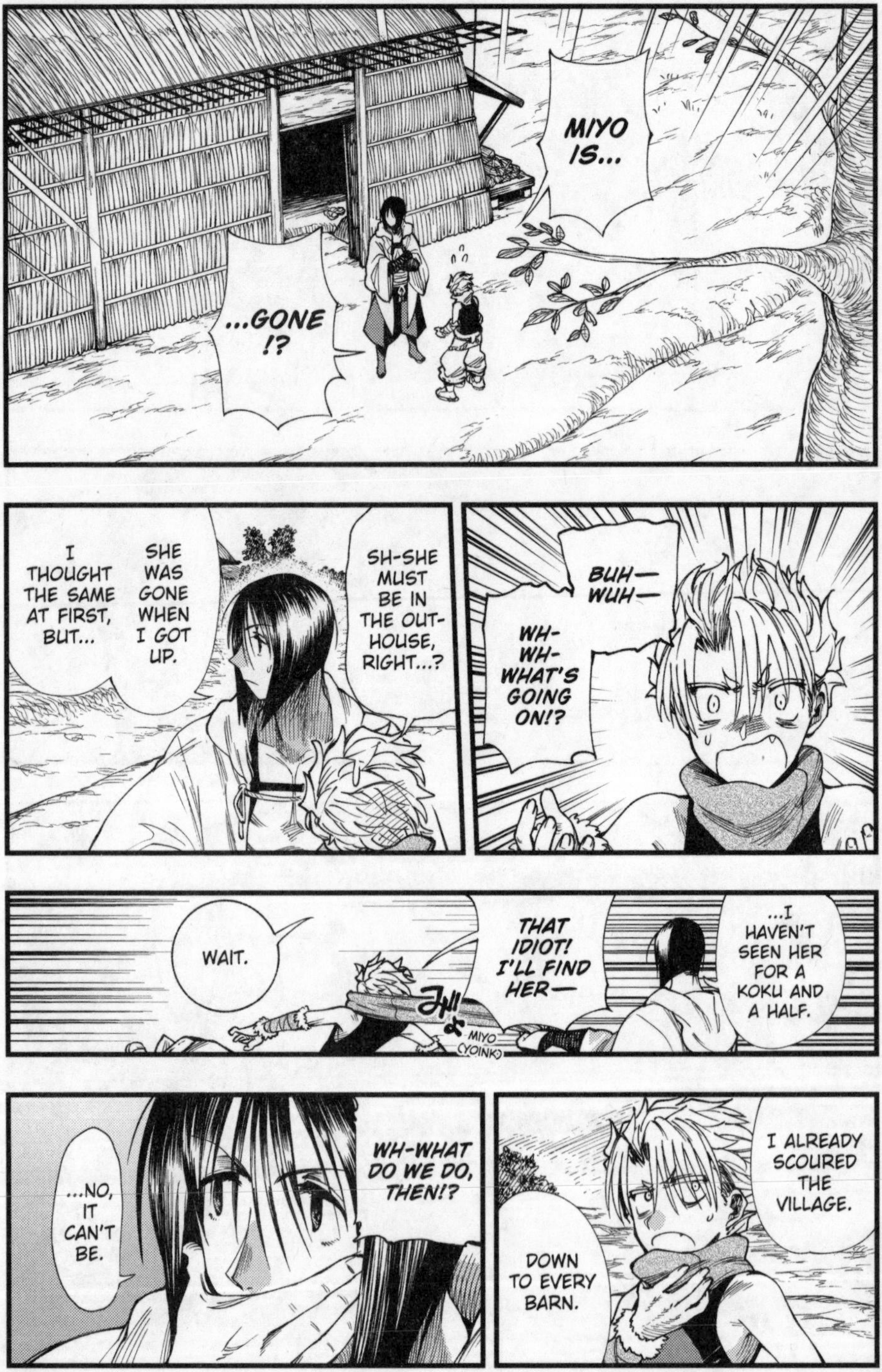
MIYO IS...
...GONE !?
BUH— WUH—
WH-WH-WHAT'S GOING ON!?
SH-SHE MUST BE IN THE OUT-HOUSE, RIGHT...?
SHE WAS GONE WHEN I GOT UP.
I THOUGHT THE SAME AT FIRST, BUT...
...I HAVEN'T SEEN HER FOR A KOKU AND A HALF.
THAT IDIOT! I'LL FIND HER—
MIYO (YOINK)
WAIT.
I ALREADY SCOURED THE VILLAGE.
DOWN TO EVERY BARN.
WH-WHAT DO WE DO, THEN!?
...NO, IT CAN'T BE.

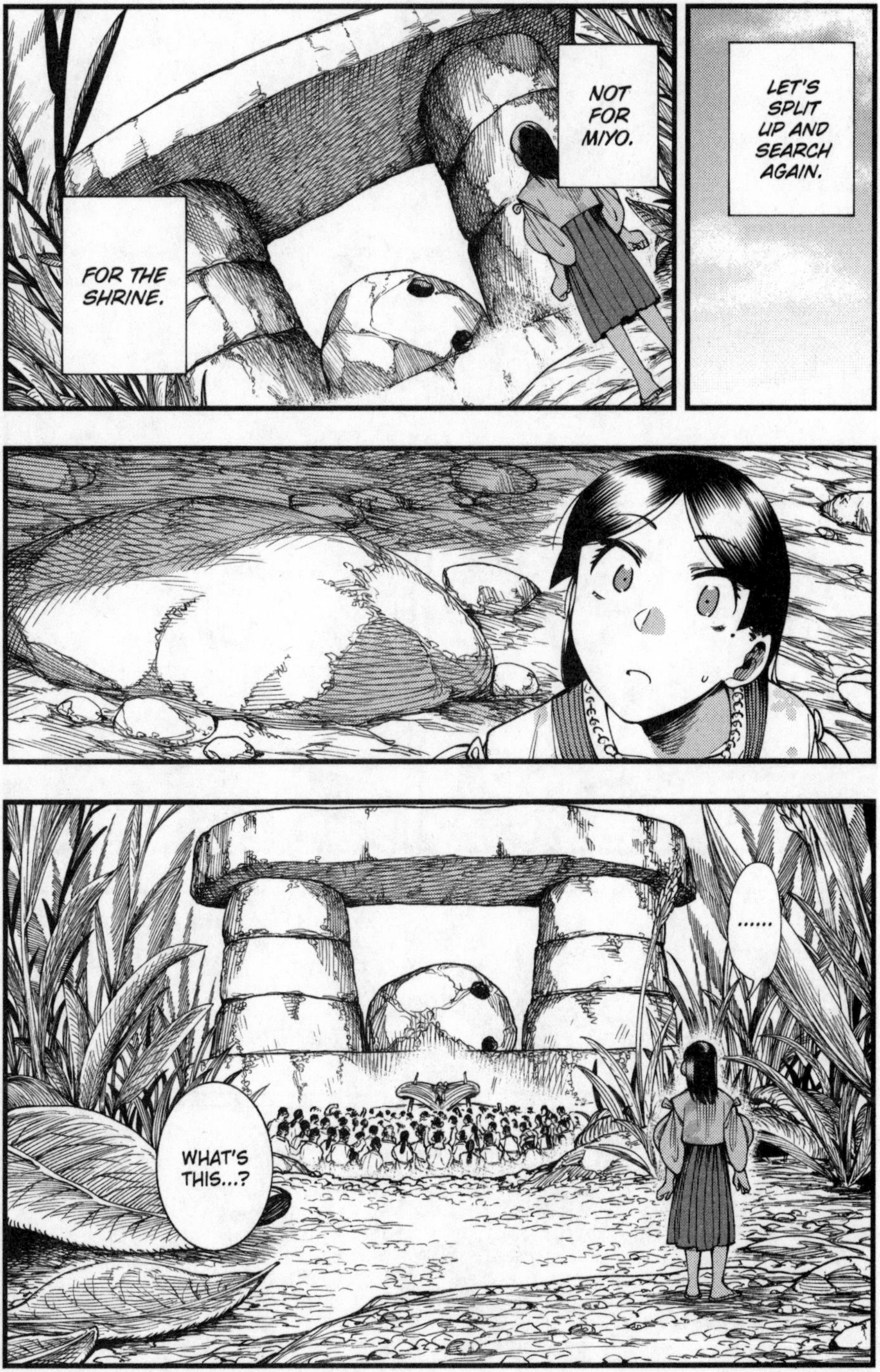
LET'S SPLIT UP AND SEARCH AGAIN.
NOT FOR MIYO.
FOR THE SHRINE.
......
WHAT'S THIS...?

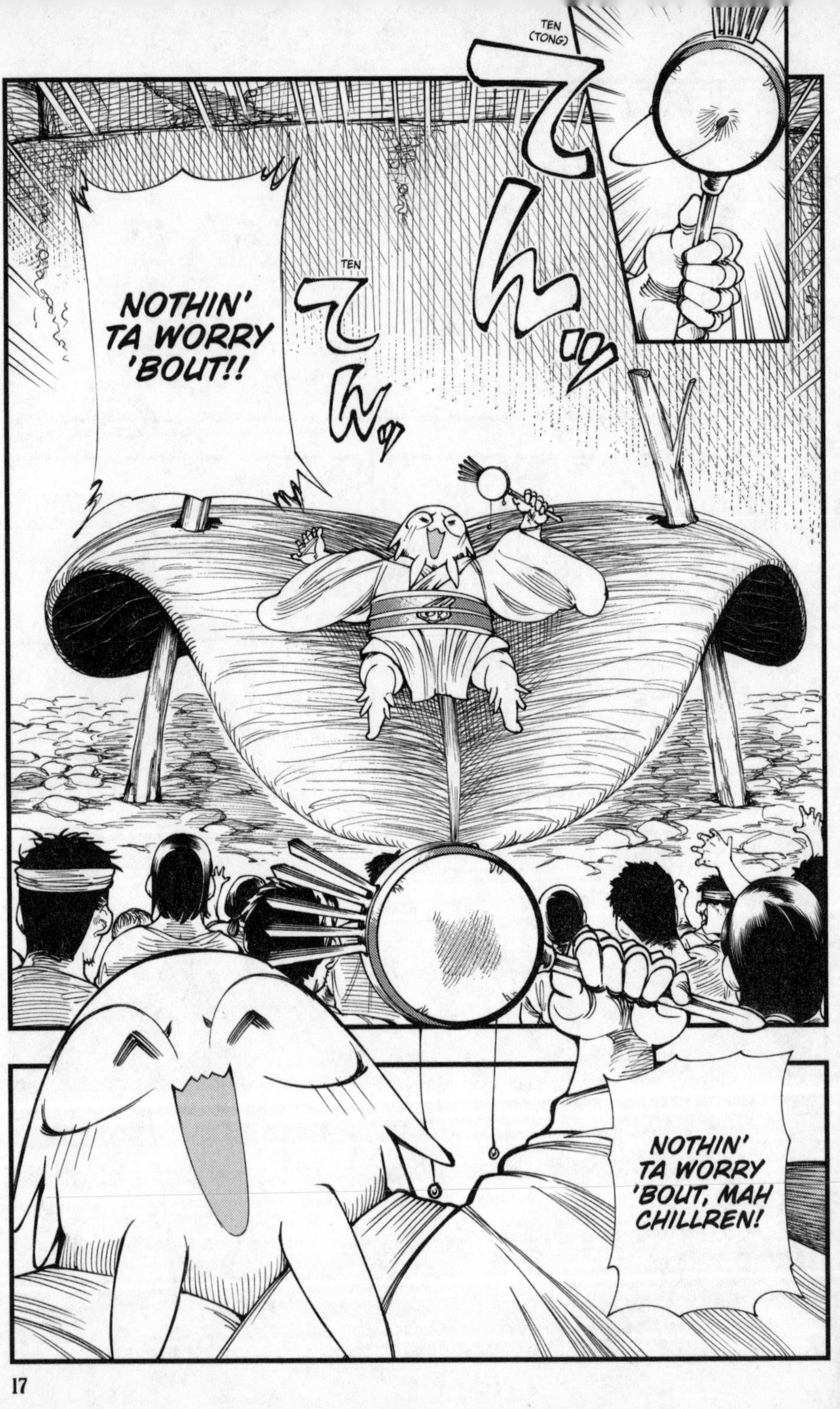
TEN (TONG)
てんッ
TEN
てんッ
NOTHIN' TA WORRY 'BOUT!!
NOTHIN' TA WORRY 'BOUT, MAH CHILLREN!

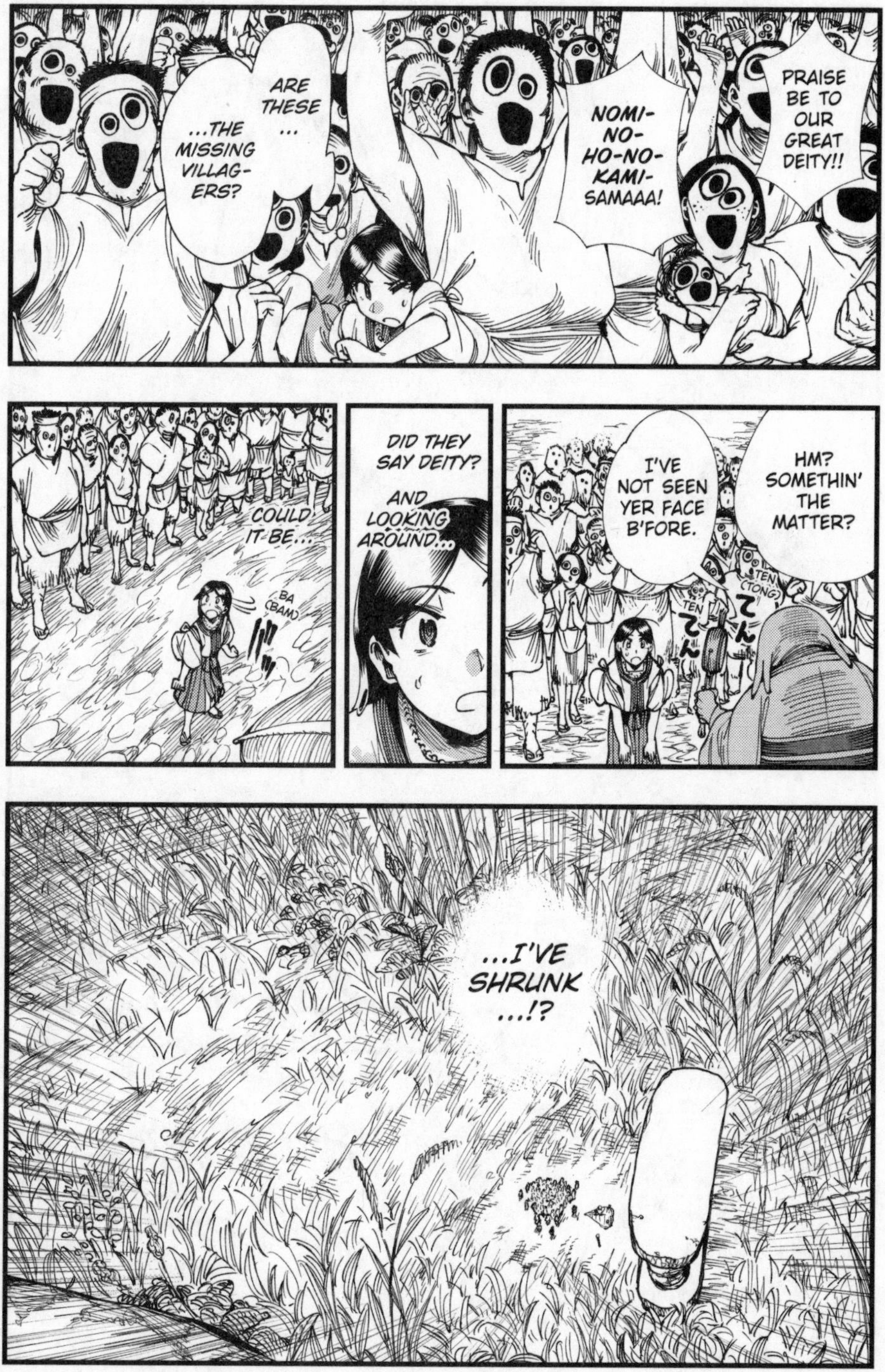
PRAISE BE TO OUR GREAT DEITY!!
NOMI-NO-HO-NO-KAMI-SAMAAA!
ARE THESE ...
...THE MISSING VILLAGERS?
HM? SOMETHIN' THE MATTER?
I'VE NOT SEEN YER FACE B'FORE.
TEN (TONG) てん
TEN てん
DID THEY SAY DEITY?
AND LOOKING AROUND...
COULD IT BE...
BA (BAM)
...I'VE SHRUNK ...!?

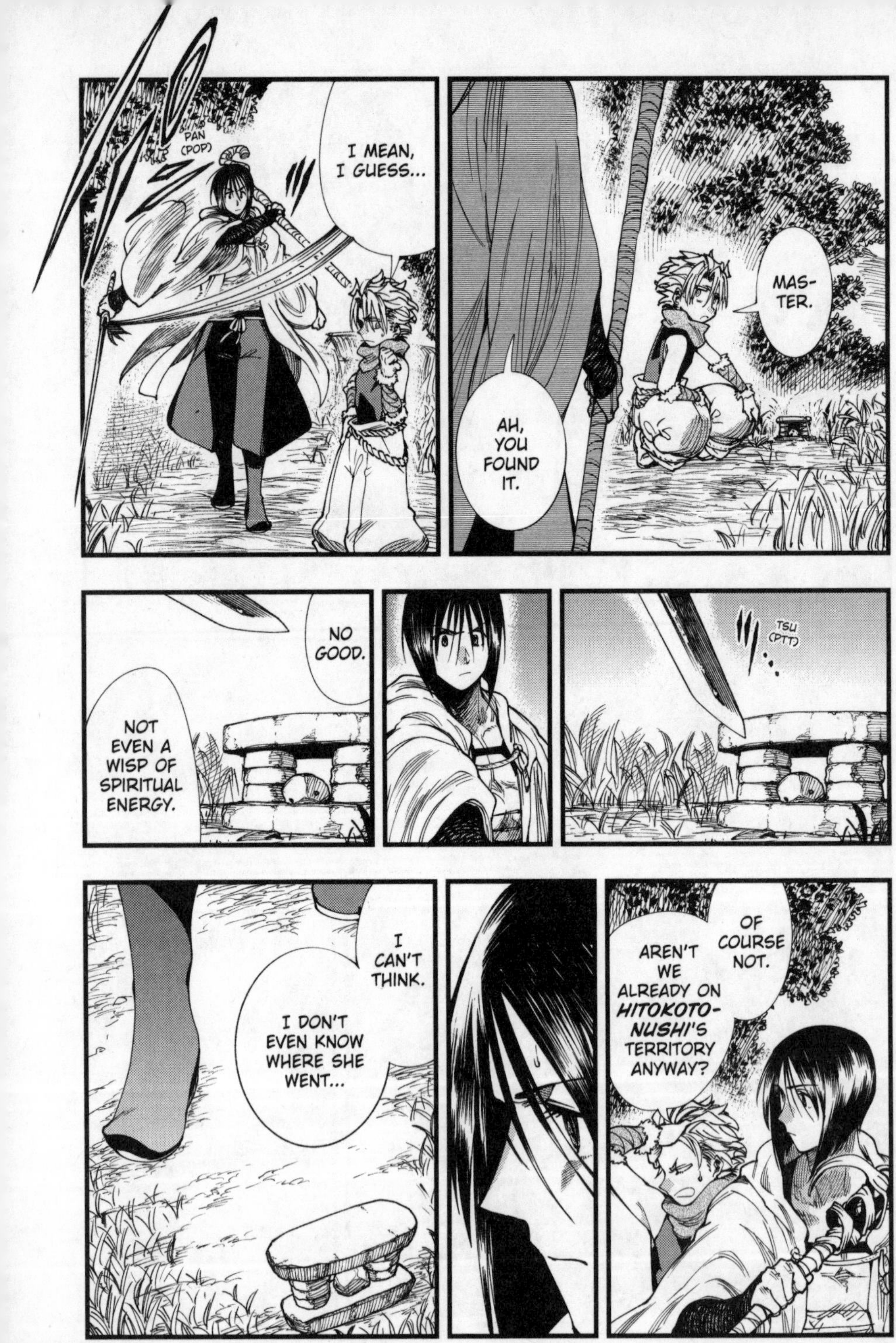
MAS-TER.
AH, YOU FOUND IT.
PAN (POP)
I MEAN, I GUESS...
TSU (PTT)
NO GOOD.
NOT EVEN A WISP OF SPIRITUAL ENERGY.
OF COURSE NOT.
AREN'T WE ALREADY ON ***HITOKOTO-NUSHI***'S TERRITORY ANYWAY?
I CAN'T THINK.
I DON'T EVEN KNOW WHERE SHE WENT...

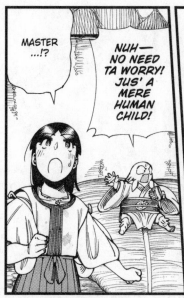

OOOO (WHOOO)
AAAH!
YEEEK!
MASTER ...!?
NUH— NO NEED TA WORRY! JUS' A MERE HUMAN CHILD!
ZEN TOO!
THEY'RE HERE LOOKING FOR ME...!
MAAAS- TEEER!!
......
HE CAN'T HEAR ME!?
DID MY VOICE SHRINK TOO...?

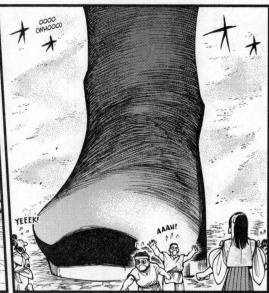

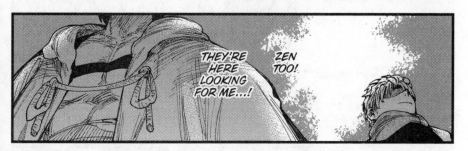

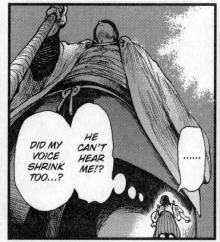

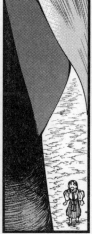

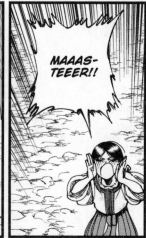

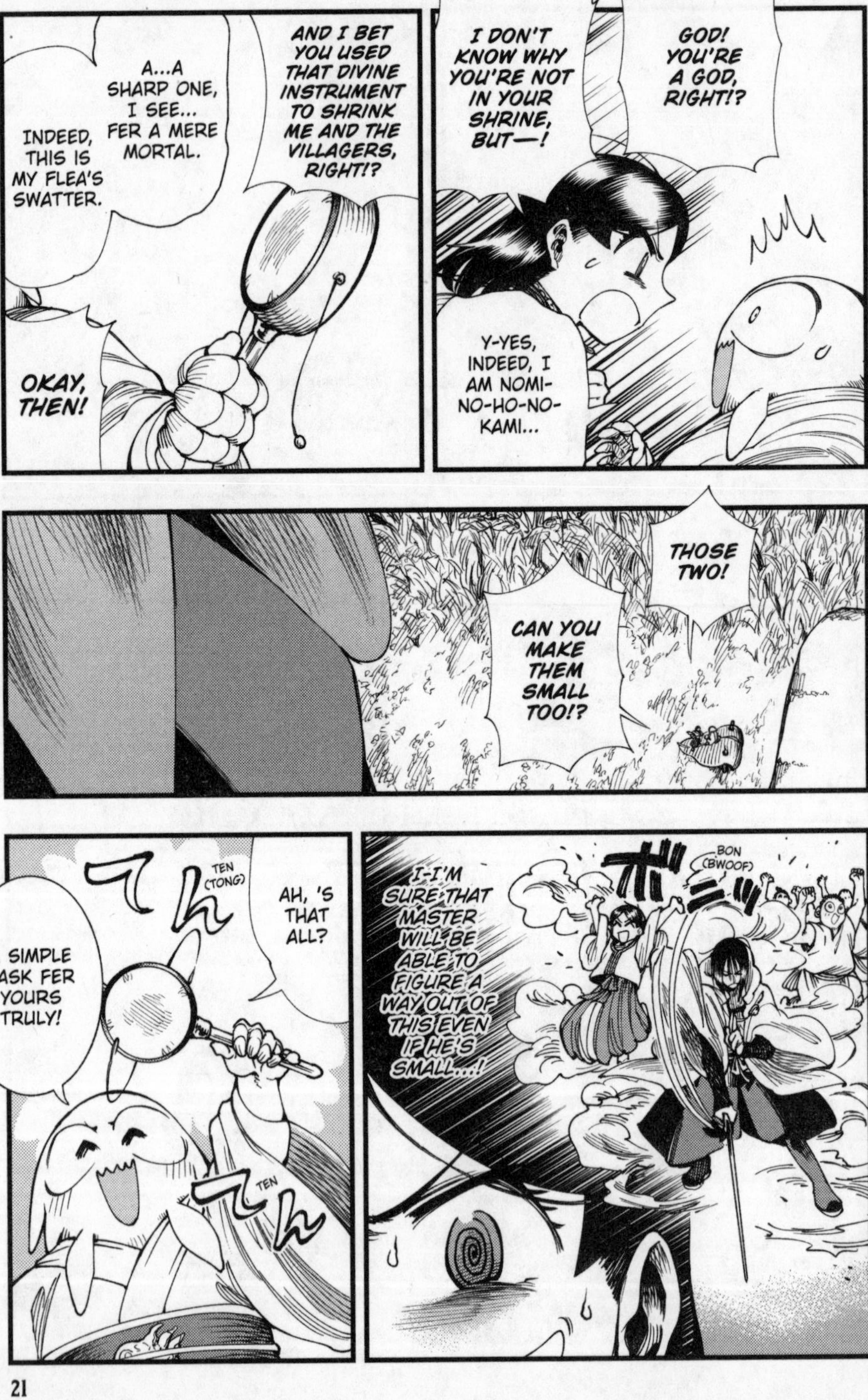
GOD! YOU'RE A GOD, RIGHT!?
I DON'T KNOW WHY YOU'RE NOT IN YOUR SHRINE, BUT—!
Y-YES, INDEED, I AM NOMI-NO-HO-NO-KAMI...
AND I BET YOU USED THAT DIVINE INSTRUMENT TO SHRINK ME AND THE VILLAGERS, RIGHT!?
A...A SHARP ONE, I SEE... FER A MERE MORTAL.
INDEED, THIS IS MY FLEA'S SWATTER.
OKAY, THEN!
THOSE TWO!
CAN YOU MAKE THEM SMALL TOO!?
BON (BWOOF)
I-I'M SURE THAT MASTER WILL BE ABLE TO FIGURE A WAY OUT OF THIS EVEN IF HE'S SMALL...!
AH, 'S THAT ALL?
TEN (TONG)
A SIMPLE TASK FER YOURS TRULY!
TEN

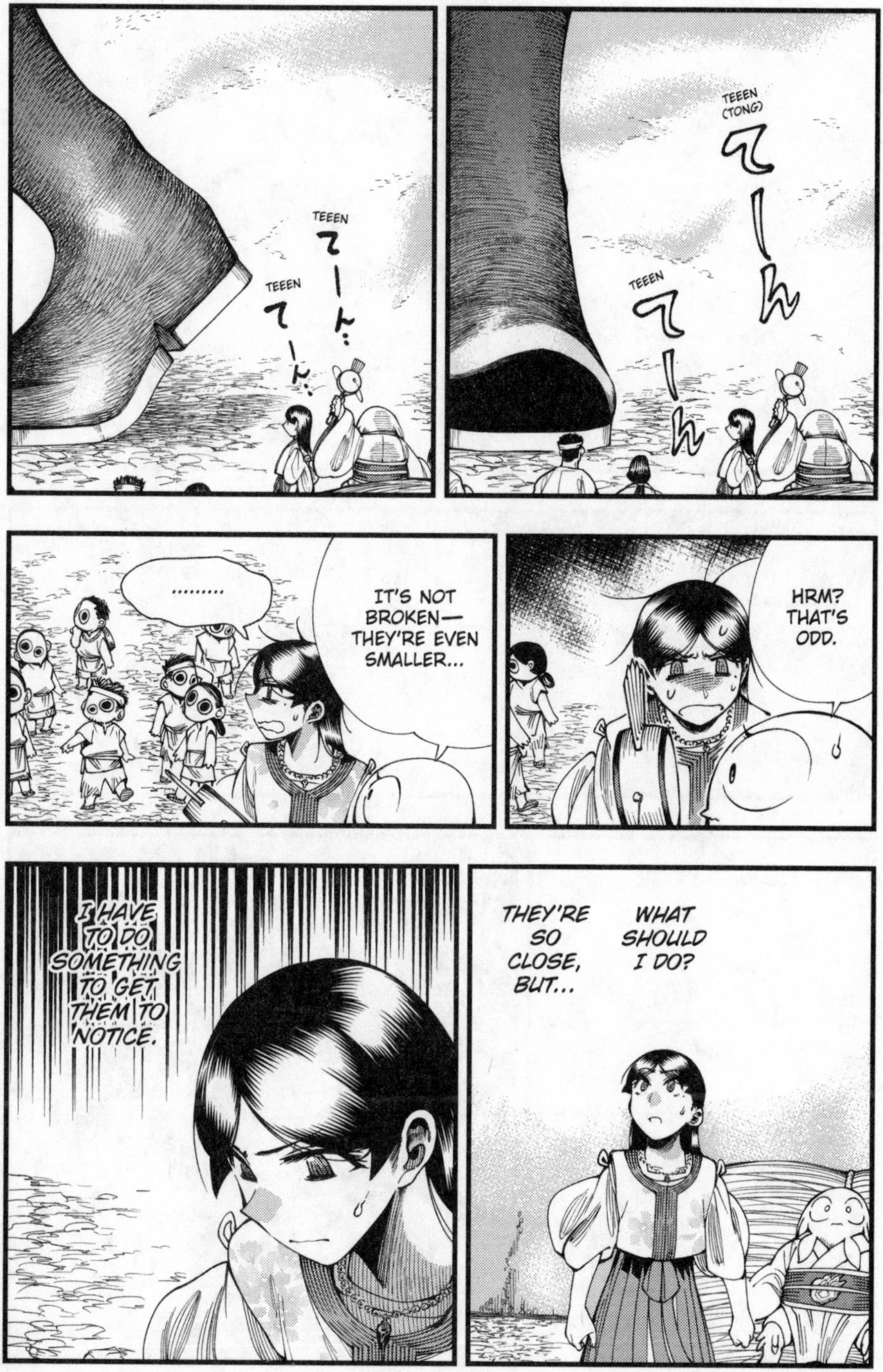
TEEEN
(TONG)
てーん
TEEEN
てーん
TEEEN
てーん
TEEEN
てーん
HRM? THAT'S ODD.
IT'S NOT BROKEN— THEY'RE EVEN SMALLER...
....
WHAT SHOULD I DO?
THEY'RE SO CLOSE, BUT...
I HAVE TO DO SOMETHING TO GET THEM TO NOTICE.

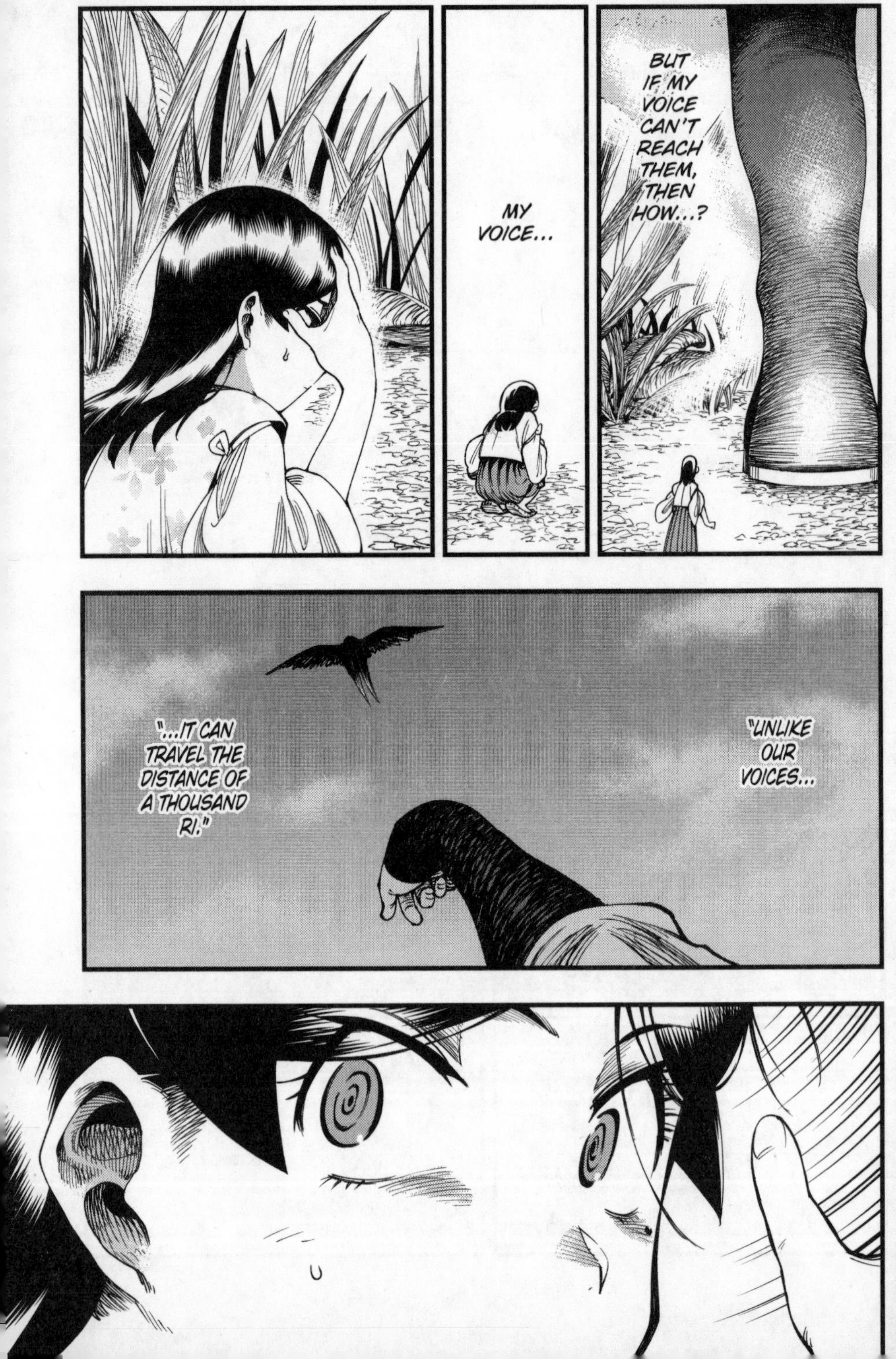
BUT IF MY VOICE CAN'T REACH THEM, THEN HOW...?
MY VOICE...
"UNLIKE OUR VOICES...
"...IT CAN TRAVEL THE DISTANCE OF A THOUSAND RI."

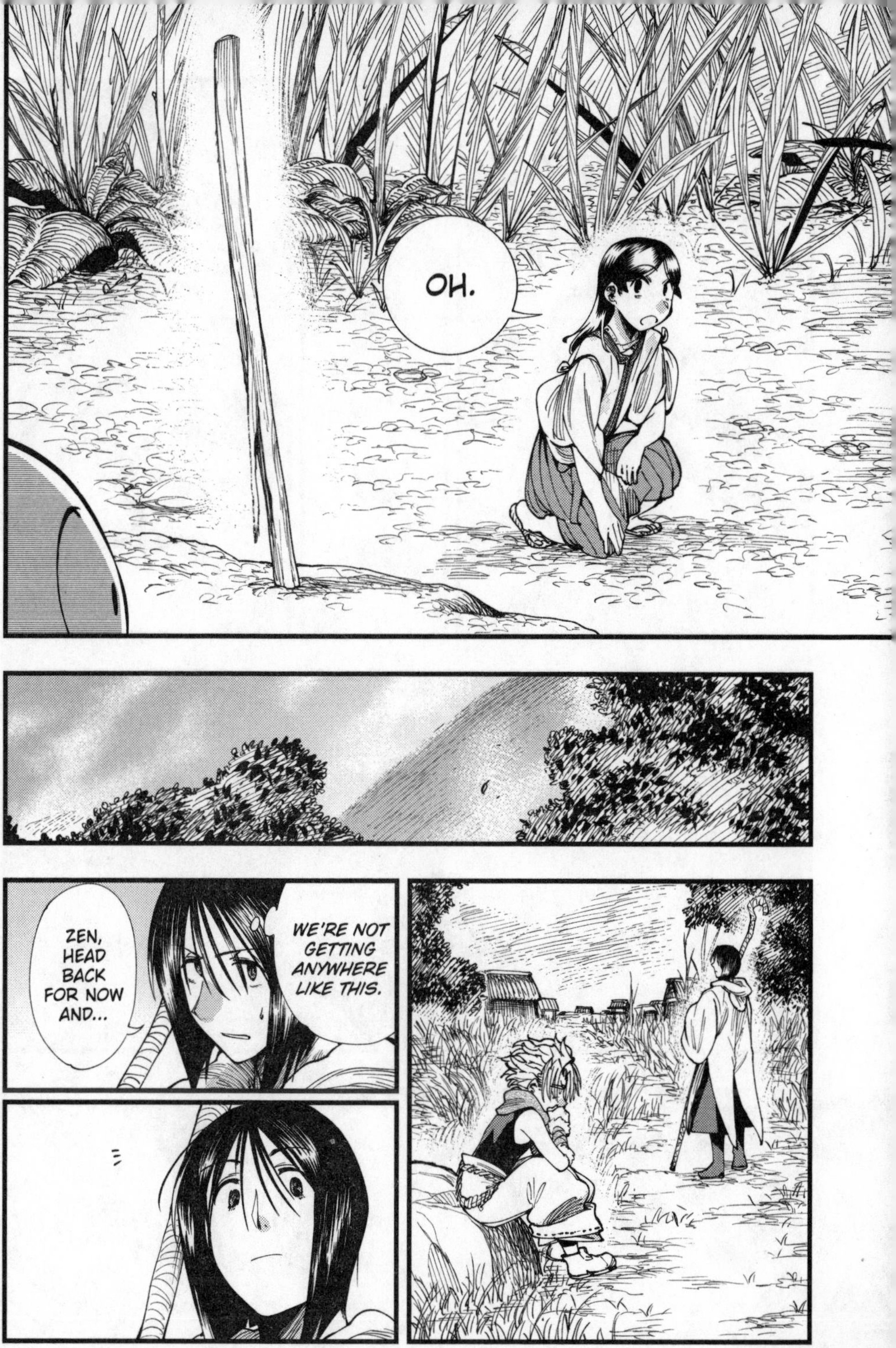
OH.
WE'RE NOT GETTING ANYWHERE LIKE THIS.
ZEN, HEAD BACK FOR NOW AND...

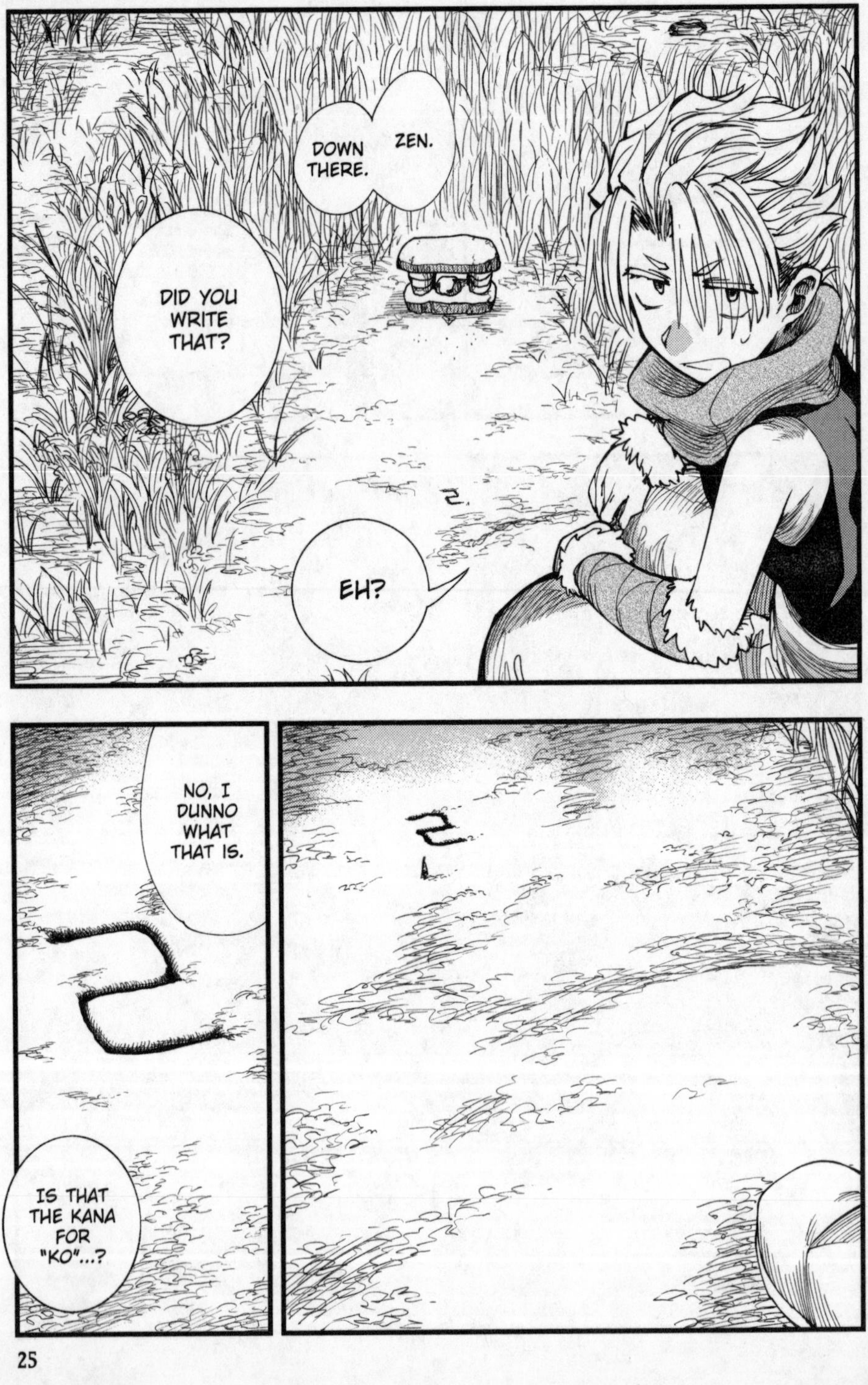
ZEN.
DOWN THERE.
DID YOU WRITE THAT?
EH?
NO, I DUNNO WHAT THAT IS.
IS THAT THE KANA FOR "KO"...?

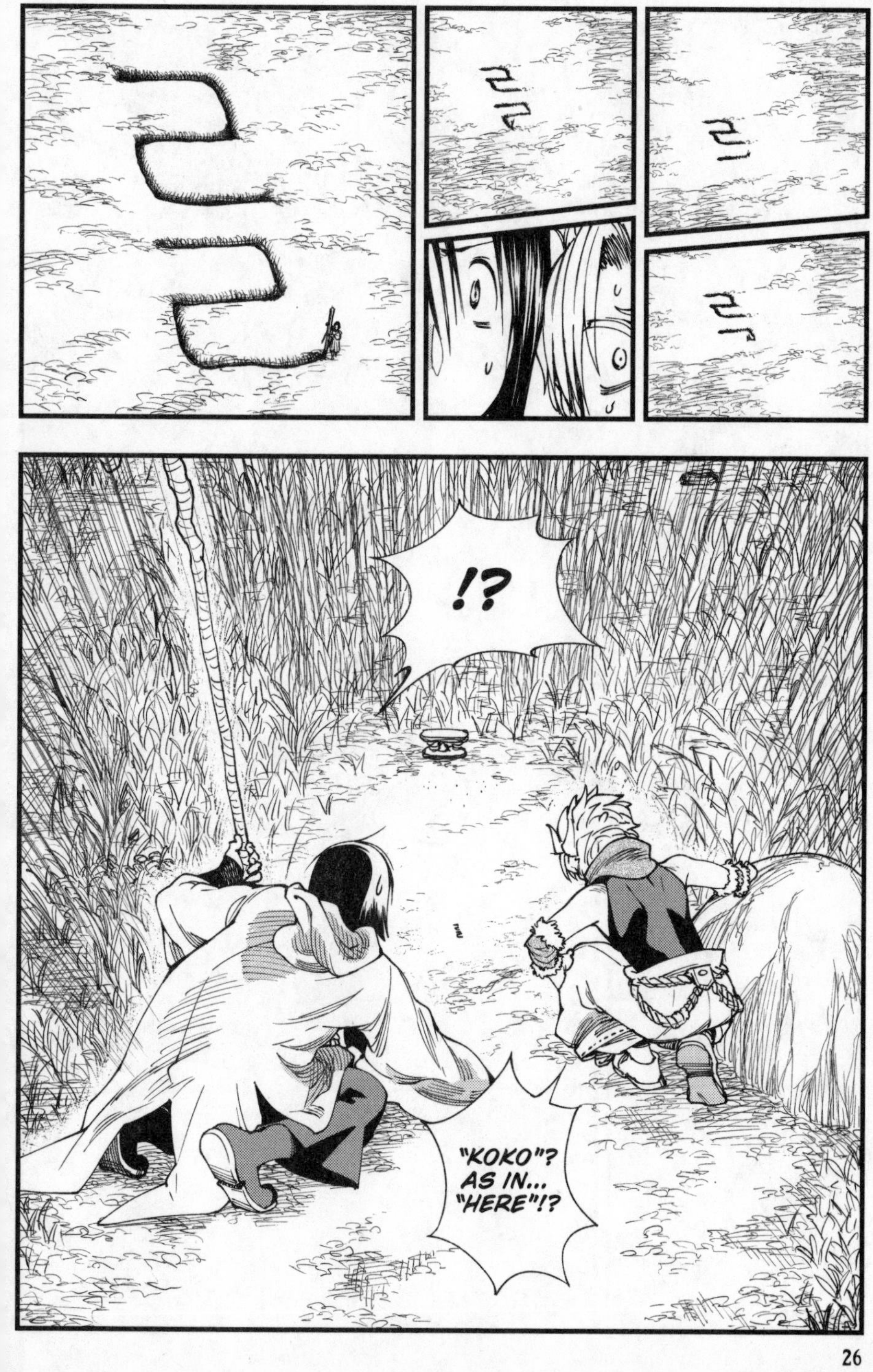
!?
"KOKO"? AS IN... "HERE"!?

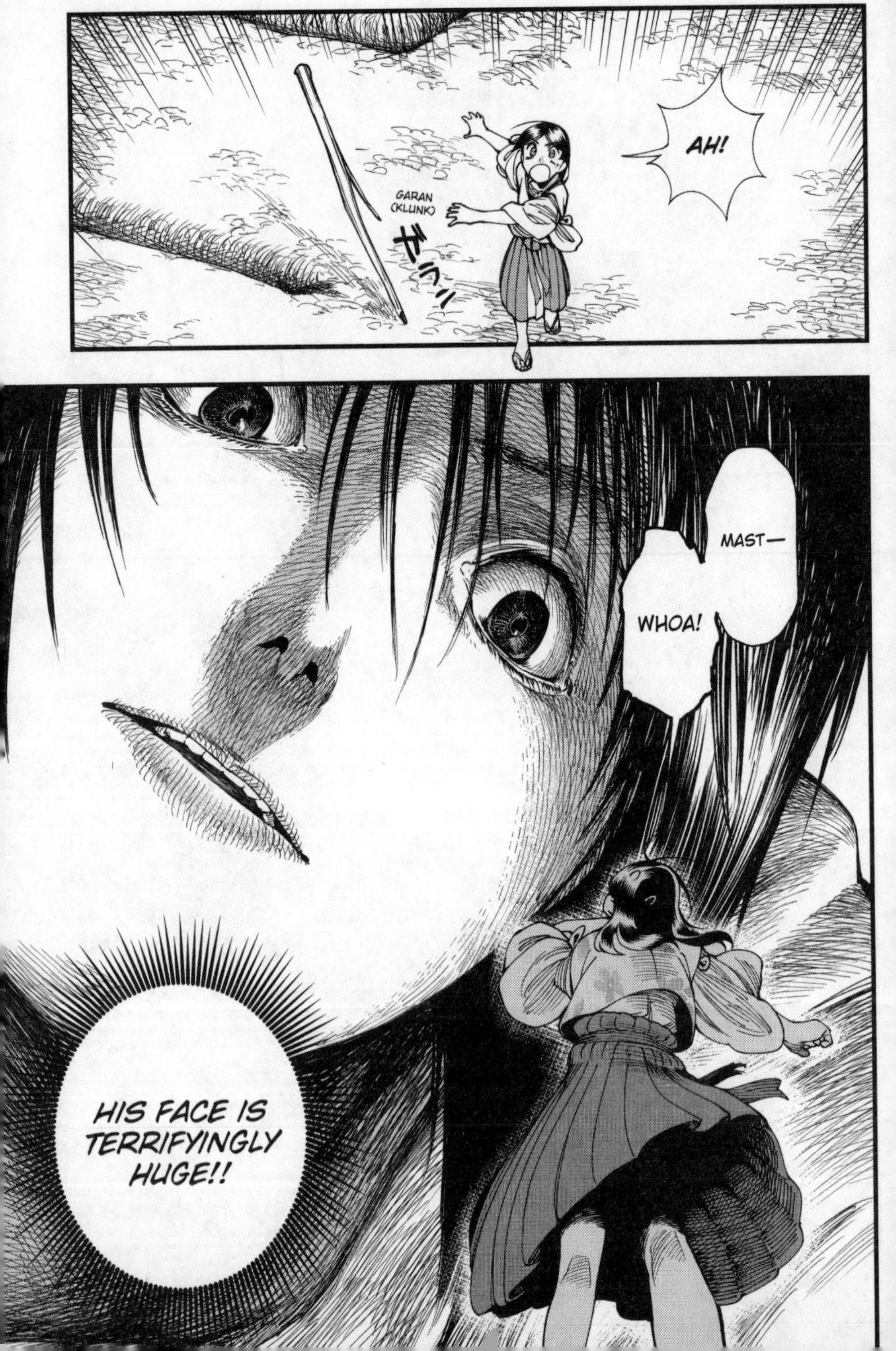
AH!
GARAN (KLUNK)
ガラン
MAST—
WHOA!
HIS FACE IS TERRIFYINGLY HUGE!!

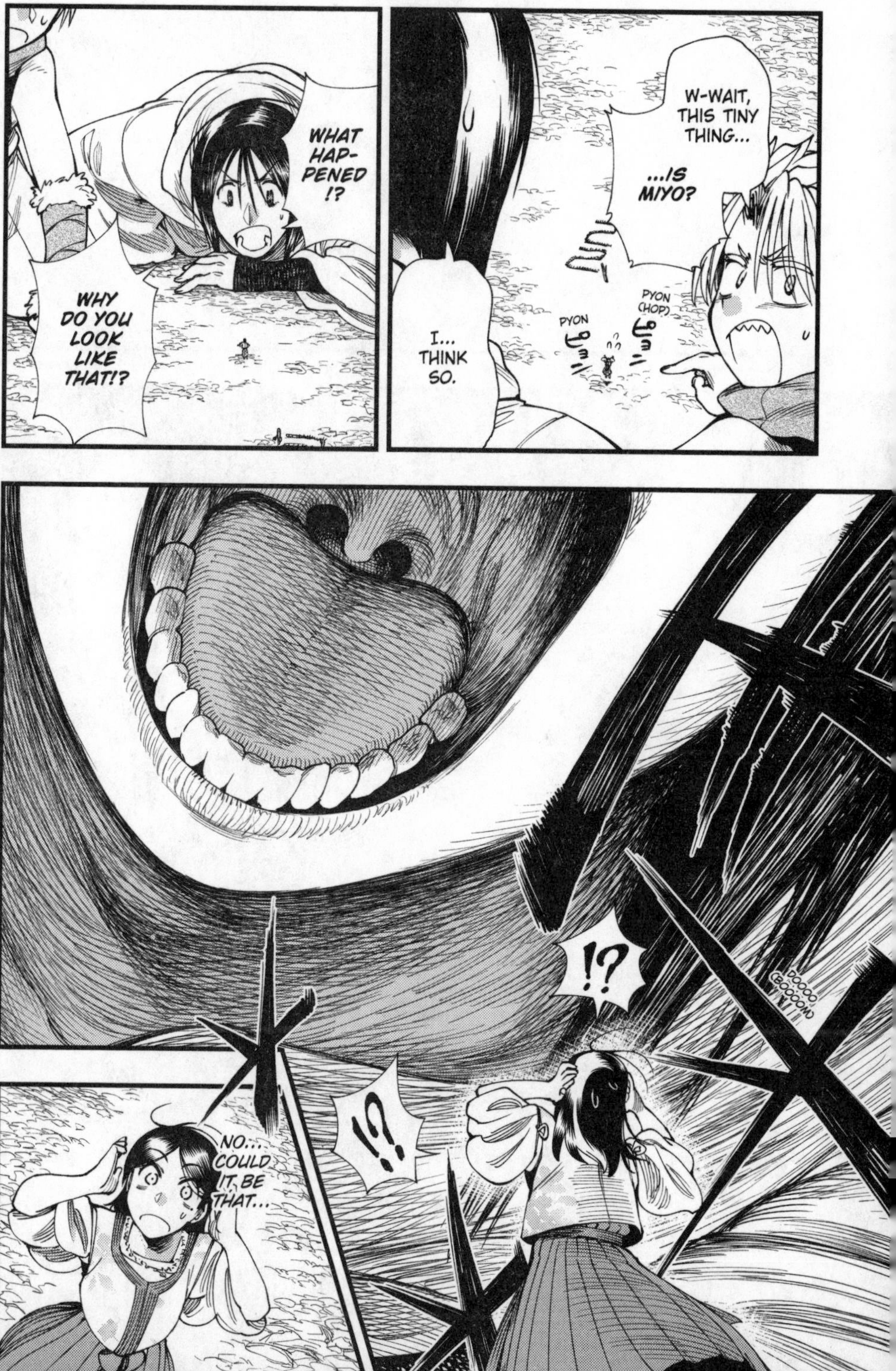
W-WAIT, THIS TINY THING...
...IS MIYO?
PYON (HOP)
PYON
I... THINK SO.
WHAT HAP-PENED!?
WHY DO YOU LOOK LIKE THAT!?
!?
DOOOO (BOOOOM)
!?
NO... COULD IT BE THAT...

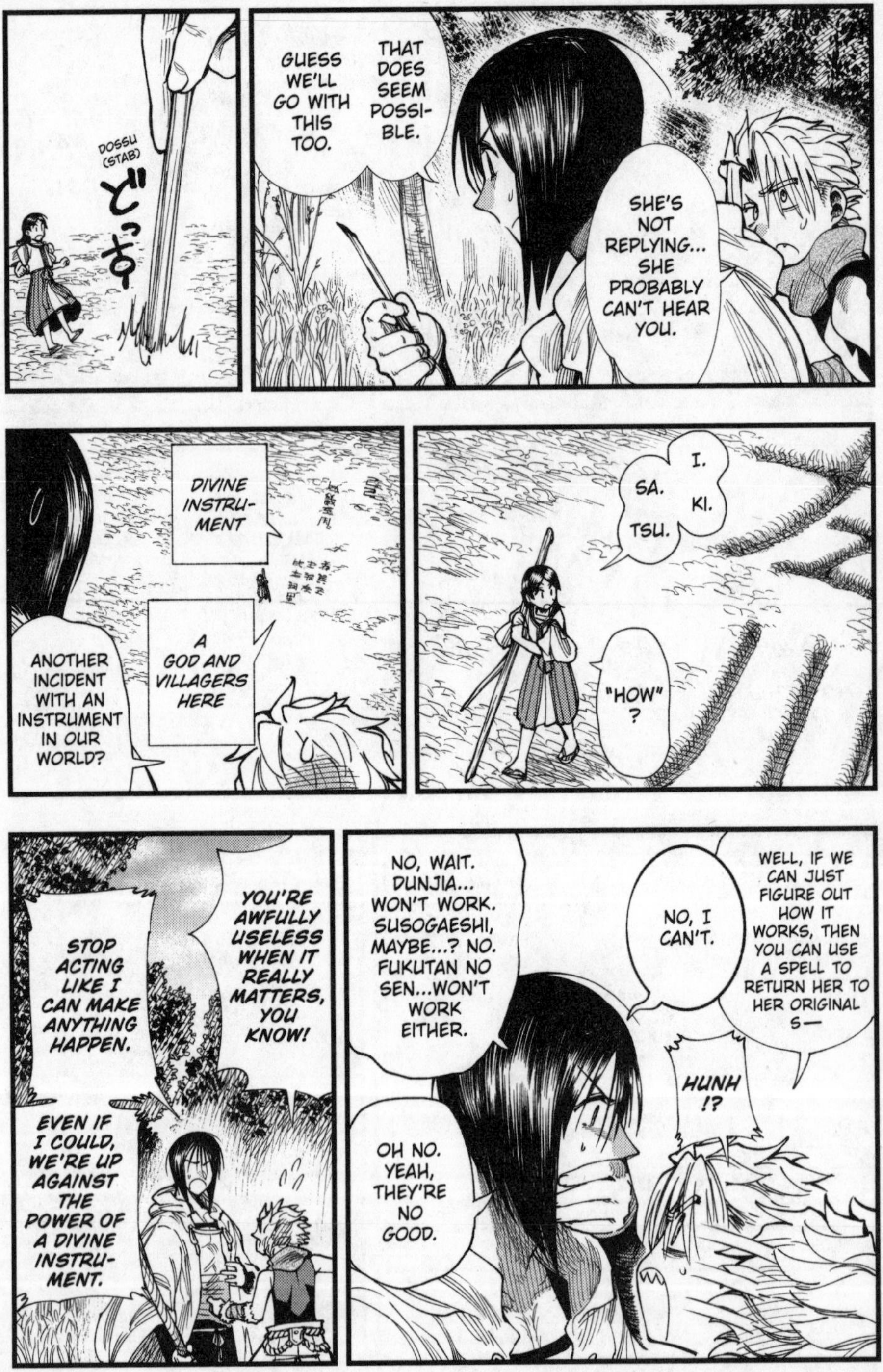
SHE'S NOT REPLYING... SHE PROBABLY CAN'T HEAR YOU.
THAT DOES SEEM POSSIBLE.
GUESS WE'LL GO WITH THIS TOO.
DOSSU (STAB)
どっす
I.
SA.
KI.
TSU.
"HOW" ?
DIVINE INSTRUMENT
A GOD AND VILLAGERS HERE
ANOTHER INCIDENT WITH AN INSTRUMENT IN OUR WORLD?
WELL, IF WE CAN JUST FIGURE OUT HOW IT WORKS, THEN YOU CAN USE A SPELL TO RETURN HER TO HER ORIGINAL S—
NO, I CAN'T.
NO, WAIT. DUNJIA... WON'T WORK. SUSOGAESHI, MAYBE...? NO. FUKUTAN NO SEN...WON'T WORK EITHER.
HUNH !?
OH NO. YEAH, THEY'RE NO GOOD.
YOU'RE AWFULLY USELESS WHEN IT REALLY MATTERS, YOU KNOW!
STOP ACTING LIKE I CAN MAKE ANYTHING HAPPEN.
EVEN IF I COULD, WE'RE UP AGAINST THE POWER OF A DIVINE INSTRUMENT.

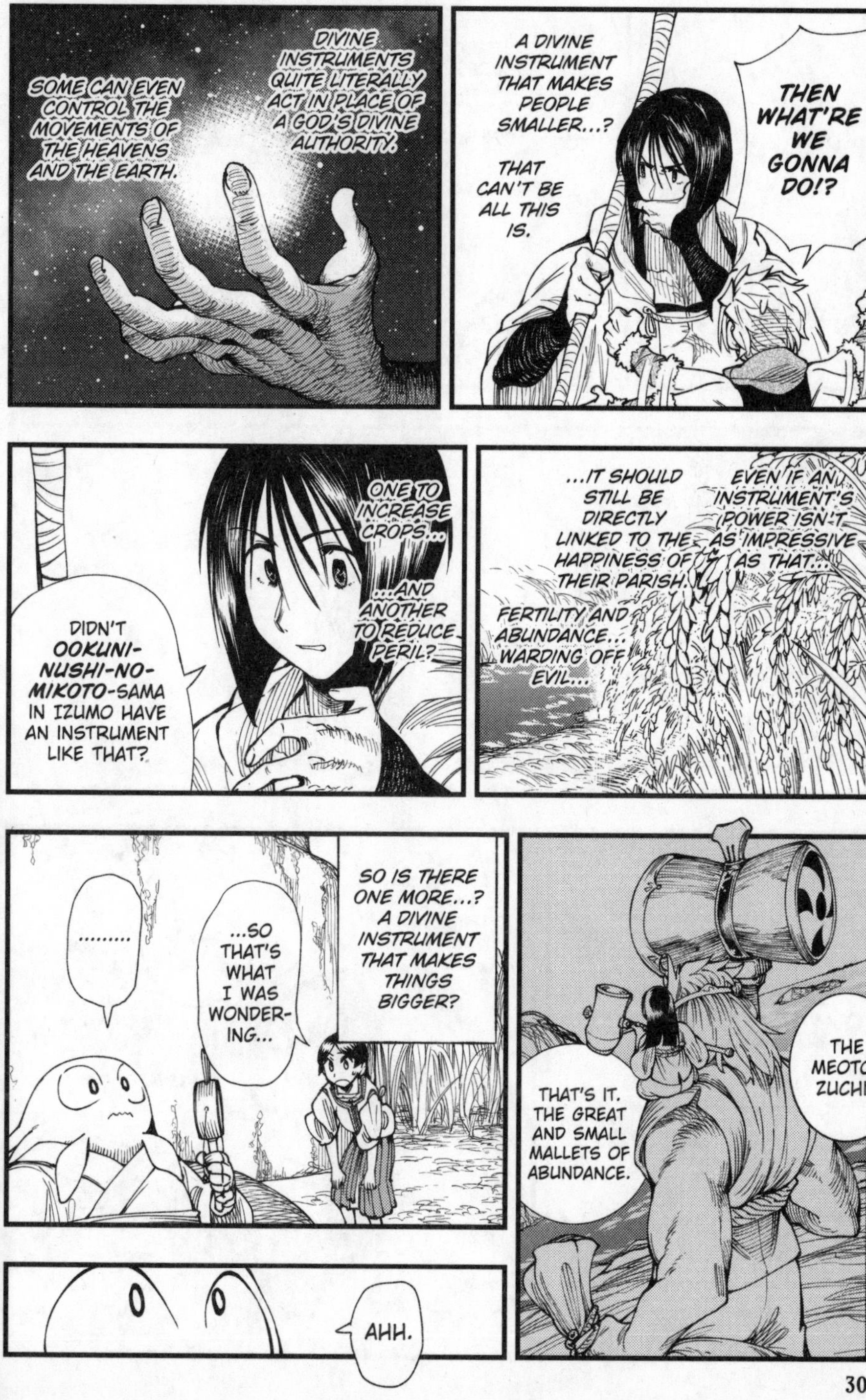
THEN WHAT'RE WE GONNA DO!?
A DIVINE INSTRUMENT THAT MAKES PEOPLE SMALLER...?
THAT CAN'T BE ALL THIS IS.
DIVINE INSTRUMENTS QUITE LITERALLY ACT IN PLACE OF A GOD'S DIVINE AUTHORITY.
SOME CAN EVEN CONTROL THE MOVEMENTS OF THE HEAVENS AND THE EARTH.
EVEN IF AN INSTRUMENT'S POWER ISN'T AS IMPRESSIVE AS THAT...
...IT SHOULD STILL BE DIRECTLY LINKED TO THE HAPPINESS OF THEIR PARISH.
FERTILITY AND ABUNDANCE... WARDING OFF EVIL...
ONE TO INCREASE CROPS...
...AND ANOTHER TO REDUCE PERIL?
DIDN'T OOKUNI-NUSHI-NO-MIKOTO-SAMA IN IZUMO HAVE AN INSTRUMENT LIKE THAT?
THE MEOTO-ZUCHI?
THAT'S IT. THE GREAT AND SMALL MALLETS OF ABUNDANCE.
SO IS THERE ONE MORE...? A DIVINE INSTRUMENT THAT MAKES THINGS BIGGER?
...SO THAT'S WHAT I WAS WONDERING...
....
AHH.

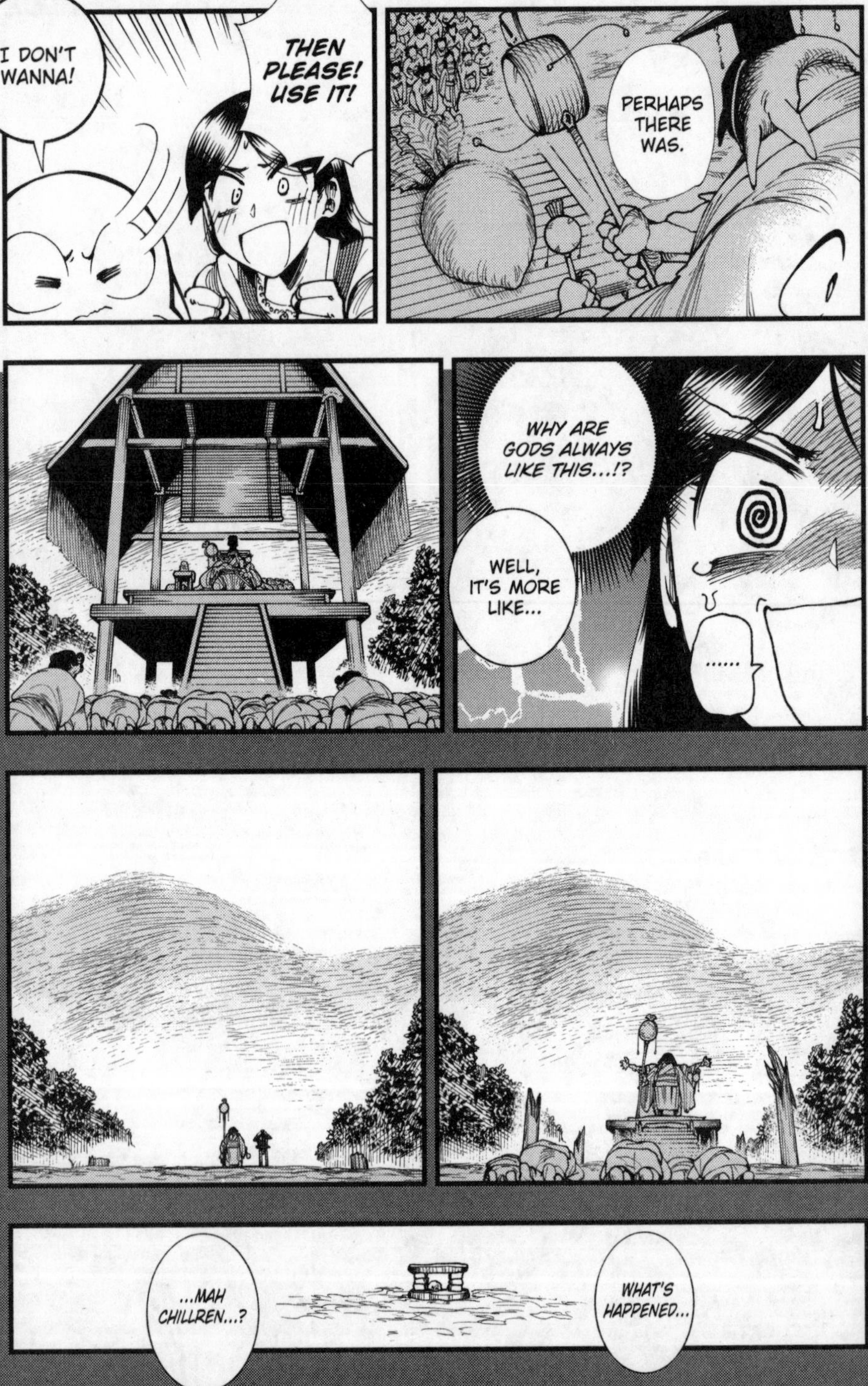
PERHAPS THERE WAS.
THEN PLEASE! USE IT!
I DON'T WANNA!
WHY ARE GODS ALWAYS LIKE THIS...!?
WELL, IT'S MORE LIKE...
......
WHAT'S HAPPENED...
...MAH CHILLREN...?

とーん…
TOOON (BONG)
WHY DON'T YA VISIT? WHERE'S YER RESPECT?
HAVE YA FORGOTTEN THOSE SPLENNID DAYS?
HAVE YA FORGOTTEN THE SOUND OF THIS GREAT DRUM THAT ASSURES PROSPERITY?
とーん…
TOOON
I SWING IT AGAIN AND AGAIN...
...BUT THEIR ADORATION NEVER GROWS.
AHH... THIS...
THIS AWFUL THING...
I NEVER...
TEN (TONG)
...WANT TO SEE IT AGAIN...!!

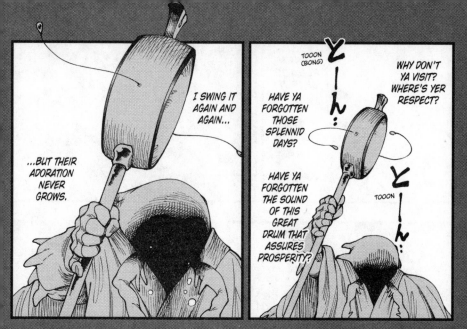

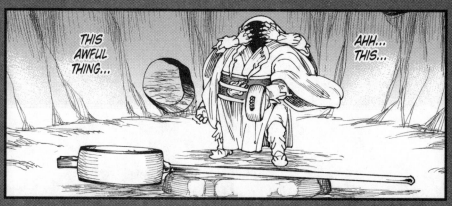

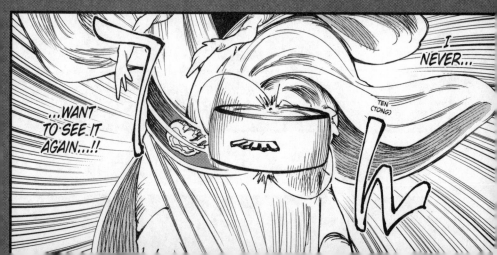

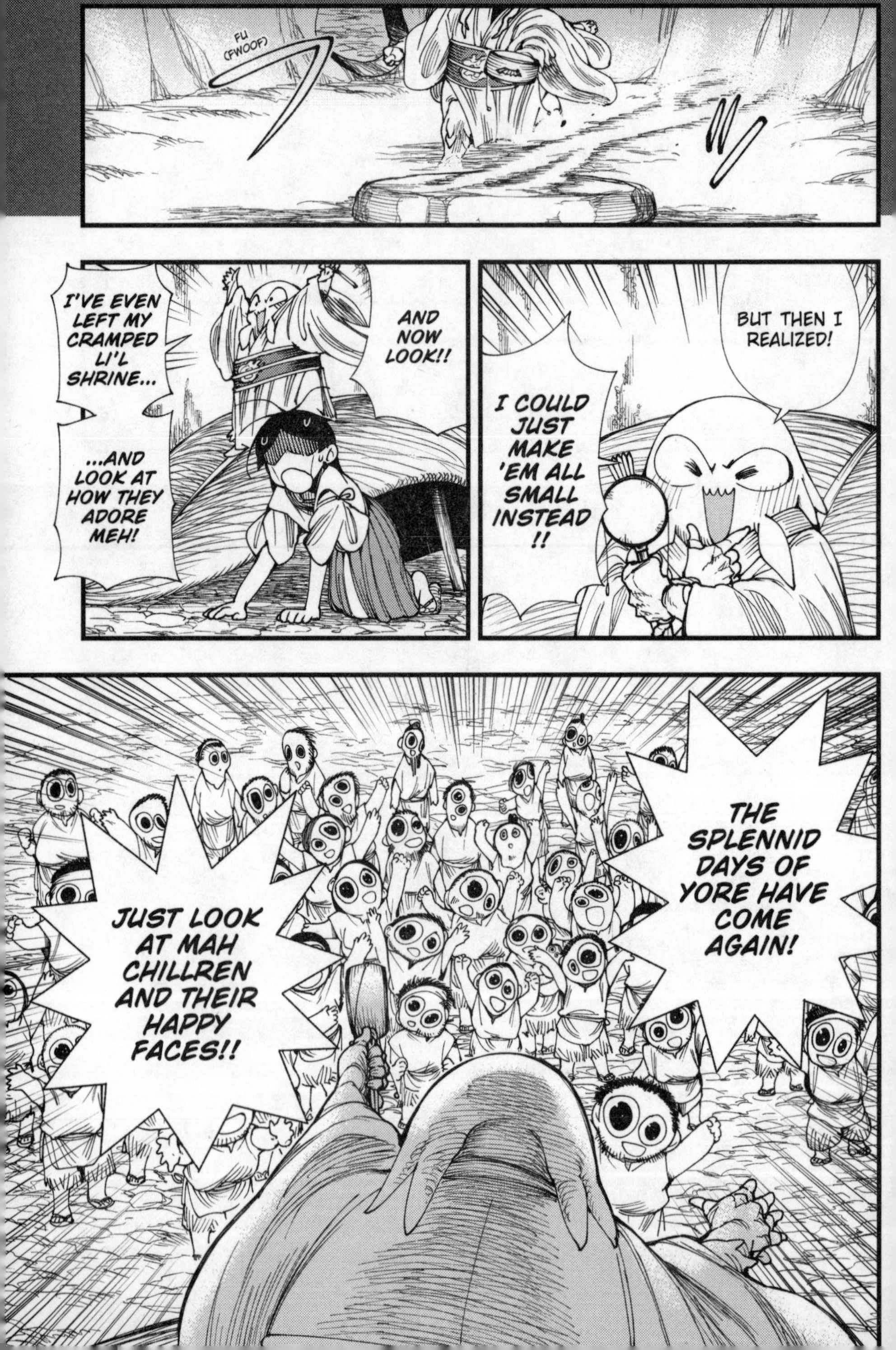
FU
(FWOOF)
BUT THEN I REALIZED!
I COULD JUST MAKE 'EM ALL SMALL INSTEAD!!
AND NOW LOOK!!
I'VE EVEN LEFT MY CRAMPED LI'L SHRINE...
...AND LOOK AT HOW THEY ADORE MEH!
THE SPLENNID DAYS OF YORE HAVE COME AGAIN!
JUST LOOK AT MAH CHILLREN AND THEIR HAPPY FACES!!

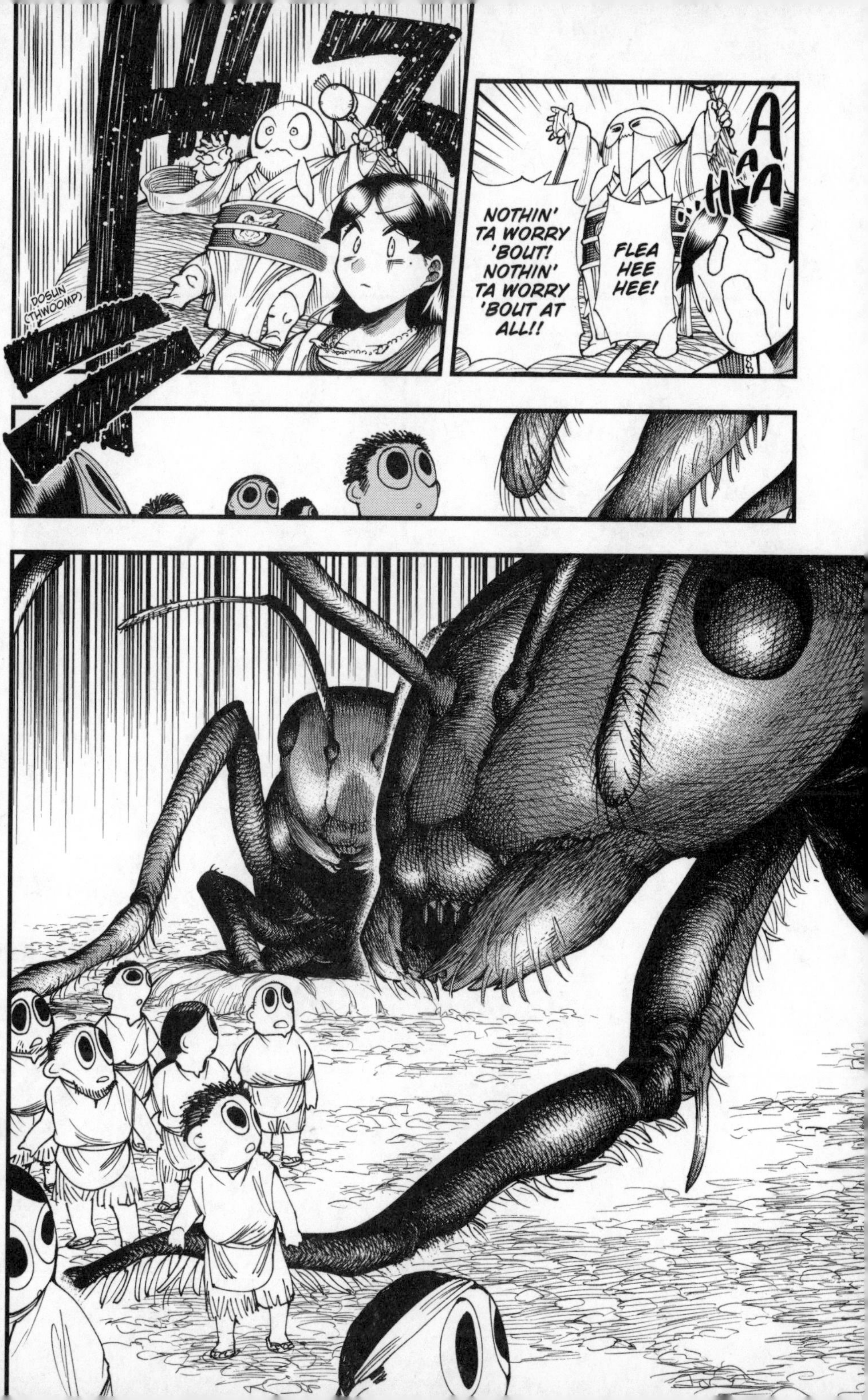
AAA...HA
FLEA HEE HEE!
NOTHIN' TA WORRY 'BOUT! NOTHIN' TA WORRY 'BOUT AT ALL!!
DOSUN (THWOOMP)

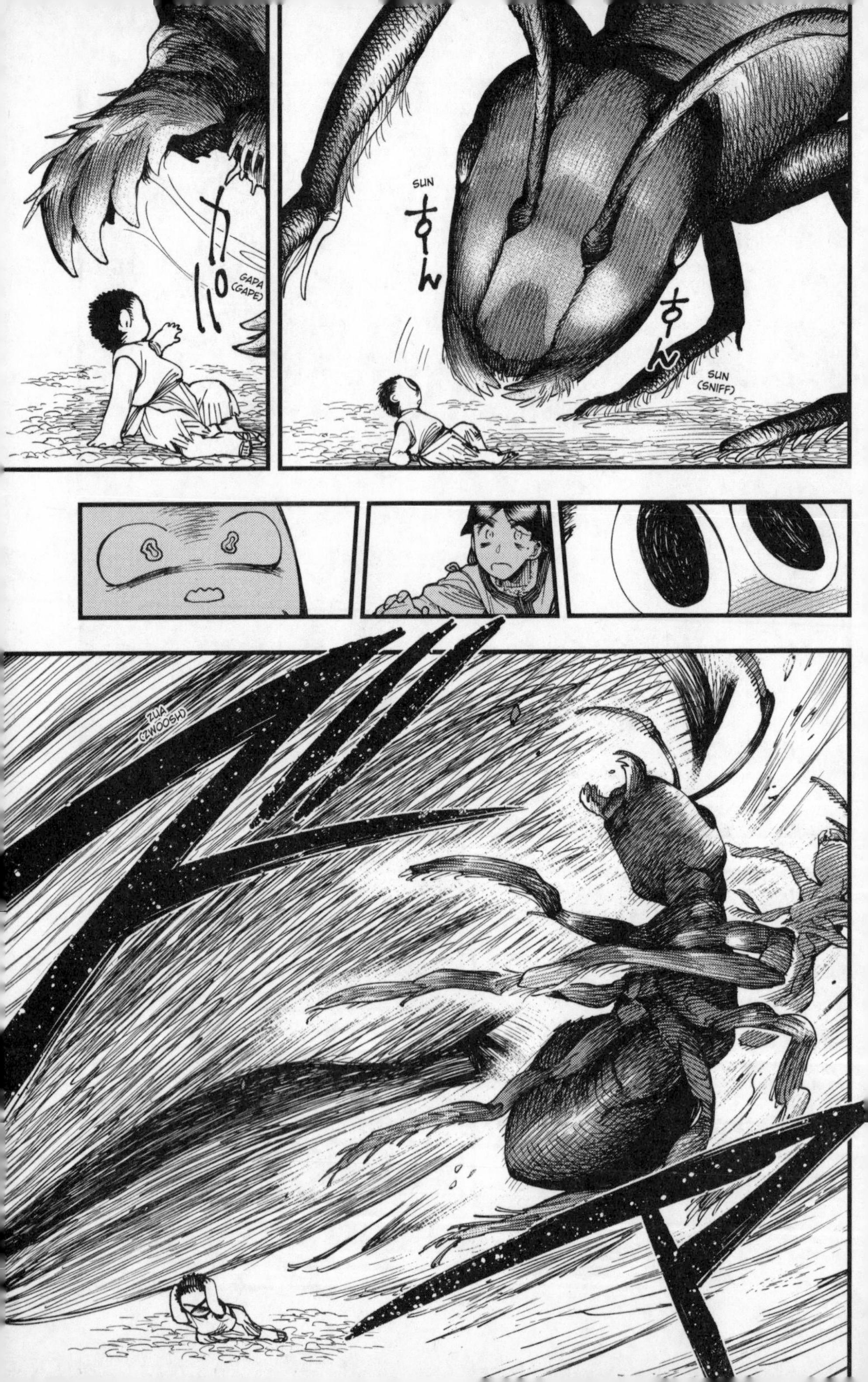
SUN
すん
すん
SUN (SNIFF)
GAPA (GAPE)
ZUA (ZWOOSH)

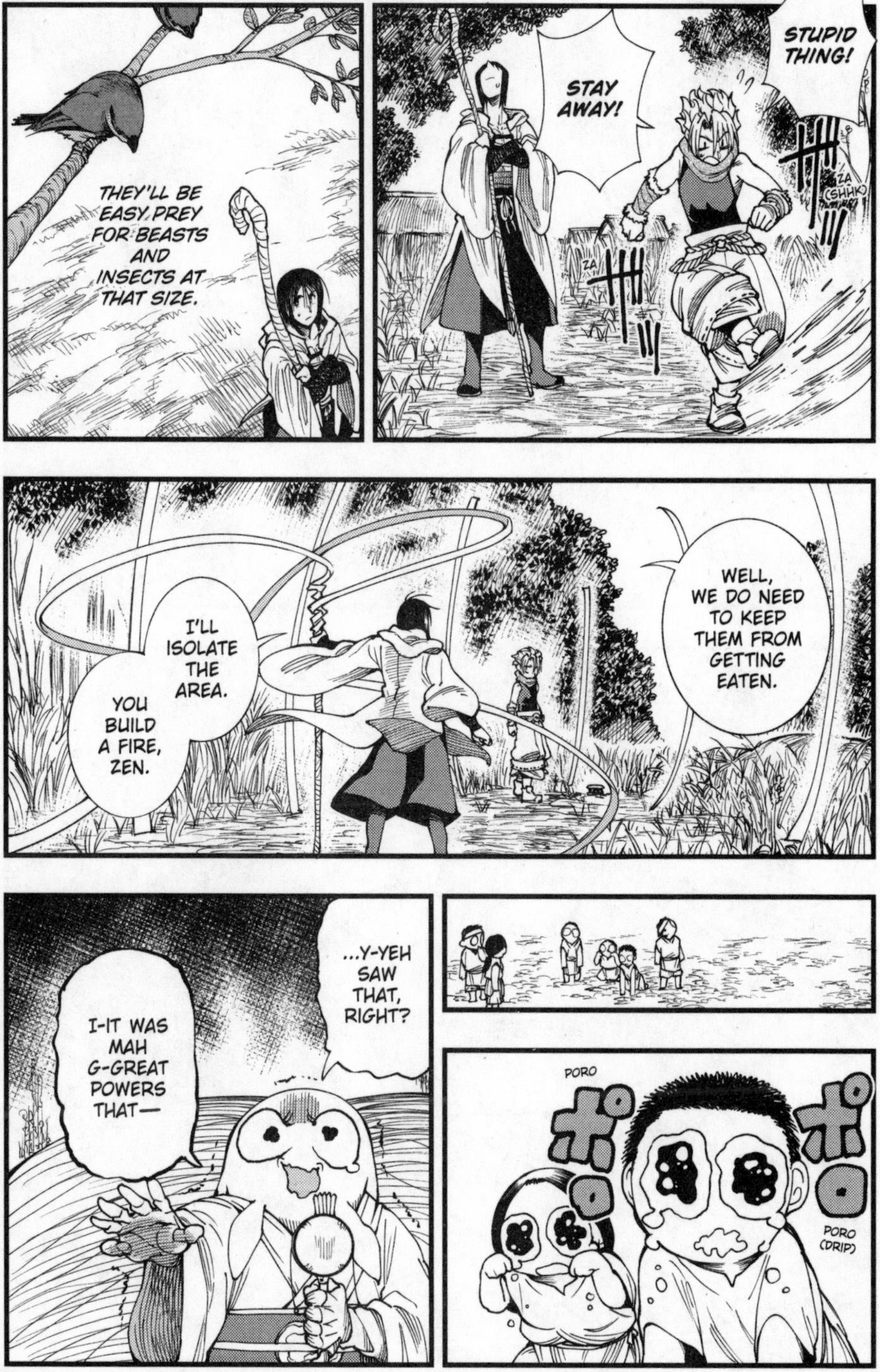
STUPID THING!
STAY AWAY!
ZA (SHHK)
ZA
THEY'LL BE EASY PREY FOR BEASTS AND INSECTS AT THAT SIZE.
WELL, WE DO NEED TO KEEP THEM FROM GETTING EATEN.
I'LL ISOLATE THE AREA.
YOU BUILD A FIRE, ZEN.
PORO
PORO (DRIP)
...Y-YEH SAW THAT, RIGHT?
I-IT WAS MAH G-GREAT POWERS THAT—

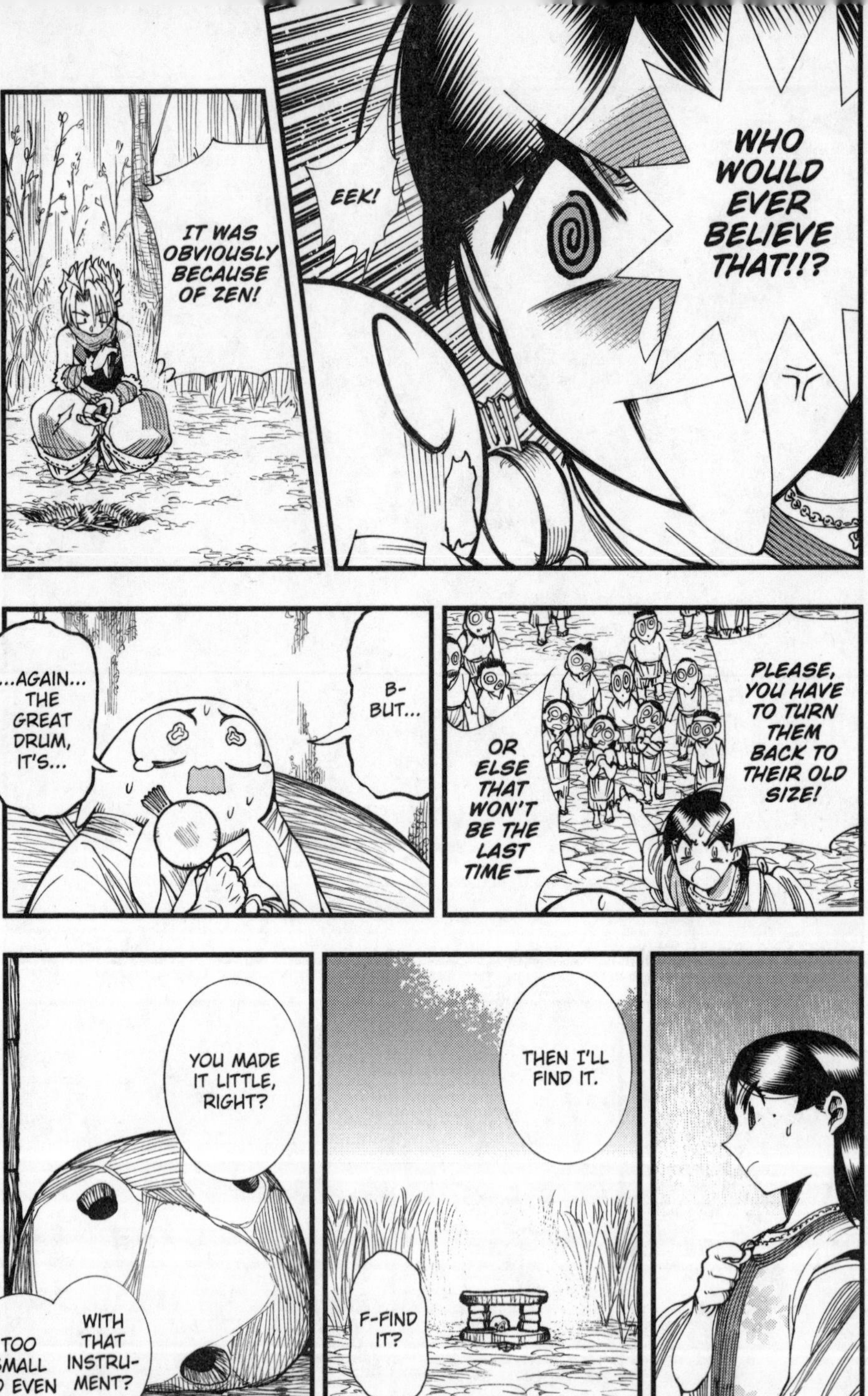
WHO WOULD EVER BELIEVE THAT!!?
EEK!
IT WAS OBVIOUSLY BECAUSE OF ZEN!
PLEASE, YOU HAVE TO TURN THEM BACK TO THEIR OLD SIZE!
OR ELSE THAT WON'T BE THE LAST TIME—
B-BUT...
...AGAIN... THE GREAT DRUM, IT'S...
THEN I'LL FIND IT.
F-FIND IT?
YOU MADE IT LITTLE, RIGHT?
WITH THAT INSTRUMENT?
TOO SMALL TO EVEN SEE?

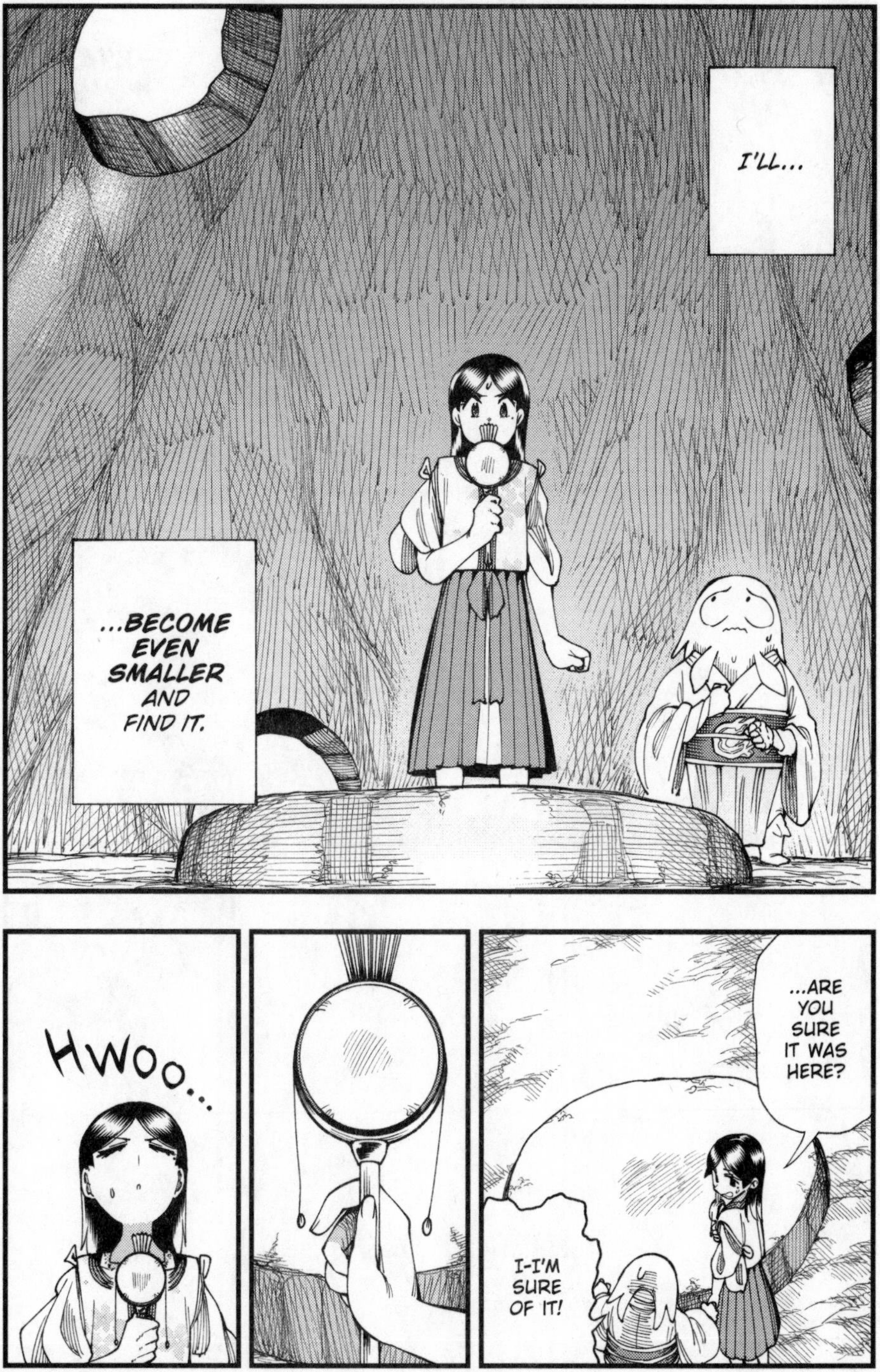
I'LL...
...BECOME EVEN SMALLER AND FIND IT.
...ARE YOU SURE IT WAS HERE?
I-I'M SURE OF IT!
HWOO...

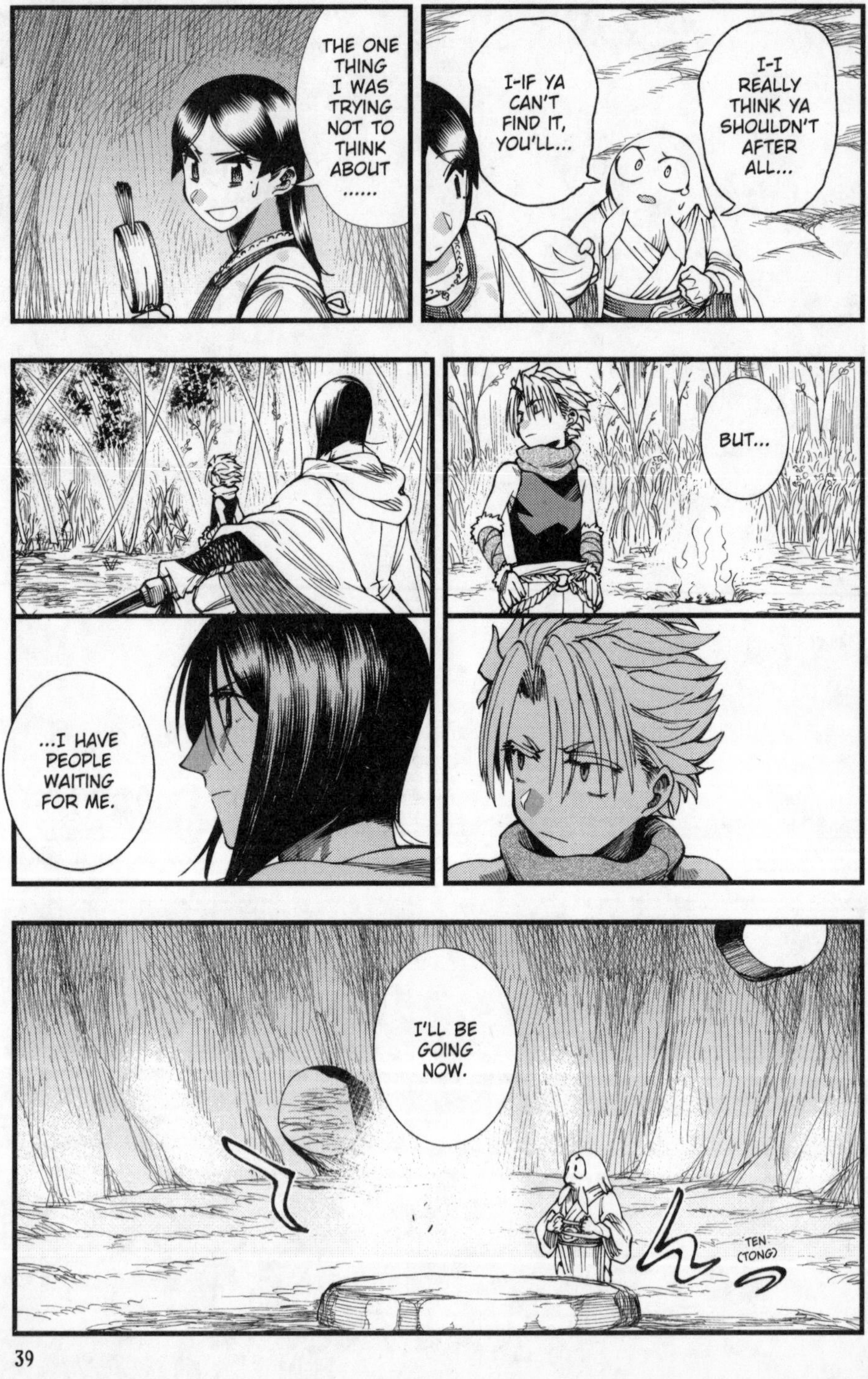
I-I REALLY THINK YA SHOULDN'T AFTER ALL...
I-IF YA CAN'T FIND IT, YOU'LL...
THE ONE THING I WAS TRYING NOT TO THINK ABOUT ......
BUT...
...I HAVE PEOPLE WAITING FOR ME.
I'LL BE GOING NOW.
TEN (TONG)

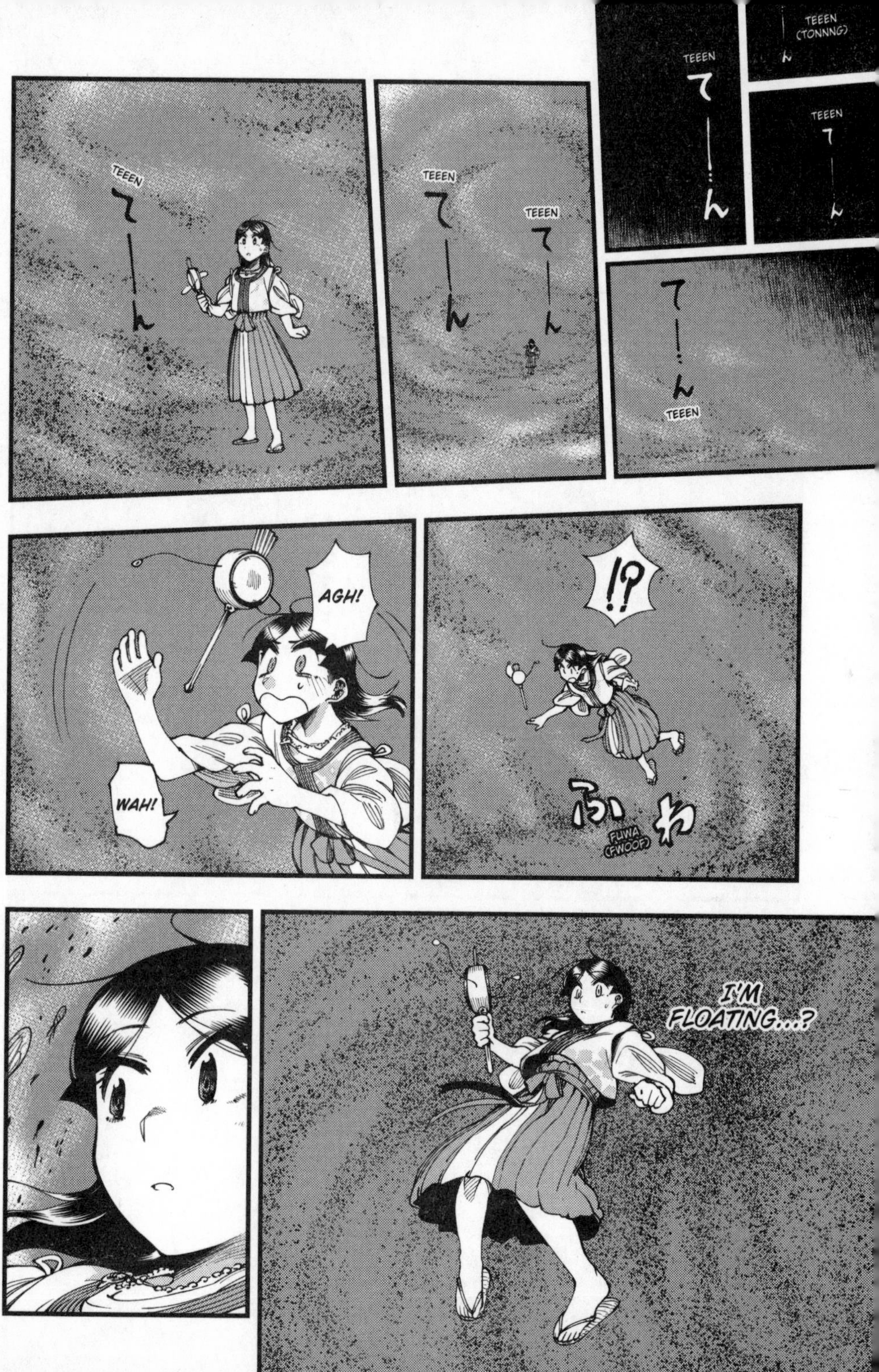
TEEEN (TONNNG)
ん
TEEEN
てーん
TEEEN
てーん
てーん
TEEEN
TEEEN
てーん
TEEEN
てーん
TEEEN
てーん
!?
ふわ
FUWA (FWOOF)
AGH!
WAH!
I'M FLOATING...?

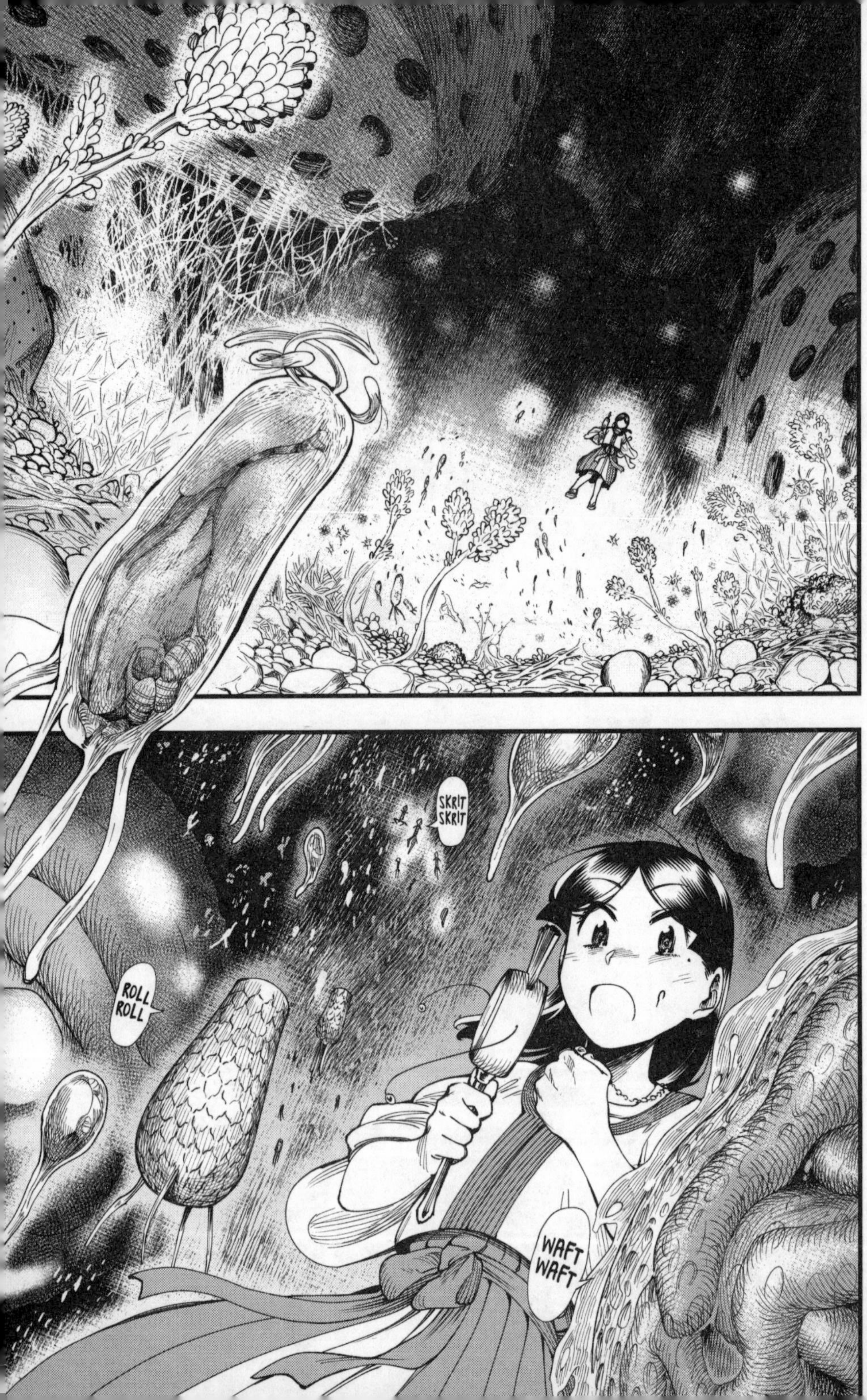
SKRIT SKRIT
ROLL ROLL
WAFT WAFT

BULGE BULGE
SWELL SWELL
FLAP FLAP
SLIDE SLIDE
SNAP SNAP
KRAK KRAK
TURN TURN
SPIN SPIN
TURN TURN
SHAKE SHAKE

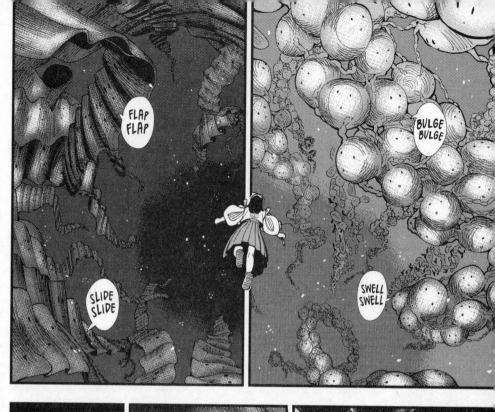

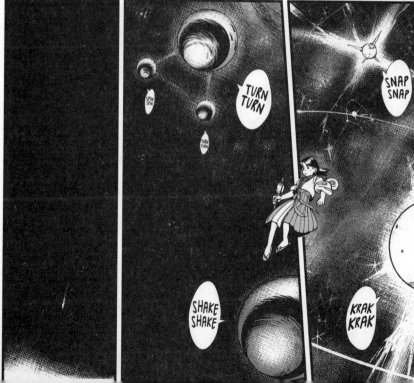

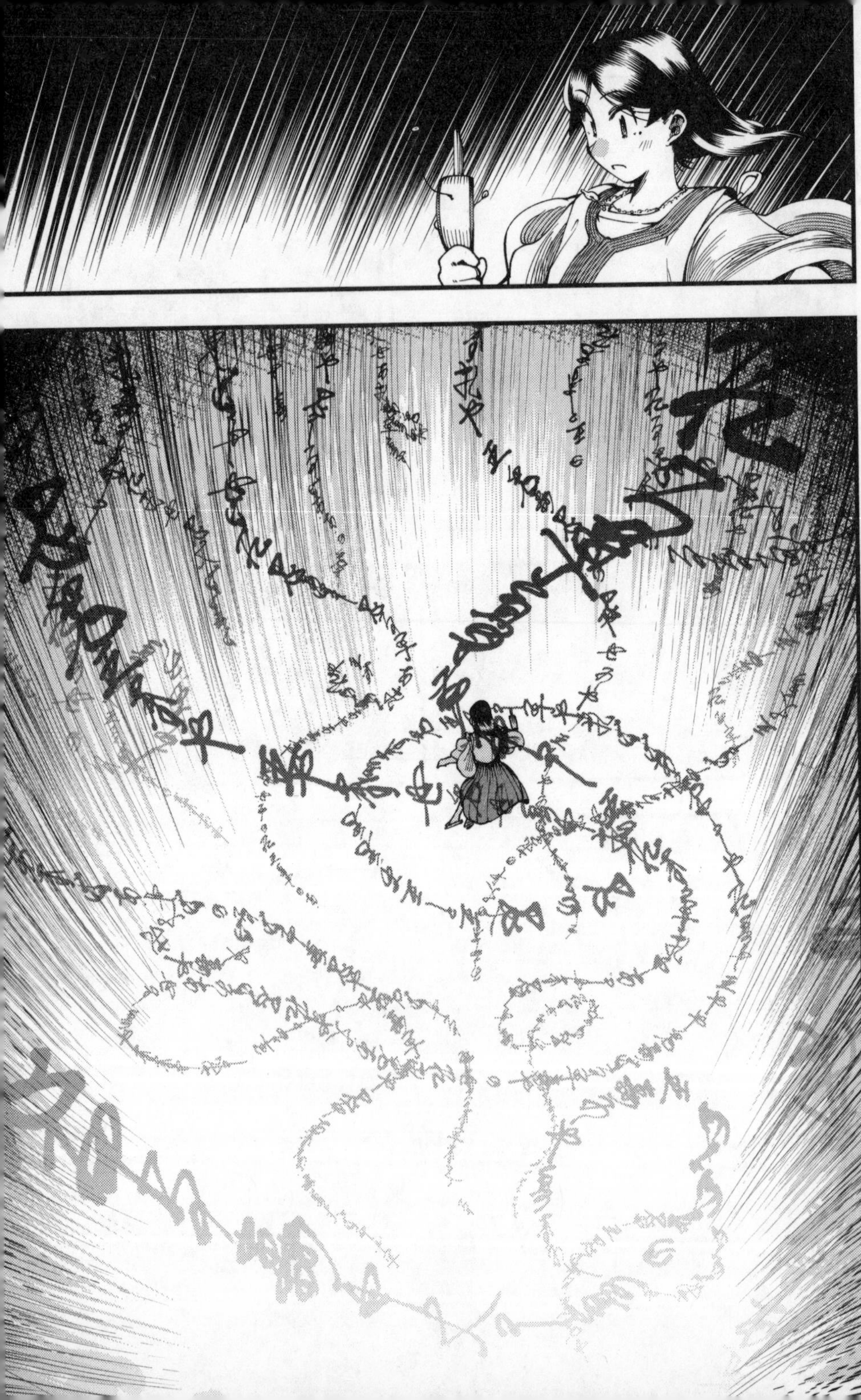

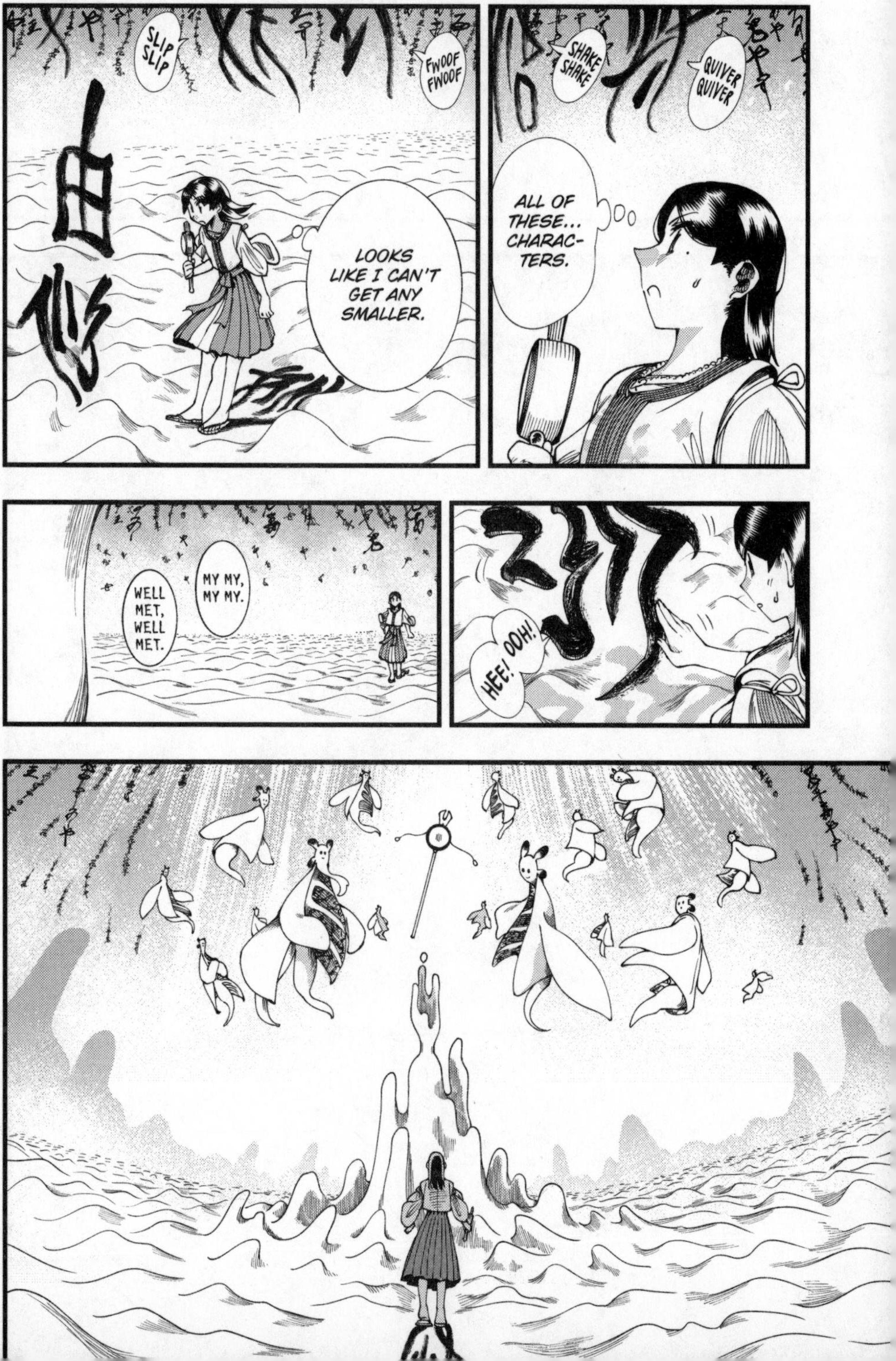
QUIVER QUIVER
SHAKE SHAKE
ALL OF THESE... CHARAC-TERS.
FWOOF FWOOF
SLIP SLIP
LOOKS LIKE I CAN'T GET ANY SMALLER.
HEE! OOH!
MY MY, MY MY.
WELL MET, WELL MET.

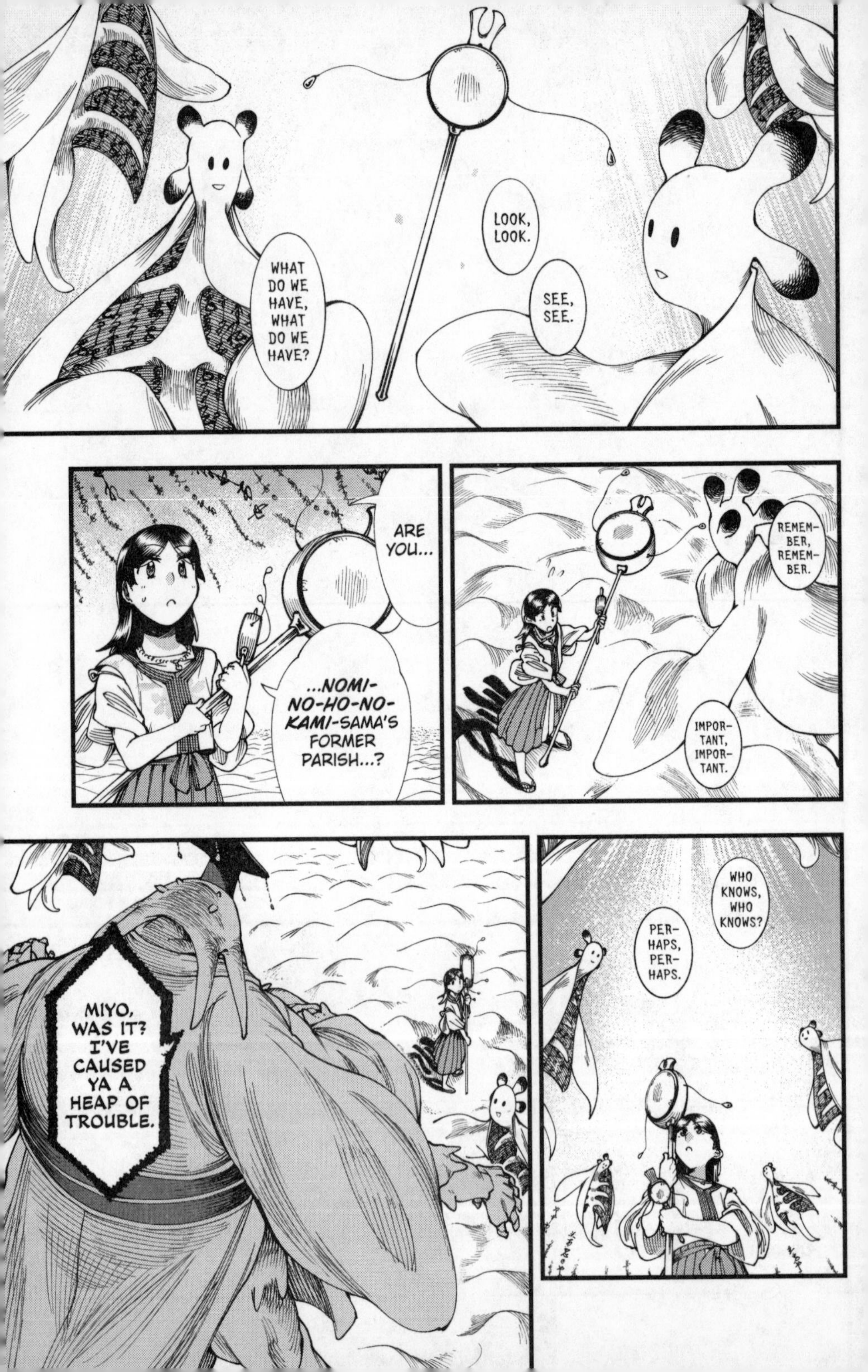

LOOK, LOOK.
SEE, SEE.
WHAT DO WE HAVE, WHAT DO WE HAVE?
REMEMBER, REMEMBER.
IMPORTANT, IMPORTANT.
ARE YOU...
...*NOMI-NO-HO-NO-KAMI*-SAMA'S FORMER PARISH...?
WHO KNOWS, WHO KNOWS?
PERHAPS, PERHAPS.
MIYO, WAS IT? I'VE CAUSED YA A HEAP OF TROUBLE.

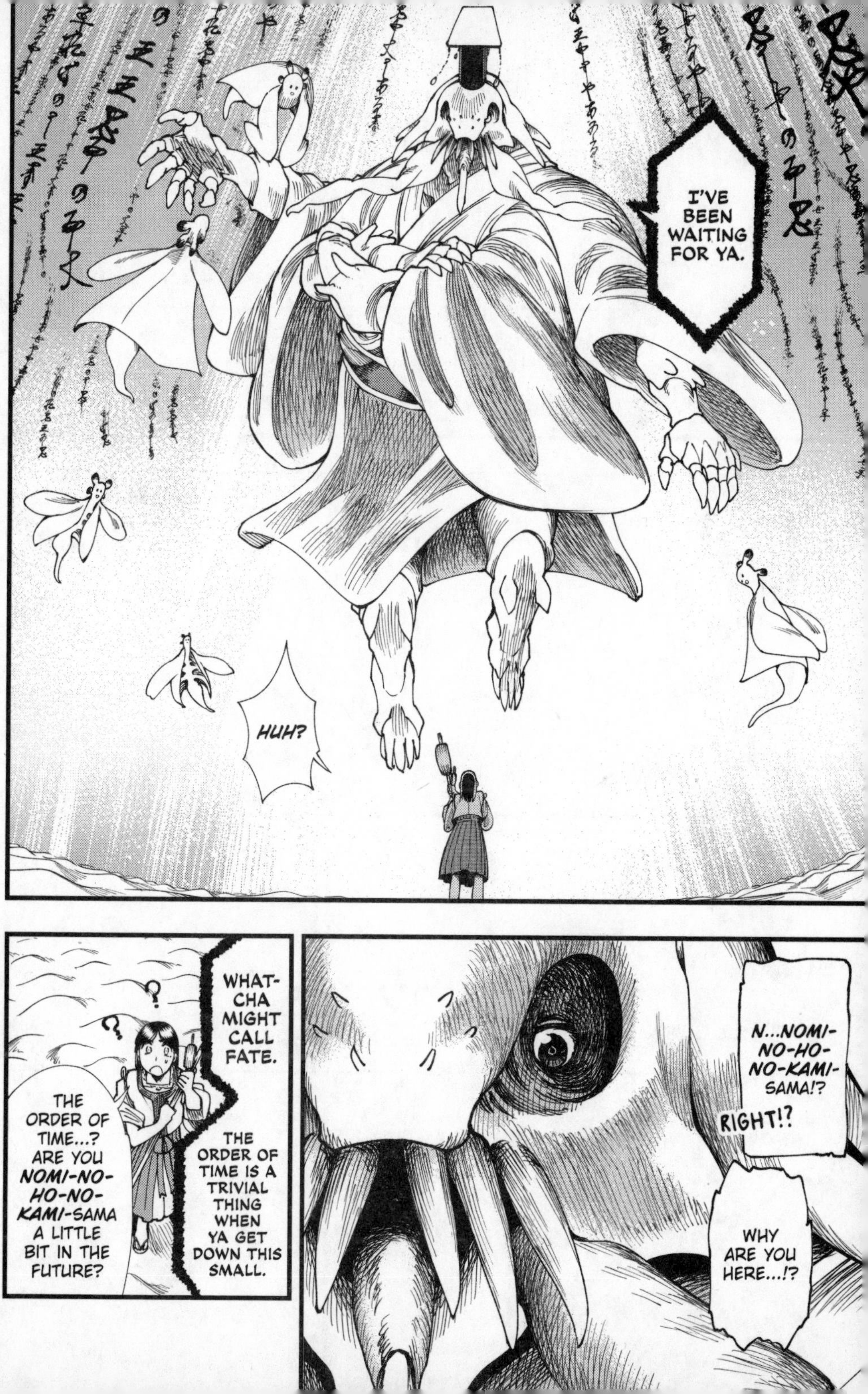
I'VE BEEN WAITING FOR YA.
HUH?
N...NOMI-NO-HO-NO-KAMI-SAMA!?
RIGHT!?
WHY ARE YOU HERE...!?
WHAT-CHA MIGHT CALL FATE.
THE ORDER OF TIME IS A TRIVIAL THING WHEN YA GET DOWN THIS SMALL.
THE ORDER OF TIME...? ARE YOU NOMI-NO-HO-NO-KAMI-SAMA A LITTLE BIT IN THE FUTURE?

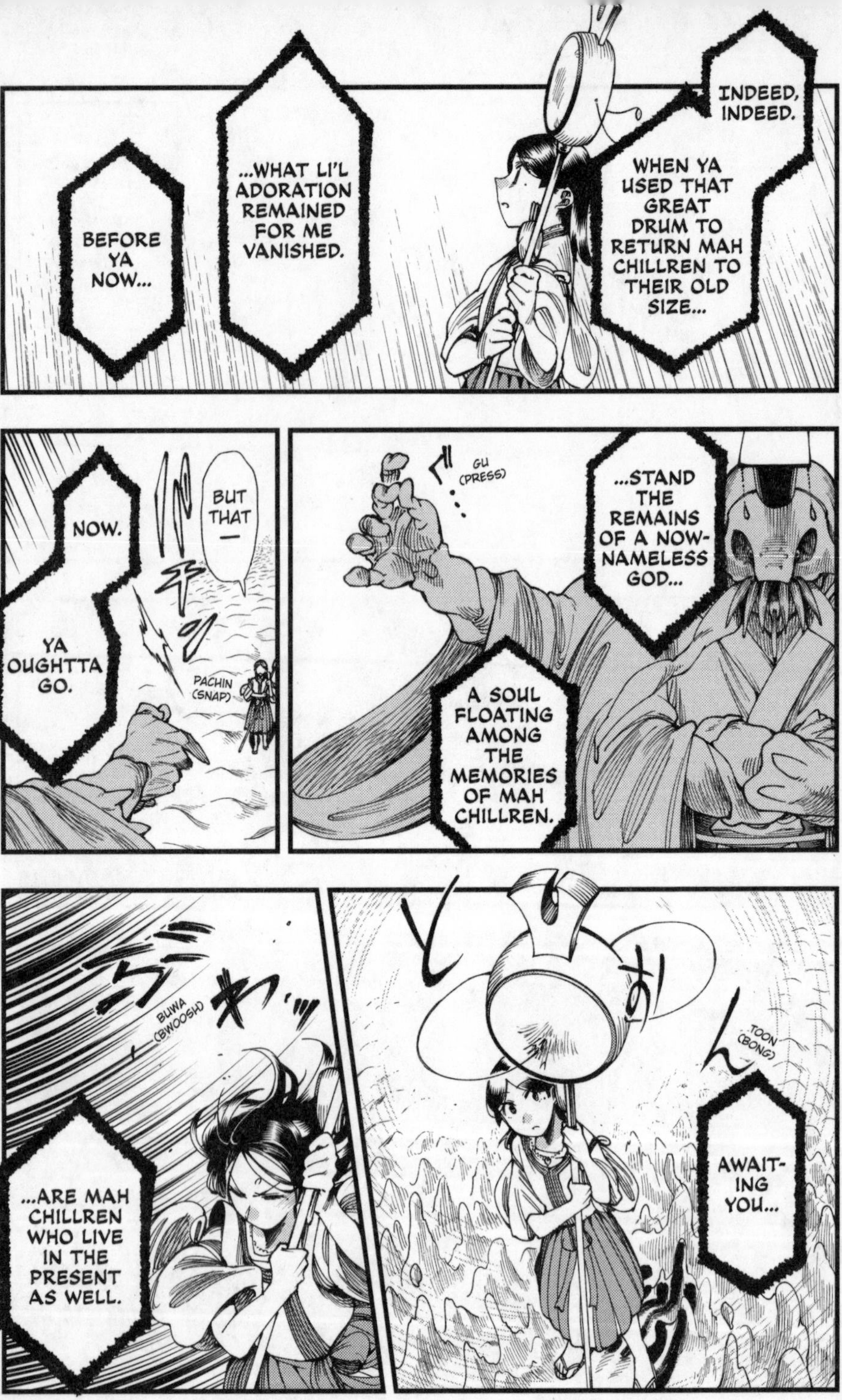
INDEED, INDEED.
WHEN YA USED THAT GREAT DRUM TO RETURN MAH CHILLREN TO THEIR OLD SIZE...
...WHAT LI'L ADORATION REMAINED FOR ME VANISHED.
BEFORE YA NOW...
...STAND THE REMAINS OF A NOW-NAMELESS GOD...
GU (PRESS)
A SOUL FLOATING AMONG THE MEMORIES OF MAH CHILLREN.
BUT THAT—
PACHIN (SNAP)
NOW.
YA OUGHTTA GO.
TOON (BONG)
AWAIT-ING YOU...
BUWA (BWOOSH)
...ARE MAH CHILLREN WHO LIVE IN THE PRESENT AS WELL.

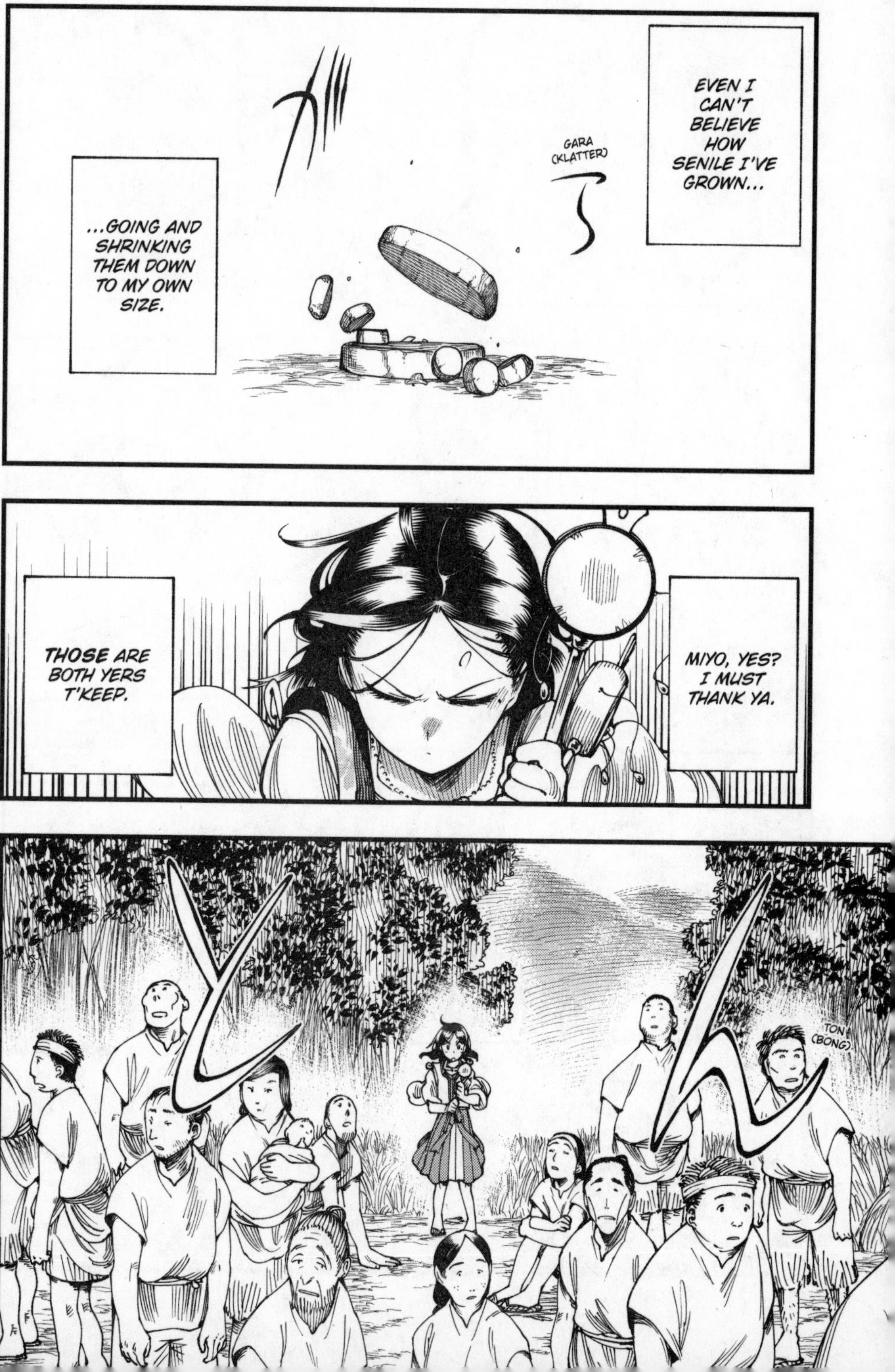
EVEN I CAN'T BELIEVE HOW SENILE I'VE GROWN...
GARA (KLATTER)
...GOING AND SHRINKING THEM DOWN TO MY OWN SIZE.
MIYO, YES? I MUST THANK YA.
THOSE ARE BOTH YERS T'KEEP.
TON (BONG)

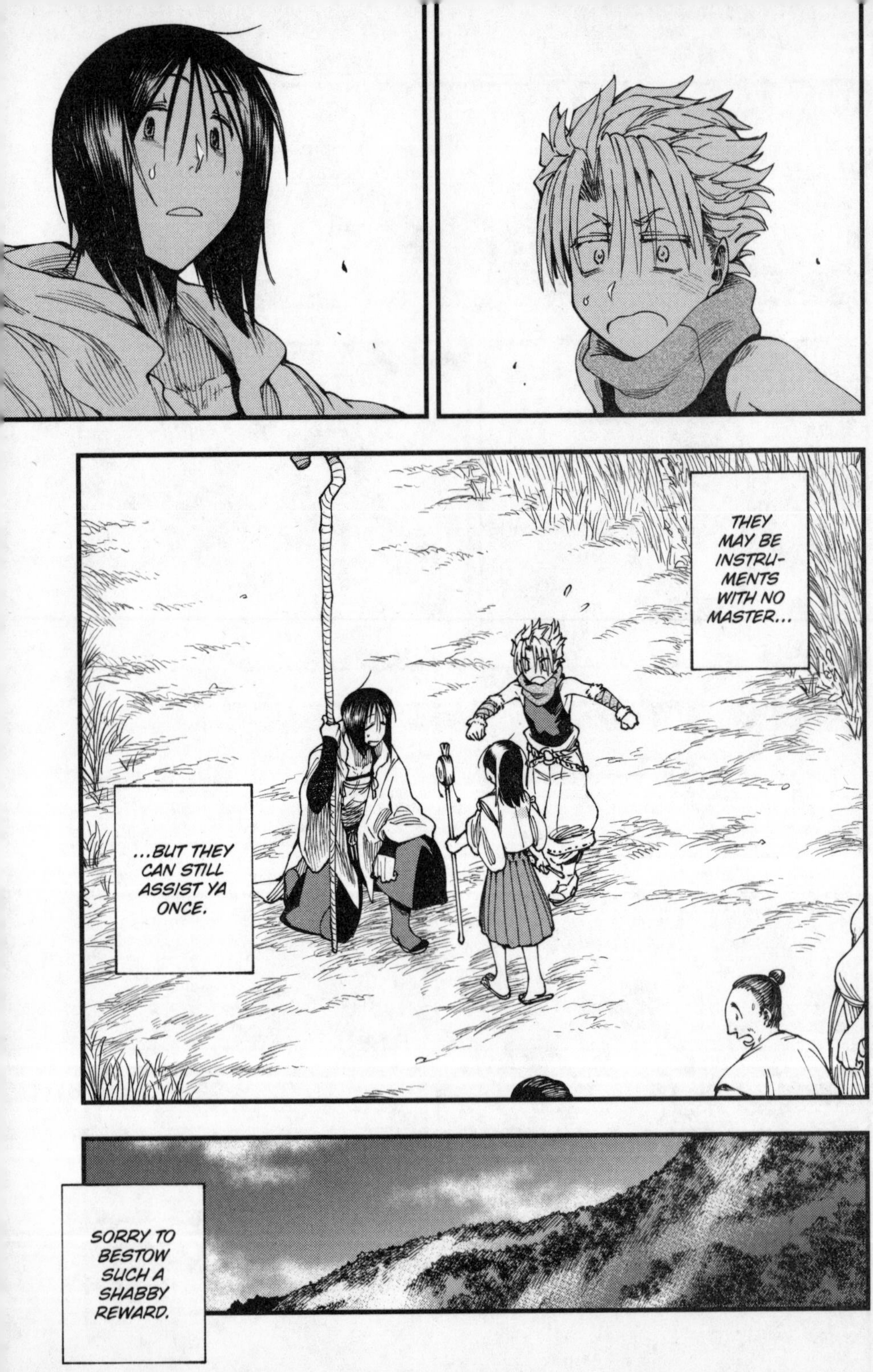
THEY MAY BE INSTRU-MENTS WITH NO MASTER...
...BUT THEY CAN STILL ASSIST YA ONCE.
SORRY TO BESTOW SUCH A SHABBY REWARD.

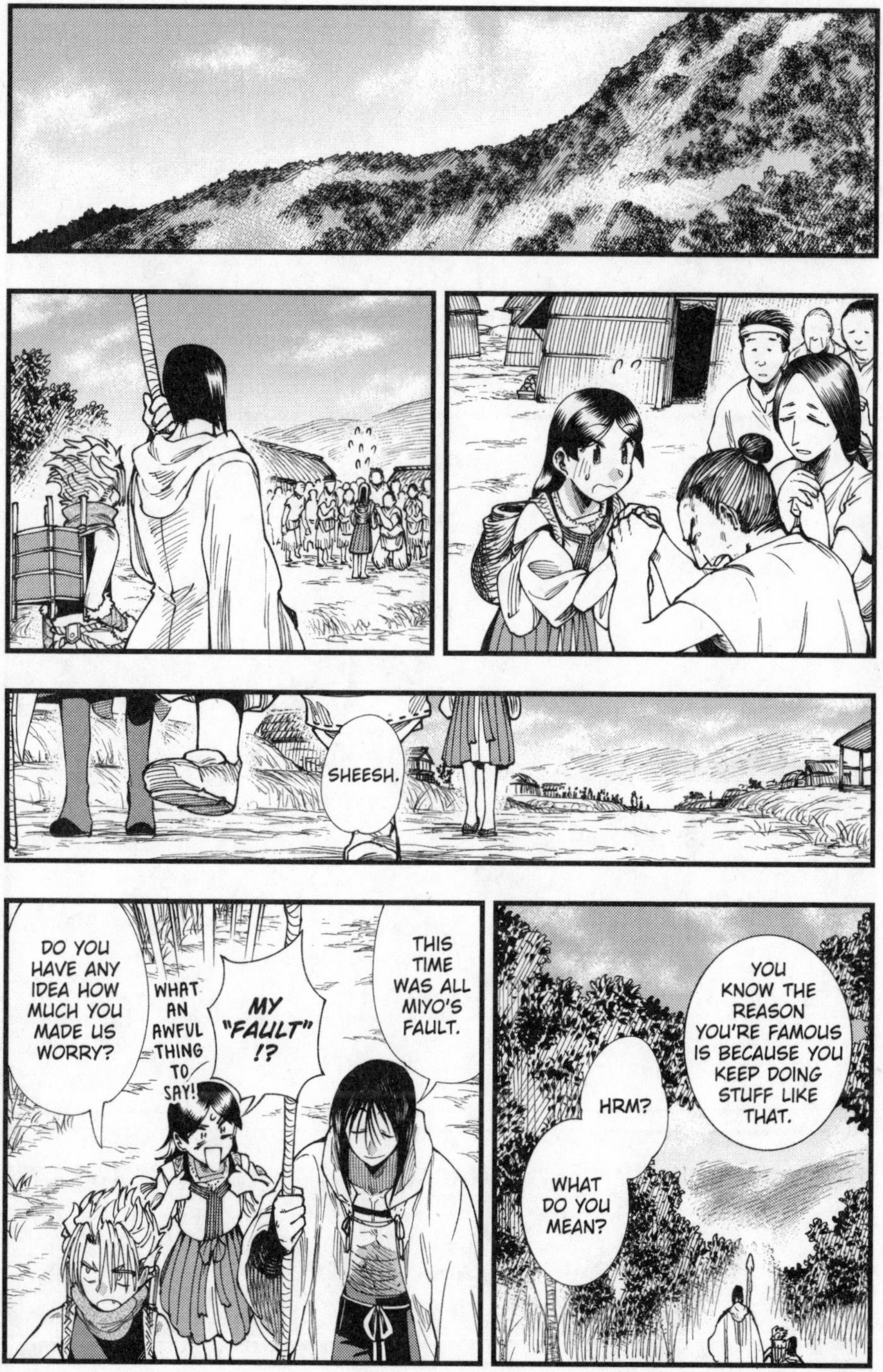
SHEESH.
YOU KNOW THE REASON YOU'RE FAMOUS IS BECAUSE YOU KEEP DOING STUFF LIKE THAT.
HRM?
WHAT DO YOU MEAN?
THIS TIME WAS ALL MIYO'S FAULT.
MY "FAULT"!?
WHAT AN AWFUL THING TO SAY!
DO YOU HAVE ANY IDEA HOW MUCH YOU MADE US WORRY?

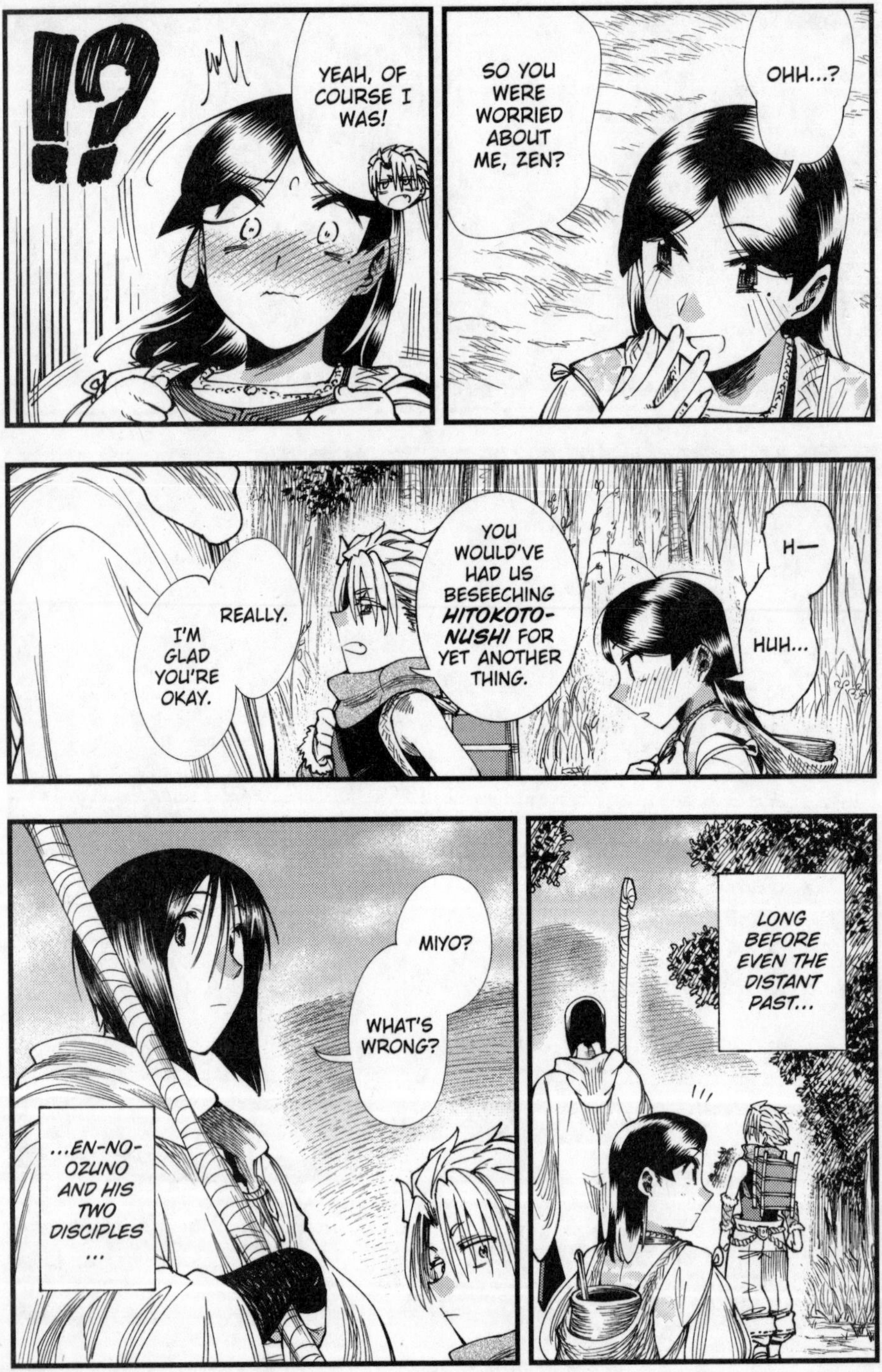
OHH...?
SO YOU WERE WORRIED ABOUT ME, ZEN?
YEAH, OF COURSE I WAS!
!?
H—
HUH...
YOU WOULD'VE HAD US BESEECHING *HITOKOTO-NUSHI* FOR YET ANOTHER THING.
REALLY.
I'M GLAD YOU'RE OKAY.
LONG BEFORE EVEN THE DISTANT PAST...
MIYO?
WHAT'S WRONG?
...EN-NO-OZUNO AND HIS TWO DISCIPLES...

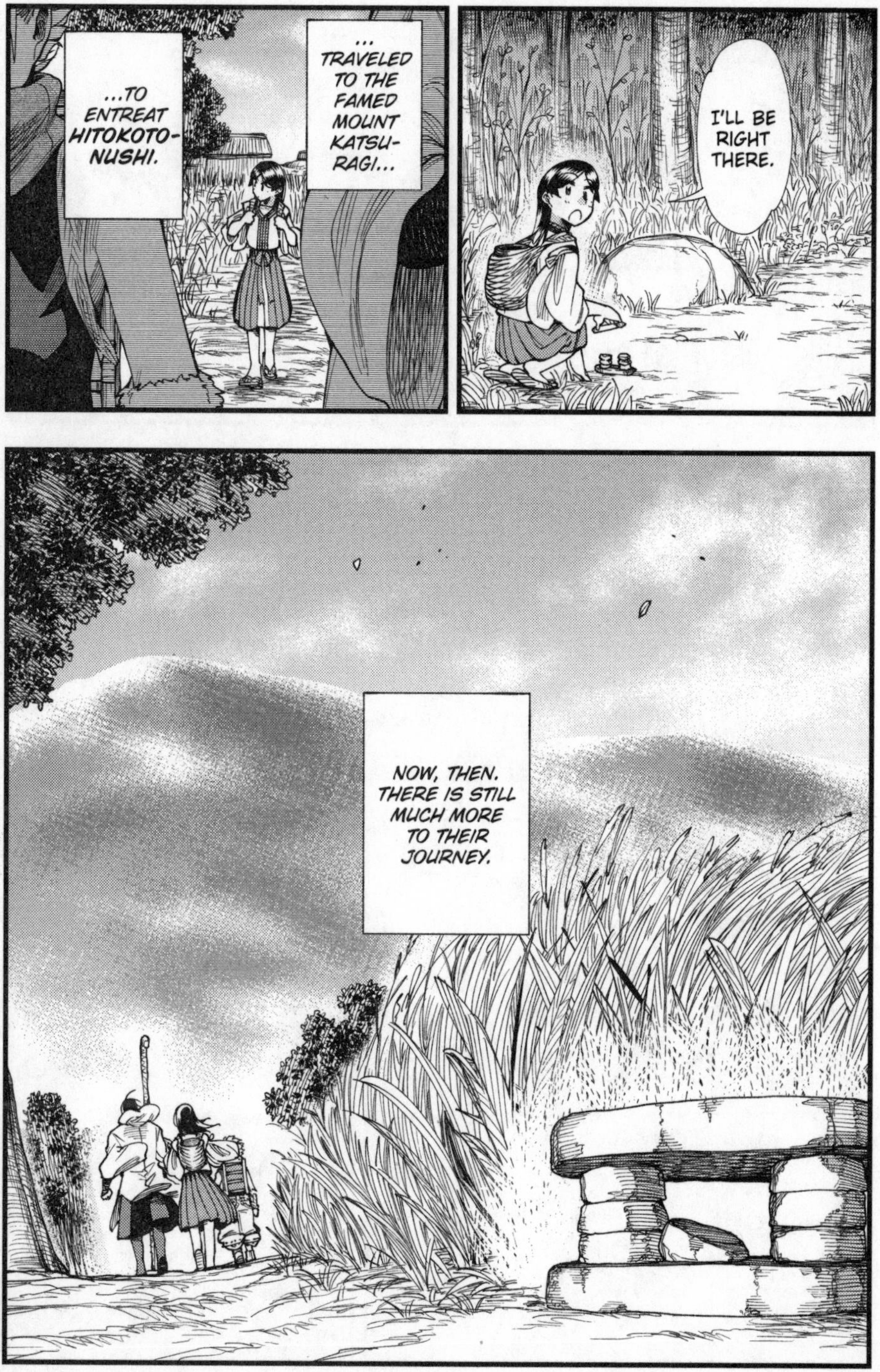
I'LL BE RIGHT THERE.
...TRAVELED TO THE FAMED MOUNT KATSURAGI...
...TO ENTREAT HITOKOTO-NUSHI.
NOW, THEN. THERE IS STILL MUCH MORE TO THEIR JOURNEY.

CHAPTER VII ❤ END

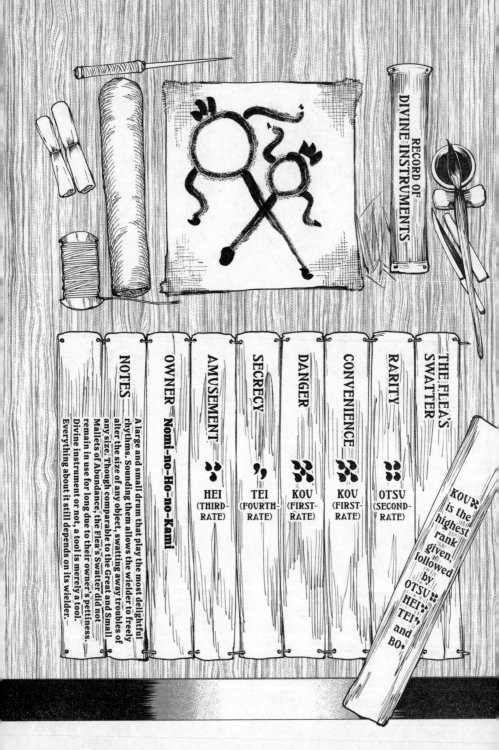

RECORD OF DIVINE INSTRUMENTS

THE FLEA'S SWATTER

RARITY	OTSU (SECOND-RATE)
CONVENIENCE	KOU (FIRST-RATE)
DANGER	KOU (FIRST-RATE)
SECRECY	TEI (FOURTH-RATE)
AMUSEMENT	HEI (THIRD-RATE)

OWNER **Nomi-no-Ho-no-Kami**

NOTES — A large and small drum that play the most delightful rhythms. Sounding them allows the wielder to freely alter the size of any object, swatting away troubles of any size. Though comparable to the Great and Small Mallets of Abundance, the Flea's Swatter did not remain in use for long due to their owner's pettiness. Divine instrument or not, a tool is merely a tool. Everything about it still depends on its wielder.

KOU is the highest rank given, followed by OTSU, HEI, TEI, and BO,

Touge Oni

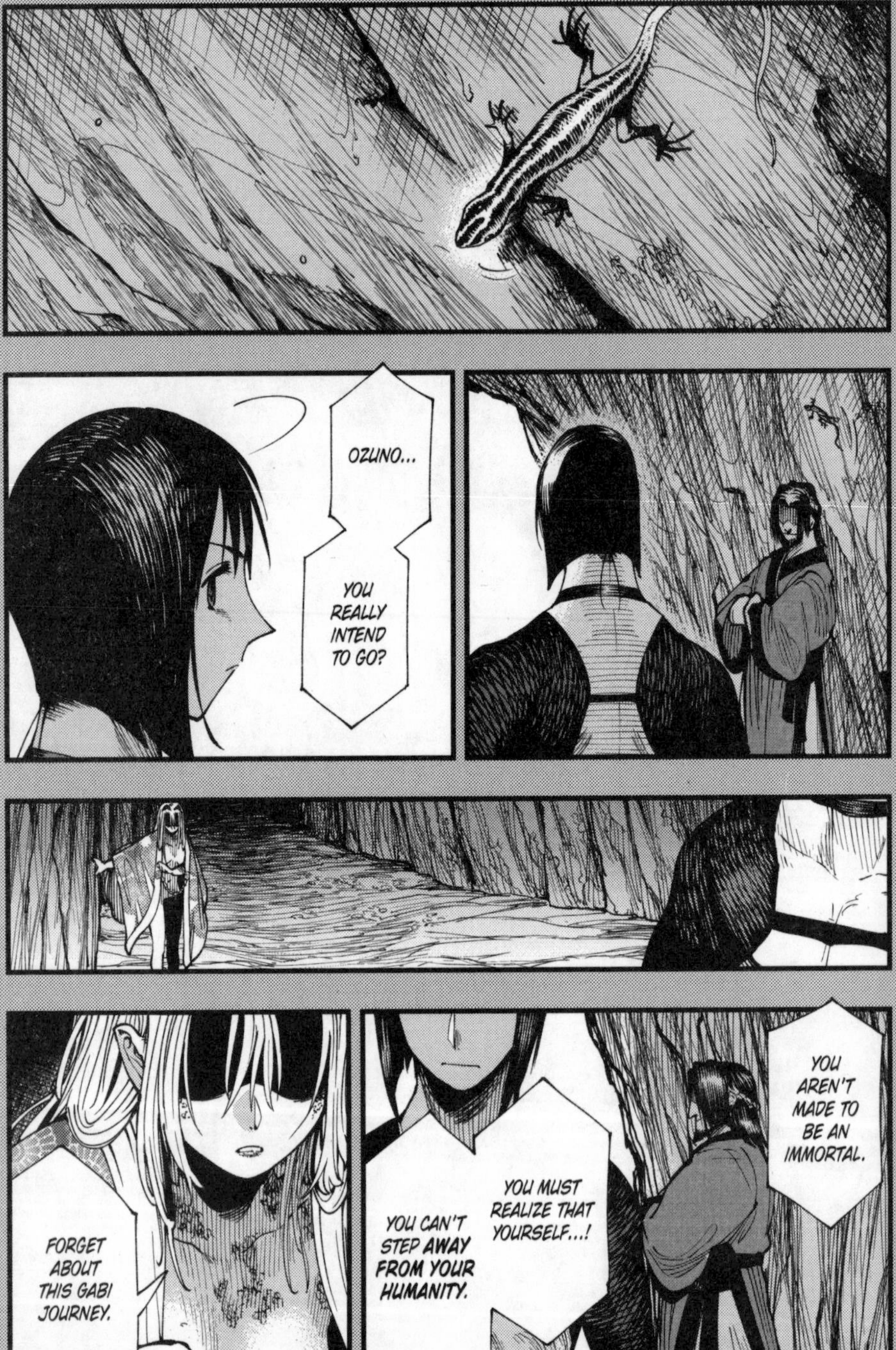
OZUNO...
YOU REALLY INTEND TO GO?
YOU AREN'T MADE TO BE AN IMMORTAL.
YOU MUST REALIZE THAT YOURSELF...!
YOU CAN'T STEP AWAY FROM YOUR HUMANITY.
FORGET ABOUT THIS GABI JOURNEY.

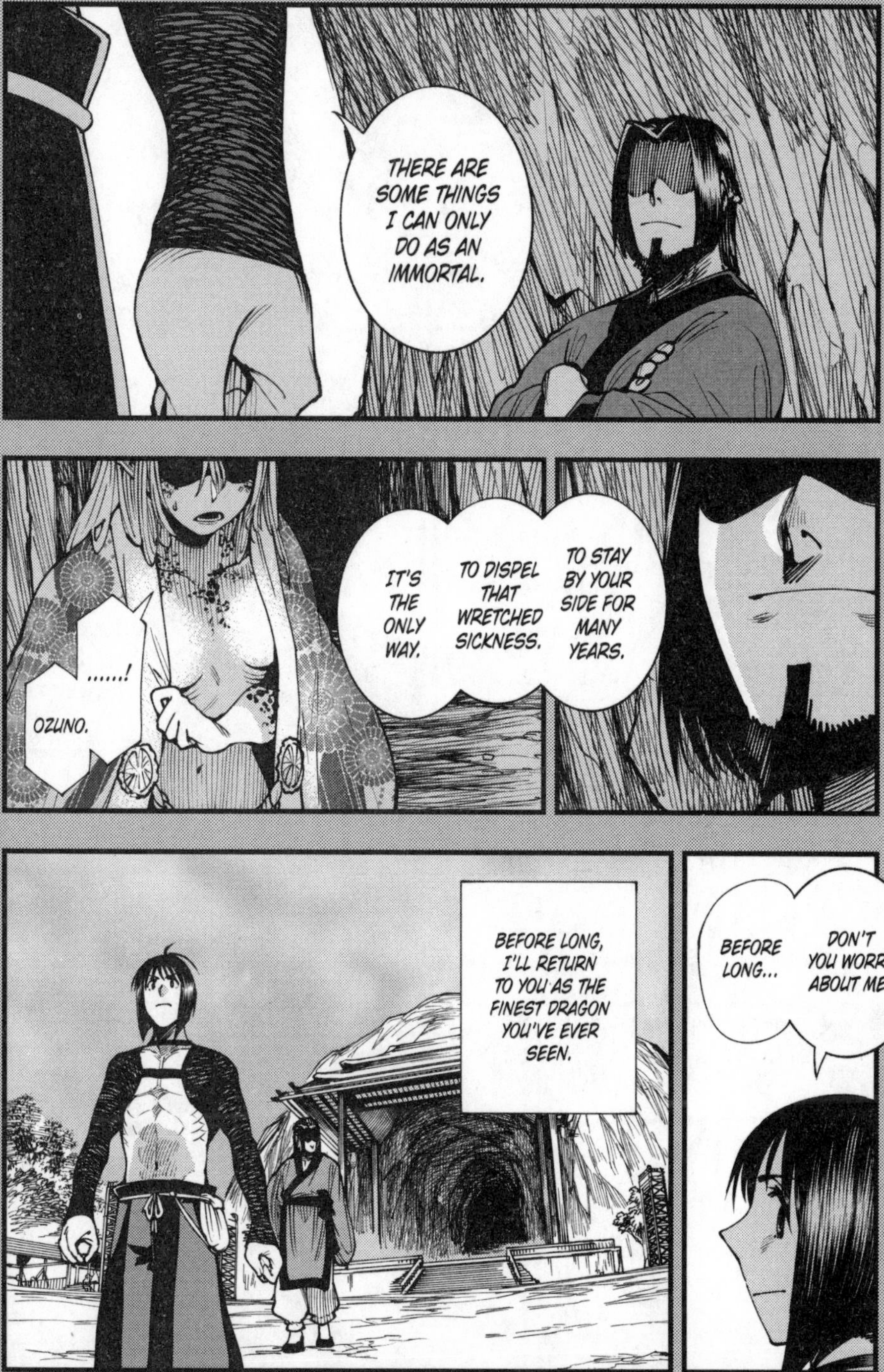
THERE ARE SOME THINGS I CAN ONLY DO AS AN IMMORTAL.
TO STAY BY YOUR SIDE FOR MANY YEARS.
TO DISPEL THAT WRETCHED SICKNESS.
IT'S THE ONLY WAY.
......!
OZUNO.
DON'T YOU WORRY ABOUT ME.
BEFORE LONG...
BEFORE LONG, I'LL RETURN TO YOU AS THE FINEST DRAGON YOU'VE EVER SEEN.

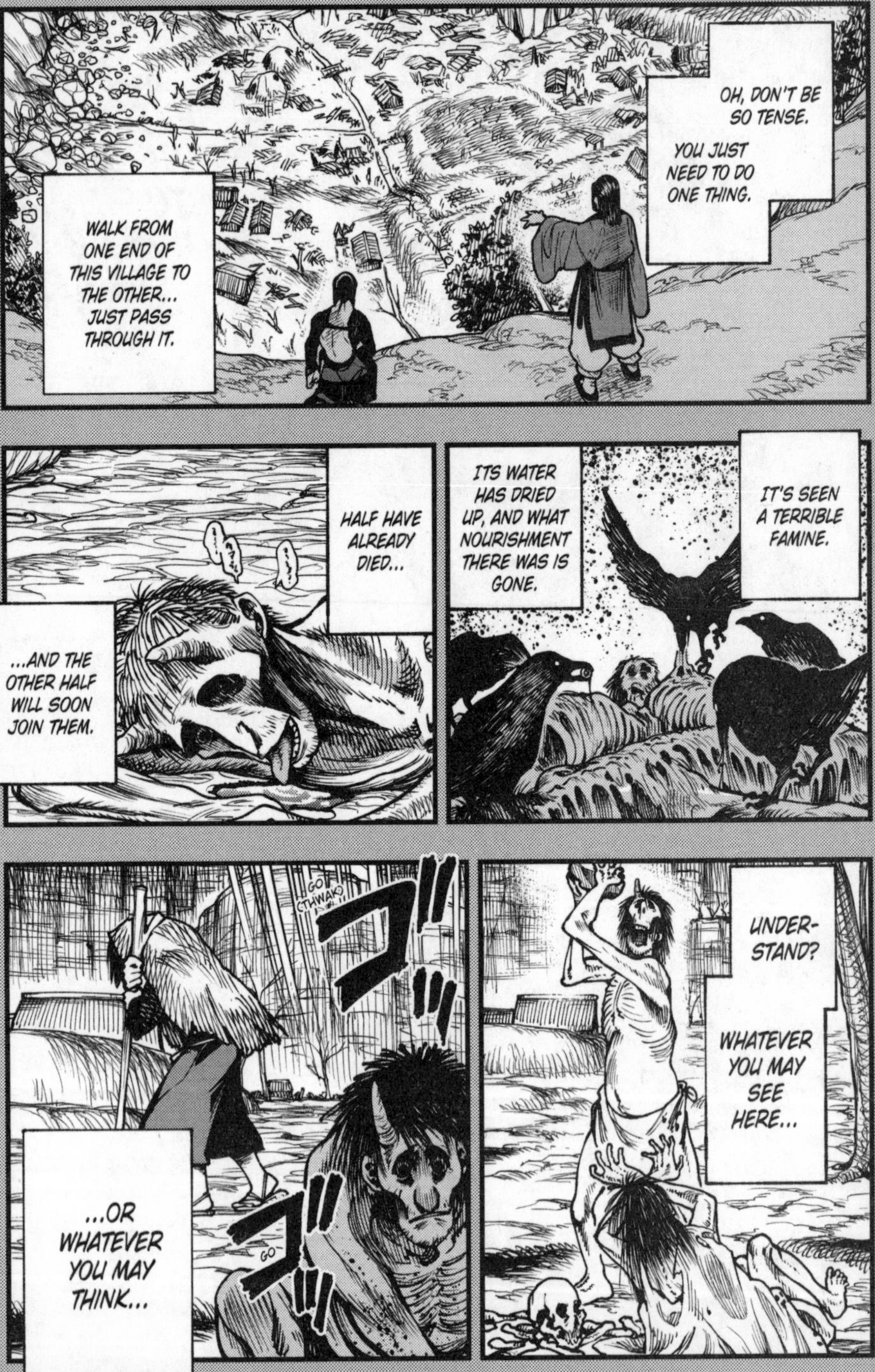
OH, DON'T BE SO TENSE.
YOU JUST NEED TO DO ONE THING.
WALK FROM ONE END OF THIS VILLAGE TO THE OTHER... JUST PASS THROUGH IT.
IT'S SEEN A TERRIBLE FAMINE.
ITS WATER HAS DRIED UP, AND WHAT NOURISHMENT THERE WAS IS GONE.
HALF HAVE ALREADY DIED...
...AND THE OTHER HALF WILL SOON JOIN THEM.
UNDER-STAND?
WHATEVER YOU MAY SEE HERE...
GO (THWAK)
GO
...OR WHATEVER YOU MAY THINK...

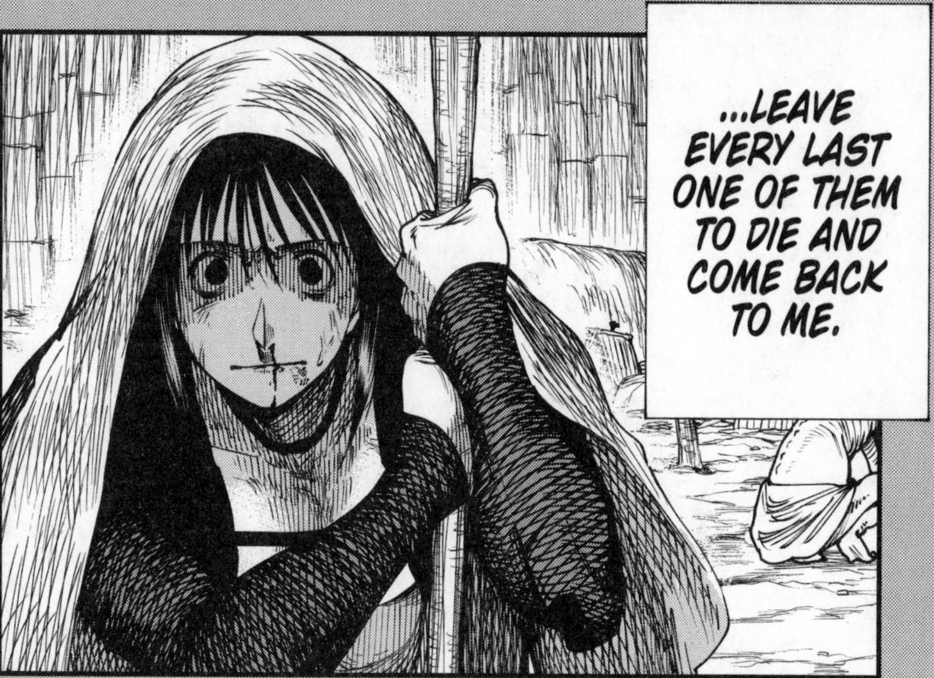
...LEAVE EVERY LAST ONE OF THEM TO DIE AND COME BACK TO ME.

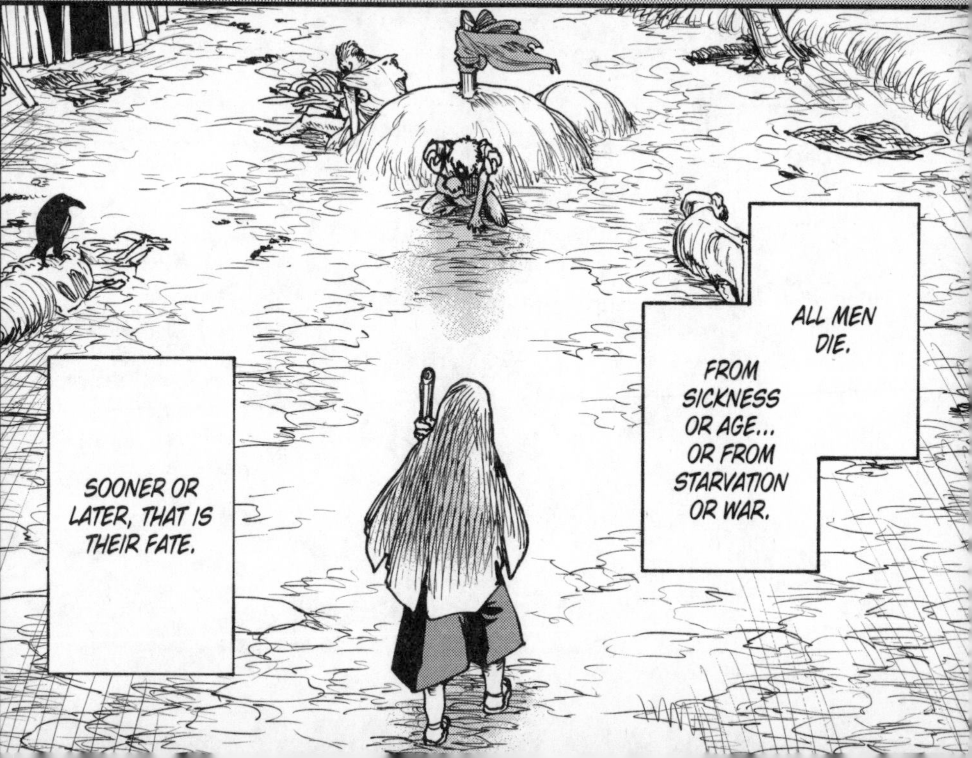
ALL MEN DIE.
FROM SICKNESS OR AGE... OR FROM STARVATION OR WAR.
SOONER OR LATER, THAT IS THEIR FATE.

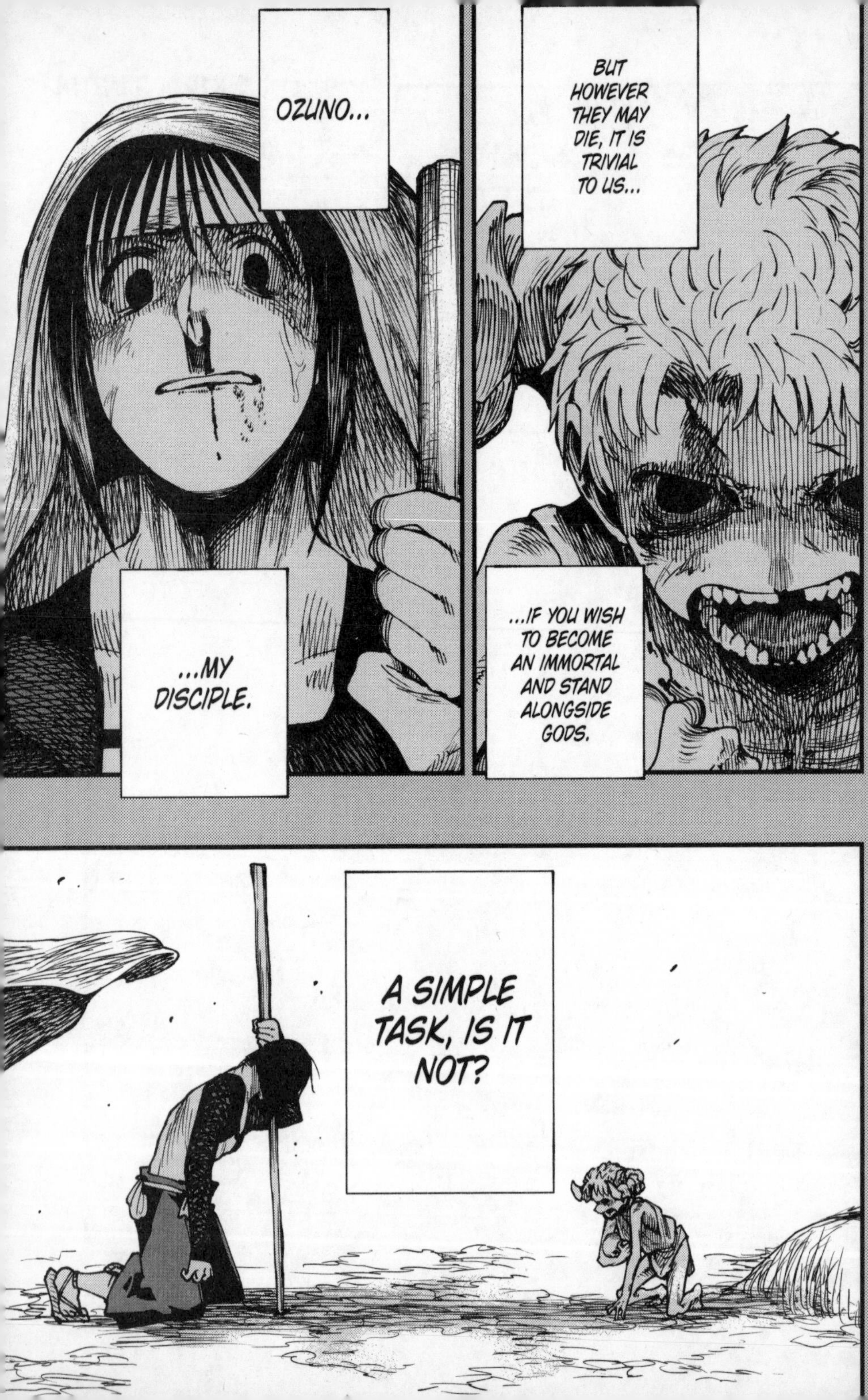
BUT HOWEVER THEY MAY DIE, IT IS TRIVIAL TO US...
...IF YOU WISH TO BECOME AN IMMORTAL AND STAND ALONGSIDE GODS.
OZUNO...
...MY DISCIPLE.
A SIMPLE TASK, IS IT NOT?

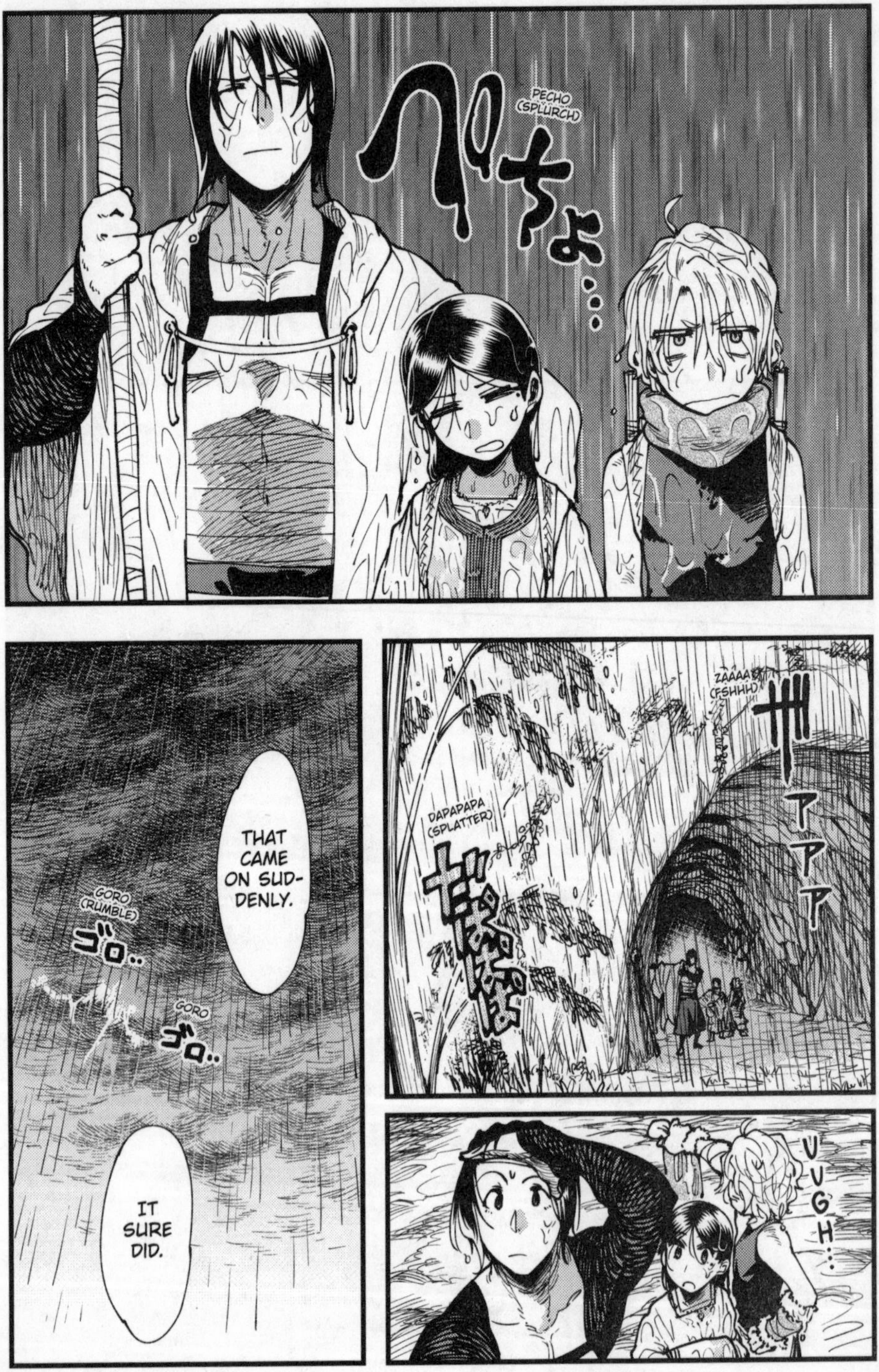
PECHO (SPLURCH)
ぺちょ…
ZAAAA (FSHHH)
ザアア
DAPAPAPA (SPLATTER)
だぱぱぱ
UUGH...
THAT CAME ON SUD-DENLY.
GORO (RUMBLE)
ゴロ..
GORO
ゴロ..
IT SURE DID.

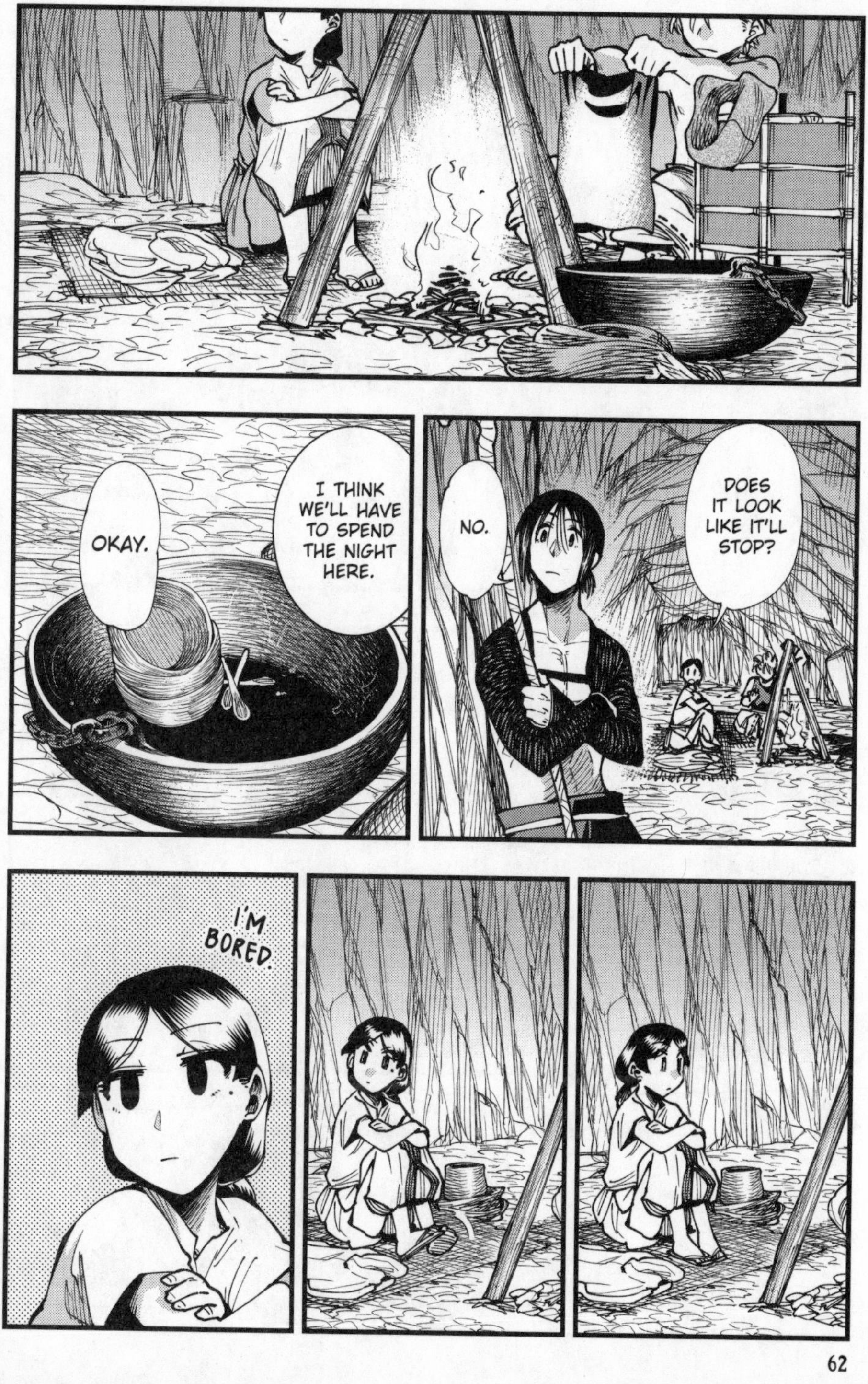
DOES IT LOOK LIKE IT'LL STOP?
NO.
I THINK WE'LL HAVE TO SPEND THE NIGHT HERE.
OKAY.
I'M BORED.

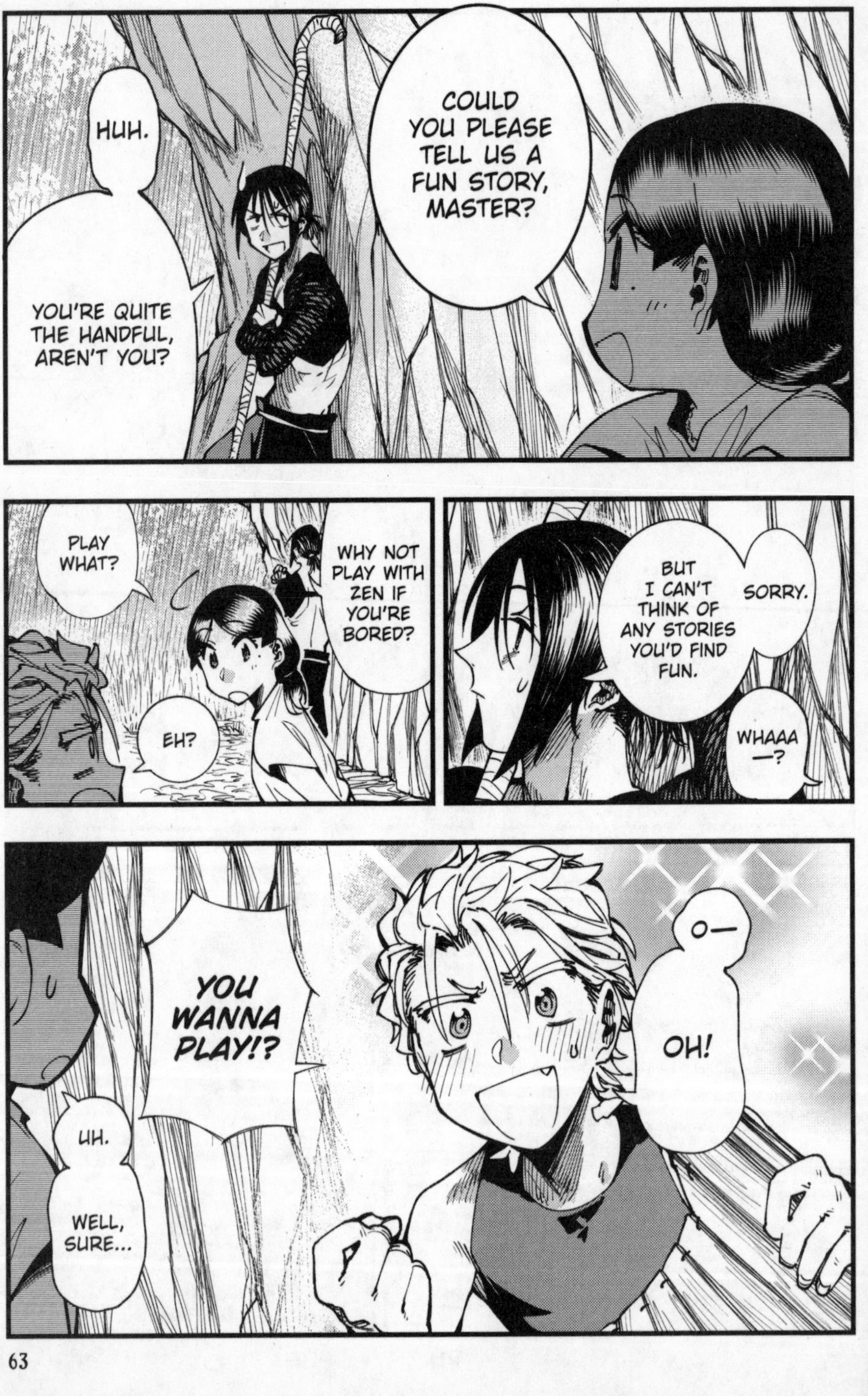
COULD YOU PLEASE TELL US A FUN STORY, MASTER?
HUH.
YOU'RE QUITE THE HANDFUL, AREN'T YOU?
SORRY.
BUT I CAN'T THINK OF ANY STORIES YOU'D FIND FUN.
WHAAA—?
WHY NOT PLAY WITH ZEN IF YOU'RE BORED?
PLAY WHAT?
EH?
O—
OH!
YOU WANNA PLAY!?
UH.
WELL, SURE...

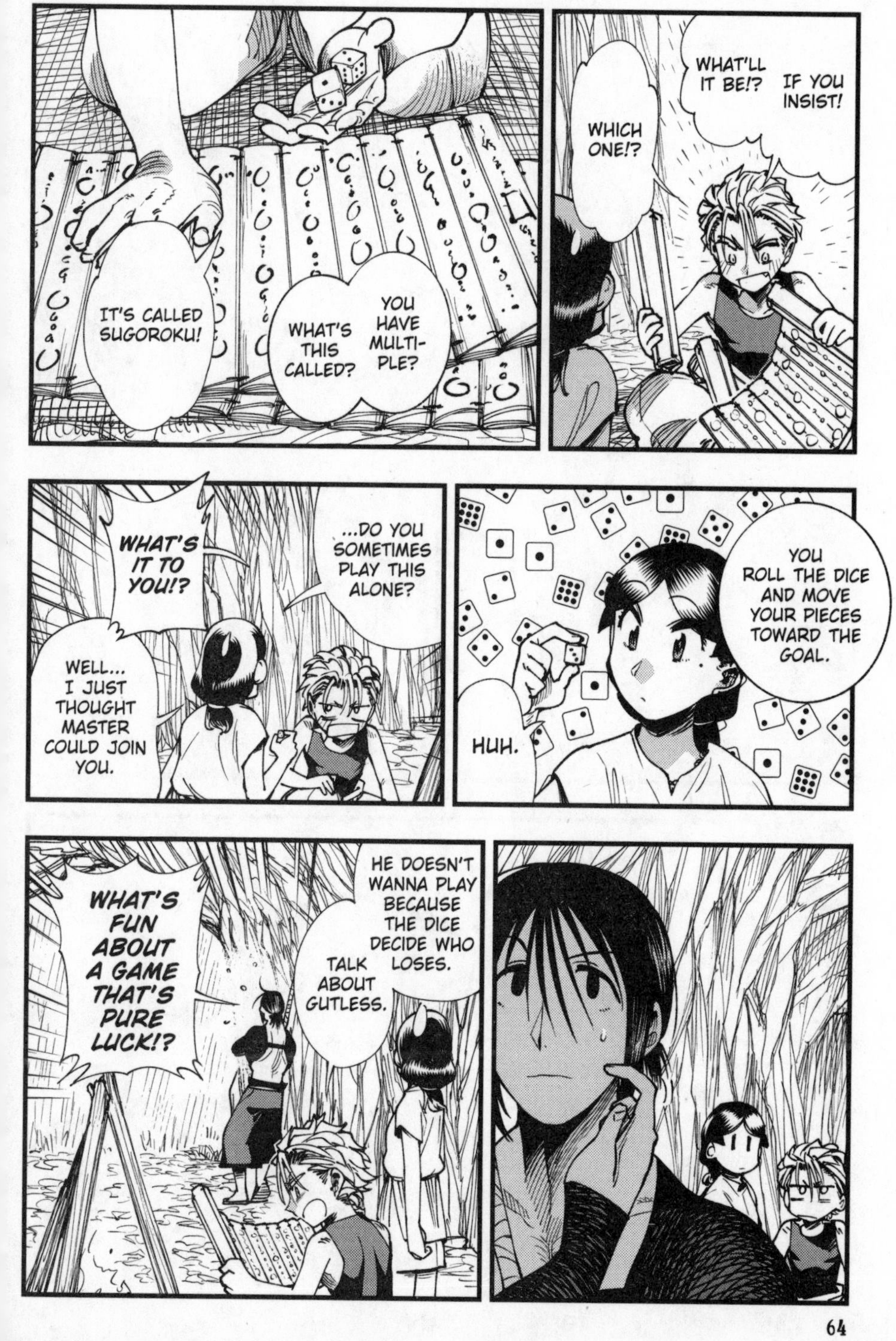
WHAT'LL IT BE!?
IF YOU INSIST!
WHICH ONE!?
YOU HAVE MULTI-PLE?
WHAT'S THIS CALLED?
IT'S CALLED SUGOROKU!
YOU ROLL THE DICE AND MOVE YOUR PIECES TOWARD THE GOAL.
HUH.
...DO YOU SOMETIMES PLAY THIS ALONE?
WHAT'S IT TO YOU!?
WELL... I JUST THOUGHT MASTER COULD JOIN YOU.
HE DOESN'T WANNA PLAY BECAUSE THE DICE DECIDE WHO LOSES.
TALK ABOUT GUTLESS.
WHAT'S FUN ABOUT A GAME THAT'S PURE LUCK!?

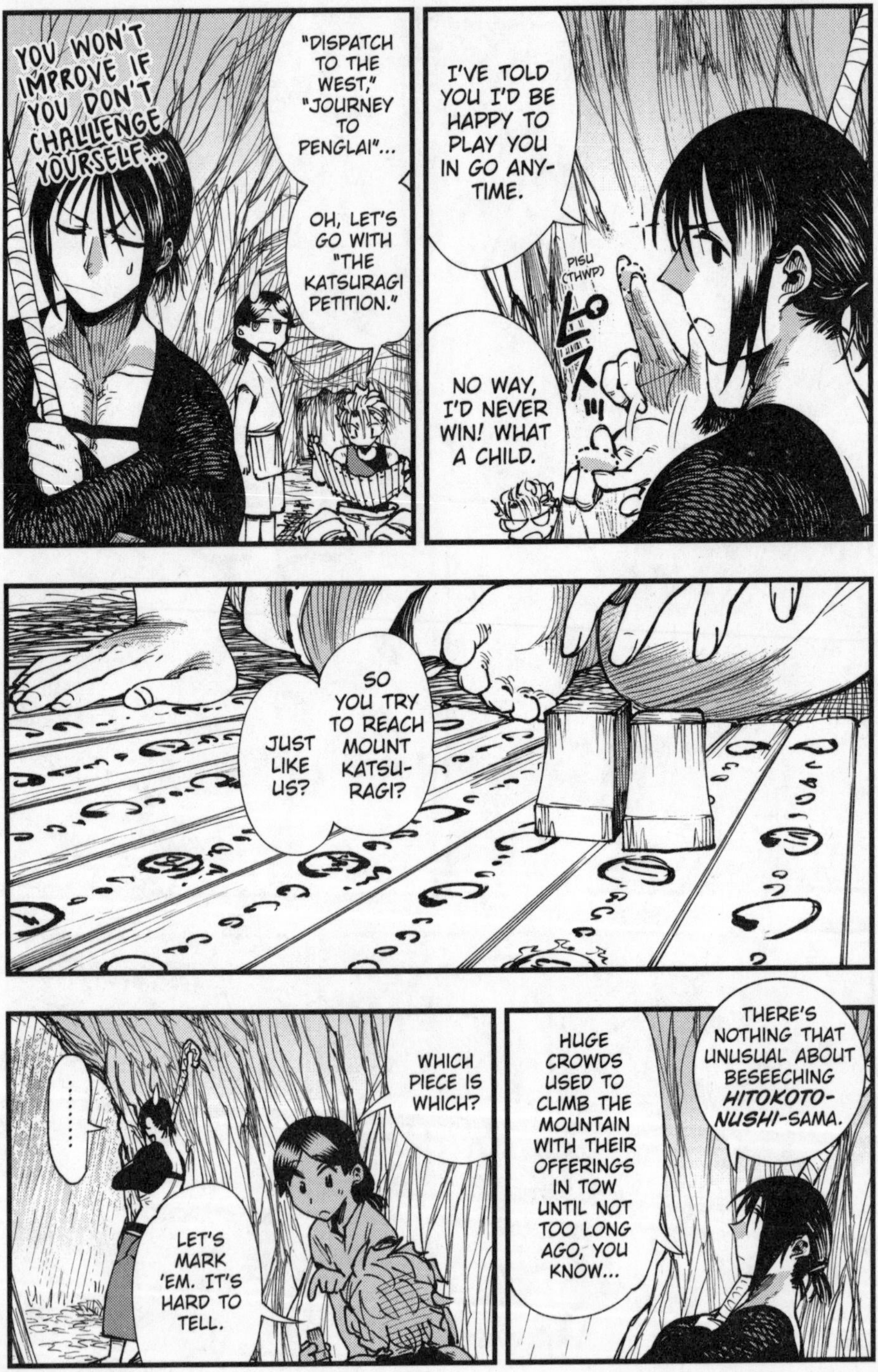
I'VE TOLD YOU I'D BE HAPPY TO PLAY YOU IN GO ANY-TIME.
PISU (THWP)
ピスッ
NO WAY, I'D NEVER WIN! WHAT A CHILD.
"DISPATCH TO THE WEST," "JOURNEY TO PENGLAI"...
OH, LET'S GO WITH "THE KATSURAGI PETITION."
YOU WON'T IMPROVE IF YOU DON'T CHALLENGE YOURSELF...
SO YOU TRY TO REACH MOUNT KATSU-RAGI?
JUST LIKE US?
THERE'S NOTHING THAT UNUSUAL ABOUT BESEECHING *HITOKOTO-NUSHI*-SAMA.
HUGE CROWDS USED TO CLIMB THE MOUNTAIN WITH THEIR OFFERINGS IN TOW UNTIL NOT TOO LONG AGO, YOU KNOW...
WHICH PIECE IS WHICH?
LET'S MARK 'EM. IT'S HARD TO TELL.
......

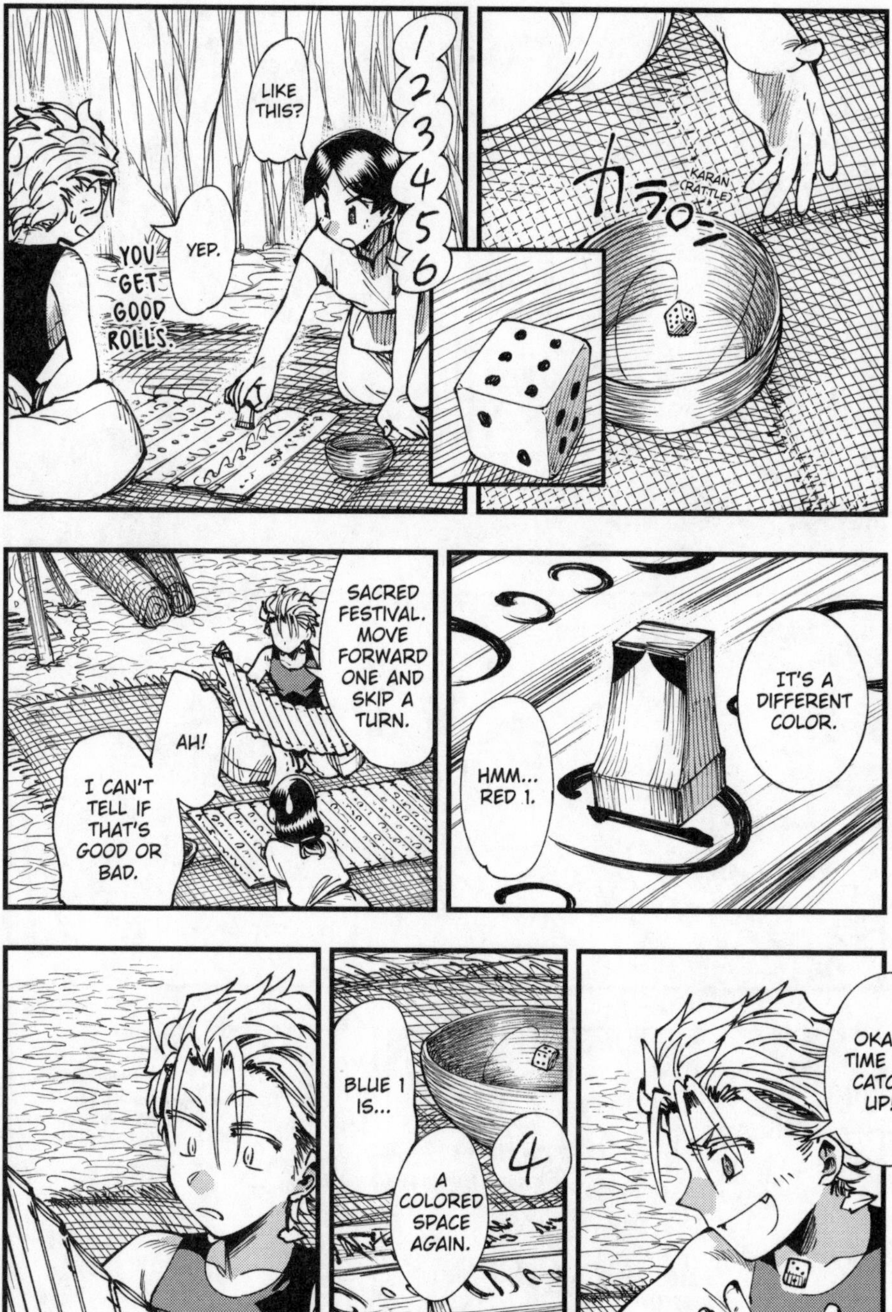
KARAN (RATTLE)
1
2
3
4
5
6
LIKE THIS?
YEP.
YOU GET GOOD ROLLS.
IT'S A DIFFERENT COLOR.
HMM... RED 1.
SACRED FESTIVAL. MOVE FORWARD ONE AND SKIP A TURN.
AH!
I CAN'T TELL IF THAT'S GOOD OR BAD.
OKAY, TIME TO CATCH UP!
4
BLUE 1 IS...
A COLORED SPACE AGAIN.

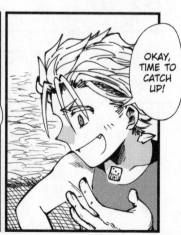

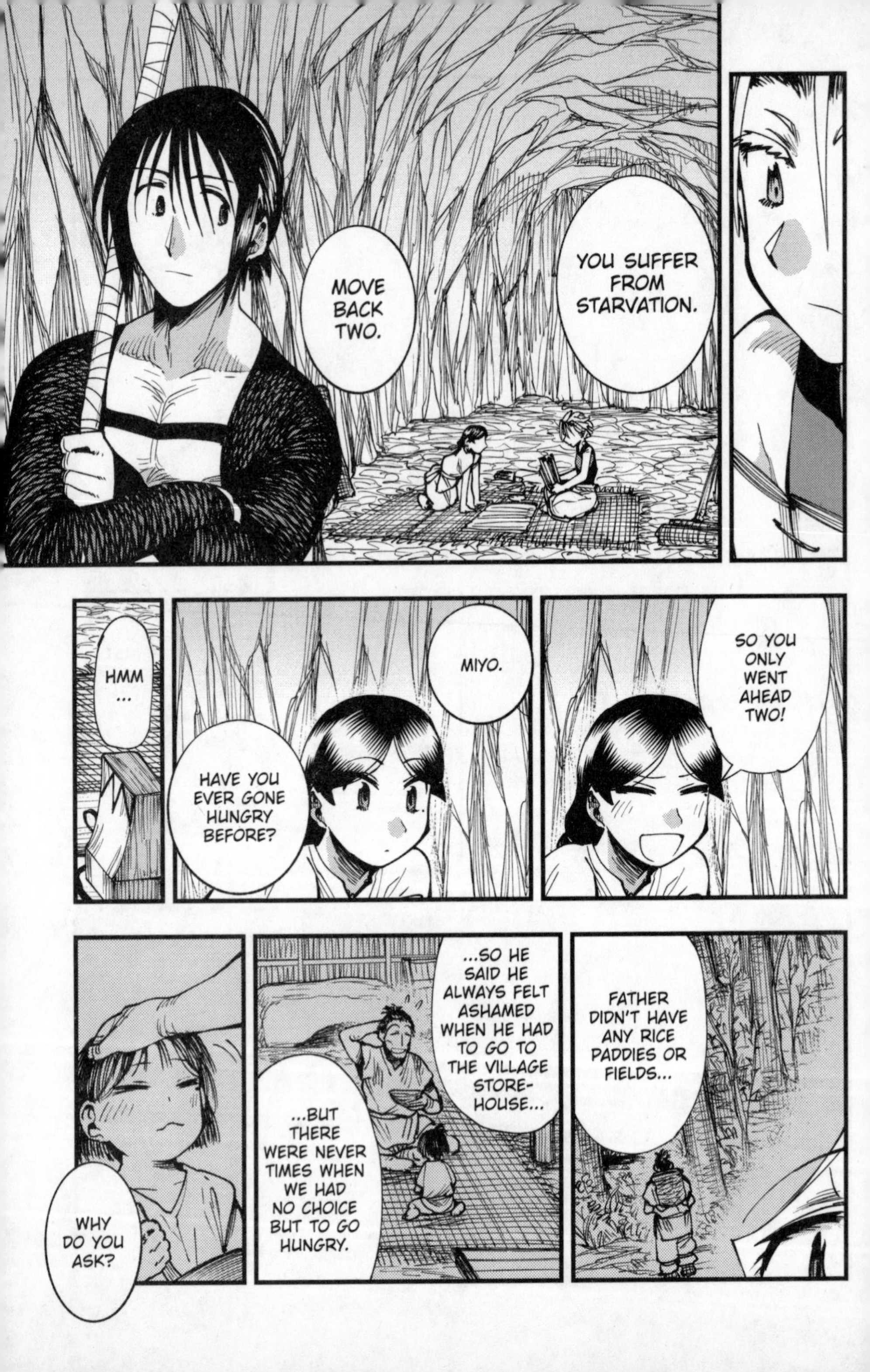
YOU SUFFER FROM STARVATION.
MOVE BACK TWO.
SO YOU ONLY WENT AHEAD TWO!
MIYO.
HAVE YOU EVER GONE HUNGRY BEFORE?
HMM ...
FATHER DIDN'T HAVE ANY RICE PADDIES OR FIELDS...
...SO HE SAID HE ALWAYS FELT ASHAMED WHEN HE HAD TO GO TO THE VILLAGE STORE-HOUSE...
...BUT THERE WERE NEVER TIMES WHEN WE HAD NO CHOICE BUT TO GO HUNGRY.
WHY DO YOU ASK?

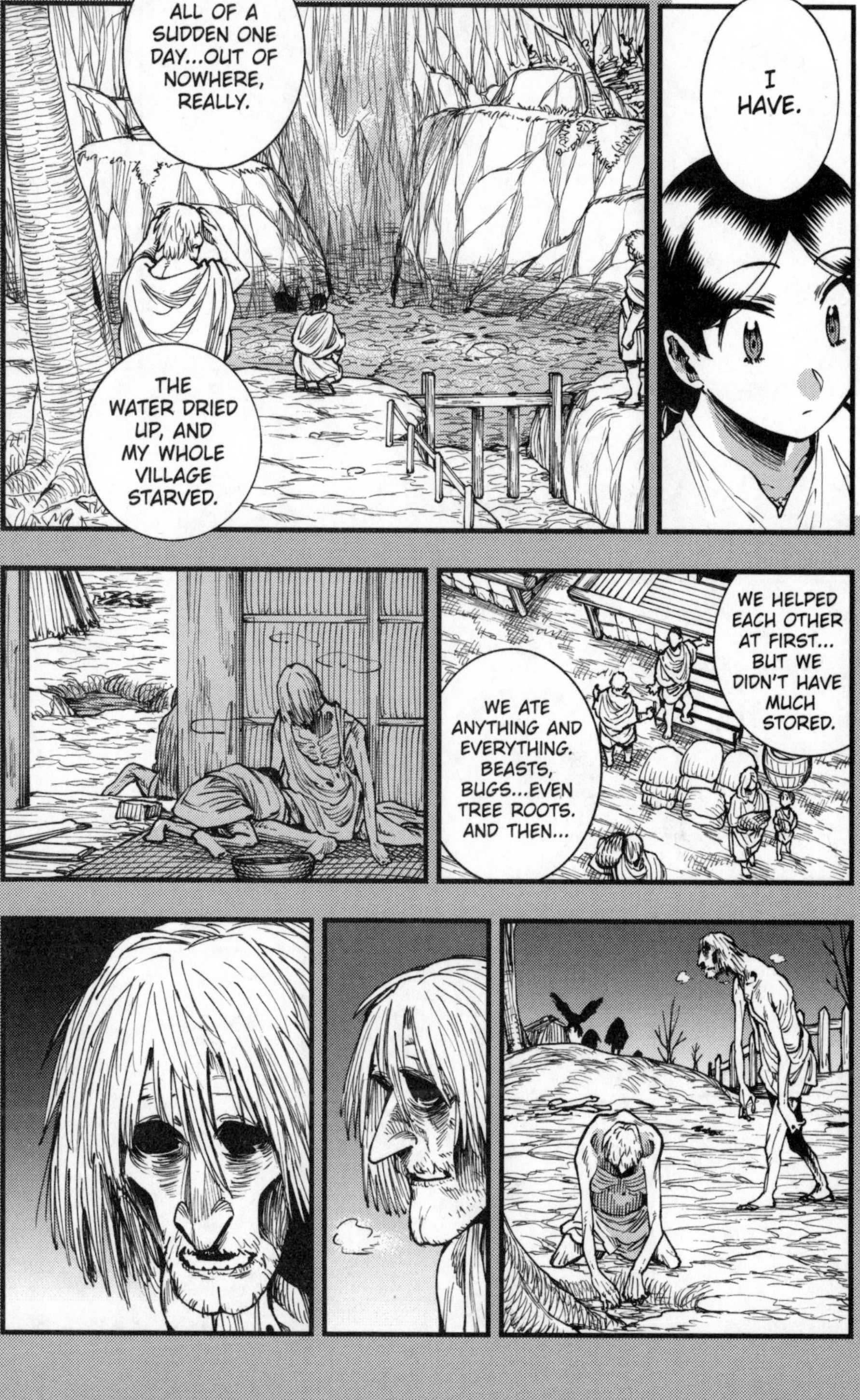
I HAVE.
ALL OF A SUDDEN ONE DAY...OUT OF NOWHERE, REALLY.
THE WATER DRIED UP, AND MY WHOLE VILLAGE STARVED.
WE HELPED EACH OTHER AT FIRST... BUT WE DIDN'T HAVE MUCH STORED.
WE ATE ANYTHING AND EVERYTHING. BEASTS, BUGS...EVEN TREE ROOTS. AND THEN...

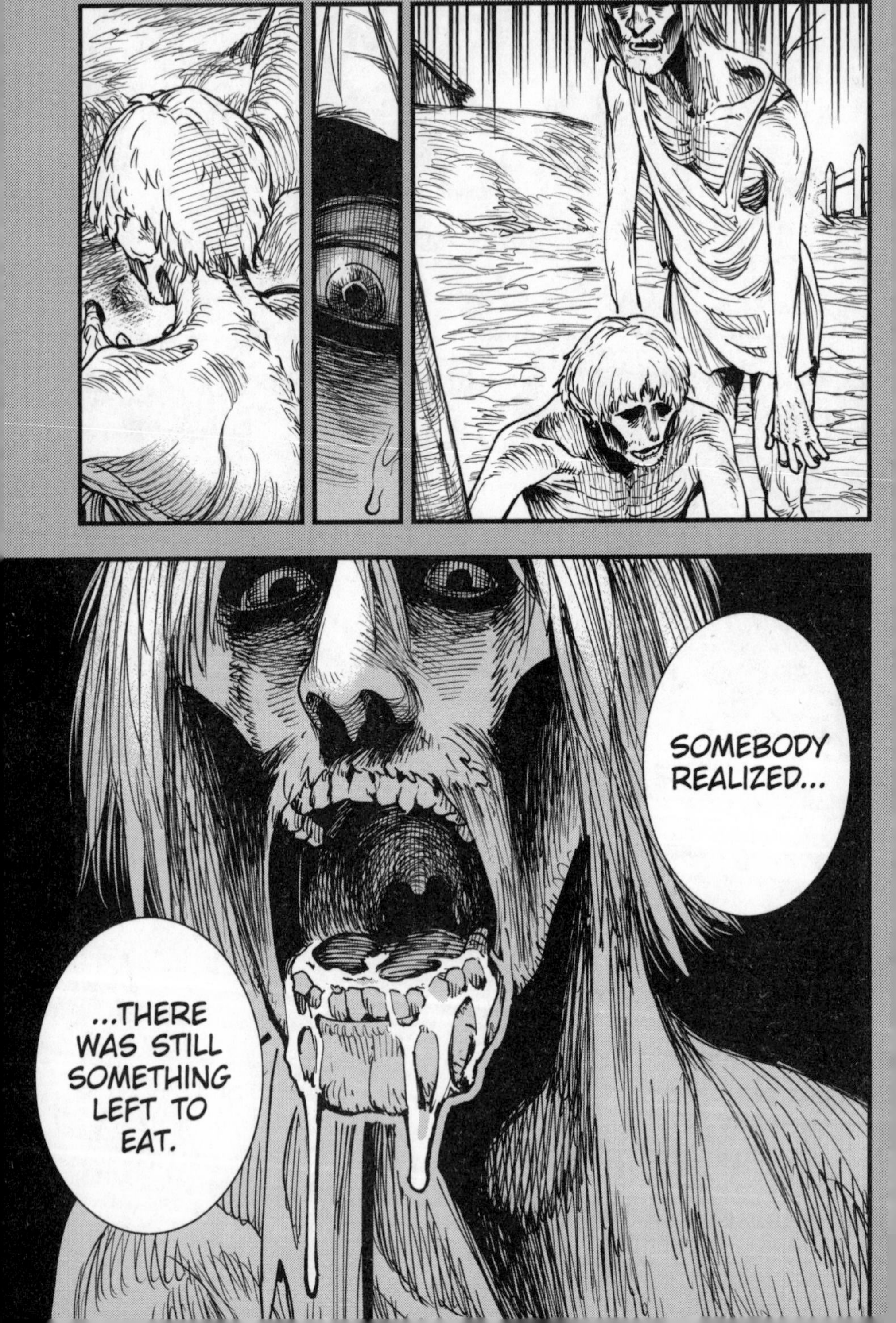
SOMEBODY REALIZED...
...THERE WAS STILL SOMETHING LEFT TO EAT.

MUSHIRI
(RRRIP)
CHIRI
(FWIRL)
CHIRI
PAKI
(KRACKLE)
PAKI

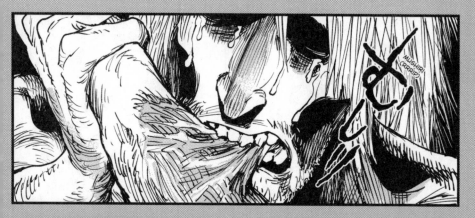

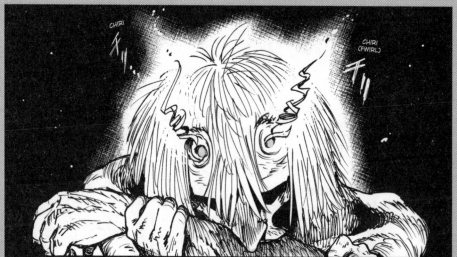

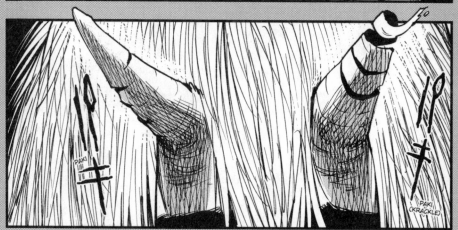

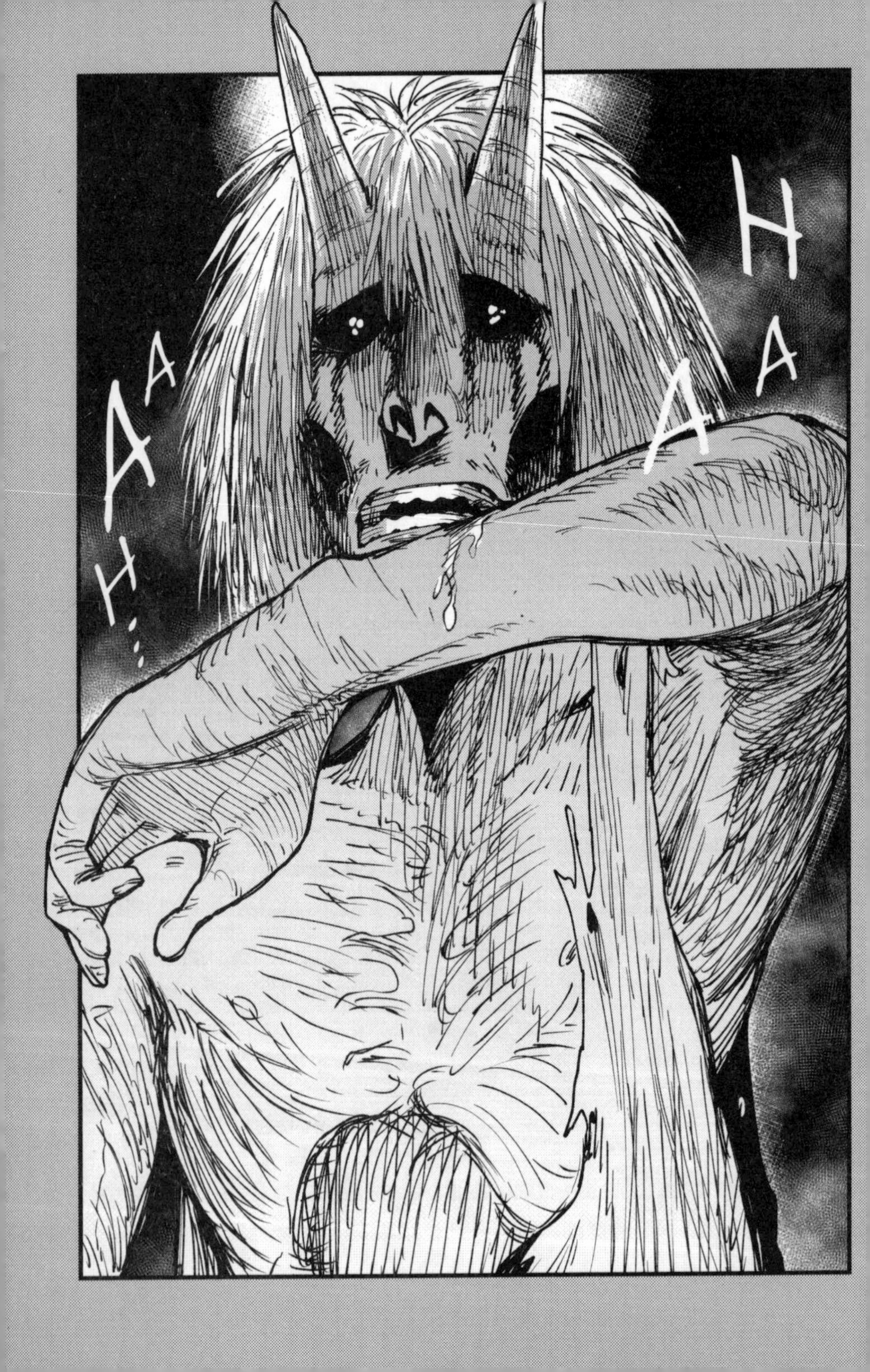
HAA
AAH...

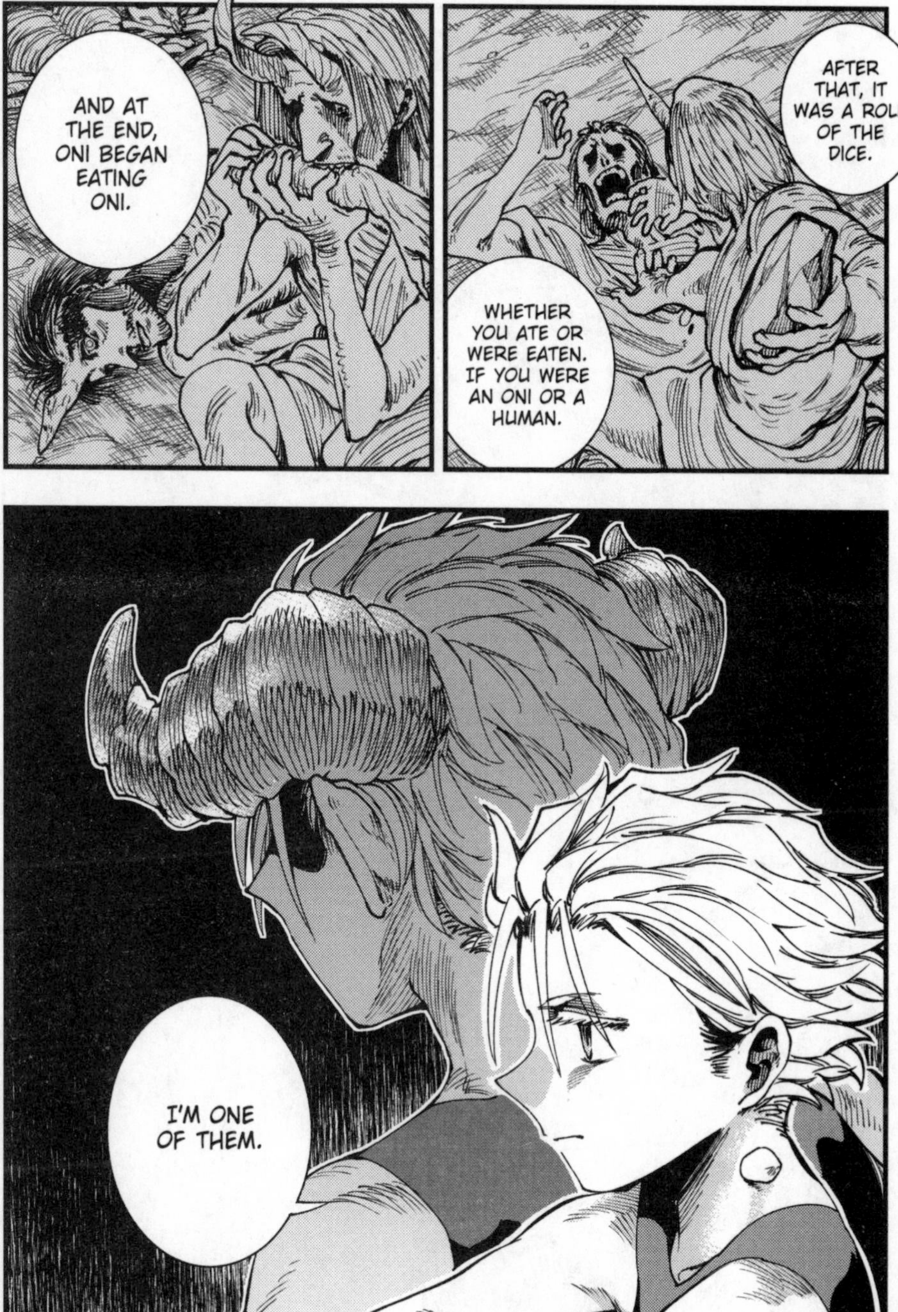
AND AT THE END, ONI BEGAN EATING ONI.
AFTER THAT, IT WAS A ROLL OF THE DICE.
WHETHER YOU ATE OR WERE EATEN. IF YOU WERE AN ONI OR A HUMAN.
I'M ONE OF THEM.

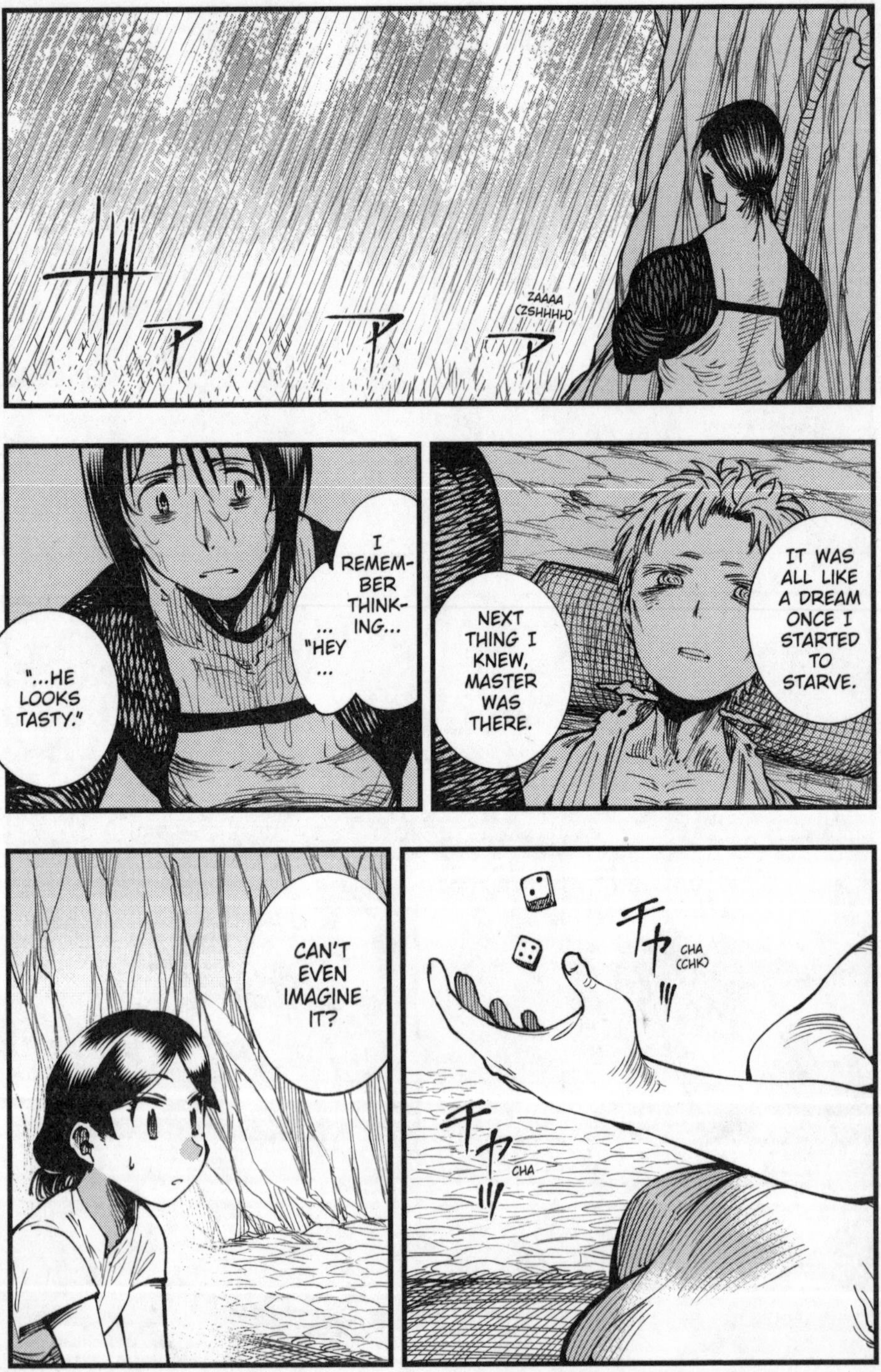
ZAAAA (ZSHHHH)
IT WAS ALL LIKE A DREAM ONCE I STARTED TO STARVE.
NEXT THING I KNEW, MASTER WAS THERE.
I REMEMBER THINKING... ... "HEY ...
"...HE LOOKS TASTY."
チャ
CHA (CHK)
チャ
CHA
CAN'T EVEN IMAGINE IT?

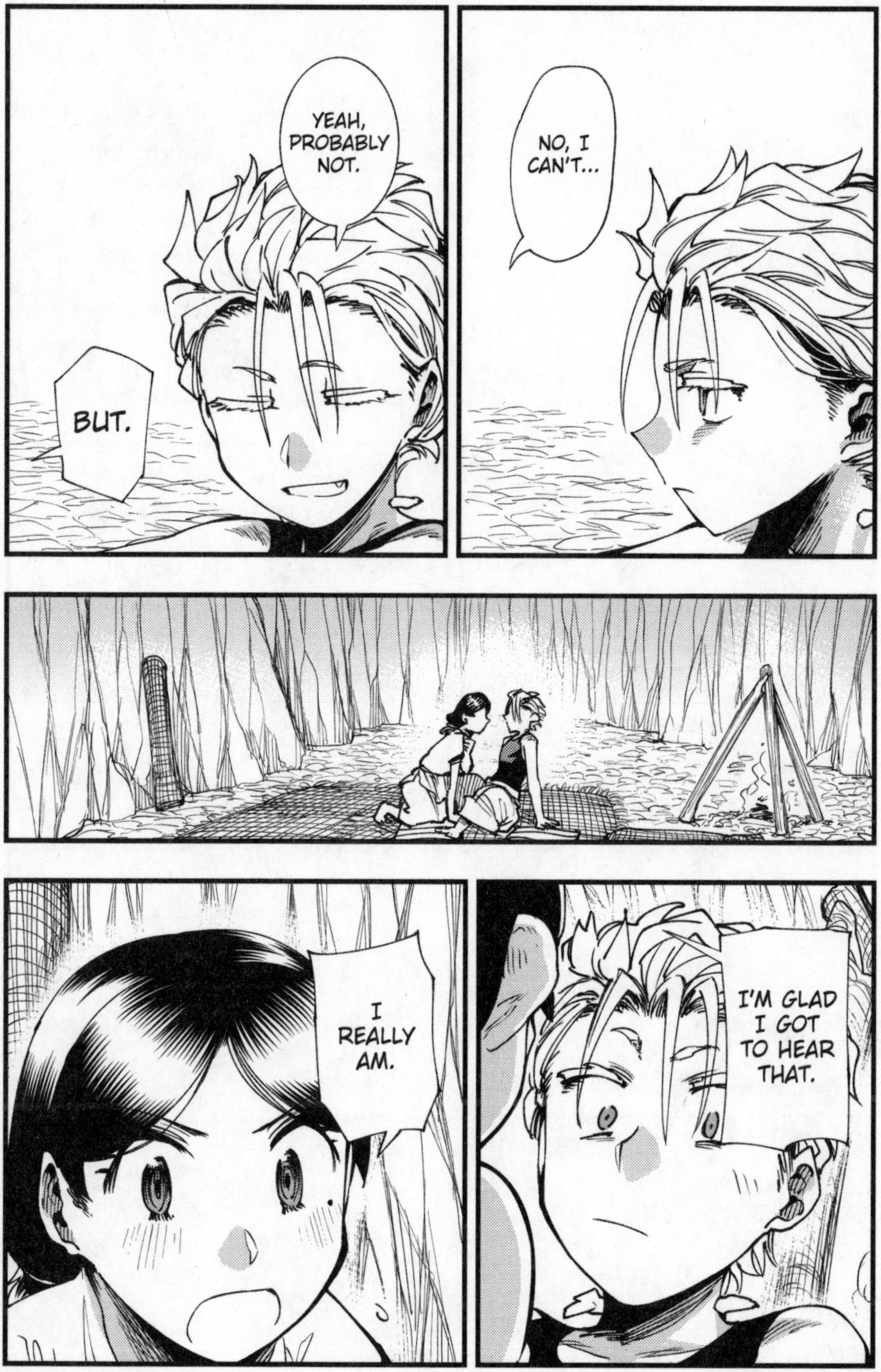
NO, I CAN'T...
YEAH, PROBABLY NOT.
BUT.
I'M GLAD I GOT TO HEAR THAT.
I REALLY AM.

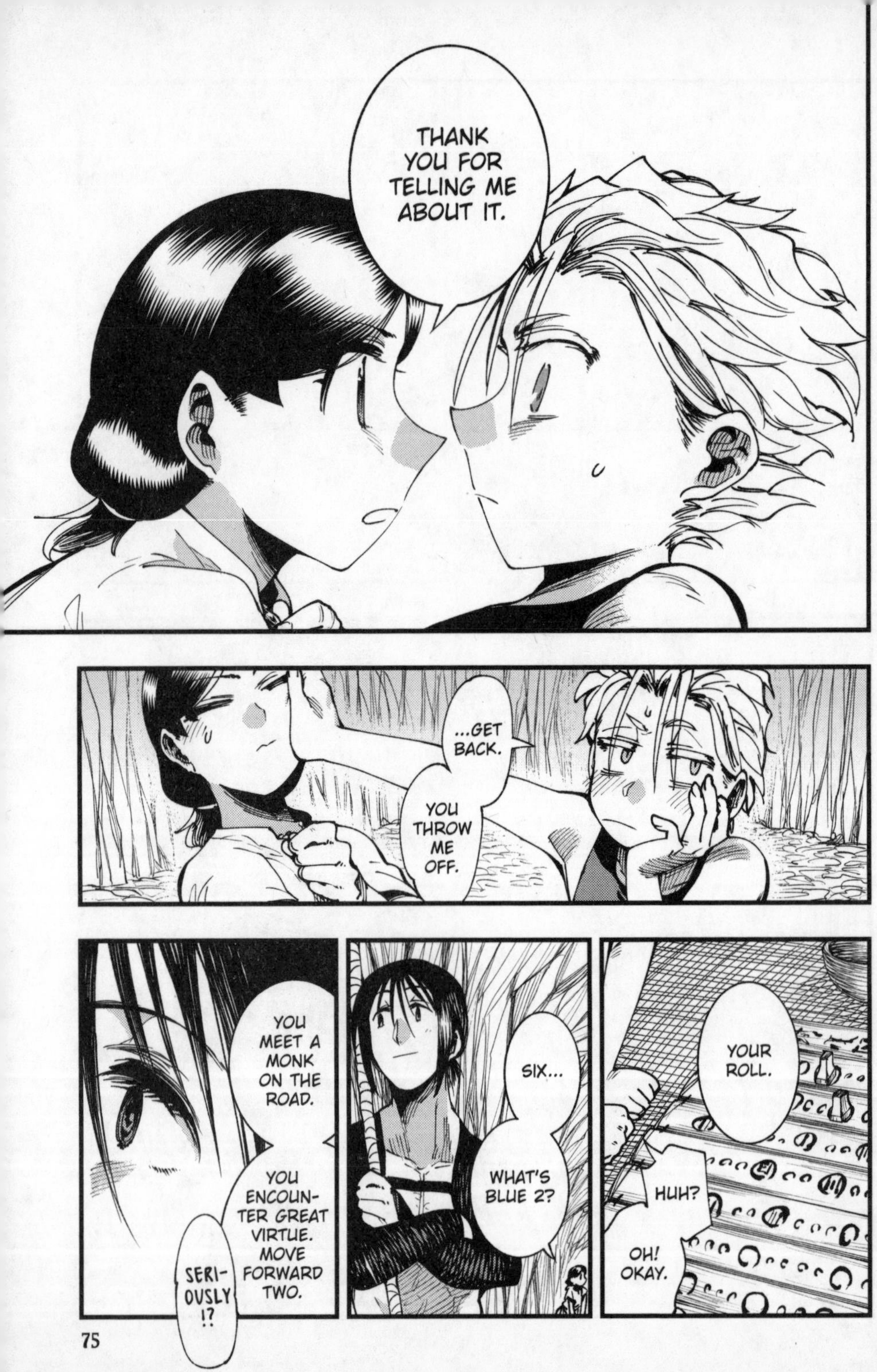
THANK YOU FOR TELLING ME ABOUT IT.
...GET BACK.
YOU THROW ME OFF.
YOUR ROLL.
HUH?
OH! OKAY.
SIX...
WHAT'S BLUE 2?
YOU MEET A MONK ON THE ROAD.
YOU ENCOUNTER GREAT VIRTUE. MOVE FORWARD TWO.
SERIOUSLY!?

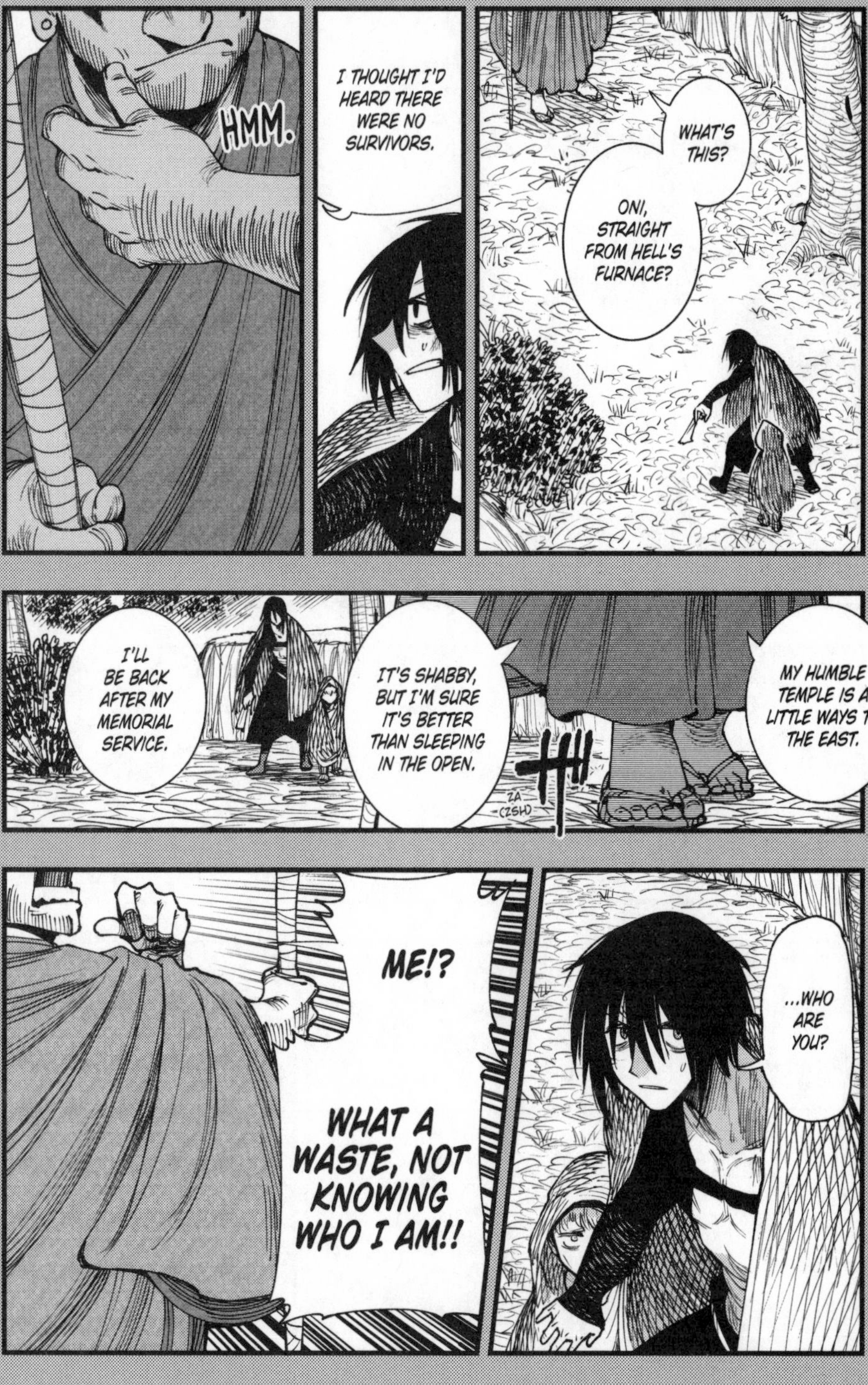
WHAT'S THIS?
ONI, STRAIGHT FROM HELL'S FURNACE?
I THOUGHT I'D HEARD THERE WERE NO SURVIVORS.
HMM.
MY HUMBLE TEMPLE IS A LITTLE WAYS TO THE EAST.
ZA (ZSH)
IT'S SHABBY, BUT I'M SURE IT'S BETTER THAN SLEEPING IN THE OPEN.
I'LL BE BACK AFTER MY MEMORIAL SERVICE.
...WHO ARE YOU?
ME!?
WHAT A WASTE, NOT KNOWING WHO I AM!!

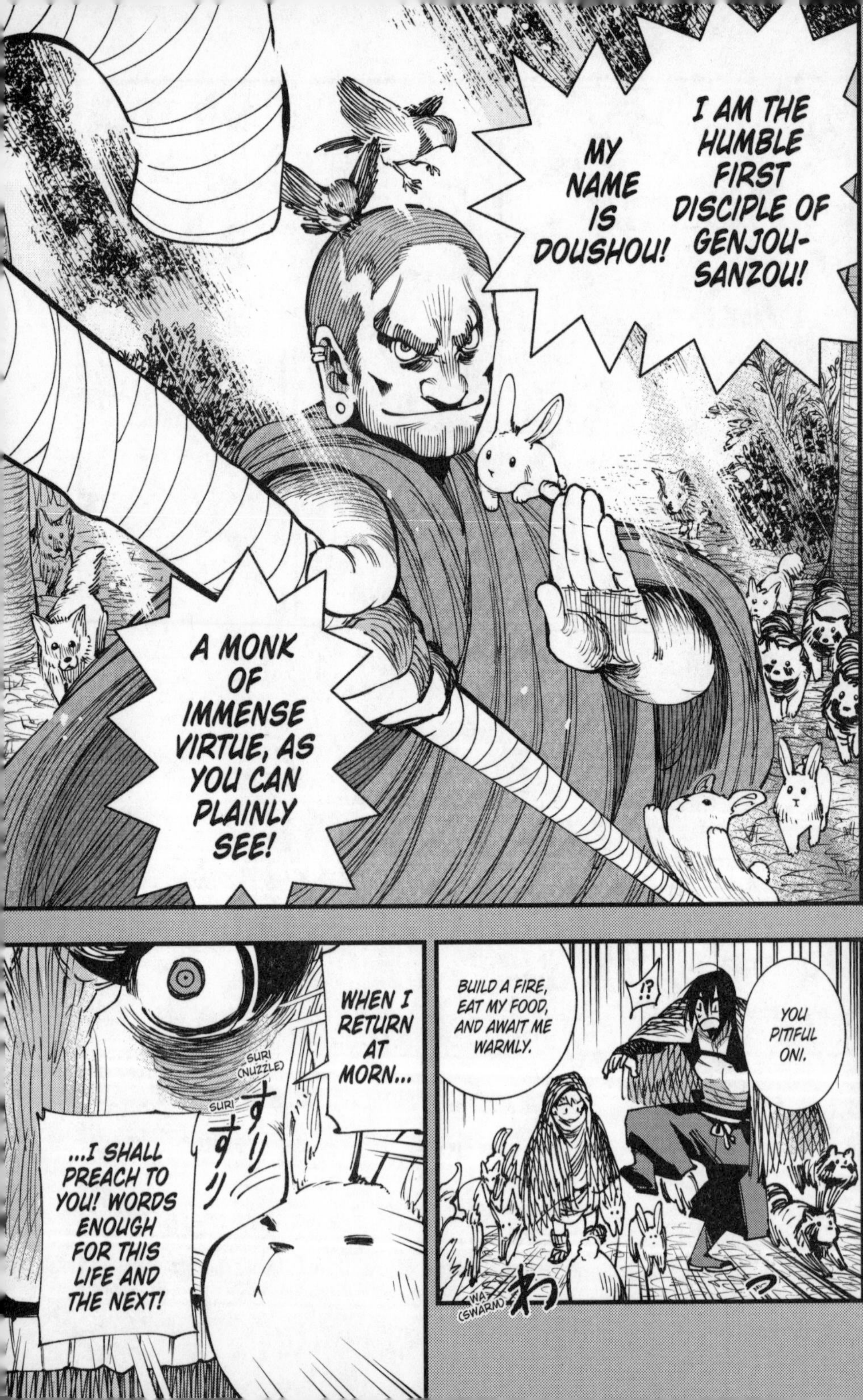
I AM THE HUMBLE FIRST DISCIPLE OF GENJOU-SANZOU!
MY NAME IS DOUSHOU!
A MONK OF IMMENSE VIRTUE, AS YOU CAN PLAINLY SEE!
YOU PITIFUL ONI.
!?
BUILD A FIRE, EAT MY FOOD, AND AWAIT ME WARMLY.
わ
WA (SWARM)
WHEN I RETURN AT MORN...
すり
SURI (NUZZLE)
すり
SURI
...I SHALL PREACH TO YOU! WORDS ENOUGH FOR THIS LIFE AND THE NEXT!

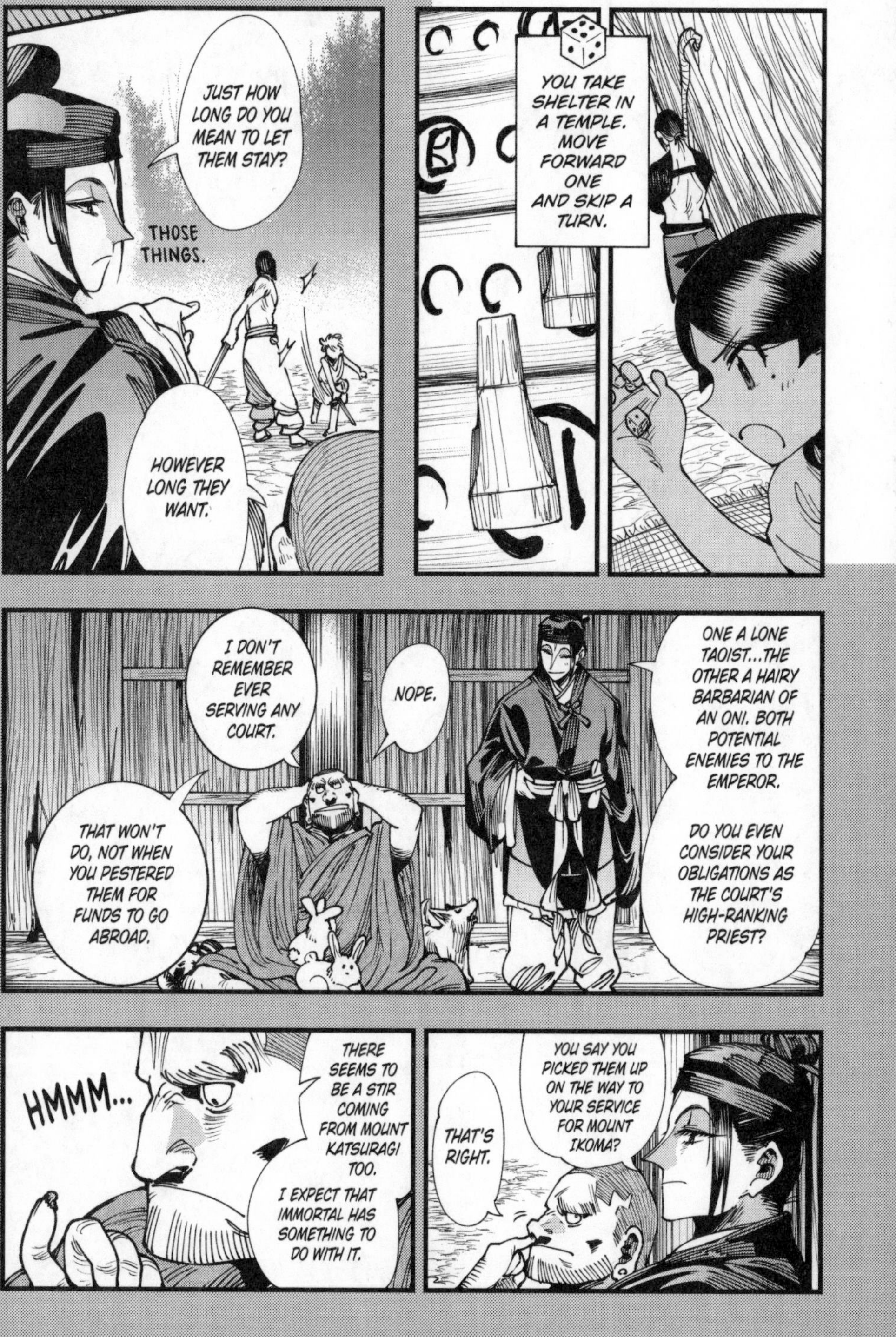
YOU TAKE SHELTER IN A TEMPLE. MOVE FORWARD ONE AND SKIP A TURN.
JUST HOW LONG DO YOU MEAN TO LET THEM STAY?
THOSE THINGS.
HOWEVER LONG THEY WANT.
ONE A LONE TAOIST...THE OTHER A HAIRY BARBARIAN OF AN ONI. BOTH POTENTIAL ENEMIES TO THE EMPEROR.
DO YOU EVEN CONSIDER YOUR OBLIGATIONS AS THE COURT'S HIGH-RANKING PRIEST?
NOPE.
I DON'T REMEMBER EVER SERVING ANY COURT.
THAT WON'T DO, NOT WHEN YOU PESTERED THEM FOR FUNDS TO GO ABROAD.
YOU SAY YOU PICKED THEM UP ON THE WAY TO YOUR SERVICE FOR MOUNT IKOMA?
THAT'S RIGHT.
THERE SEEMS TO BE A STIR COMING FROM MOUNT KATSURAGI TOO.
HMMM...
I EXPECT THAT IMMORTAL HAS SOMETHING TO DO WITH IT.

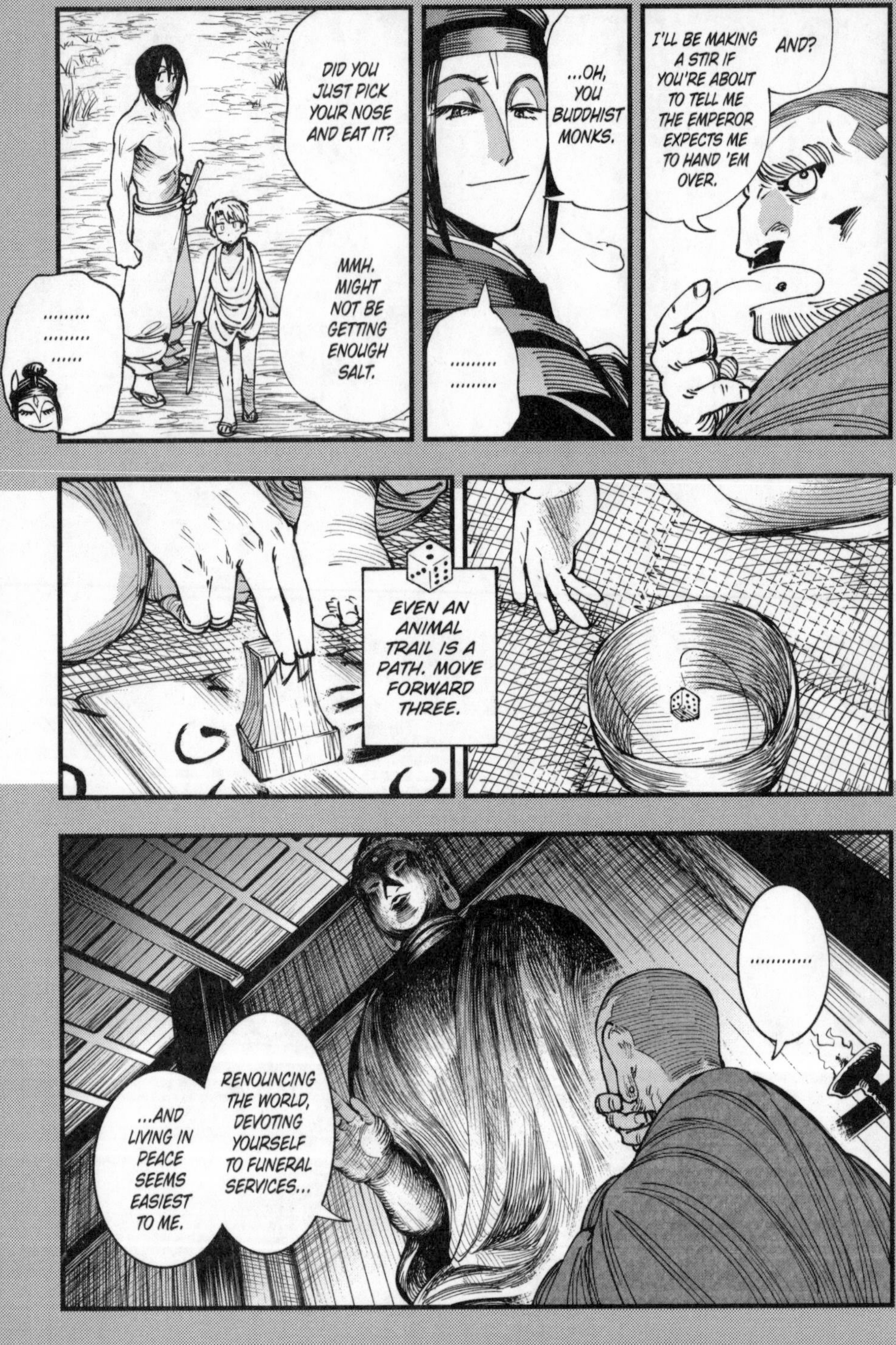
AND?
I'LL BE MAKING A STIR IF YOU'RE ABOUT TO TELL ME THE EMPEROR EXPECTS ME TO HAND 'EM OVER.
...OH, YOU BUDDHIST MONKS.
....
DID YOU JUST PICK YOUR NOSE AND EAT IT?
MMH. MIGHT NOT BE GETTING ENOUGH SALT.
....
EVEN AN ANIMAL TRAIL IS A PATH. MOVE FORWARD THREE.
....
RENOUNCING THE WORLD, DEVOTING YOURSELF TO FUNERAL SERVICES...
...AND LIVING IN PEACE SEEMS EASIEST TO ME.

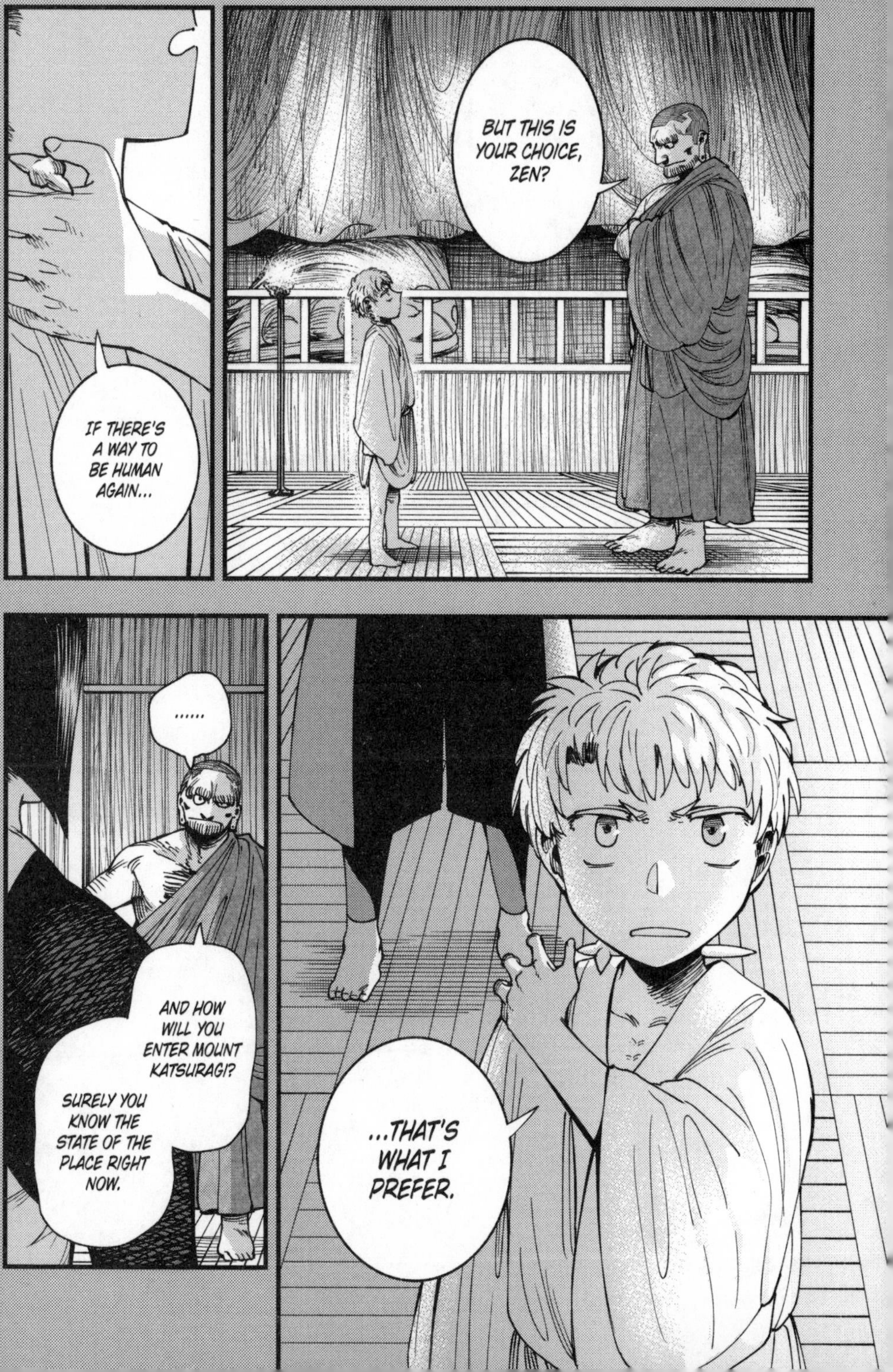
BUT THIS IS YOUR CHOICE, ZEN?
IF THERE'S A WAY TO BE HUMAN AGAIN...
...THAT'S WHAT I PREFER.
......
AND HOW WILL YOU ENTER MOUNT KATSURAGI?
SURELY YOU KNOW THE STATE OF THE PLACE RIGHT NOW.

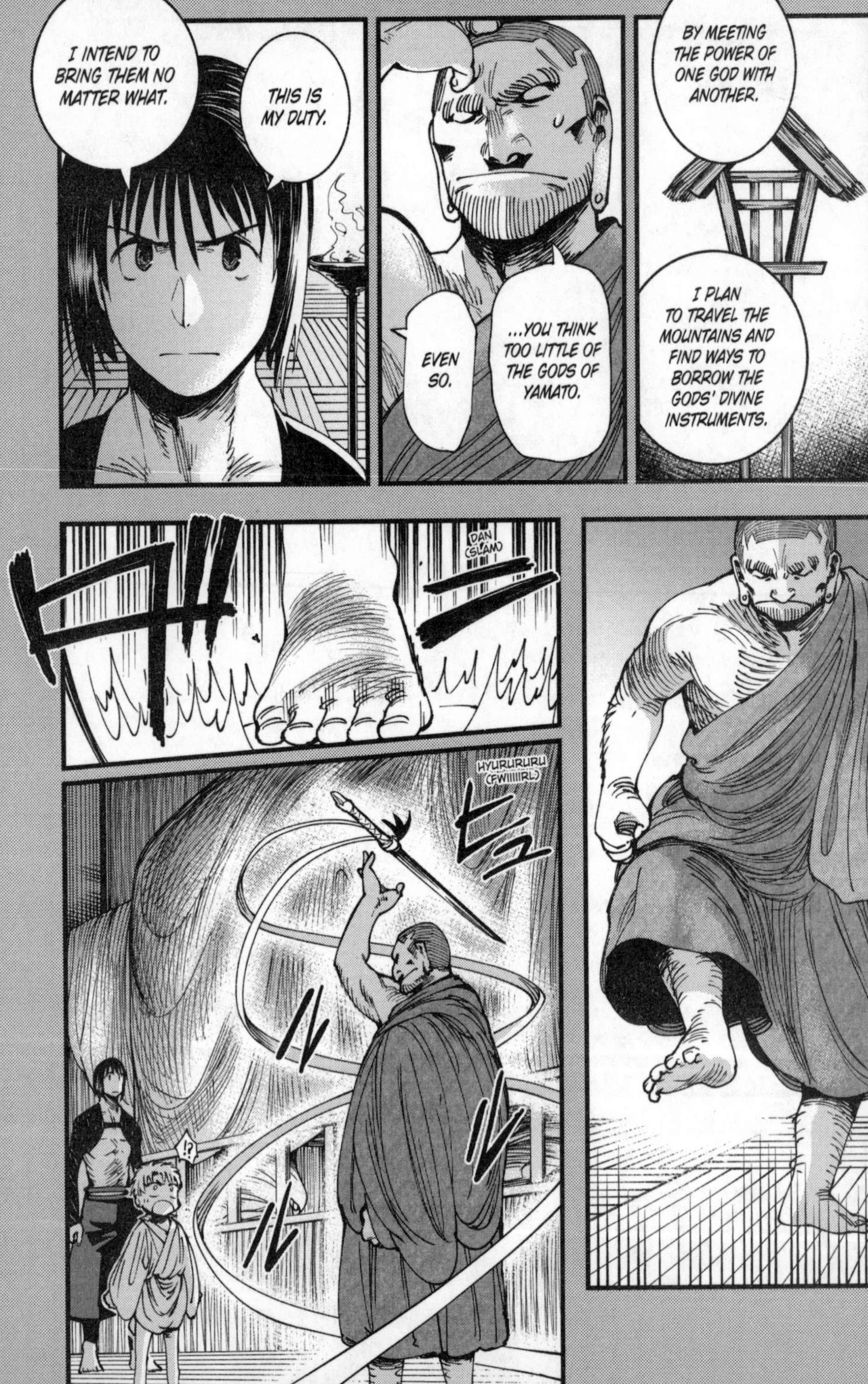
BY MEETING THE POWER OF ONE GOD WITH ANOTHER.
I PLAN TO TRAVEL THE MOUNTAINS AND FIND WAYS TO BORROW THE GODS' DIVINE INSTRUMENTS.
...YOU THINK TOO LITTLE OF THE GODS OF YAMATO.
EVEN SO.
I INTEND TO BRING THEM NO MATTER WHAT.
THIS IS MY DUTY.
DAN (SLAM)
HYURURURU (FWIIIIRL)
!?

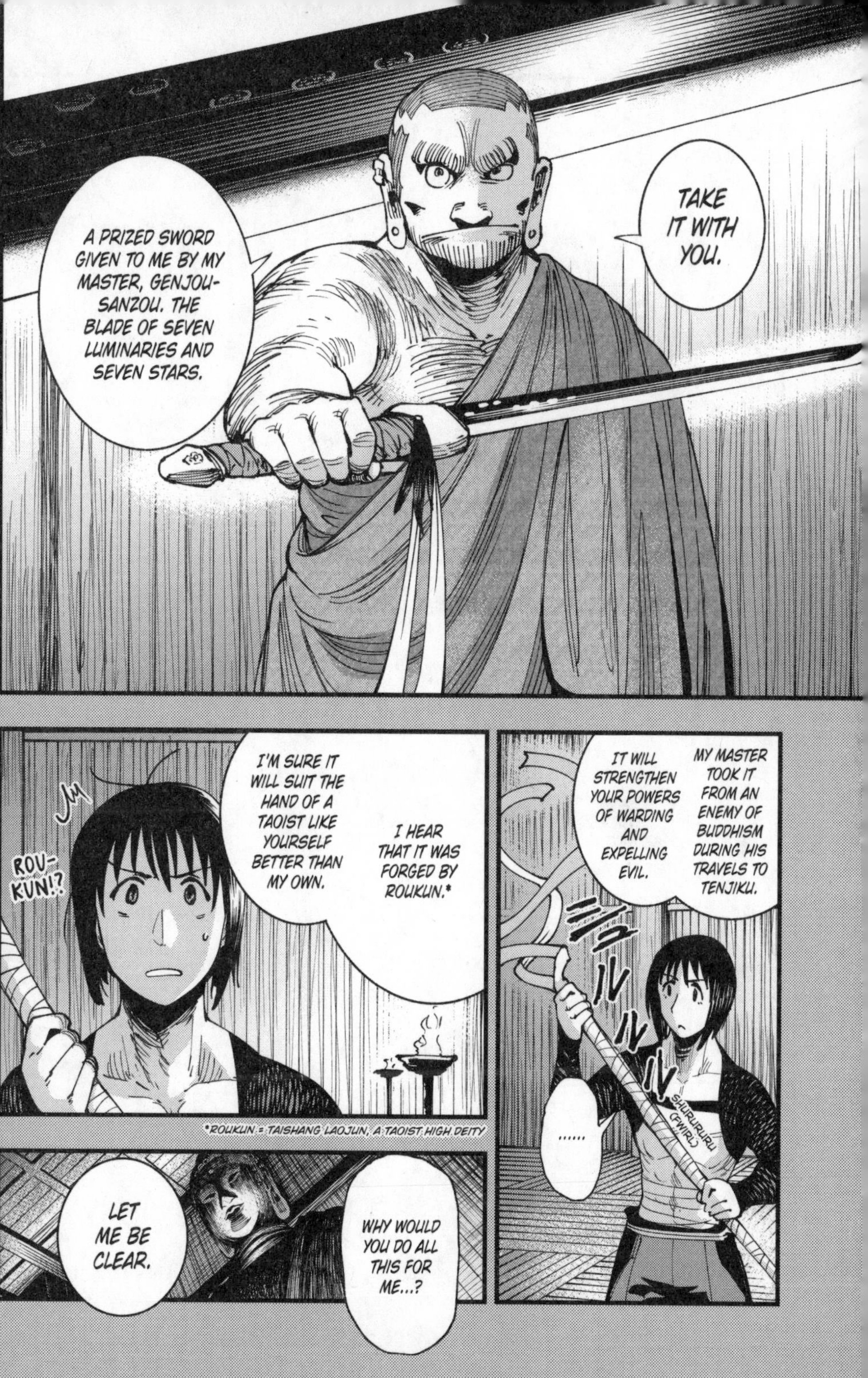
TAKE IT WITH YOU.
A PRIZED SWORD GIVEN TO ME BY MY MASTER, GENJOU-SANZOU. THE BLADE OF SEVEN LUMINARIES AND SEVEN STARS.
MY MASTER TOOK IT FROM AN ENEMY OF BUDDHISM DURING HIS TRAVELS TO TENJIKU.
IT WILL STRENGTHEN YOUR POWERS OF WARDING AND EXPELLING EVIL.
SHURURURU (FWIRL)
......
I HEAR THAT IT WAS FORGED BY ROUKUN.*
I'M SURE IT WILL SUIT THE HAND OF A TAOIST LIKE YOURSELF BETTER THAN MY OWN.
ROU-KUN!?
*ROUKUN = TAISHANG LAOJUN, A TAOIST HIGH DEITY
WHY WOULD YOU DO ALL THIS FOR ME...?
LET ME BE CLEAR.

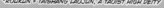

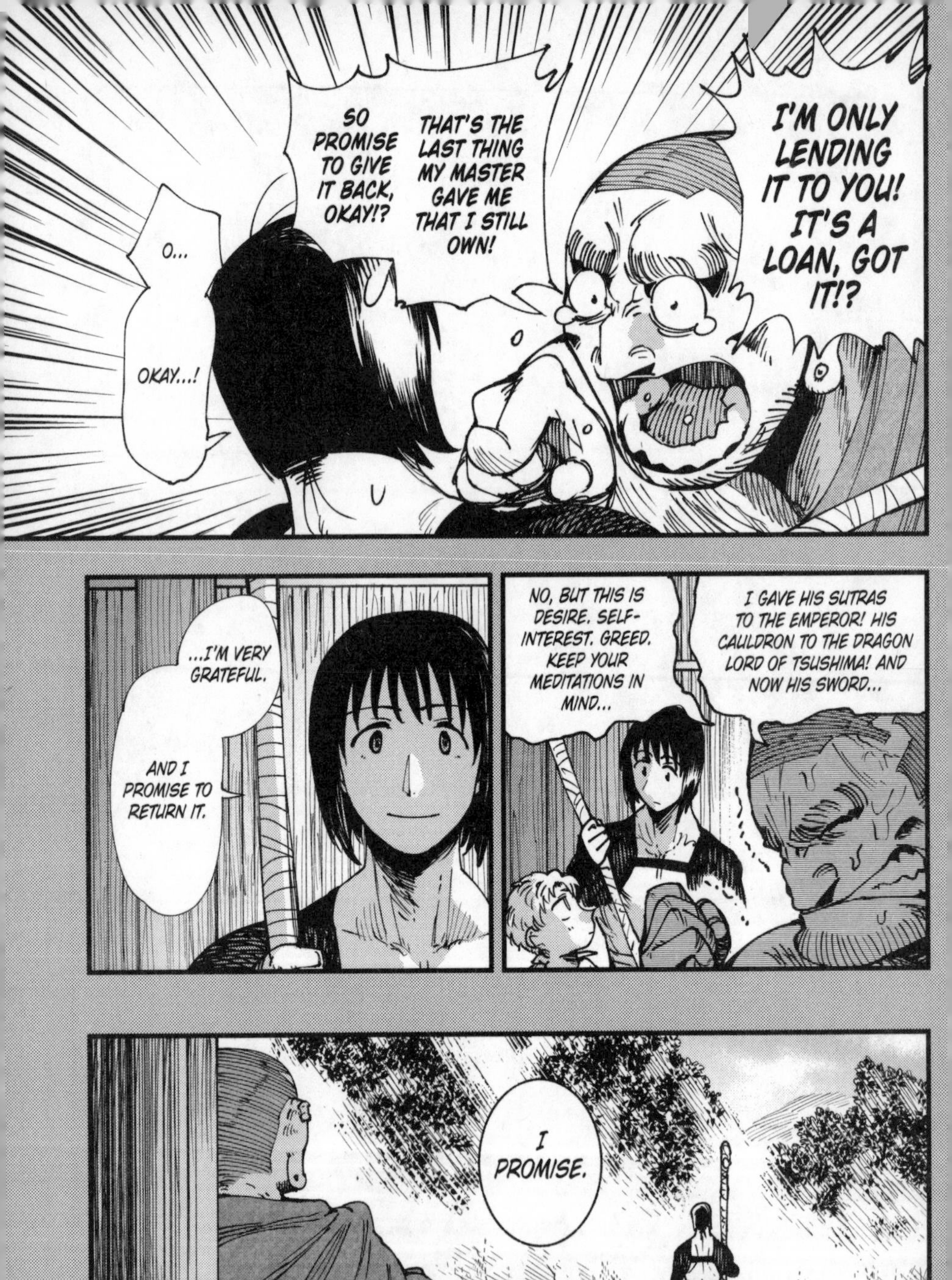
I'M ONLY LENDING IT TO YOU! IT'S A LOAN, GOT IT!?
THAT'S THE LAST THING MY MASTER GAVE ME THAT I STILL OWN!
SO PROMISE TO GIVE IT BACK, OKAY!?
O... OKAY...!
I GAVE HIS SUTRAS TO THE EMPEROR! HIS CAULDRON TO THE DRAGON LORD OF TSUSHIMA! AND NOW HIS SWORD...
NO, BUT THIS IS DESIRE. SELF-INTEREST. GREED. KEEP YOUR MEDITATIONS IN MIND...
...I'M VERY GRATEFUL.
AND I PROMISE TO RETURN IT.
I PROMISE.

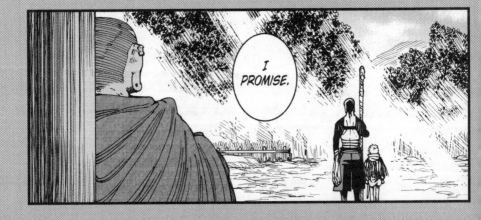

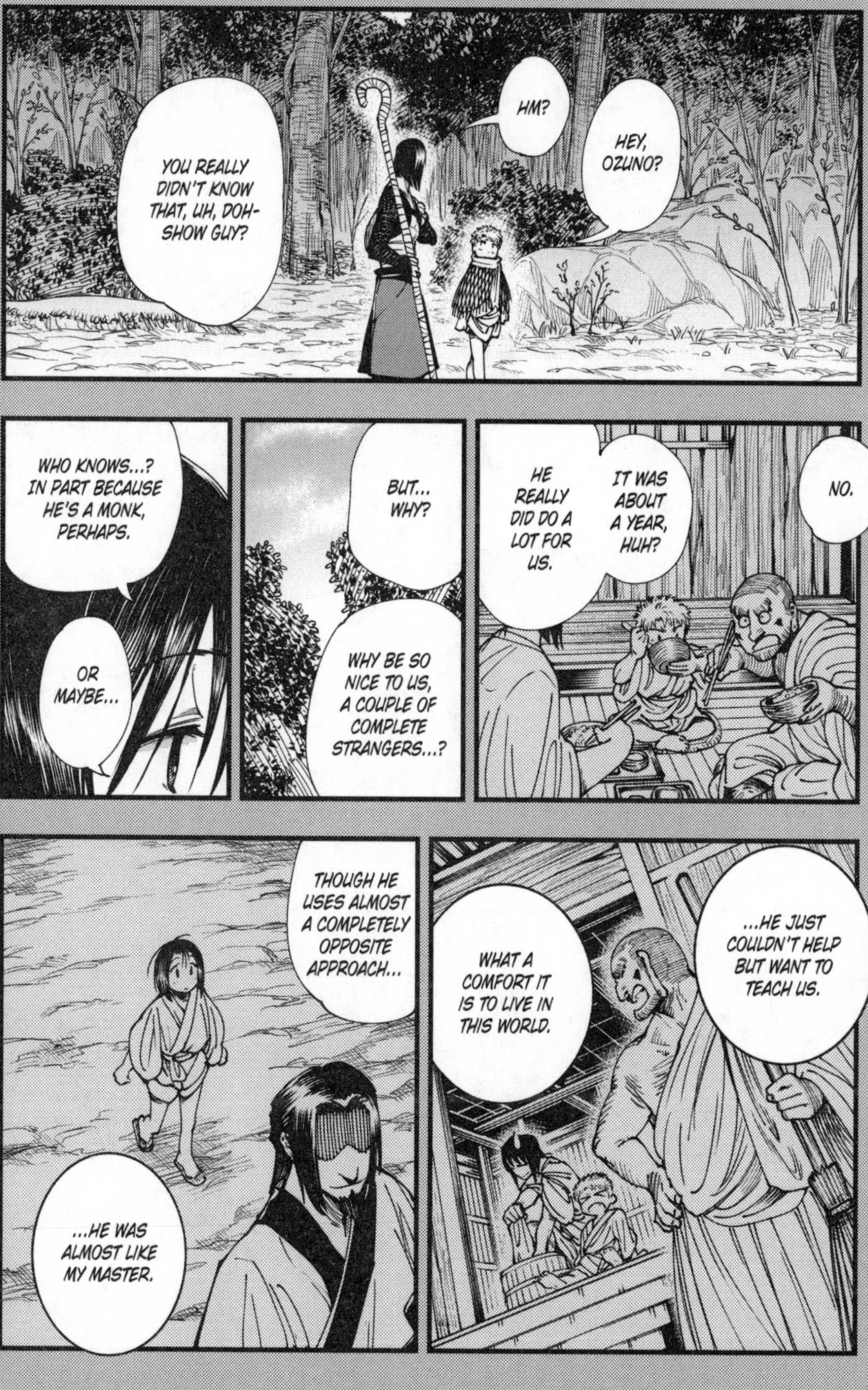
HEY, OZUNO?
HM?
YOU REALLY DIDN'T KNOW THAT, UH, DOH-SHOW GUY?
NO.
IT WAS ABOUT A YEAR, HUH?
HE REALLY DID DO A LOT FOR US.
BUT... WHY?
WHY BE SO NICE TO US, A COUPLE OF COMPLETE STRANGERS...?
WHO KNOWS...? IN PART BECAUSE HE'S A MONK, PERHAPS.
OR MAYBE...
...HE JUST COULDN'T HELP BUT WANT TO TEACH US.
WHAT A COMFORT IT IS TO LIVE IN THIS WORLD.
THOUGH HE USES ALMOST A COMPLETELY OPPOSITE APPROACH...
...HE WAS ALMOST LIKE MY MASTER.

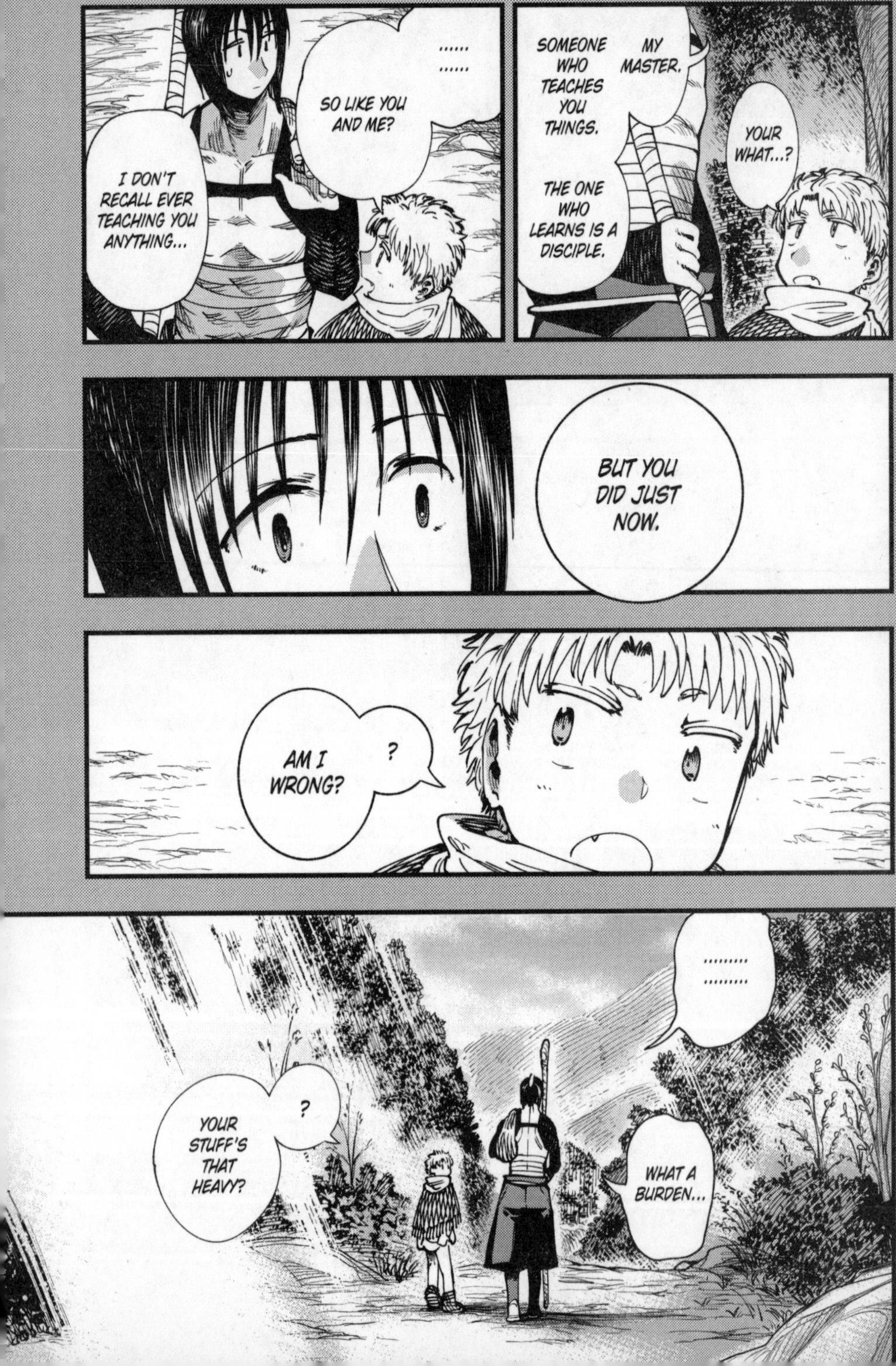
MY MASTER.
YOUR WHAT...?
SOMEONE WHO TEACHES YOU THINGS.
THE ONE WHO LEARNS IS A DISCIPLE.
......
......
SO LIKE YOU AND ME?
I DON'T RECALL EVER TEACHING YOU ANYTHING...
BUT YOU DID JUST NOW.
?
AM I WRONG?
....
....
WHAT A BURDEN...
?
YOUR STUFF'S THAT HEAVY?

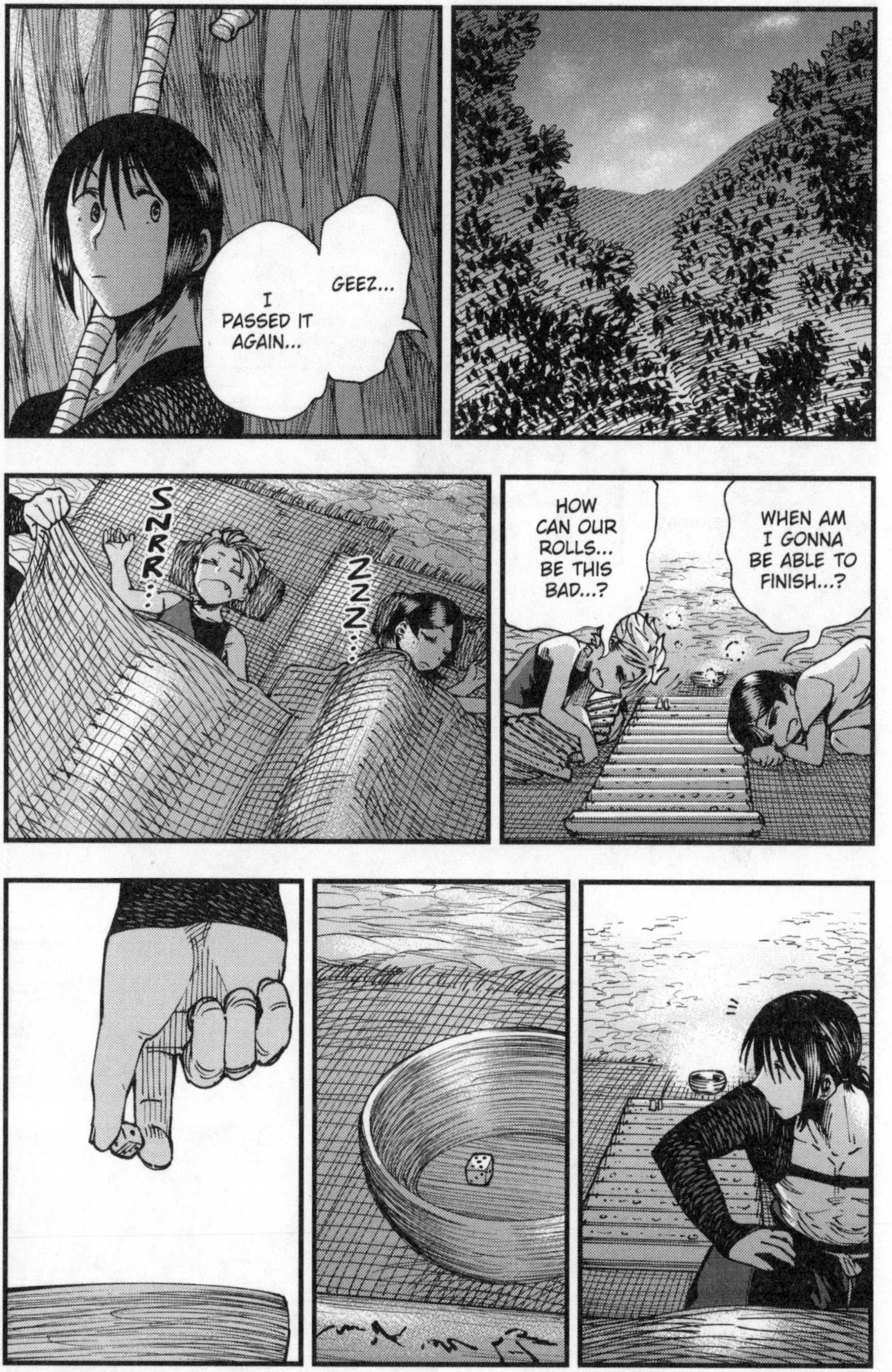
GEEZ...
I PASSED IT AGAIN...
WHEN AM I GONNA BE ABLE TO FINISH...?
HOW CAN OUR ROLLS... BE THIS BAD...?
ZZZ...
SNRR...

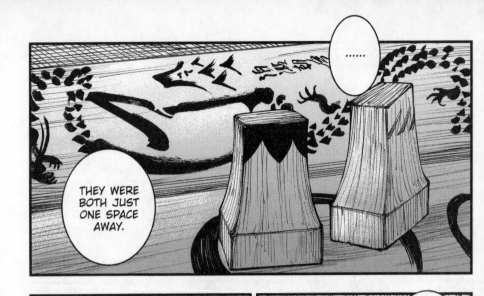

......

THEY WERE BOTH JUST ONE SPACE AWAY.

HMPH!

"THE KATSURAGI PETITION"... HUH.

PASHA
STHWAP!

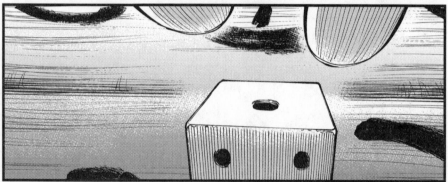

THE RAIN HAS ENDED.

MAY THE SHINING HEAVENS GUIDE YOUR FATE.

YAWN...

CHAPTER VIII ❤ END

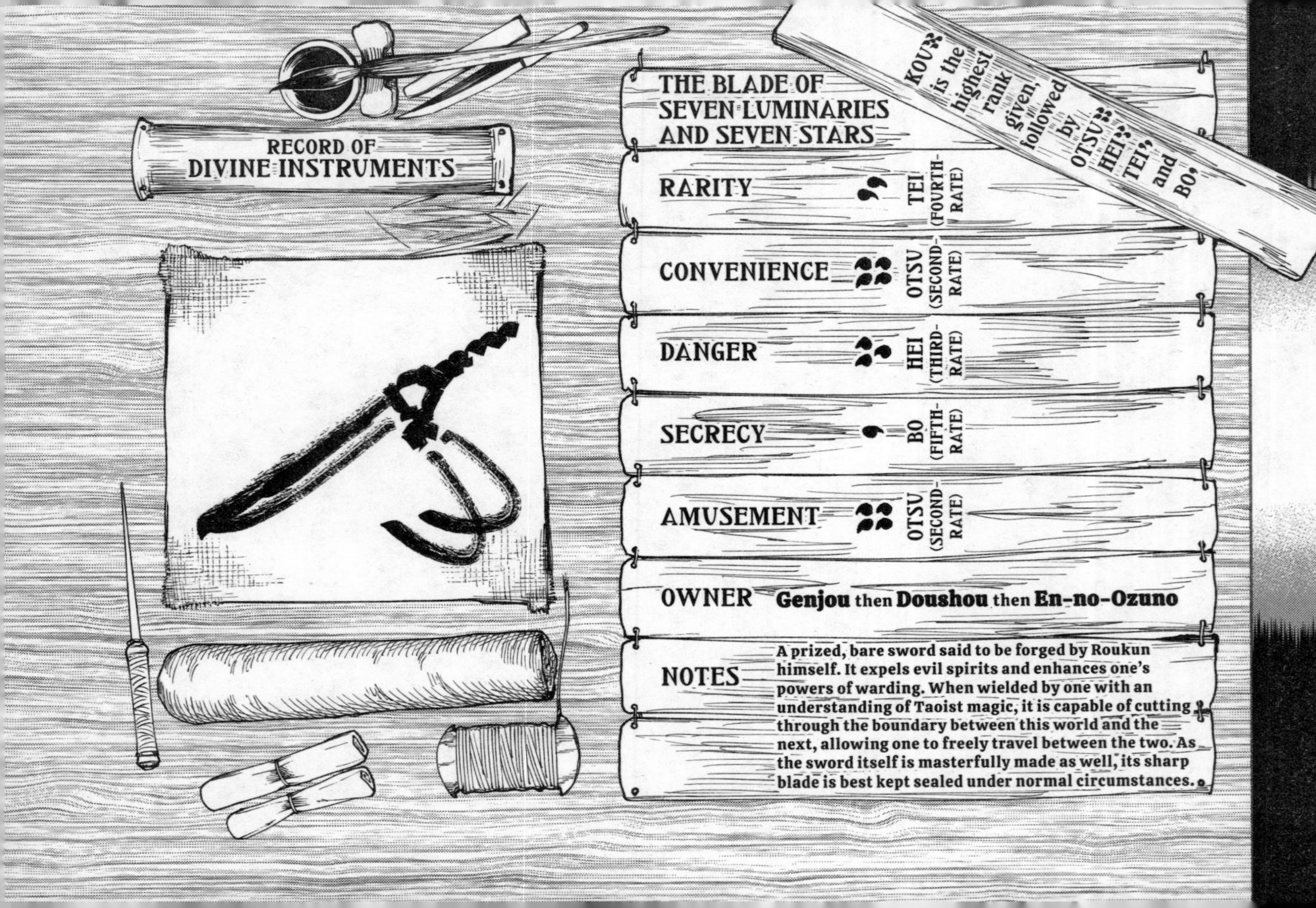
RECORD OF DIVINE INSTRUMENTS
THE BLADE OF SEVEN LUMINARIES AND SEVEN STARS
KOU is the highest rank given, followed by OTSU, HEI, TEI, and BO.
RARITY TEI (FOURTH-RATE)
CONVENIENCE OTSU (SECOND-RATE)
DANGER HEI (THIRD-RATE)
SECRECY BO (FIFTH-RATE)
AMUSEMENT OTSU (SECOND-RATE)
OWNER Genjou then Doushou then En-no-Ozuno
NOTES A prized, bare sword said to be forged by Roukun himself. It expels evil spirits and enhances one's powers of warding. When wielded by one with an understanding of Taoist magic, it is capable of cutting through the boundary between this world and the next, allowing one to freely travel between the two. As the sword itself is masterfully made as well, its sharp blade is best kept sealed under normal circumstances.

Touge Oni

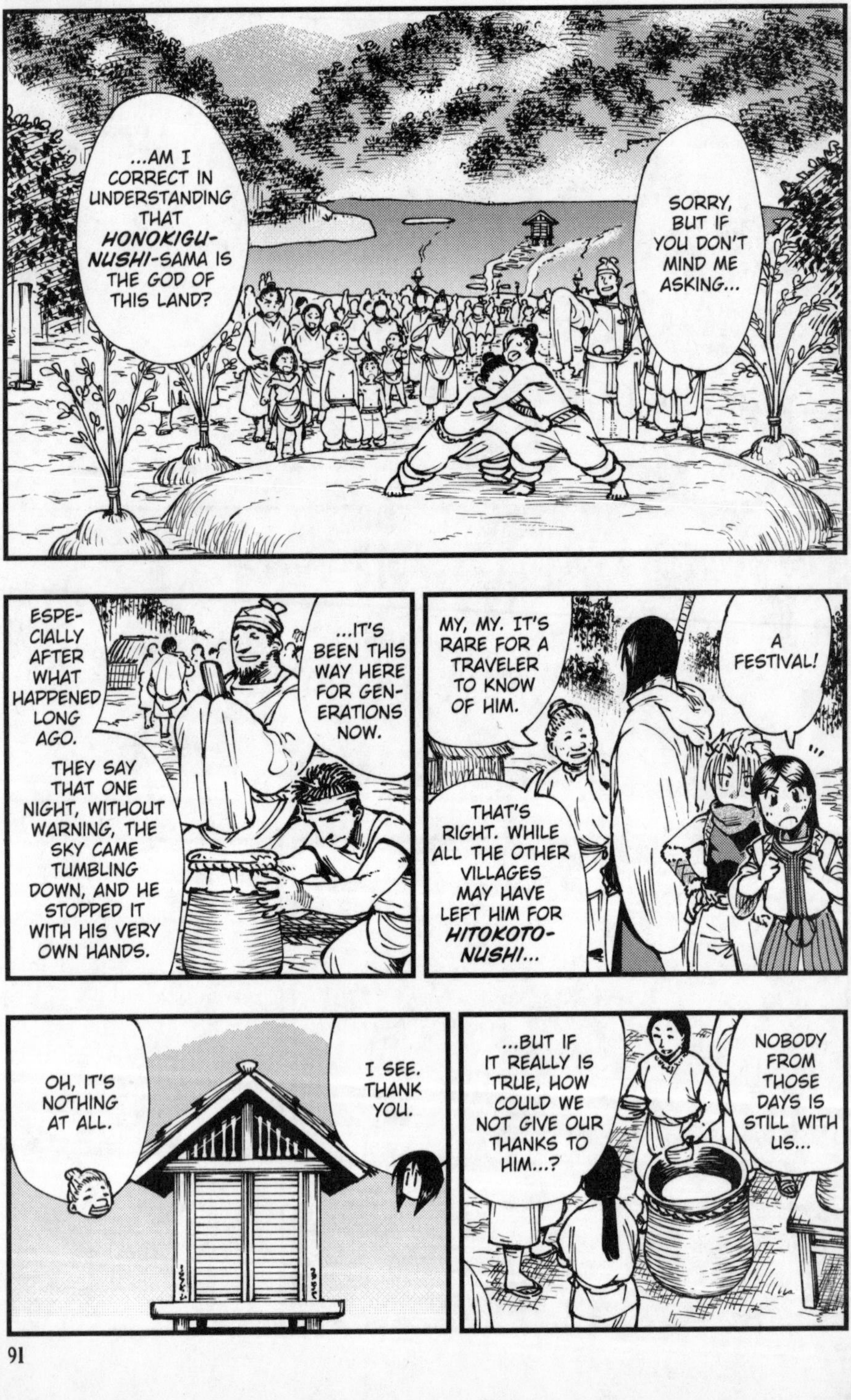
SORRY, BUT IF YOU DON'T MIND ME ASKING...
...AM I CORRECT IN UNDERSTANDING THAT *HONOKIGUNUSHI*-SAMA IS THE GOD OF THIS LAND?
A FESTIVAL!
...
MY, MY. IT'S RARE FOR A TRAVELER TO KNOW OF HIM.
THAT'S RIGHT. WHILE ALL THE OTHER VILLAGES MAY HAVE LEFT HIM FOR *HITOKOTONUSHI*...
...IT'S BEEN THIS WAY HERE FOR GENERATIONS NOW.
ESPECIALLY AFTER WHAT HAPPENED LONG AGO.
THEY SAY THAT ONE NIGHT, WITHOUT WARNING, THE SKY CAME TUMBLING DOWN, AND HE STOPPED IT WITH HIS VERY OWN HANDS.
NOBODY FROM THOSE DAYS IS STILL WITH US...
...BUT IF IT REALLY IS TRUE, HOW COULD WE NOT GIVE OUR THANKS TO HIM...?
I SEE. THANK YOU.
OH, IT'S NOTHING AT ALL.

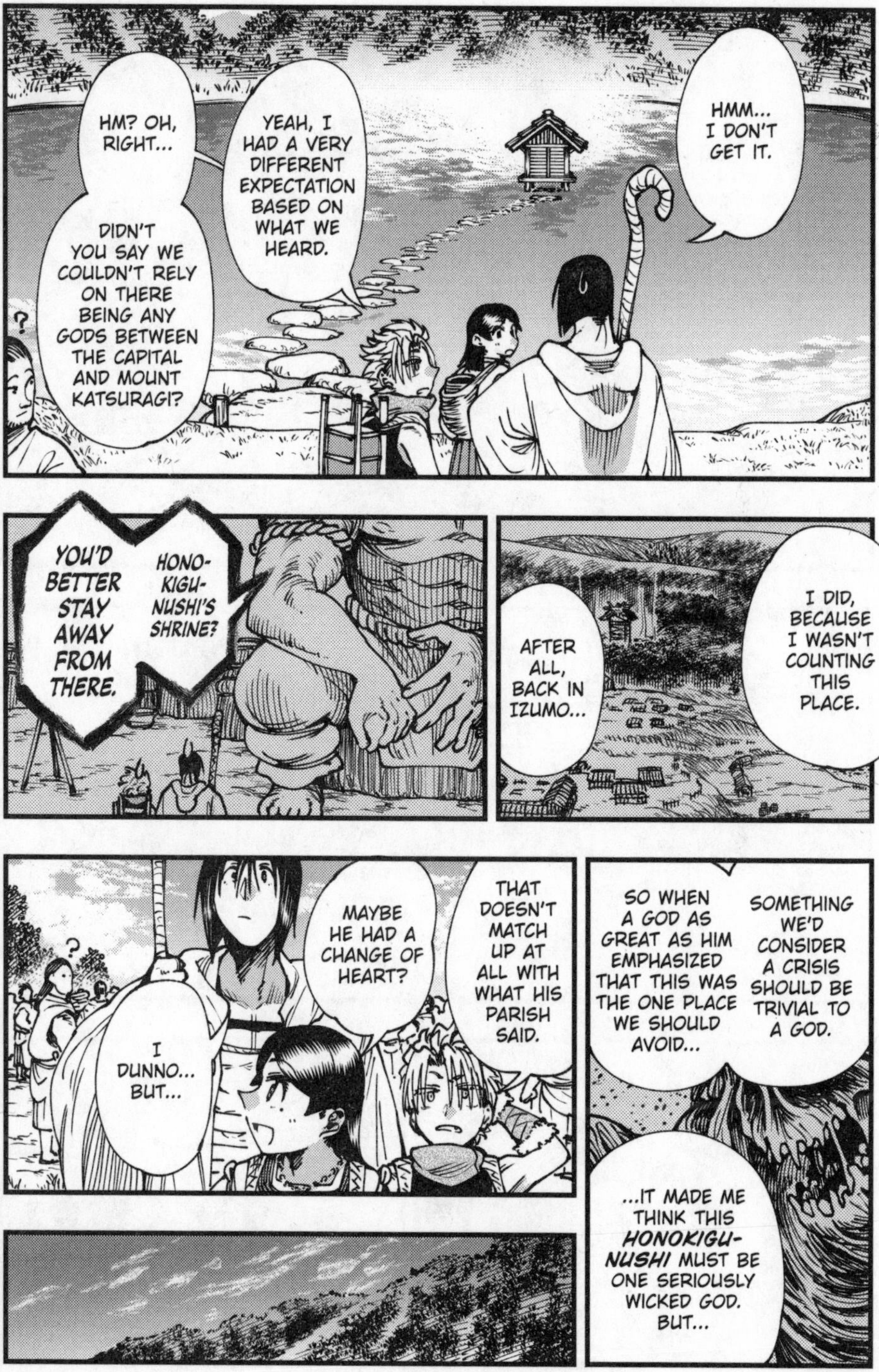
HMM... I DON'T GET IT.
YEAH, I HAD A VERY DIFFERENT EXPECTATION BASED ON WHAT WE HEARD.
HM? OH, RIGHT...
DIDN'T YOU SAY WE COULDN'T RELY ON THERE BEING ANY GODS BETWEEN THE CAPITAL AND MOUNT KATSURAGI?
?
I DID, BECAUSE I WASN'T COUNTING THIS PLACE.
AFTER ALL, BACK IN IZUMO...
HONO-KIGU-NUSHI'S SHRINE?
YOU'D BETTER STAY AWAY FROM THERE.
SOMETHING WE'D CONSIDER A CRISIS SHOULD BE TRIVIAL TO A GOD.
SO WHEN A GOD AS GREAT AS HIM EMPHASIZED THAT THIS WAS THE ONE PLACE WE SHOULD AVOID...
...IT MADE ME THINK THIS *HONOKIGU-NUSHI* MUST BE ONE SERIOUSLY WICKED GOD. BUT...
THAT DOESN'T MATCH UP AT ALL WITH WHAT HIS PARISH SAID.
MAYBE HE HAD A CHANGE OF HEART?
?
I DUNNO... BUT...

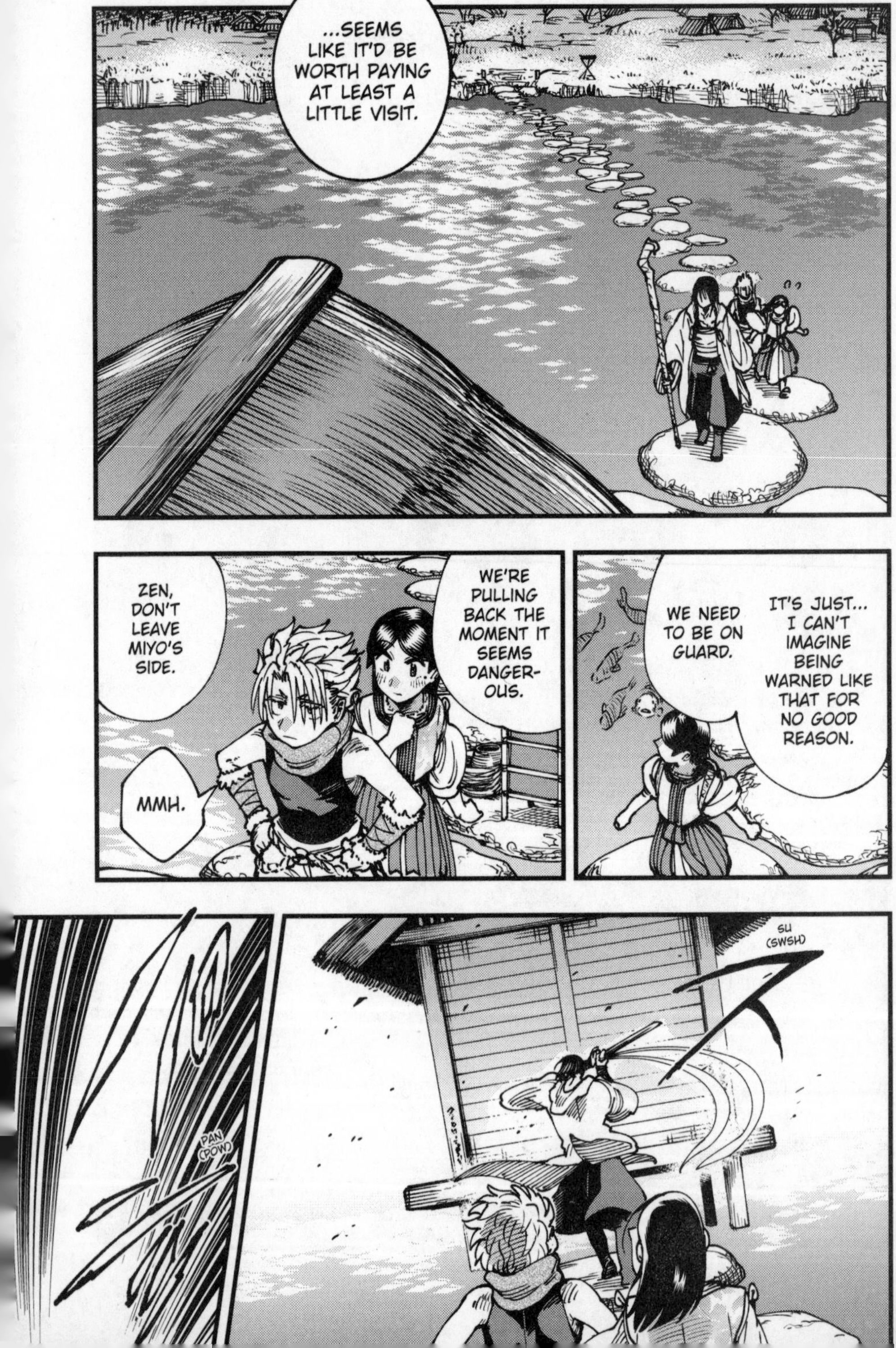
...SEEMS LIKE IT'D BE WORTH PAYING AT LEAST A LITTLE VISIT.
IT'S JUST... I CAN'T IMAGINE BEING WARNED LIKE THAT FOR NO GOOD REASON.
WE NEED TO BE ON GUARD.
WE'RE PULLING BACK THE MOMENT IT SEEMS DANGER-OUS.
ZEN, DON'T LEAVE MIYO'S SIDE.
MMH.
SU (SWSH)
PAN (POW)

CHAPTER IX THE GREAT WELL OF THE HEAVENS

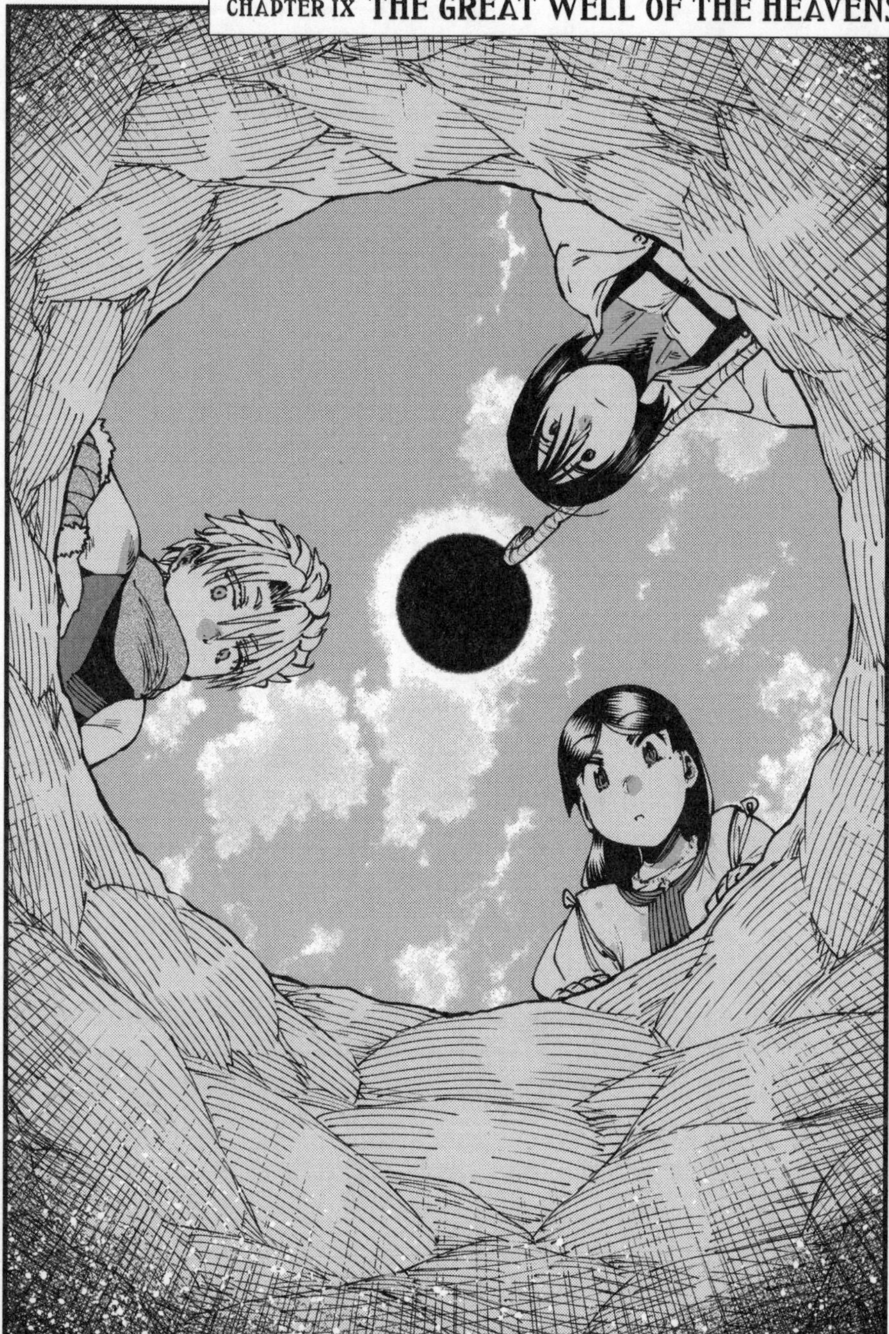

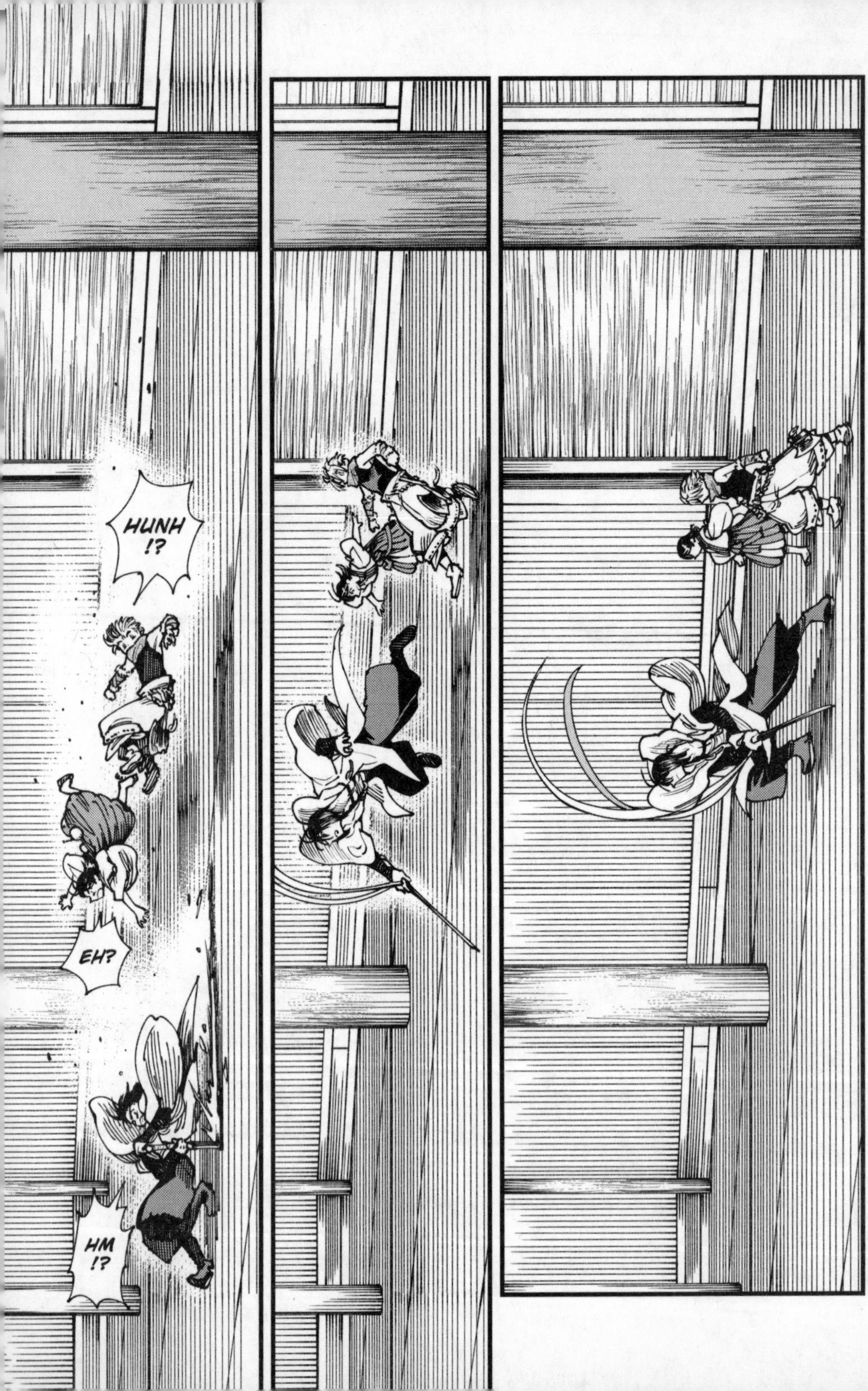
HUNH !?
EH?
HM !?

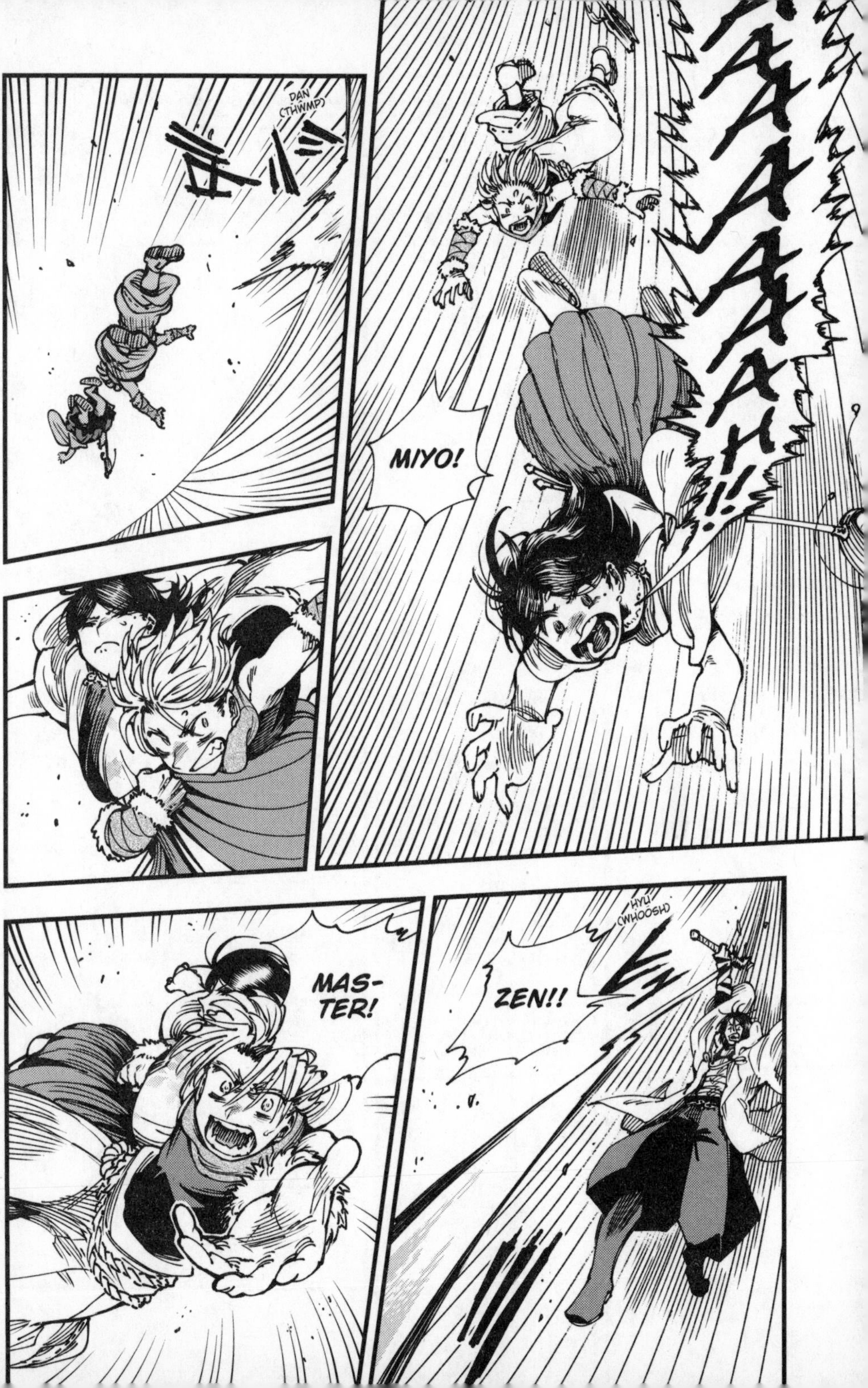
AAAAAH!!
MIYO!
DAN (THWMP)
HYU (WHOOSH)
ZEN!!
MAS-
TER!

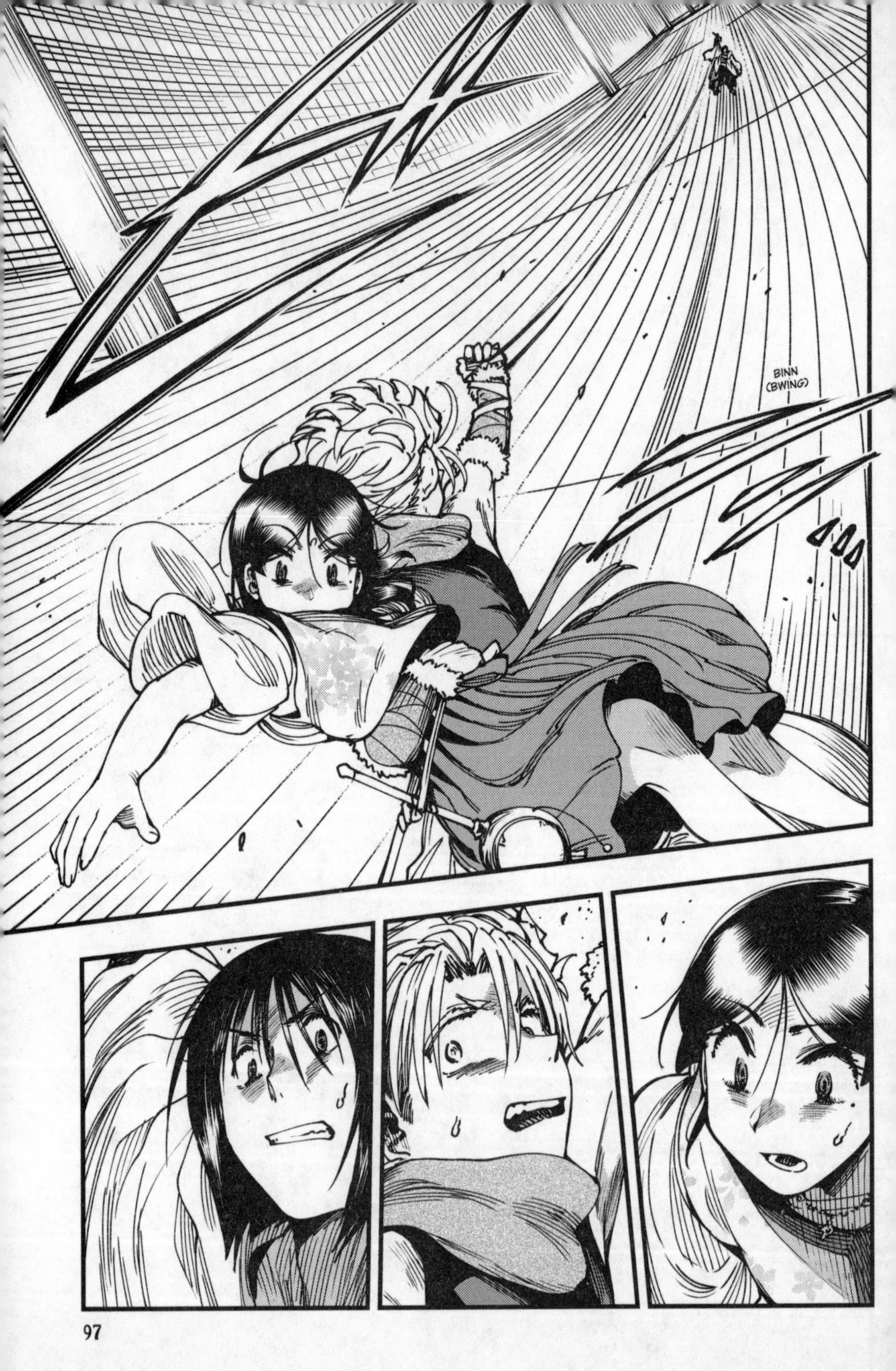
BINN
(BWING)

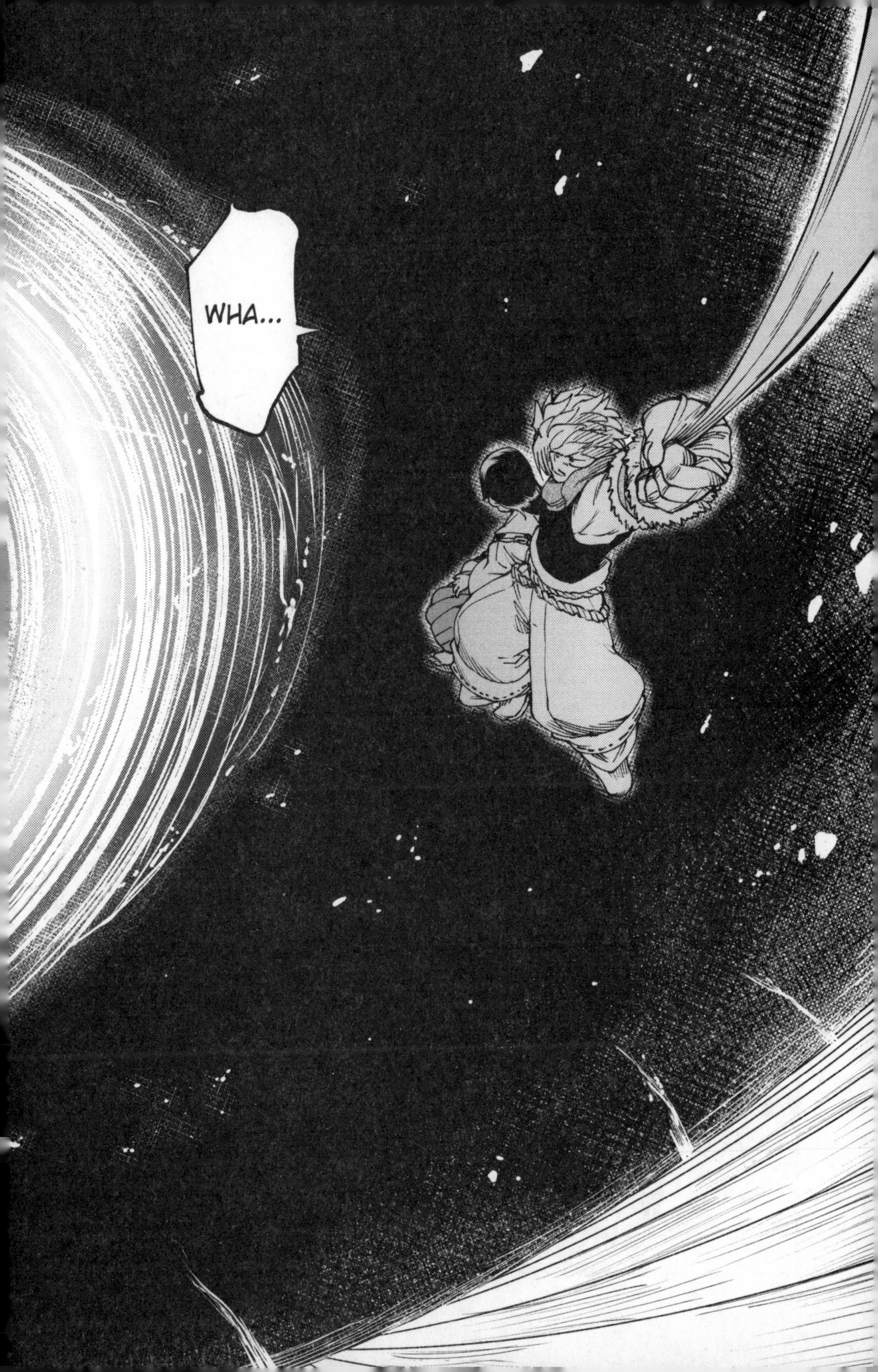
WHA...

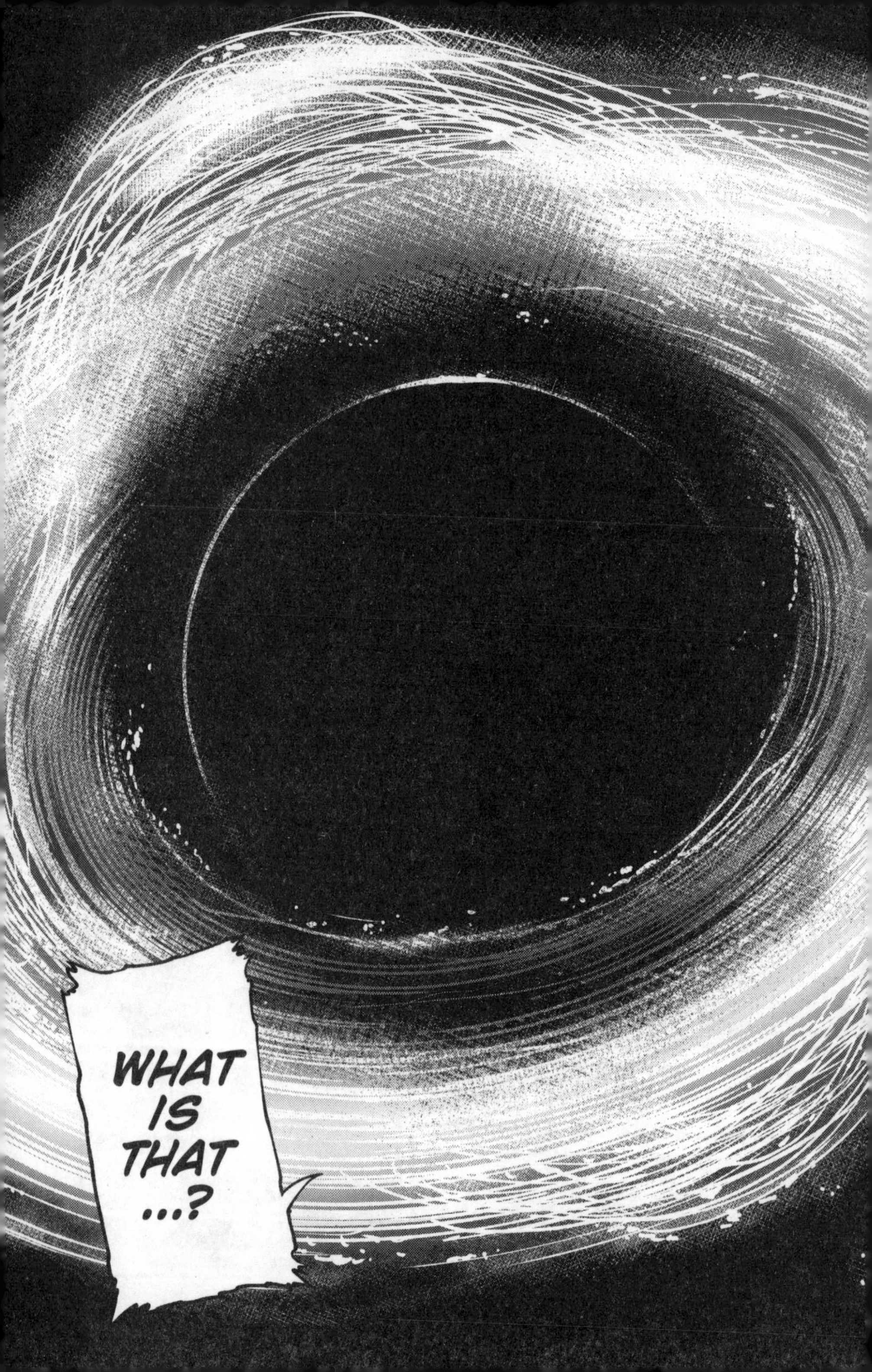
WHAT IS THAT ...?

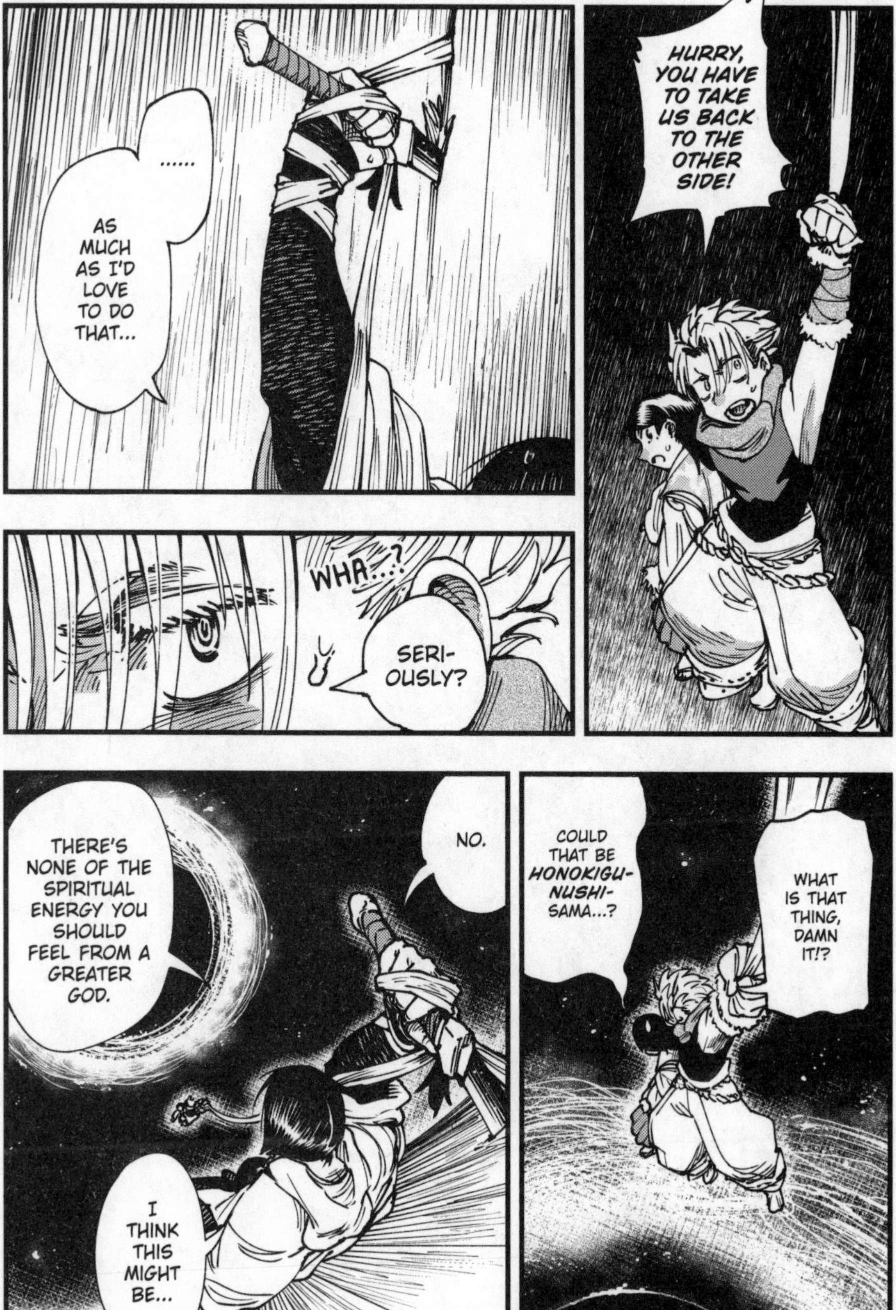
HURRY, YOU HAVE TO TAKE US BACK TO THE OTHER SIDE!
......
AS MUCH AS I'D LOVE TO DO THAT...
WHA...?
SERIOUSLY?
WHAT IS THAT THING, DAMN IT!?
COULD THAT BE *HONOKIGUNUSHI*-SAMA...?
NO.
THERE'S NONE OF THE SPIRITUAL ENERGY YOU SHOULD FEEL FROM A GREATER GOD.
I THINK THIS MIGHT BE...

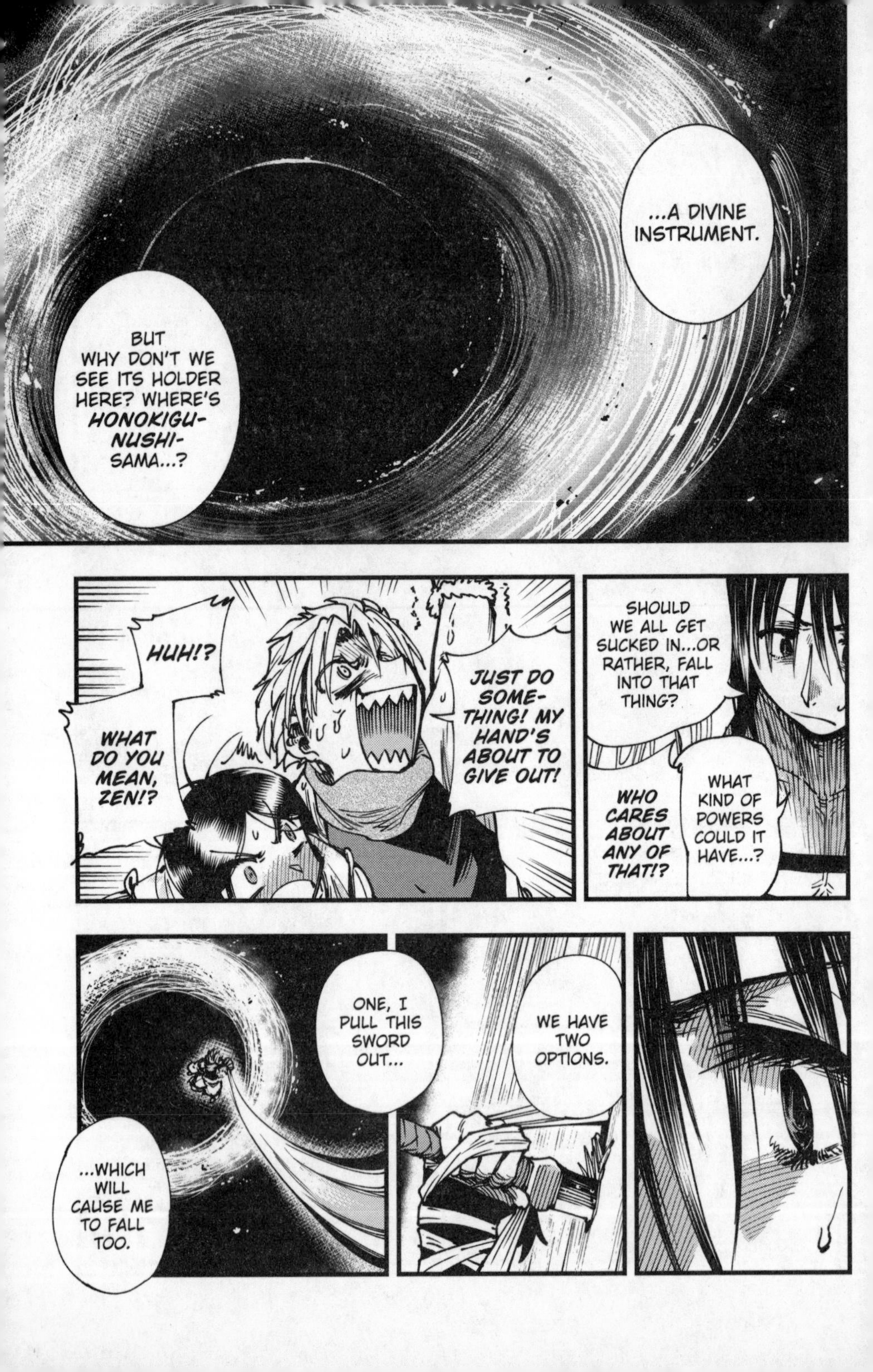
...A DIVINE INSTRUMENT.
BUT WHY DON'T WE SEE ITS HOLDER HERE? WHERE'S HONOKIGUNUSHI-SAMA...?
SHOULD WE ALL GET SUCKED IN...OR RATHER, FALL INTO THAT THING?
WHAT KIND OF POWERS COULD IT HAVE...?
WHO CARES ABOUT ANY OF THAT!?
JUST DO SOMETHING! MY HAND'S ABOUT TO GIVE OUT!
HUH!?
WHAT DO YOU MEAN, ZEN!?
WE HAVE TWO OPTIONS.
ONE, I PULL THIS SWORD OUT...
...WHICH WILL CAUSE ME TO FALL TOO.

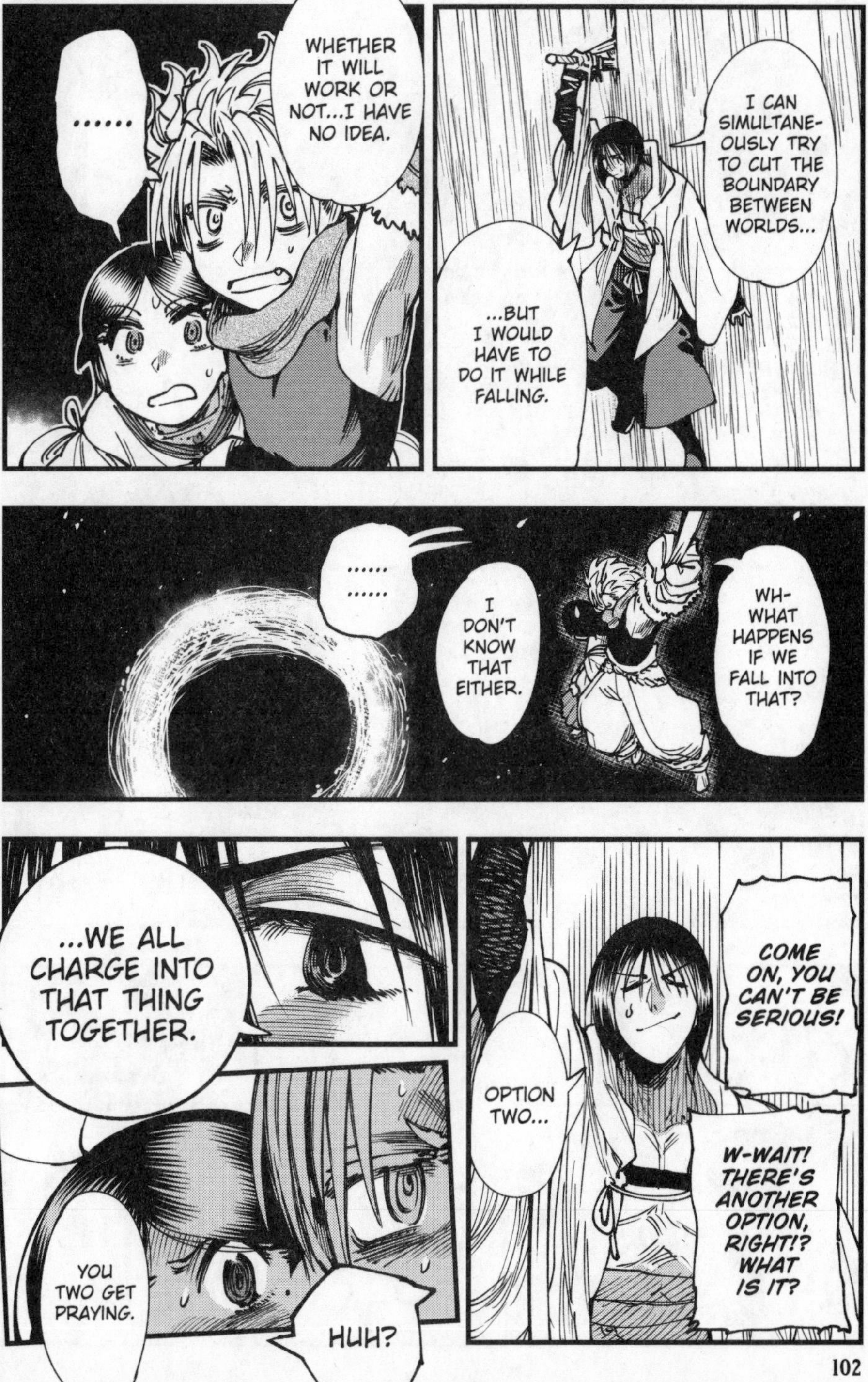
I CAN SIMULTANE-OUSLY TRY TO CUT THE BOUNDARY BETWEEN WORLDS...
...BUT I WOULD HAVE TO DO IT WHILE FALLING.
WHETHER IT WILL WORK OR NOT...I HAVE NO IDEA.
......
WH- WHAT HAPPENS IF WE FALL INTO THAT?
I DON'T KNOW THAT EITHER.
....
COME ON, YOU CAN'T BE SERIOUS!
OPTION TWO...
W-WAIT! THERE'S ANOTHER OPTION, RIGHT!? WHAT IS IT?
...WE ALL CHARGE INTO THAT THING TOGETHER.
HUH?
YOU TWO GET PRAYING.

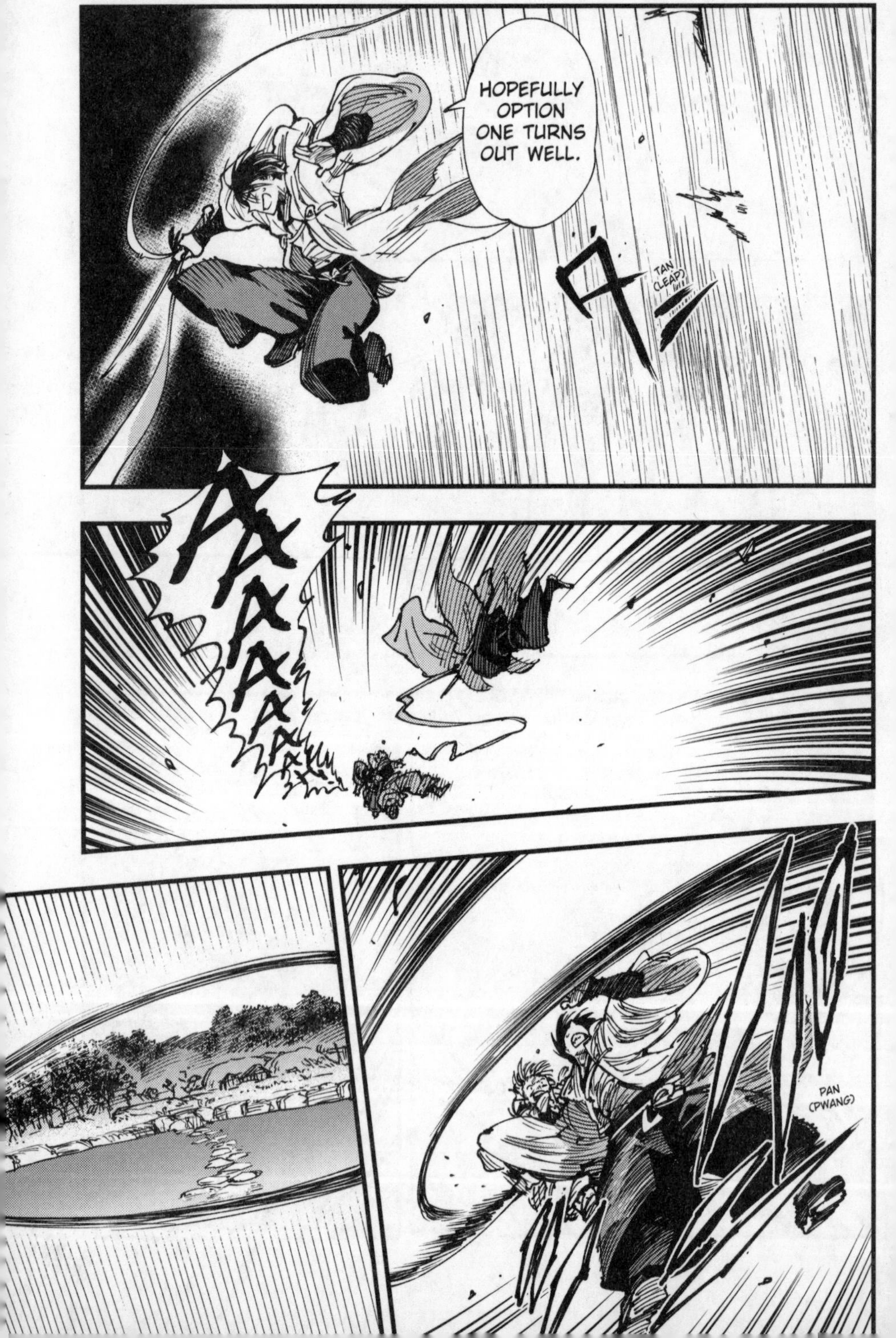
HOPEFULLY OPTION ONE TURNS OUT WELL.
TAN (LEAP)
PAN (PWANG)

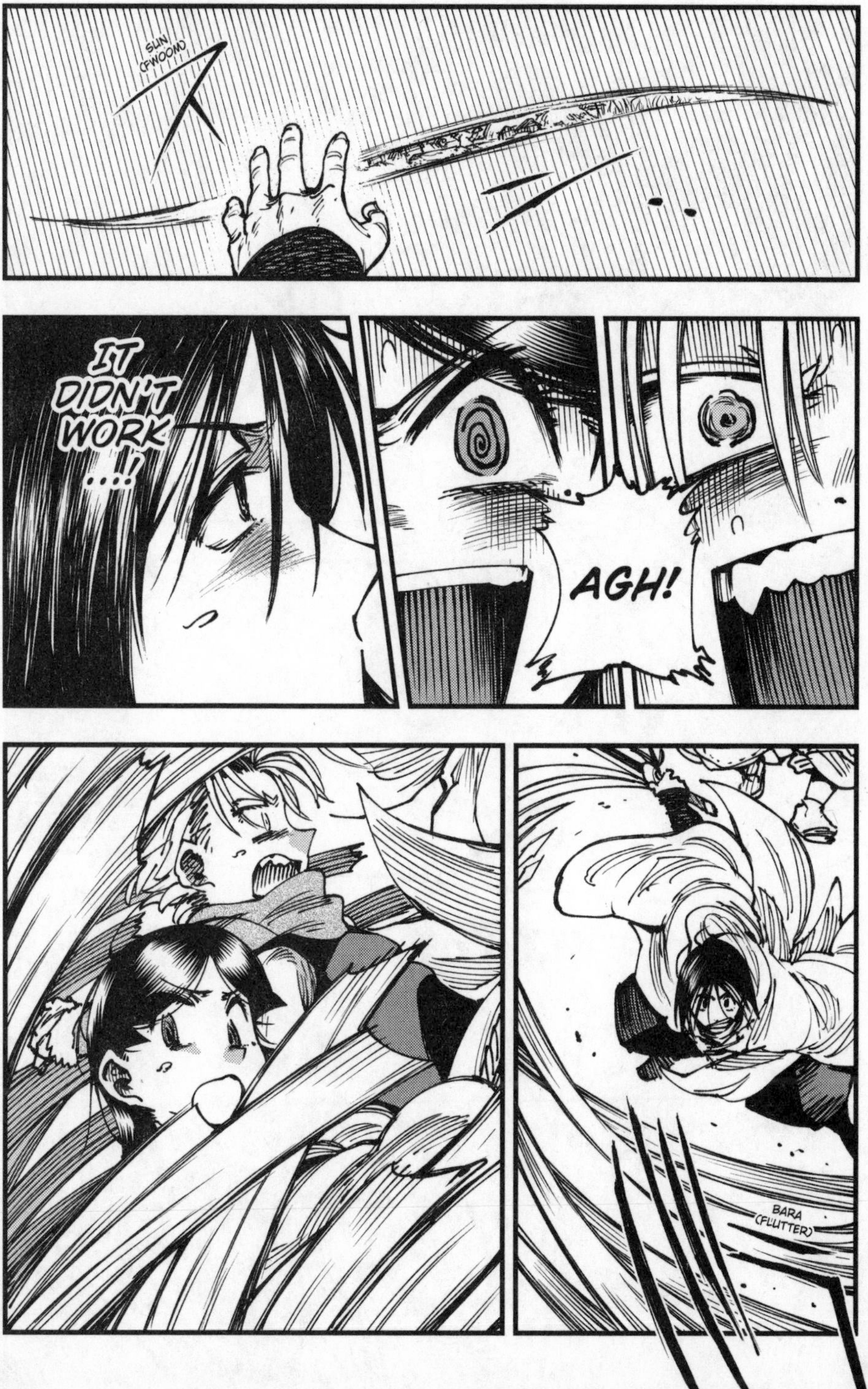
SUN (FWOOM)
AGH!
IT DIDN'T WORK ...!
BARA (FLUTTER)

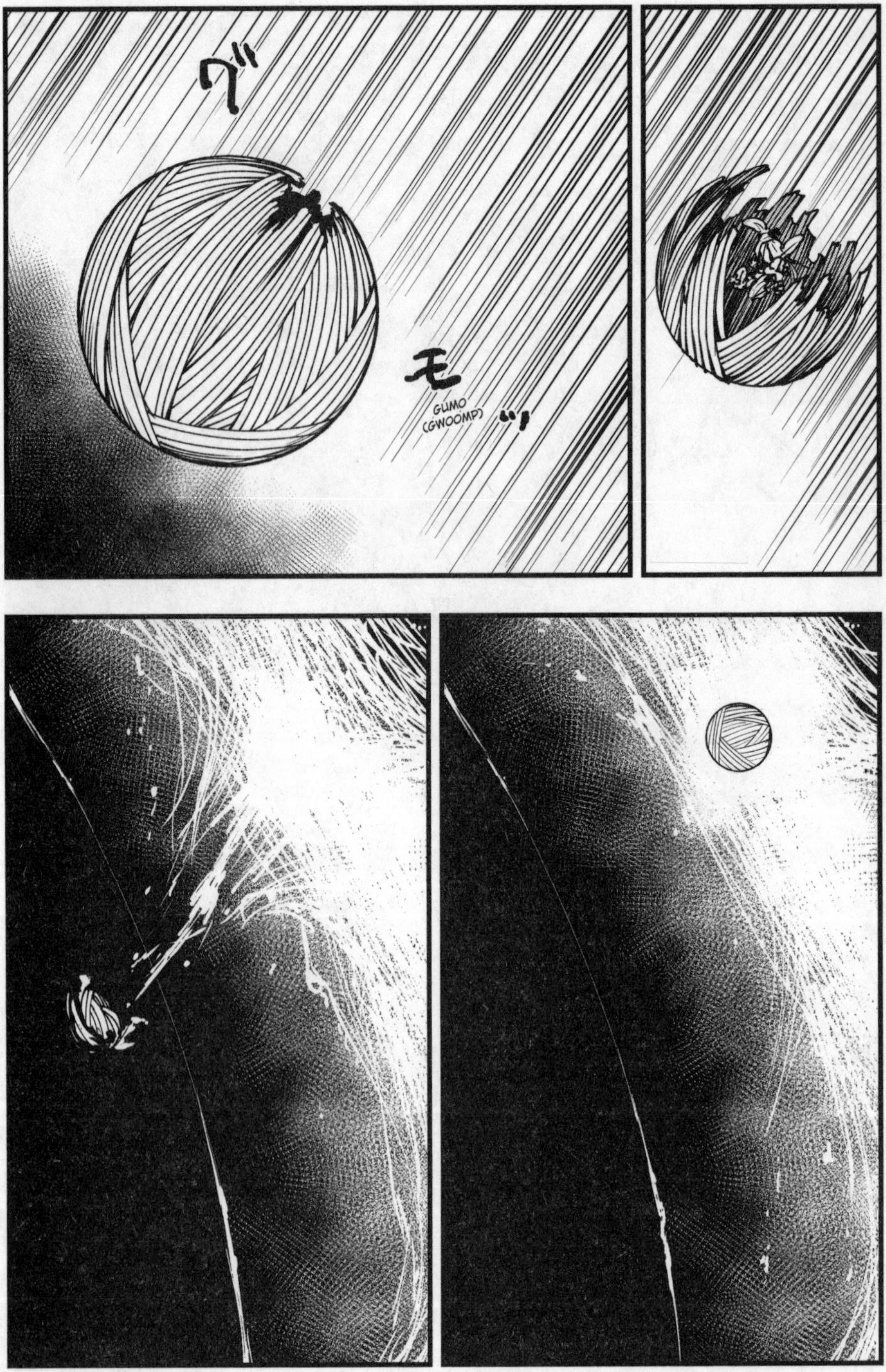
グ
モ
GUMO
(GWOOMP)
ッ

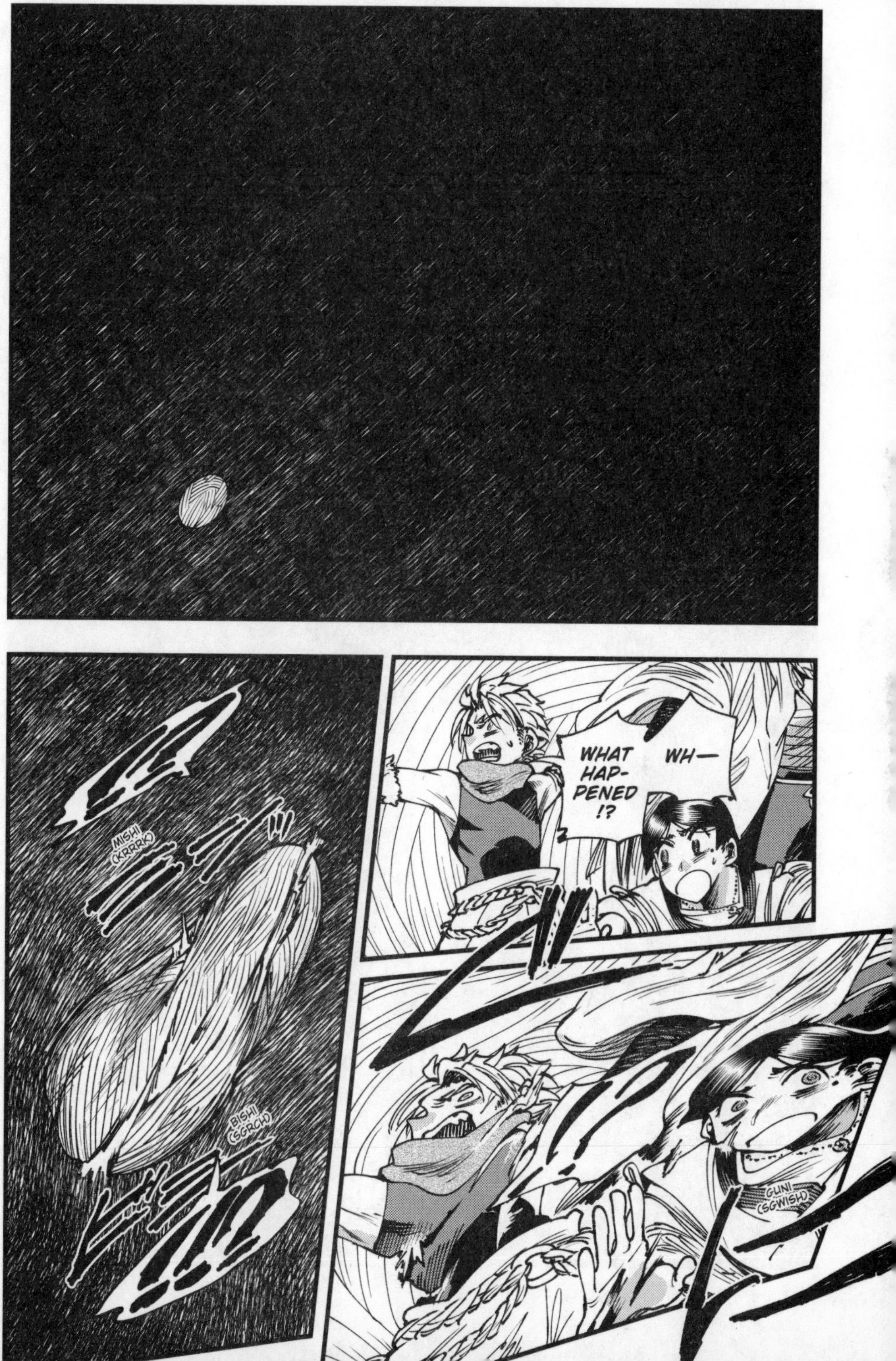
WH—
WHAT HAP-PENED !?
GUNI (SGWISH)
MISHI (KRRRK)
BISHI (SGRCH)

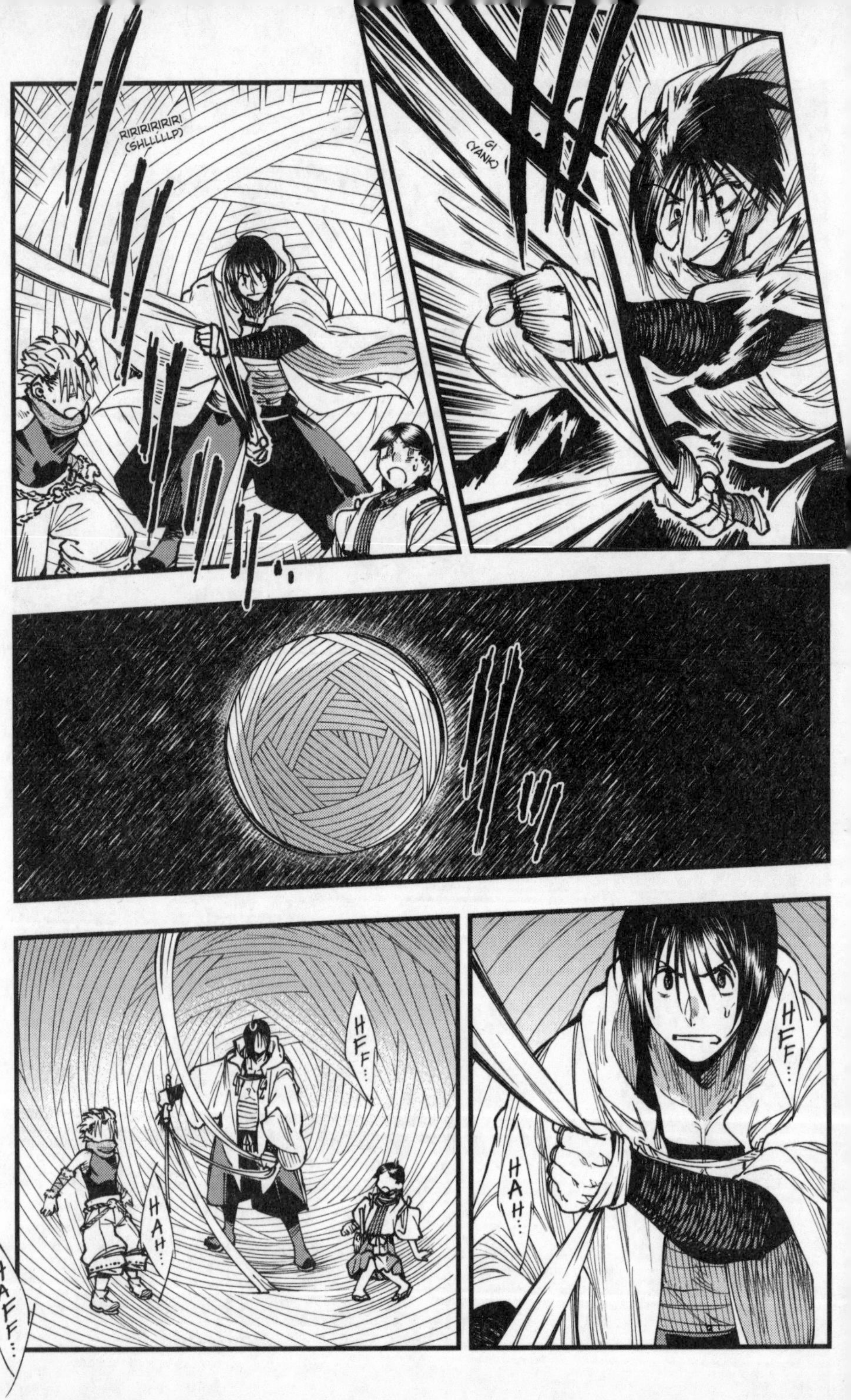
GI
(YANK)
RIRIRIRIRI
(SHLLLLLP)
HFF...
HAH...
HFF...
HAH...
HAFF...

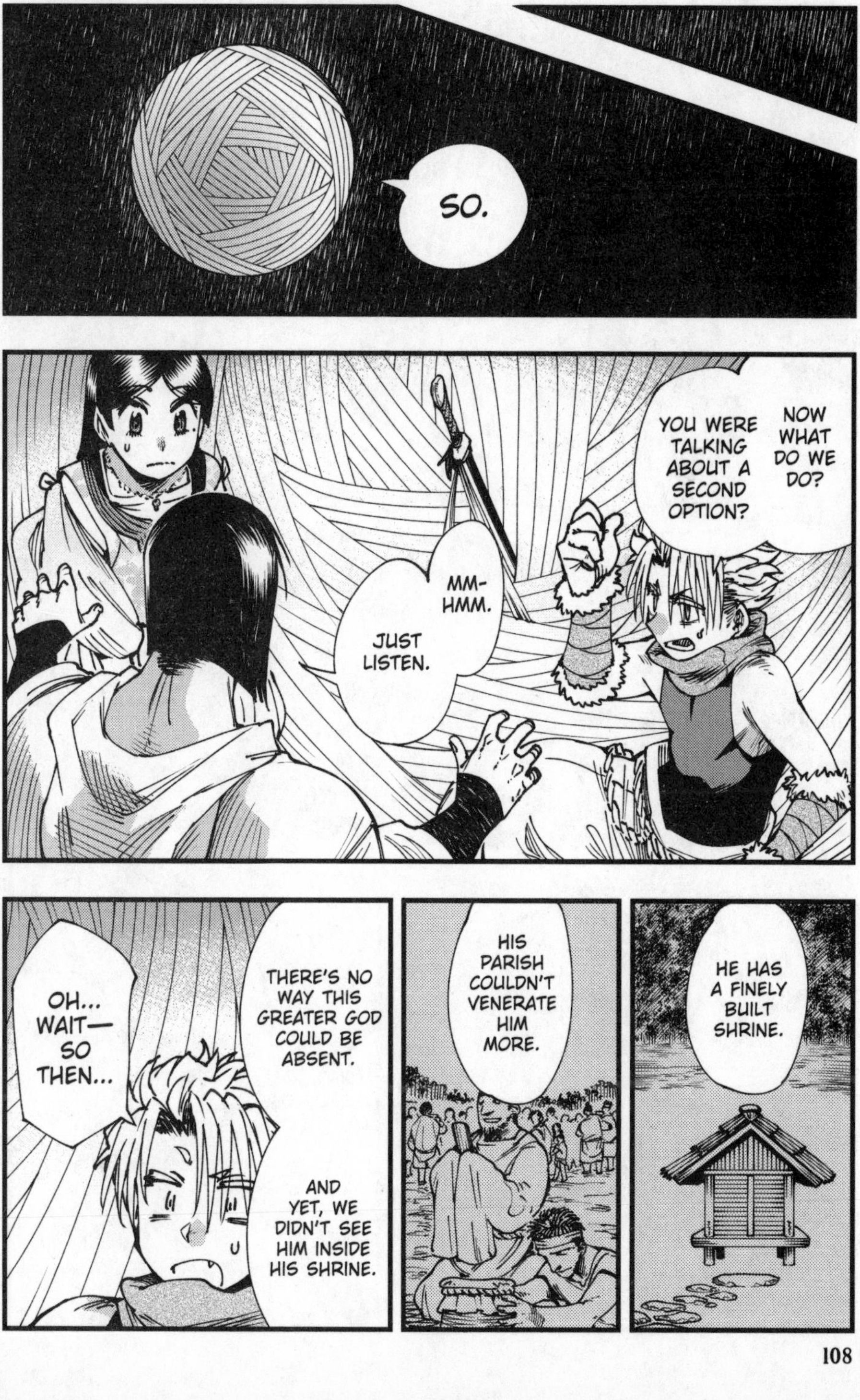
SO.
NOW WHAT DO WE DO?
YOU WERE TALKING ABOUT A SECOND OPTION?
MM-HMM.
JUST LISTEN.
HE HAS A FINELY BUILT SHRINE.
HIS PARISH COULDN'T VENERATE HIM MORE.
THERE'S NO WAY THIS GREATER GOD COULD BE ABSENT.
AND YET, WE DIDN'T SEE HIM INSIDE HIS SHRINE.
OH... WAIT— SO THEN...

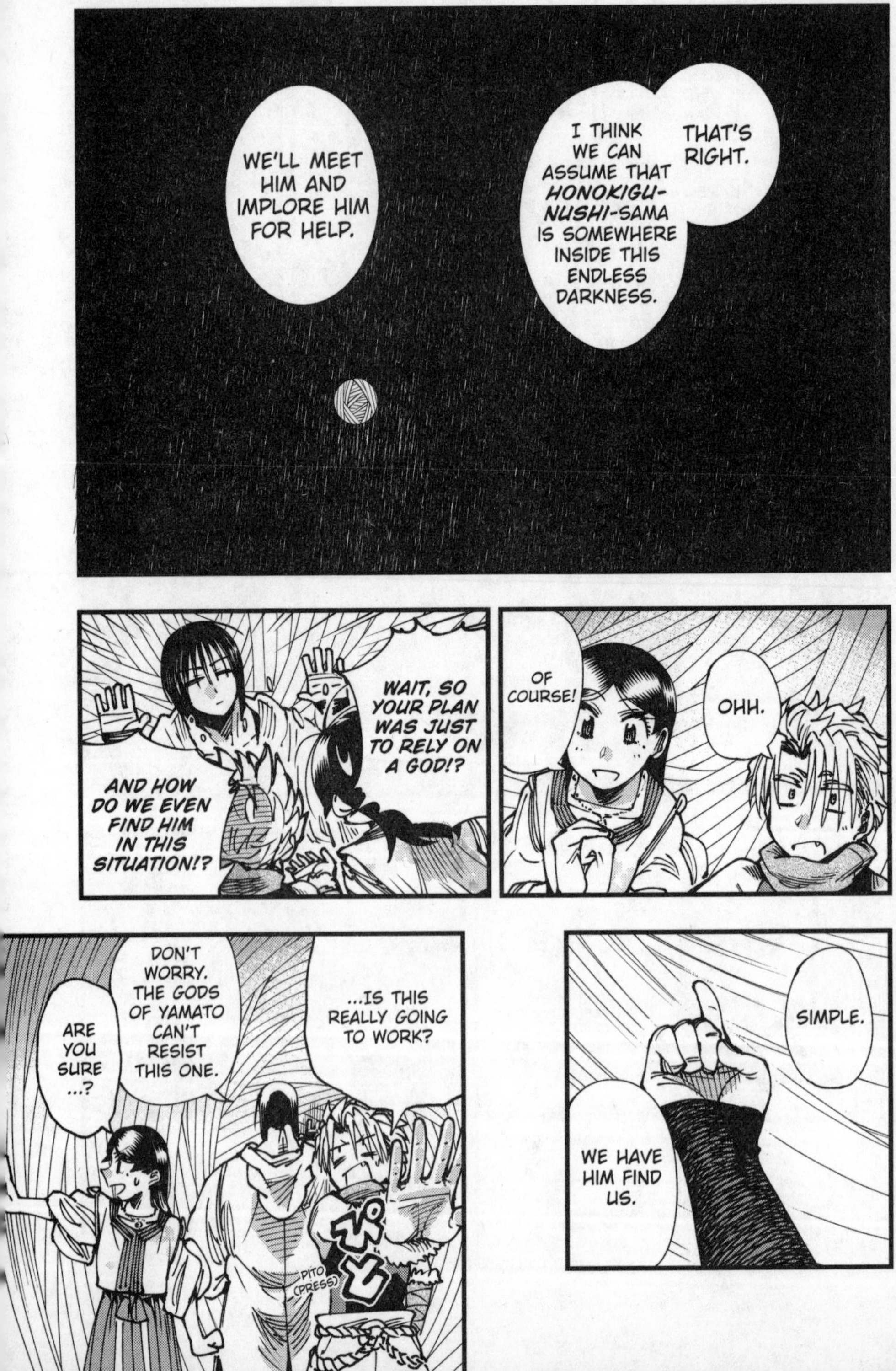
THAT'S RIGHT.
I THINK WE CAN ASSUME THAT *HONOKIGU-NUSHI*-SAMA IS SOMEWHERE INSIDE THIS ENDLESS DARKNESS.
WE'LL MEET HIM AND IMPLORE HIM FOR HELP.
OHH.
OF COURSE!
WAIT, SO YOUR PLAN WAS JUST TO RELY ON A GOD!?
AND HOW DO WE EVEN FIND HIM IN THIS SITUATION!?
SIMPLE.
WE HAVE HIM FIND US.
...IS THIS REALLY GOING TO WORK?
DON'T WORRY. THE GODS OF YAMATO CAN'T RESIST THIS ONE.
ARE YOU SURE ...?
ぴと
PITO (PRESS)

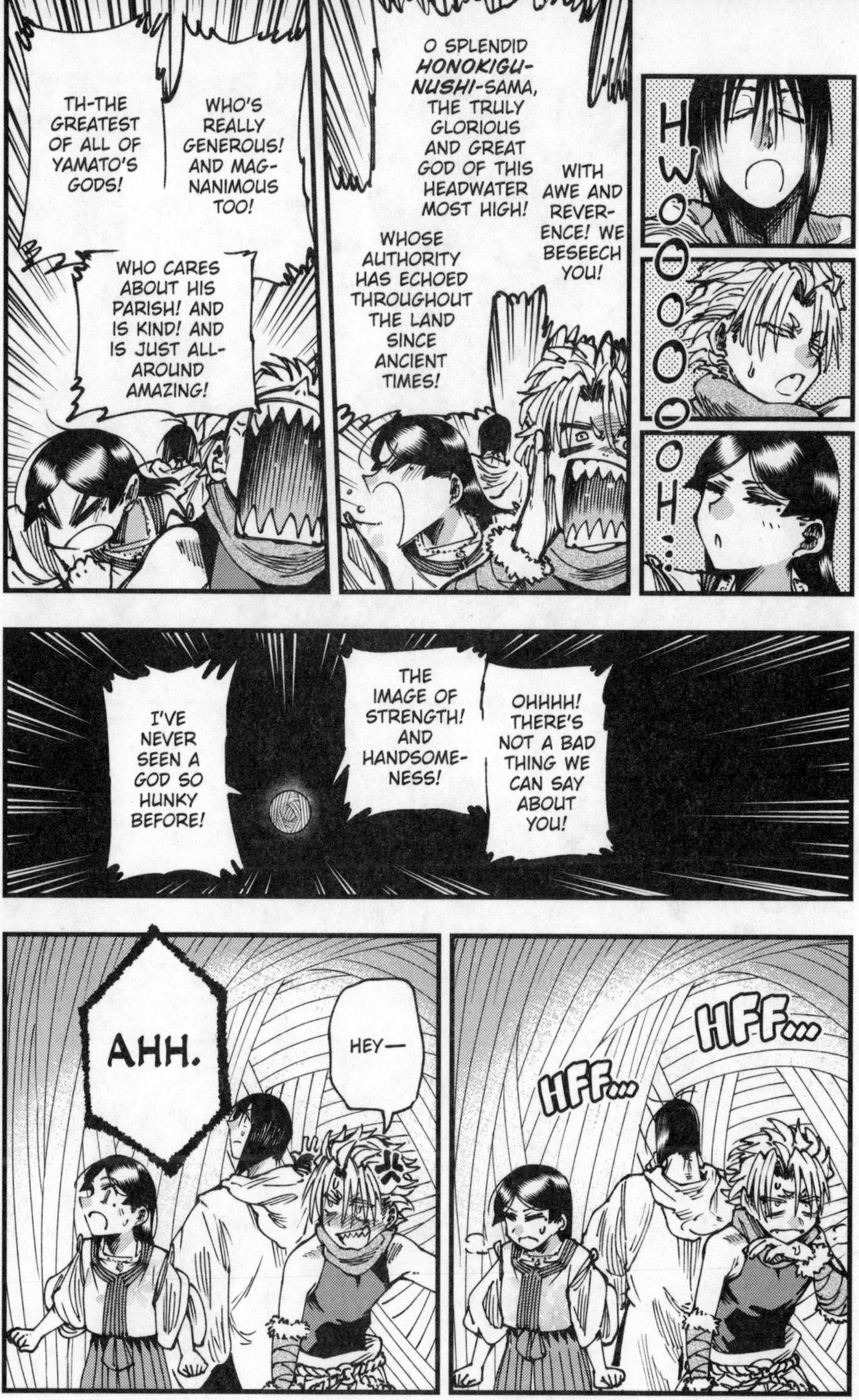
HWOOOOOOOH...
O SPLENDID HONOKIGUNUSHI-SAMA, THE TRULY GLORIOUS AND GREAT GOD OF THIS HEADWATER MOST HIGH!
WITH AWE AND REVERENCE! WE BESEECH YOU!
WHOSE AUTHORITY HAS ECHOED THROUGHOUT THE LAND SINCE ANCIENT TIMES!
WHO'S REALLY GENEROUS! AND MAGNANIMOUS TOO!
TH-THE GREATEST OF ALL OF YAMATO'S GODS!
WHO CARES ABOUT HIS PARISH! AND IS KIND! AND IS JUST ALL-AROUND AMAZING!
OHHHH! THERE'S NOT A BAD THING WE CAN SAY ABOUT YOU!
THE IMAGE OF STRENGTH! AND HANDSOMENESS!
I'VE NEVER SEEN A GOD SO HUNKY BEFORE!
HFF...
HFF...
HEY—
AHH.

WHAT A PLEASANT FEELING...
TRULY AWE-SOME...
NUAAA (SWOOOM)
I'D LIKE TO HEAR MORE...
ARE—
ARE WE IN THE PRESENCE OF HONOKIGU-NUSHI-SAMA!?
AHH...
IN-DEED.
THIS GUY HERE ...
THAT'S THIS GUY...

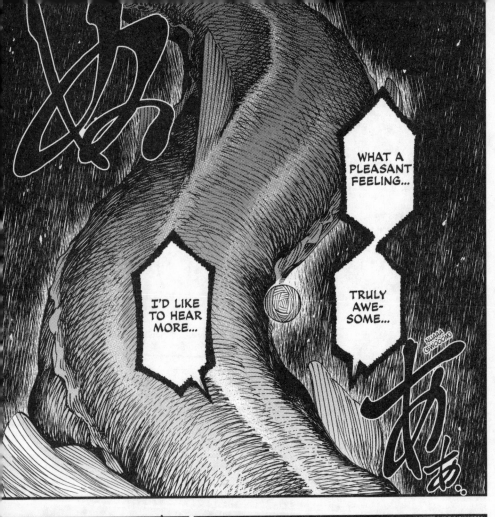

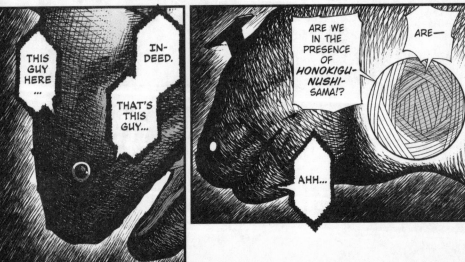

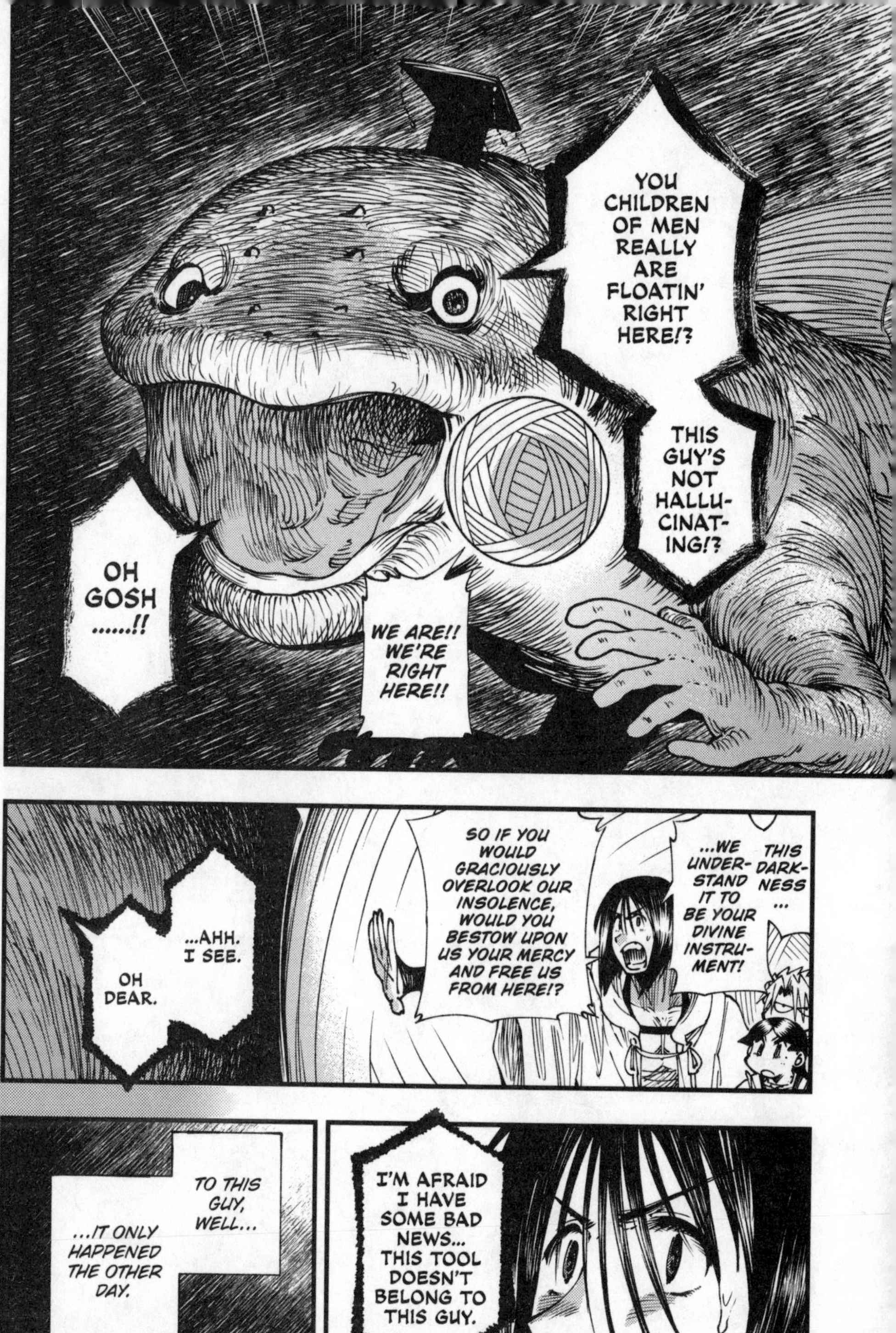
YOU CHILDREN OF MEN REALLY ARE FLOATIN' RIGHT HERE!?
THIS GUY'S NOT HALLU-CINAT-ING!?
WE ARE!! WE'RE RIGHT HERE!!
OH GOSH ......!!
THIS DARK-NESS ...
...WE UNDER-STAND IT TO BE YOUR DIVINE INSTRU-MENT!
SO IF YOU WOULD GRACIOUSLY OVERLOOK OUR INSOLENCE, WOULD YOU BESTOW UPON US YOUR MERCY AND FREE US FROM HERE!?
...AHH. I SEE.
OH DEAR.
I'M AFRAID I HAVE SOME BAD NEWS... THIS TOOL DOESN'T BELONG TO THIS GUY.
TO THIS GUY, WELL...
...IT ONLY HAPPENED THE OTHER DAY.

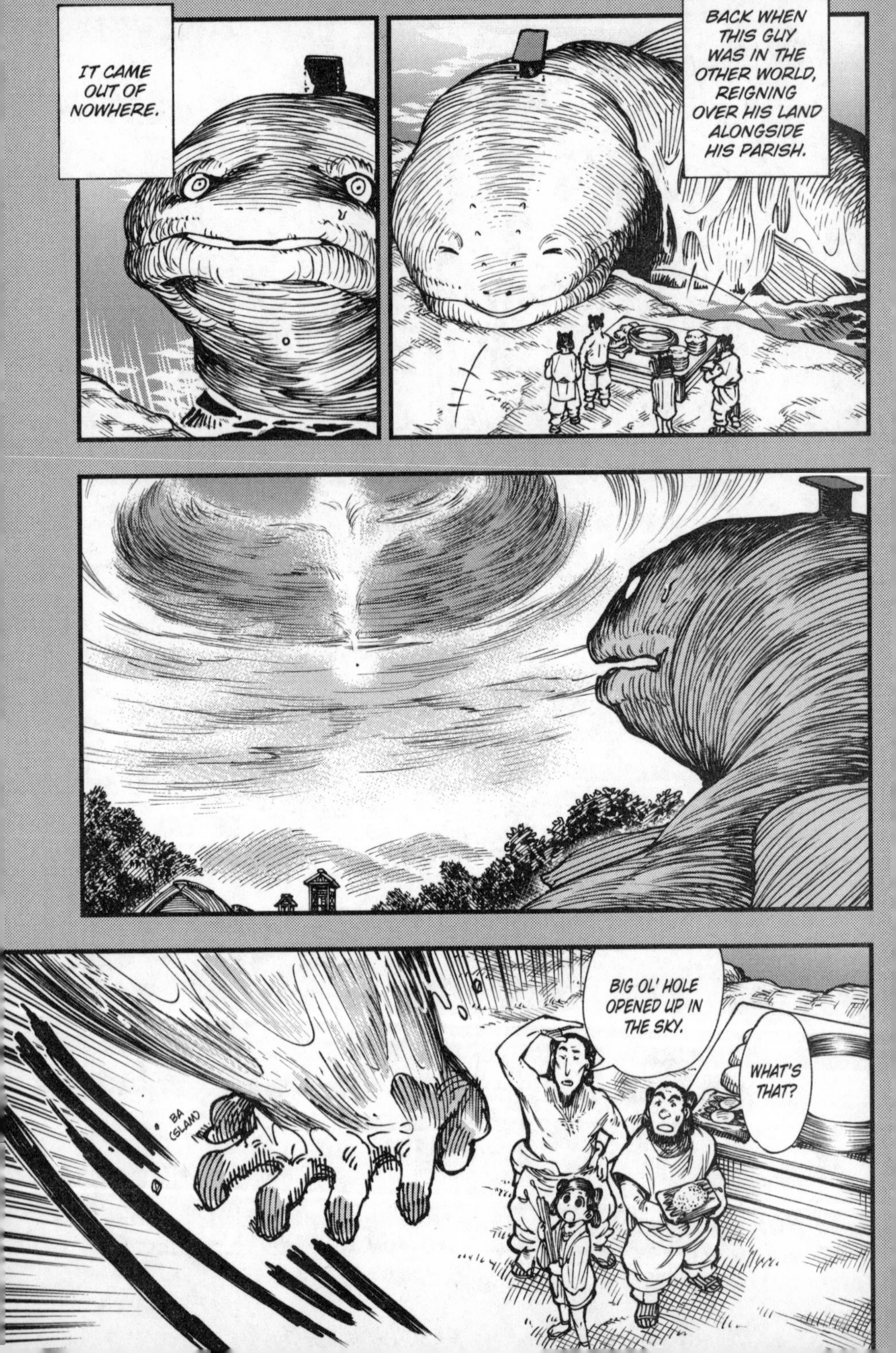
BACK WHEN THIS GUY WAS IN THE OTHER WORLD, REIGNING OVER HIS LAND ALONGSIDE HIS PARISH.
IT CAME OUT OF NOWHERE.
WHAT'S THAT?
BIG OL' HOLE OPENED UP IN THE SKY.
BA (SLAM)

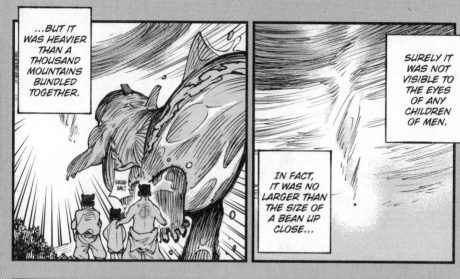

SURELY IT WAS NOT VISIBLE TO THE EYES OF ANY CHILDREN OF MEN.
IN FACT, IT WAS NO LARGER THAN THE SIZE OF A BEAN UP CLOSE...
...BUT IT WAS HEAVIER THAN A THOUSAND MOUNTAINS BUNDLED TOGETHER.
NOT A SPECK OF THIS TOWN WOULD REMAIN IF IT WERE TO FALL TO THE EARTH.
EE!
DOSU
DOSU (STOMP)
DOSU
DOSU
IT WAS BUT A STROKE OF LUCK THAT IT FELL IN A PLACE WHERE THIS GUY COULD SEE IT.
THIS GUY CAN MAKE IT!

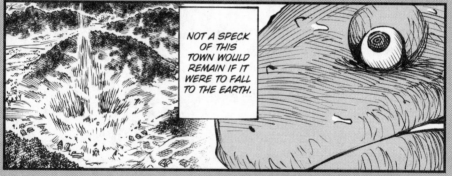

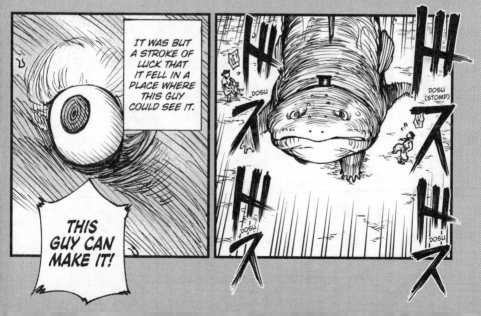

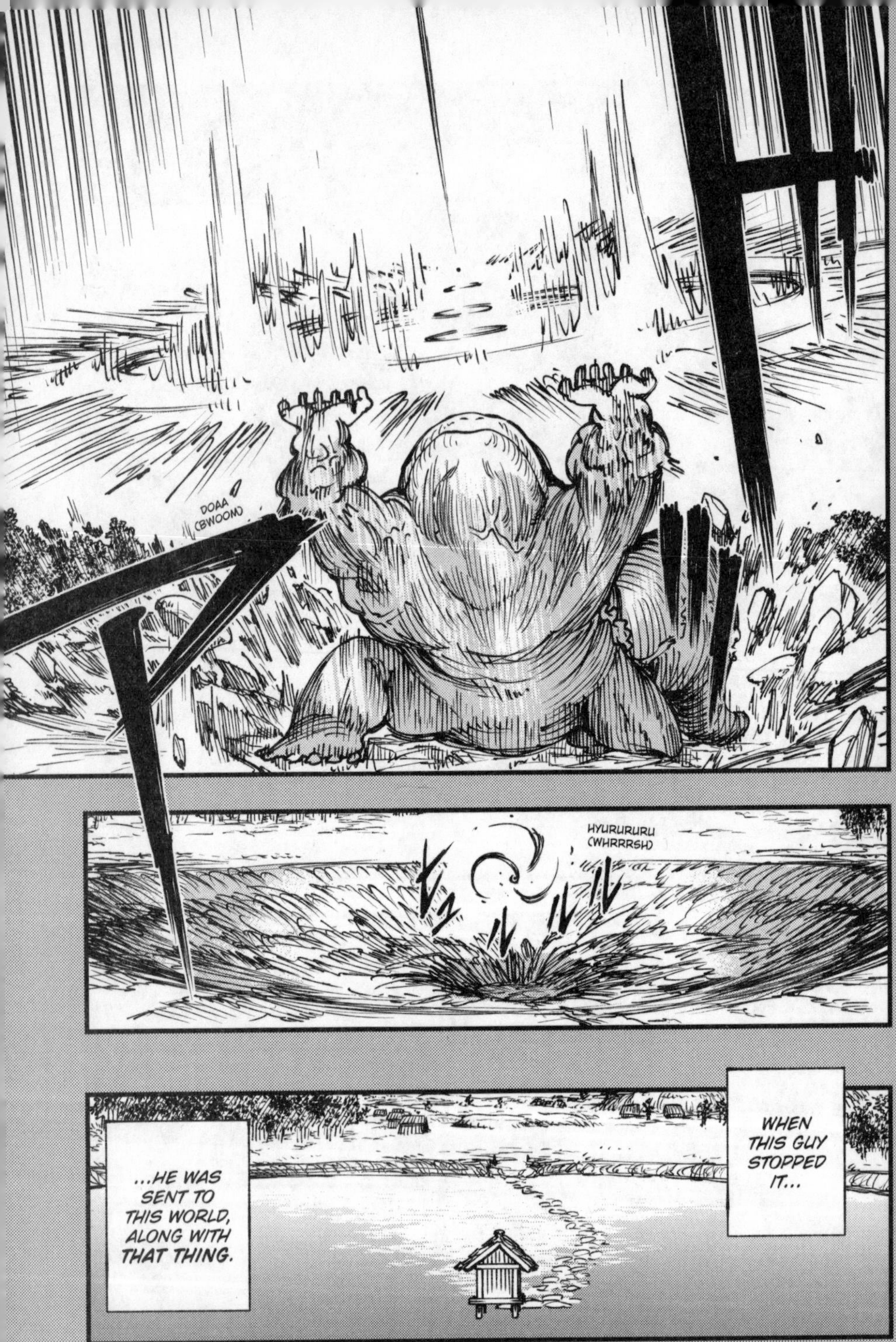
DOAA
(BWOON)
HYURURURU
(WHRRRSH)
WHEN THIS GUY STOPPED IT...
...HE WAS SENT TO THIS WORLD, ALONG WITH THAT THING.

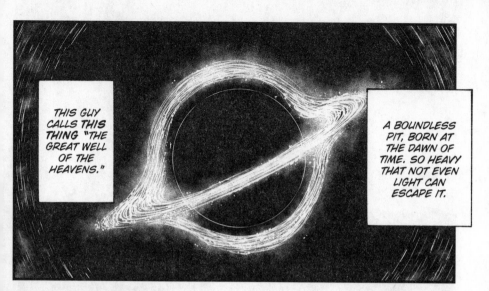

A BOUNDLESS PIT, BORN AT THE DAWN OF TIME. SO HEAVY THAT NOT EVEN LIGHT CAN ESCAPE IT.
THIS GUY CALLS THIS THING "THE GREAT WELL OF THE HEAVENS."
AND TO THIS GUY...
...ALL OF THIS HAPPENED A MERE SEVEN DAYS AGO.
HOLD ON!
HUH ...?
HUH?
YOU MENTIONED THE TIME YOU SPENT ALONGSIDE MAN IN THE OTHER WORLD...
HUH !?
THAT WAS FAR BEFORE TIME IMMEMORIAL!

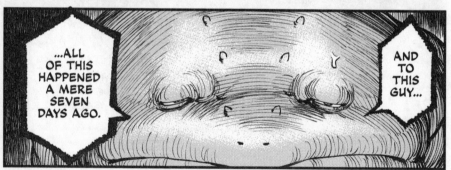

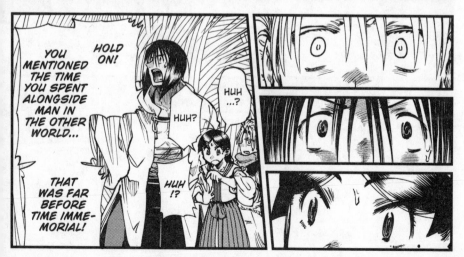

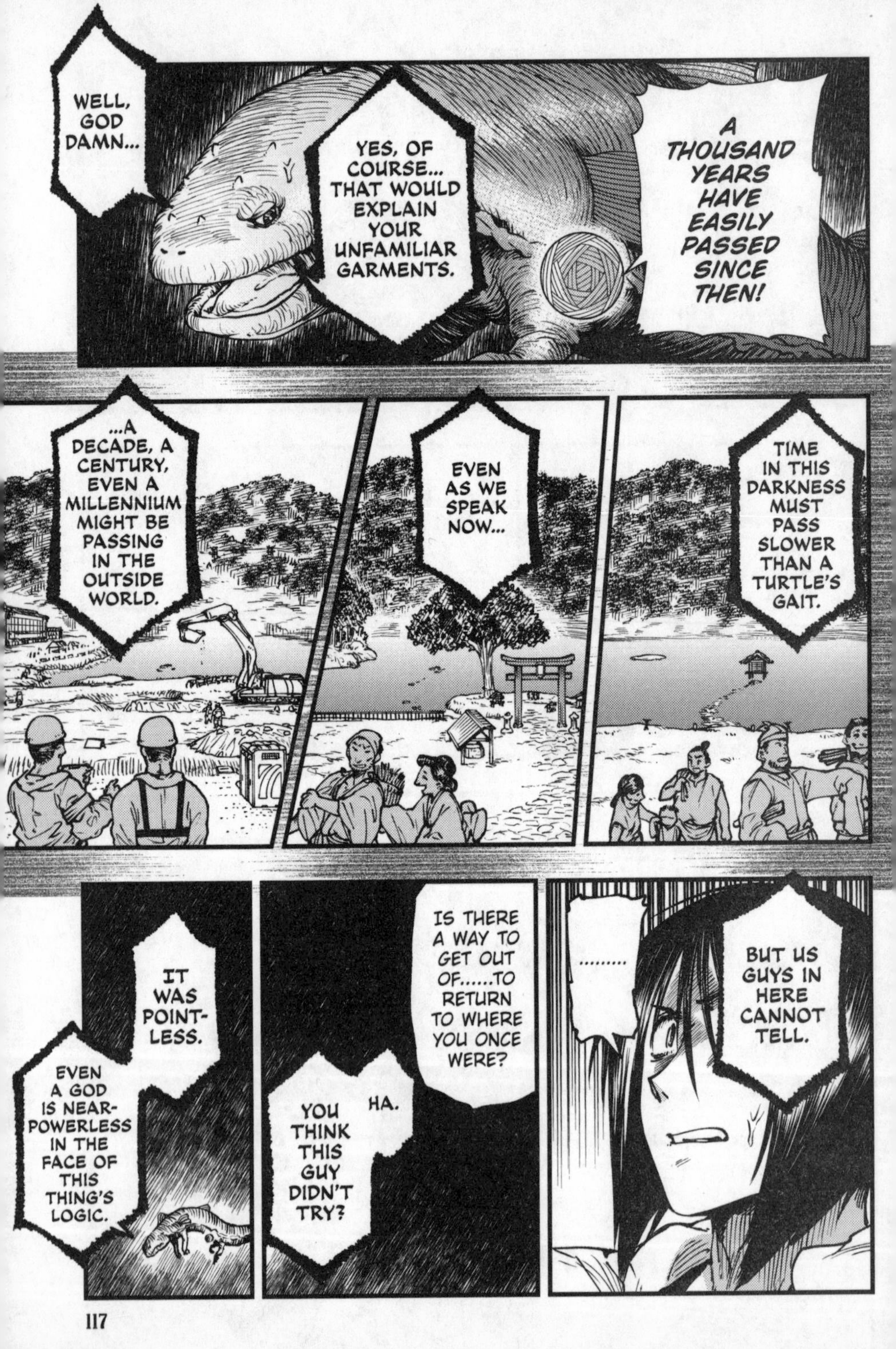
A THOUSAND YEARS HAVE EASILY PASSED SINCE THEN!
YES, OF COURSE... THAT WOULD EXPLAIN YOUR UNFAMILIAR GARMENTS.
WELL, GOD DAMN...
TIME IN THIS DARKNESS MUST PASS SLOWER THAN A TURTLE'S GAIT.
EVEN AS WE SPEAK NOW...
...A DECADE, A CENTURY, EVEN A MILLENNIUM MIGHT BE PASSING IN THE OUTSIDE WORLD.
BUT US GUYS IN HERE CANNOT TELL.
....
IS THERE A WAY TO GET OUT OF......TO RETURN TO WHERE YOU ONCE WERE?
HA.
YOU THINK THIS GUY DIDN'T TRY?
IT WAS POINTLESS.
EVEN A GOD IS NEAR-POWERLESS IN THE FACE OF THIS THING'S LOGIC.

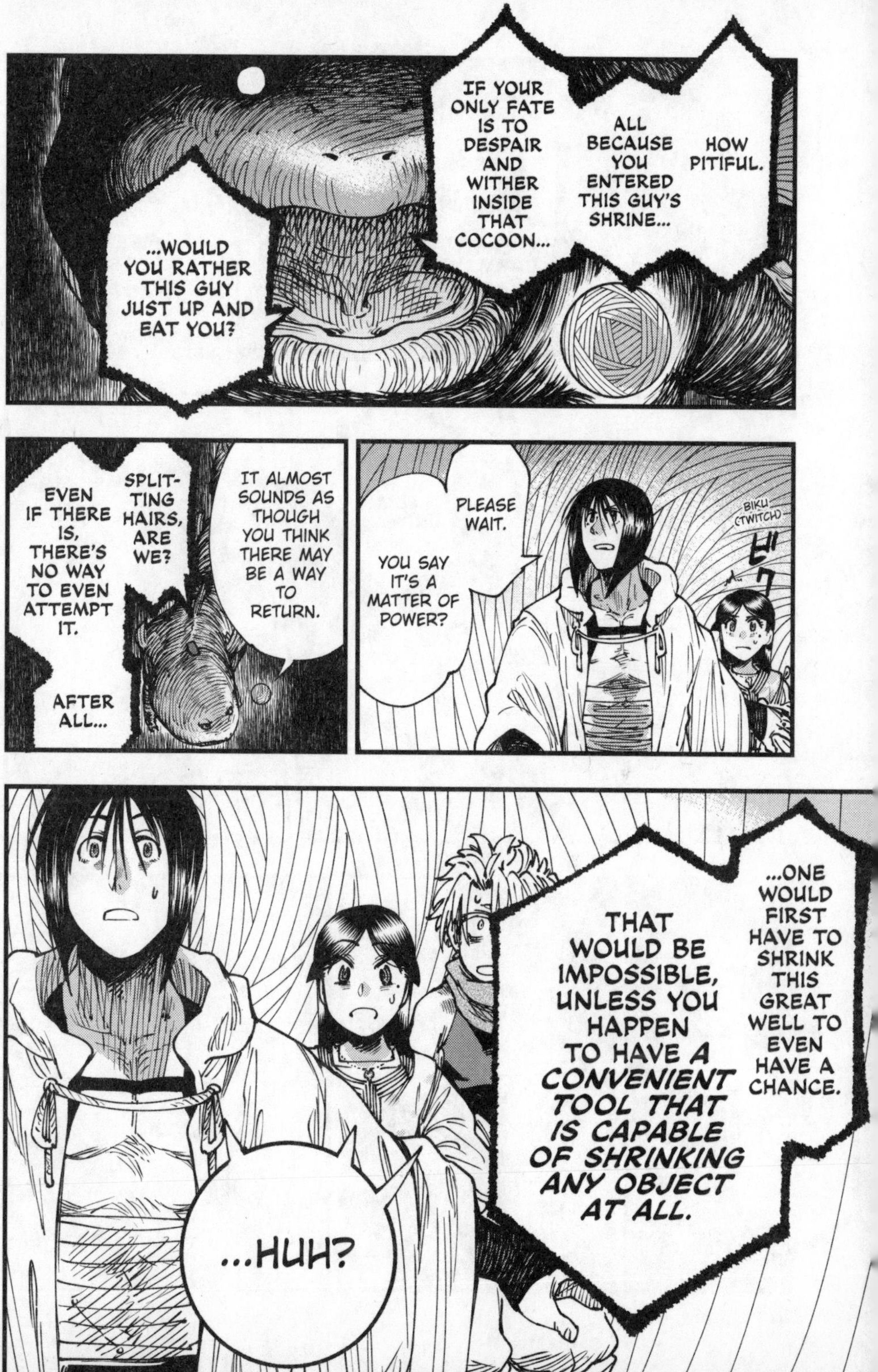
HOW PITIFUL.
ALL BECAUSE YOU ENTERED THIS GUY'S SHRINE...
IF YOUR ONLY FATE IS TO DESPAIR AND WITHER INSIDE THAT COCOON...
...WOULD YOU RATHER THIS GUY JUST UP AND EAT YOU?
BIKU (TWITCH)
PLEASE WAIT.
YOU SAY IT'S A MATTER OF POWER?
IT ALMOST SOUNDS AS THOUGH YOU THINK THERE MAY BE A WAY TO RETURN.
SPLIT-TING HAIRS, ARE WE?
EVEN IF THERE IS, THERE'S NO WAY TO EVEN ATTEMPT IT.
AFTER ALL...
...ONE WOULD FIRST HAVE TO SHRINK THIS GREAT WELL TO EVEN HAVE A CHANCE.
THAT WOULD BE IMPOSSIBLE, UNLESS YOU HAPPEN TO HAVE A *CONVENIENT TOOL THAT IS CAPABLE OF SHRINKING ANY OBJECT AT ALL.*
...HUH?

AH... UM.
WHAT IF WE TOLD YOU WE DO HAVE ONE...?
HUH? FOR REALS?
NO! THAT'S STILL NOT ENOUGH! THAT WAS ONLY A PREREQUI-SITE...!
BECAUSE ON TOP OF THAT!
THE GATE IS AT THE CENTER OF THIS GREAT WELL...
YOU WOULD AGAIN NEED A CONVENIENT TOOL THAT IS *CAPABLE OF GROWING ANY OBJECT AT ALL* TO HAVE ANY CHANCE OF—
UMM...
WE ACTUALLY HAVE ONE OF THOSE TOO...
WHAT!
THE!
FUUUUCK!!?

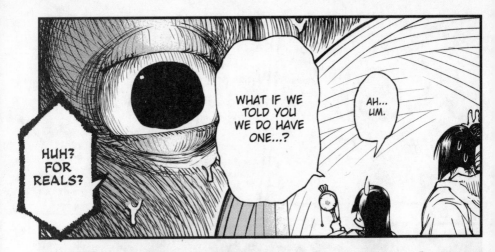

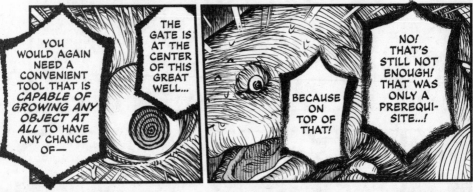

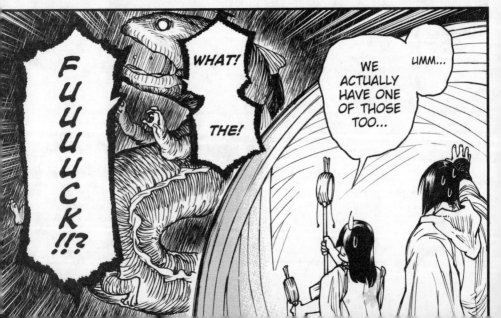

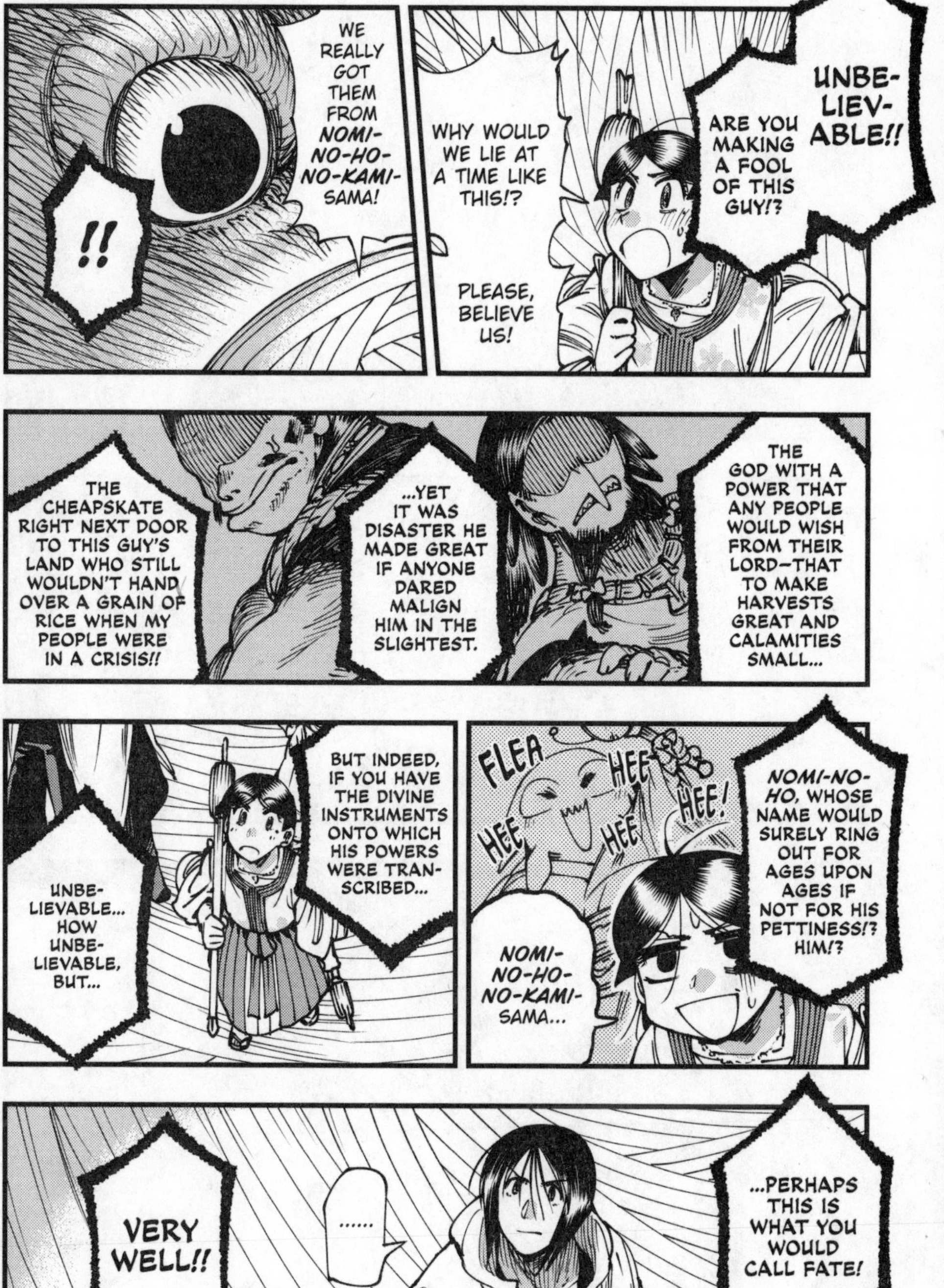
UNBE-LIEV-ABLE!!
ARE YOU MAKING A FOOL OF THIS GUY!?
WHY WOULD WE LIE AT A TIME LIKE THIS!?
PLEASE, BELIEVE US!
WE REALLY GOT THEM FROM *NOMI-NO-HO-NO-KAMI-*SAMA!
!!
THE GOD WITH A POWER THAT ANY PEOPLE WOULD WISH FROM THEIR LORD—THAT TO MAKE HARVESTS GREAT AND CALAMITIES SMALL...
...YET IT WAS DISASTER HE MADE GREAT IF ANYONE DARED MALIGN HIM IN THE SLIGHTEST.
THE CHEAPSKATE RIGHT NEXT DOOR TO THIS GUY'S LAND WHO STILL WOULDN'T HAND OVER A GRAIN OF RICE WHEN MY PEOPLE WERE IN A CRISIS!!
NOMI-NO-HO, WHOSE NAME WOULD SURELY RING OUT FOR AGES UPON AGES IF NOT FOR HIS PETTINESS!? HIM!?
FLEA
HEE HEE HEE HEE!
*NOMI-NO-HO-NO-KAMI-*SAMA...
BUT INDEED, IF YOU HAVE THE DIVINE INSTRUMENTS ONTO WHICH HIS POWERS WERE TRANSCRIBED...
UNBE-LIEVABLE... HOW UNBE-LIEVABLE, BUT...
...PERHAPS THIS IS WHAT YOU WOULD CALL FATE!
......
VERY WELL!!

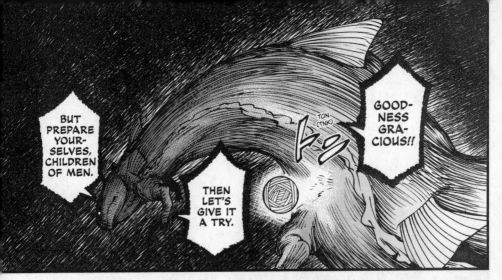

TON (TNK)
GOODNESS GRACIOUS!!
THEN LET'S GIVE IT A TRY.
BUT PREPARE YOURSELVES, CHILDREN OF MEN.
MANY DIFFICULTIES STILL AWAIT US.
CONSIDER YOUR CHANCES WORSE THAN A COIN FLIP.
I DON'T LIKE TO GAMBLE...
...BUT IT'S A LOT BETTER THAN HAVING NO SHOT AT ALL.
WE WILL BEGIN BY DIVING DEEPER INTO THIS GREAT WELL.
IF THAT COCOON RIPS, YOU WILL BE TORN APART DOWN TO YOUR SOUL.
BEKO (CRUMPLE)
BEKO
SHUTOTOTO (FSSHHT)

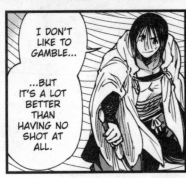

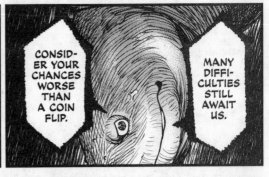

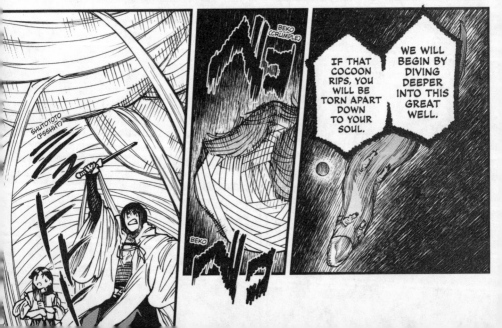

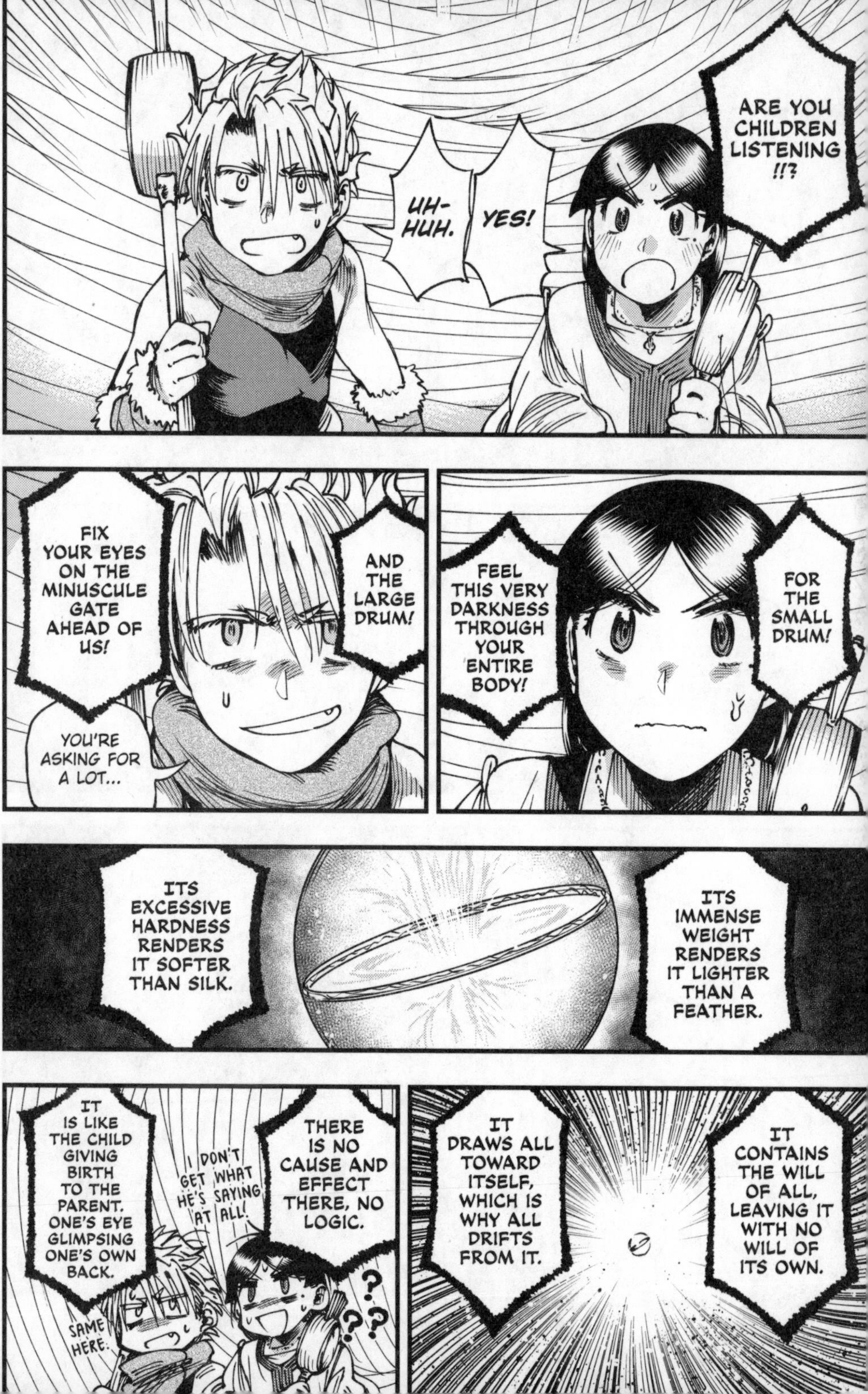
ARE YOU CHILDREN LISTENING !!?
YES!
UH-HUH.
FOR THE SMALL DRUM!
FEEL THIS VERY DARKNESS THROUGH YOUR ENTIRE BODY!
AND THE LARGE DRUM!
FIX YOUR EYES ON THE MINUSCULE GATE AHEAD OF US!
YOU'RE ASKING FOR A LOT...
ITS IMMENSE WEIGHT RENDERS IT LIGHTER THAN A FEATHER.
ITS EXCESSIVE HARDNESS RENDERS IT SOFTER THAN SILK.
IT CONTAINS THE WILL OF ALL, LEAVING IT WITH NO WILL OF ITS OWN.
IT DRAWS ALL TOWARD ITSELF, WHICH IS WHY ALL DRIFTS FROM IT.
THERE IS NO CAUSE AND EFFECT THERE, NO LOGIC.
I DON'T GET WHAT HE'S SAYING AT ALL!
IT IS LIKE THE CHILD GIVING BIRTH TO THE PARENT. ONE'S EYE GLIMPSING ONE'S OWN BACK.
???
SAME HERE.

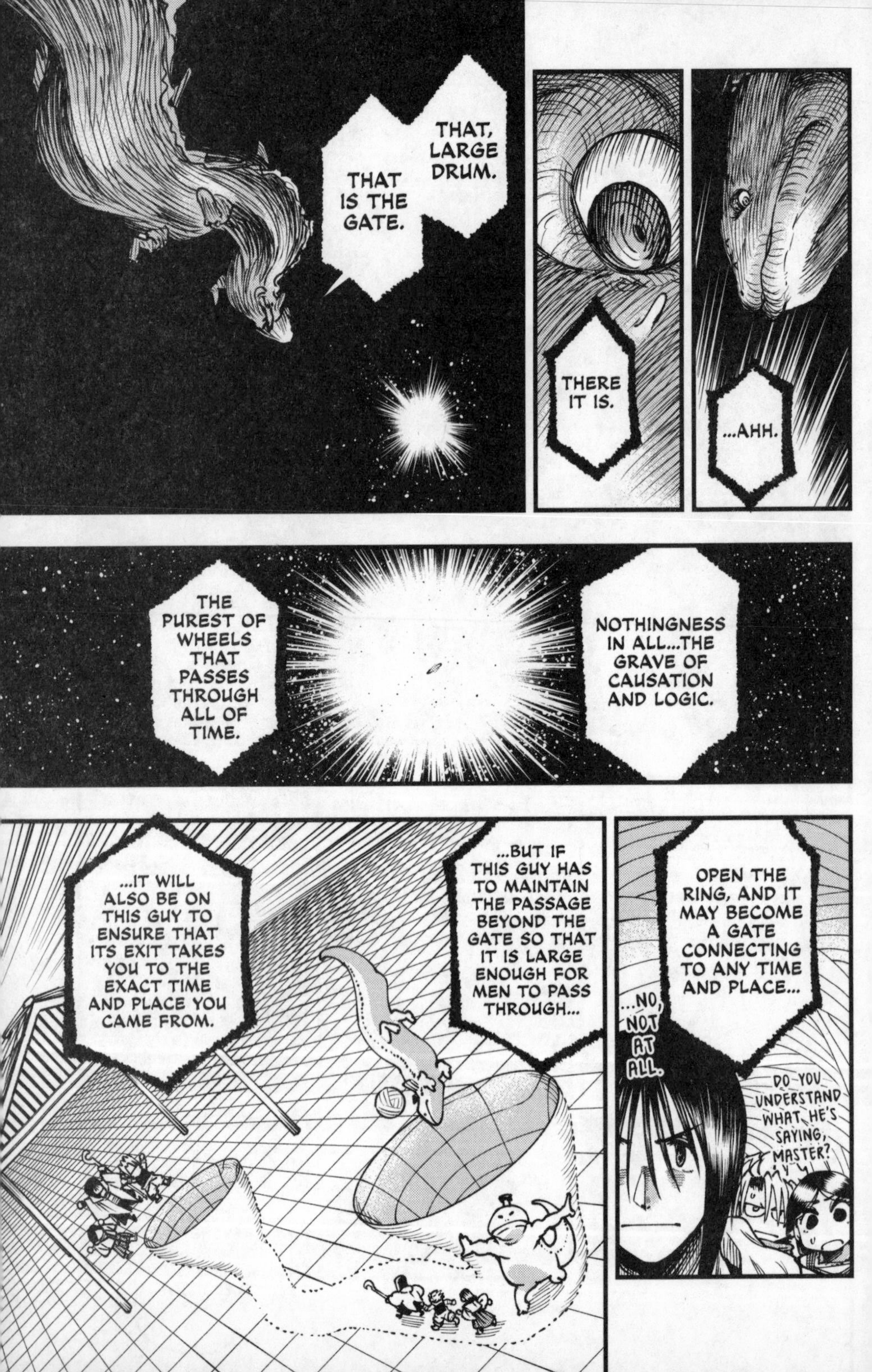
...AHH.
THERE IT IS.
THAT, LARGE DRUM.
THAT IS THE GATE.
NOTHINGNESS IN ALL...THE GRAVE OF CAUSATION AND LOGIC.
THE PUREST OF WHEELS THAT PASSES THROUGH ALL OF TIME.
OPEN THE RING, AND IT MAY BECOME A GATE CONNECTING TO ANY TIME AND PLACE...
DO YOU UNDERSTAND WHAT HE'S SAYING, MASTER?
...NO, NOT AT ALL.
...BUT IF THIS GUY HAS TO MAINTAIN THE PASSAGE BEYOND THE GATE SO THAT IT IS LARGE ENOUGH FOR MEN TO PASS THROUGH...
...IT WILL ALSO BE ON THIS GUY TO ENSURE THAT ITS EXIT TAKES YOU TO THE EXACT TIME AND PLACE YOU CAME FROM.

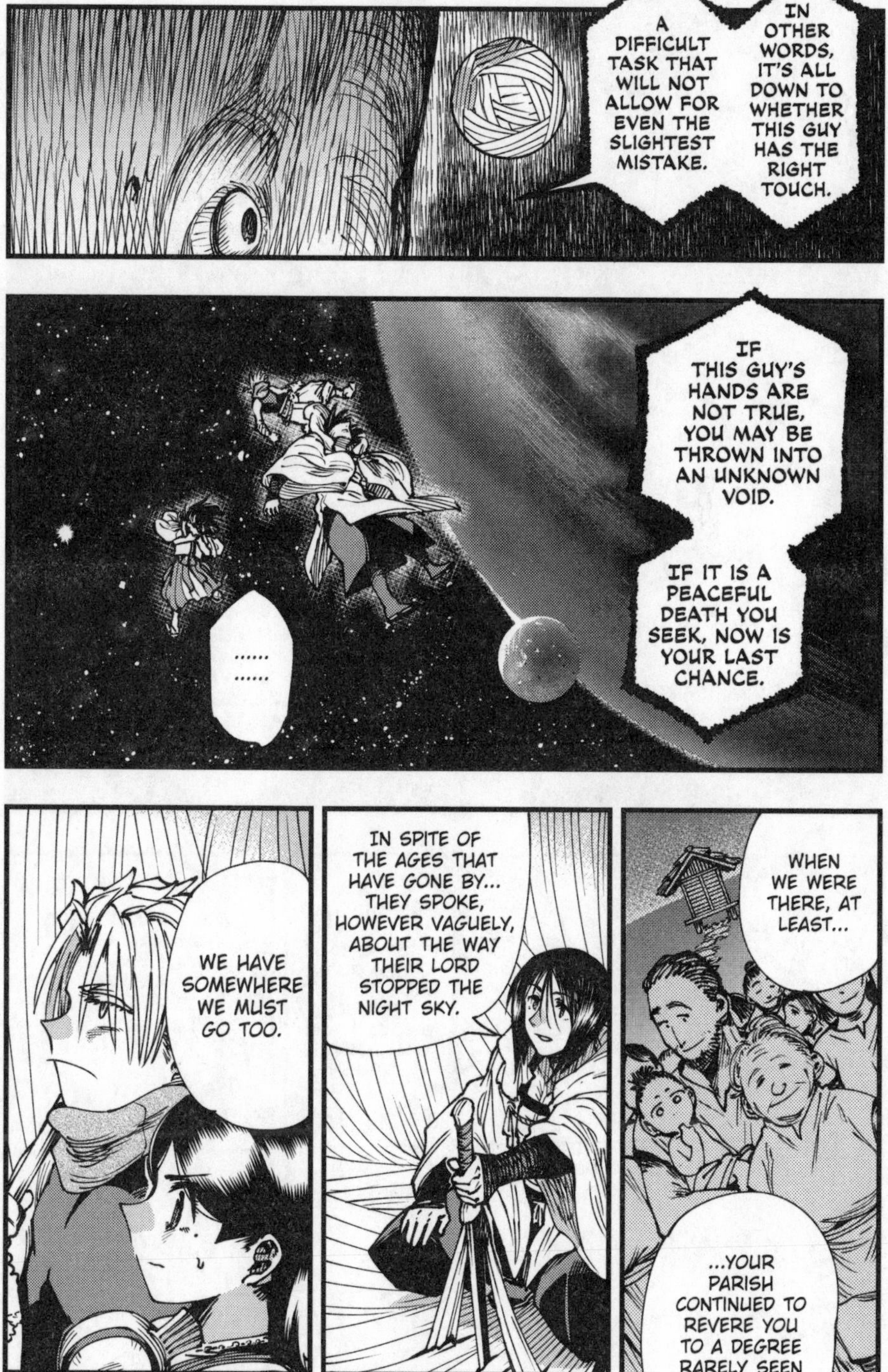
IN OTHER WORDS, IT'S ALL DOWN TO WHETHER THIS GUY HAS THE RIGHT TOUCH.
A DIFFICULT TASK THAT WILL NOT ALLOW FOR EVEN THE SLIGHTEST MISTAKE.
IF THIS GUY'S HANDS ARE NOT TRUE, YOU MAY BE THROWN INTO AN UNKNOWN VOID.
IF IT IS A PEACEFUL DEATH YOU SEEK, NOW IS YOUR LAST CHANCE.
....
WHEN WE WERE THERE, AT LEAST...
...YOUR PARISH CONTINUED TO REVERE YOU TO A DEGREE RARELY SEEN THESE DAYS.
IN SPITE OF THE AGES THAT HAVE GONE BY... THEY SPOKE, HOWEVER VAGUELY, ABOUT THE WAY THEIR LORD STOPPED THE NIGHT SKY.
WE HAVE SOMEWHERE WE MUST GO TOO.

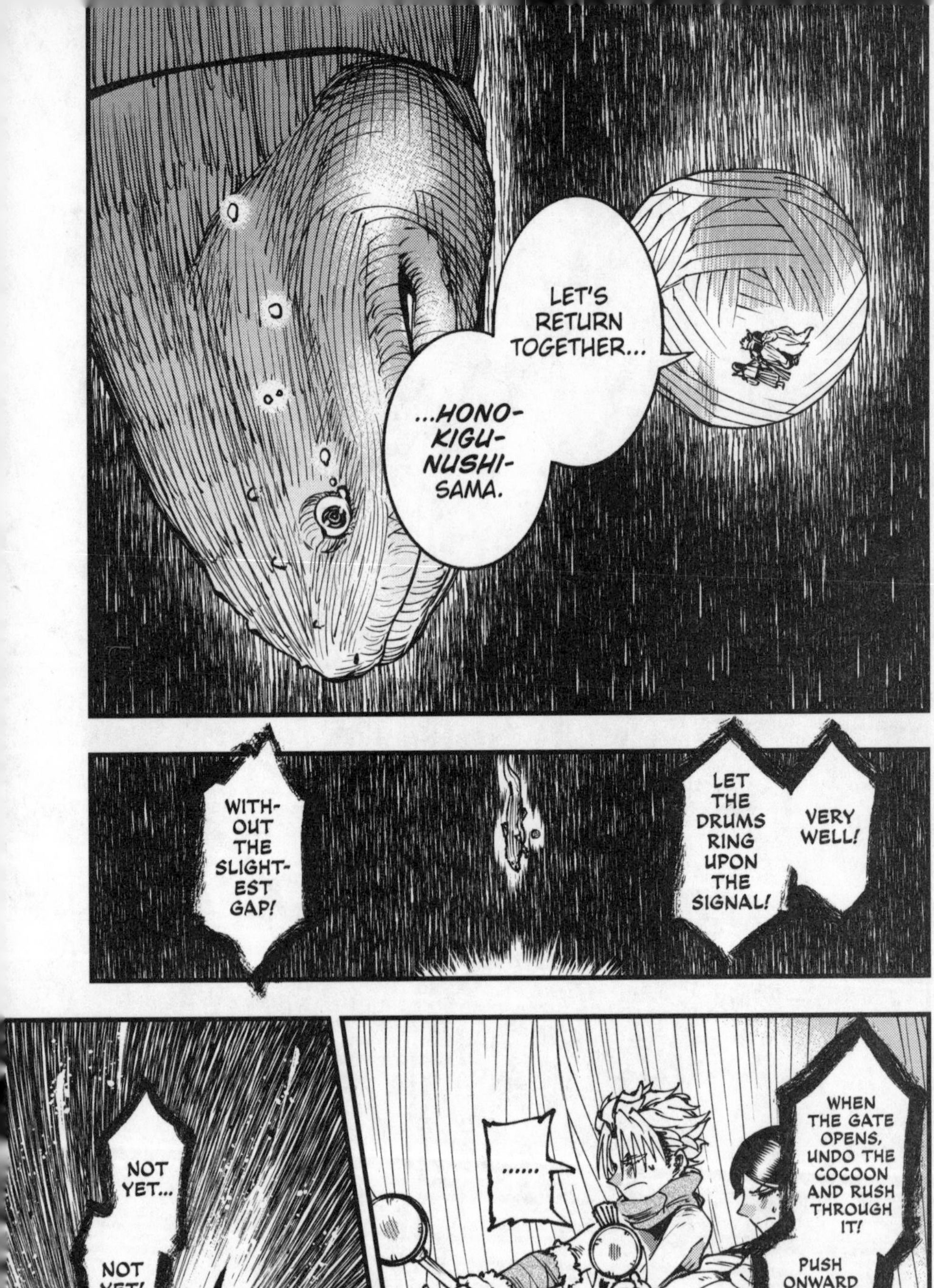
LET'S RETURN TOGETHER...
...HONO-KIGU-NUSHI-SAMA.
VERY WELL!
LET THE DRUMS RING UPON THE SIGNAL!
WITHOUT THE SLIGHTEST GAP!
WHEN THE GATE OPENS, UNDO THE COCOON AND RUSH THROUGH IT!
PUSH ONWARD TO THE END WITH ALL YOUR HEART!
......
NOT YET...
NOT YET!

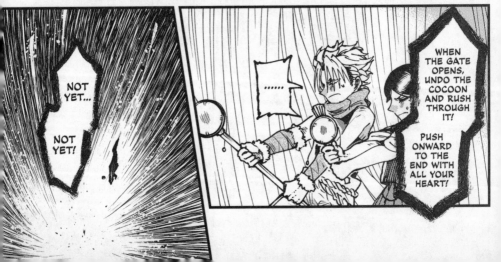

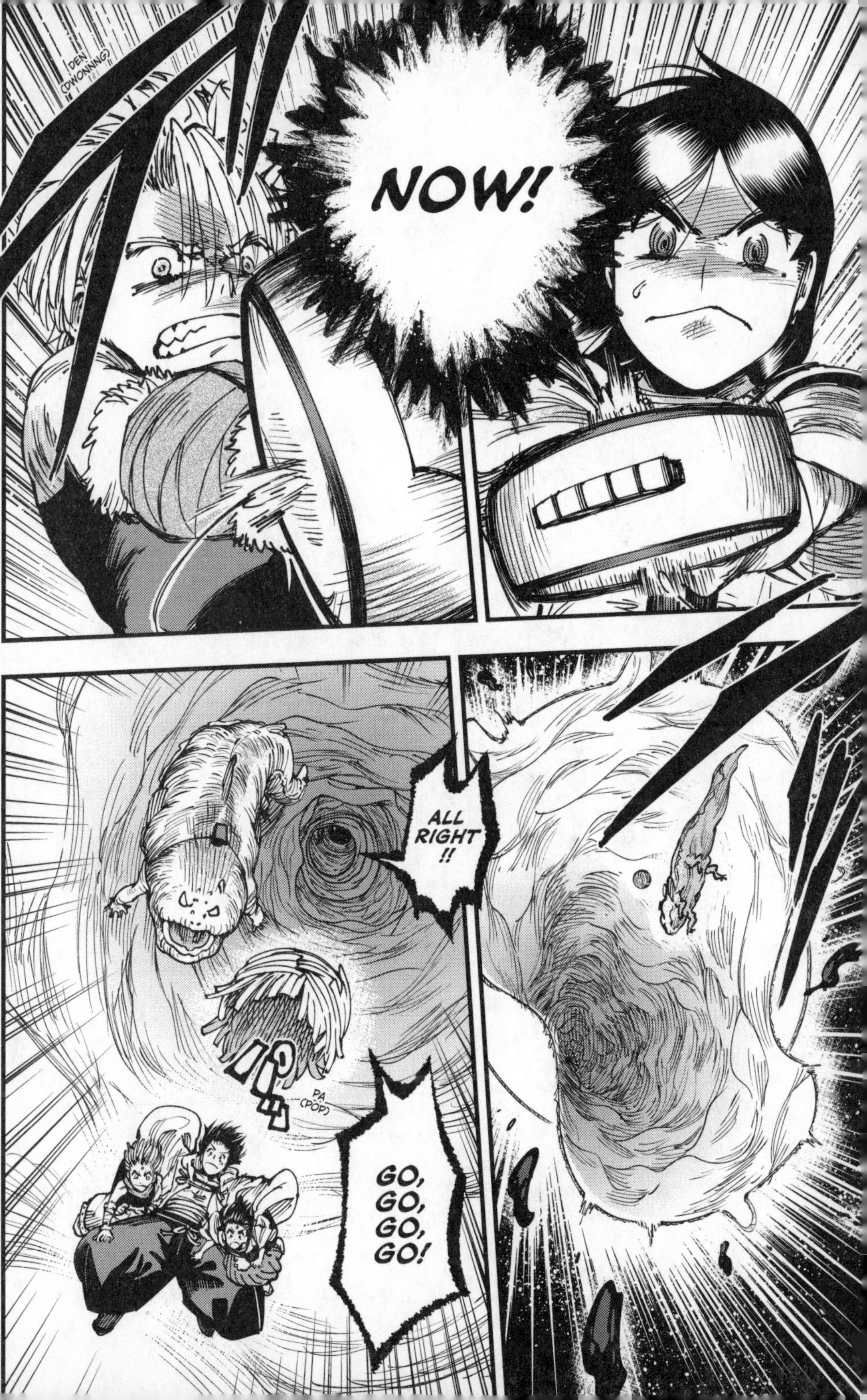
NOW!
DEN (DWONNNG)
ALL RIGHT!!
PA (POP)
GO, GO, GO, GO!

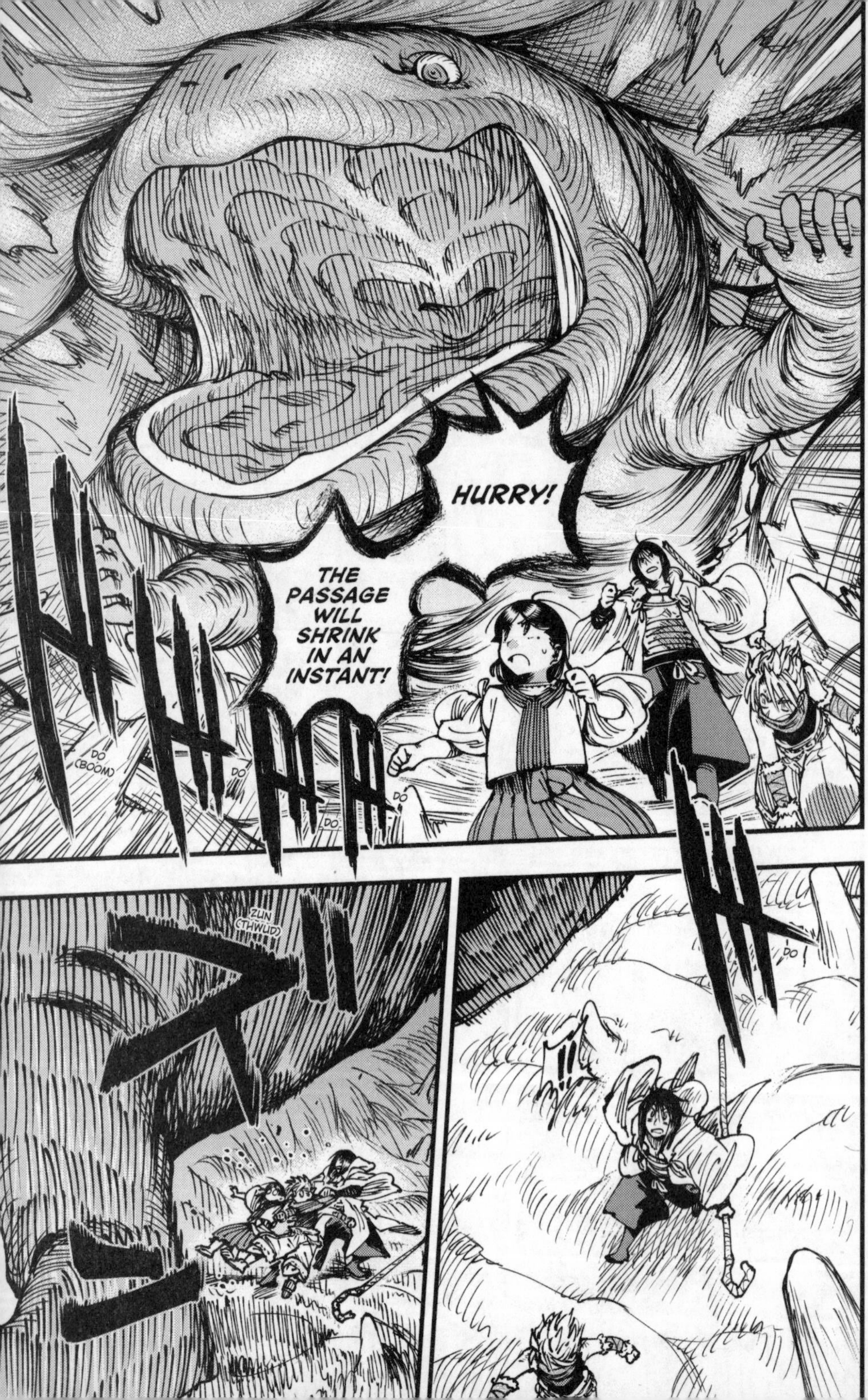
HURRY!
THE PASSAGE WILL SHRINK IN AN INSTANT!
DO (BOOM)
DO
DO
DO
DO
!!
ZUN (THWUD)

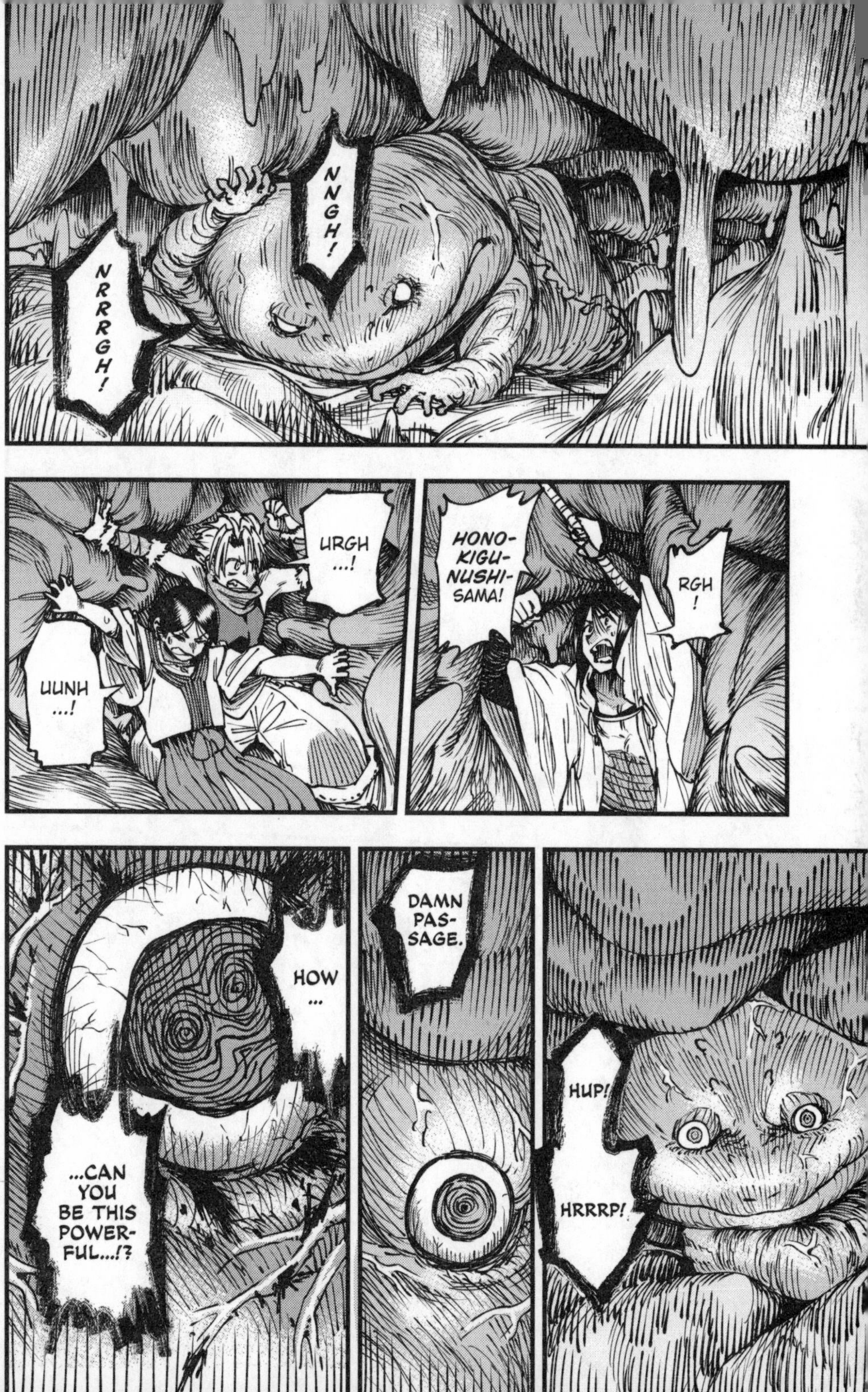
NNGH!
NRRRGH!
HONO-KIGU-NUSHI-SAMA!
RGH!
URGH...!
UUNH...!
HUP!
HRRRP!
DAMN PAS-SAGE.
HOW...
...CAN YOU BE THIS POWER-FUL...!?

NYUI
(SQUITHER)

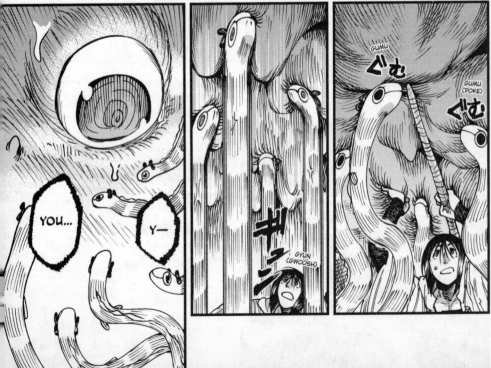

YOU...

Y—

GYUN
(GWOOSH)

GUMU

GUMU
(POKE)

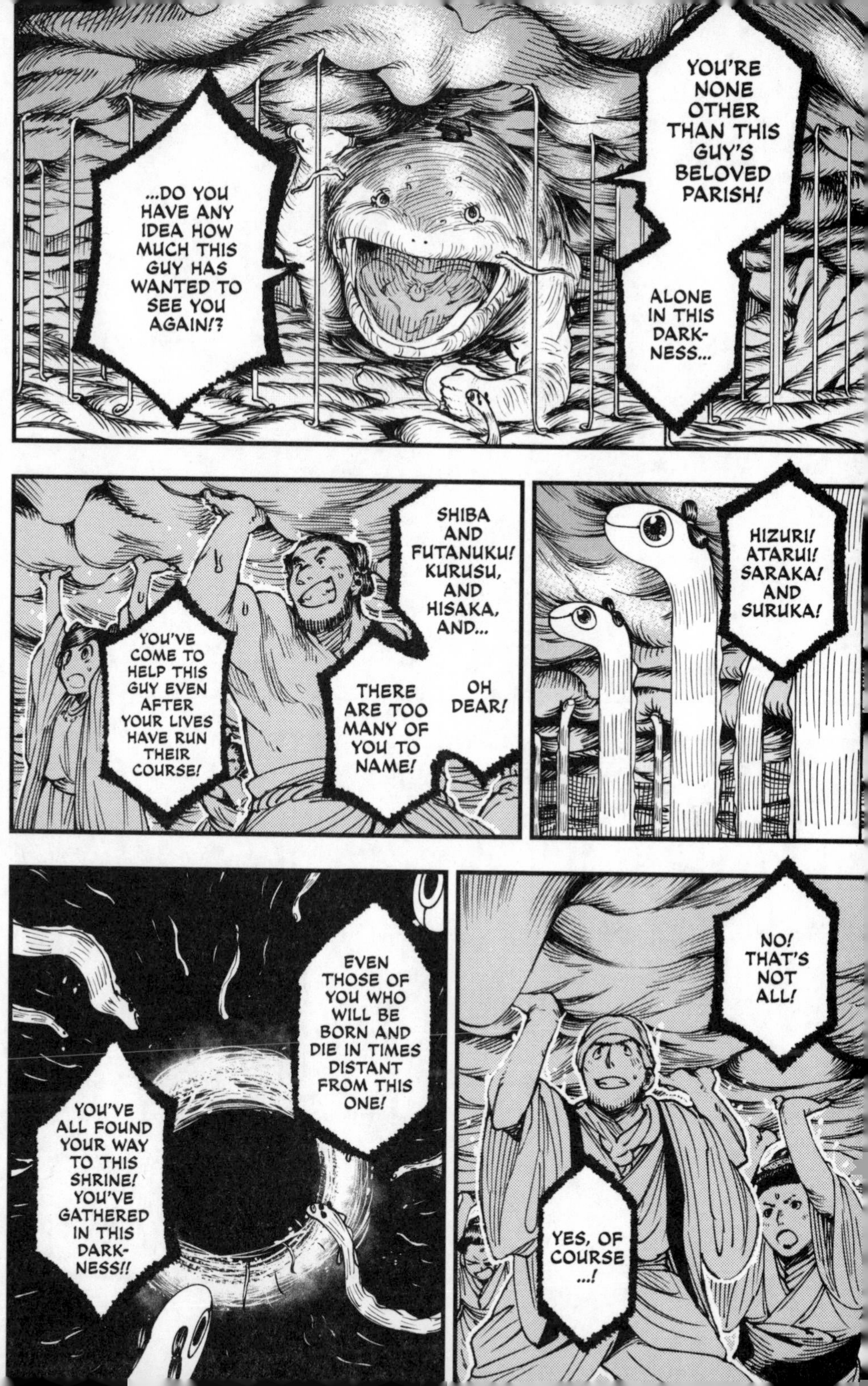
YOU'RE NONE OTHER THAN THIS GUY'S BELOVED PARISH!
ALONE IN THIS DARK-NESS...
...DO YOU HAVE ANY IDEA HOW MUCH THIS GUY HAS WANTED TO SEE YOU AGAIN!?
HIZURI! ATARUI! SARAKA! AND SURUKA!
SHIBA AND FUTANUKU! KURUSU, AND HISAKA, AND...
OH DEAR!
THERE ARE TOO MANY OF YOU TO NAME!
YOU'VE COME TO HELP THIS GUY EVEN AFTER YOUR LIVES HAVE RUN THEIR COURSE!
NO! THAT'S NOT ALL!
YES, OF COURSE ...!
EVEN THOSE OF YOU WHO WILL BE BORN AND DIE IN TIMES DISTANT FROM THIS ONE!
YOU'VE ALL FOUND YOUR WAY TO THIS SHRINE! YOU'VE GATHERED IN THIS DARK-NESS!!

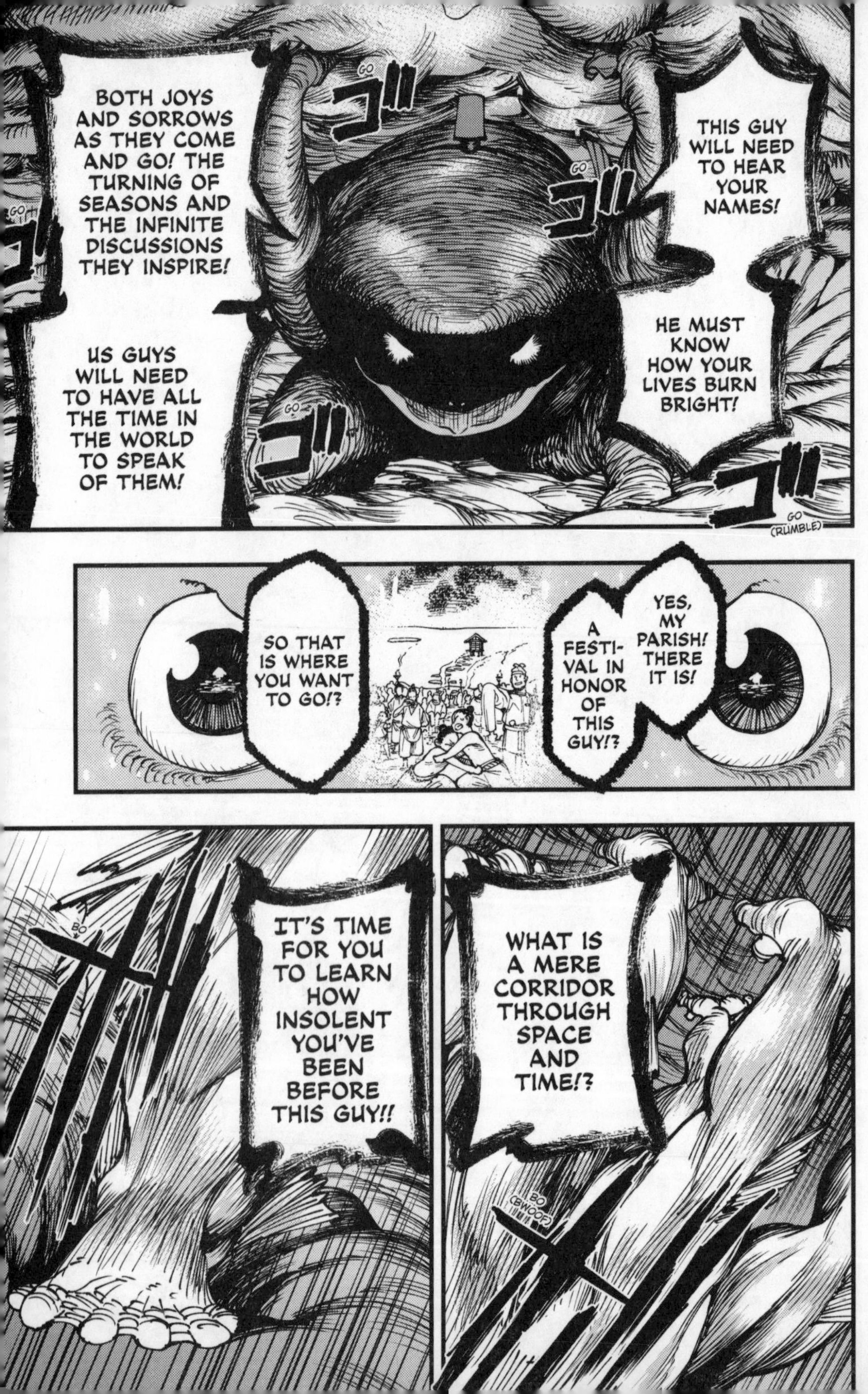
THIS GUY WILL NEED TO HEAR YOUR NAMES!
BOTH JOYS AND SORROWS AS THEY COME AND GO! THE TURNING OF SEASONS AND THE INFINITE DISCUSSIONS THEY INSPIRE!
GO
GO
GO
GO
HE MUST KNOW HOW YOUR LIVES BURN BRIGHT!
US GUYS WILL NEED TO HAVE ALL THE TIME IN THE WORLD TO SPEAK OF THEM!
GO (RUMBLE)
YES, MY PARISH! THERE IT IS!
A FESTIVAL IN HONOR OF THIS GUY!?
SO THAT IS WHERE YOU WANT TO GO!?
WHAT IS A MERE CORRIDOR THROUGH SPACE AND TIME!?
BO (BWOOF)
IT'S TIME FOR YOU TO LEARN HOW INSOLENT YOU'VE BEEN BEFORE THIS GUY!!
BO

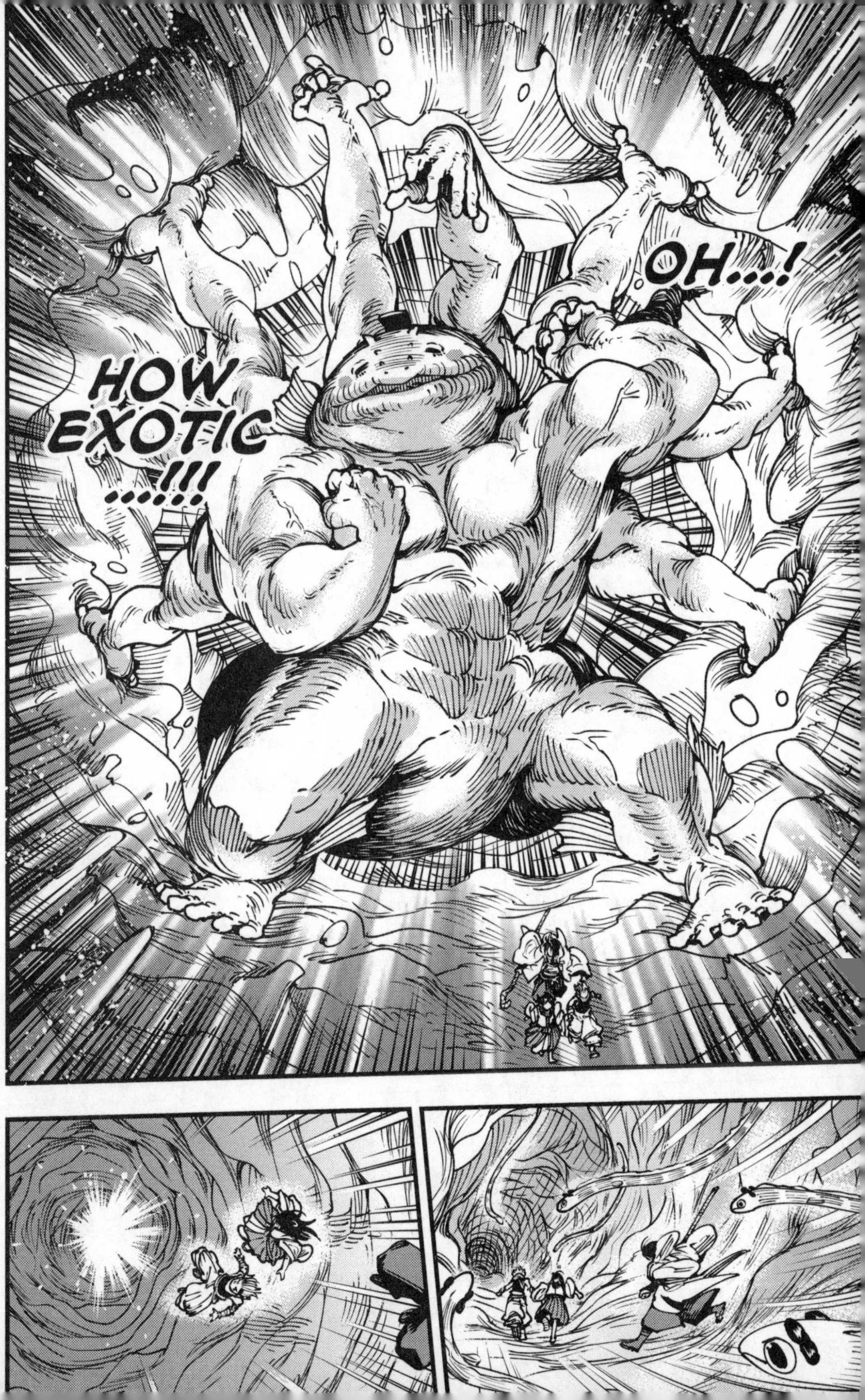
OH...!
HOW EXOTIC ....!!!

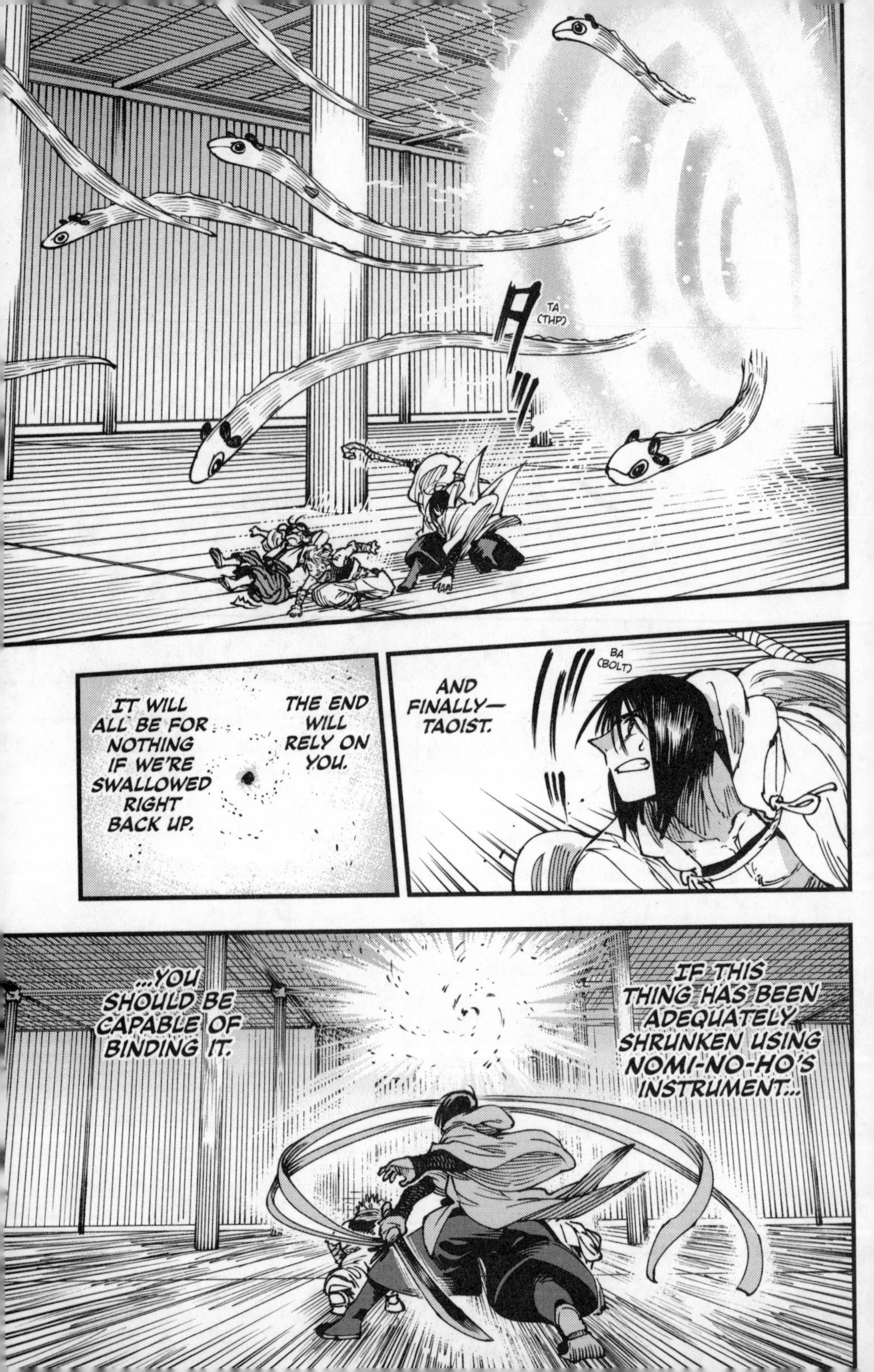
TA (THP)
BA (BOLT)
AND FINALLY— TAOIST.
THE END WILL RELY ON YOU.
IT WILL ALL BE FOR NOTHING IF WE'RE SWALLOWED RIGHT BACK UP.
IF THIS THING HAS BEEN ADEQUATELY SHRUNKEN USING NOMI-NO-HO'S INSTRUMENT...
...YOU SHOULD BE CAPABLE OF BINDING IT.

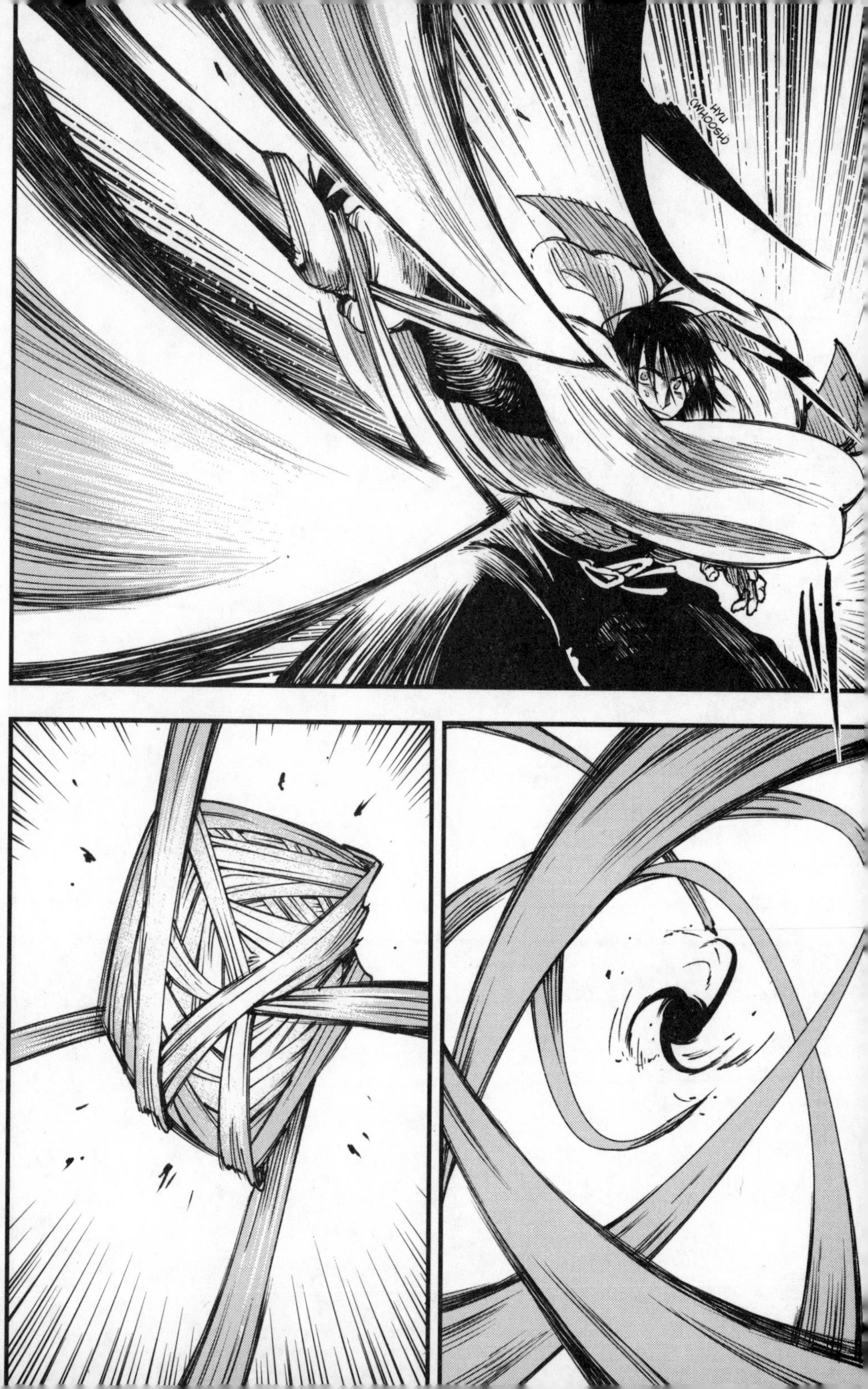
HYU
(WHOOSH)

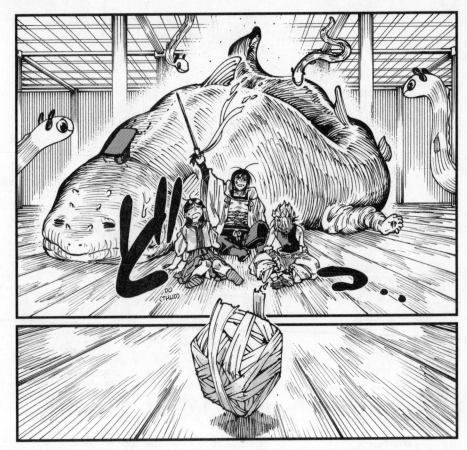

DO
(THUD)

THE
GREAT WELL
OF THE
HEAVENS...

...HAS
BEEN
EXORCISED.

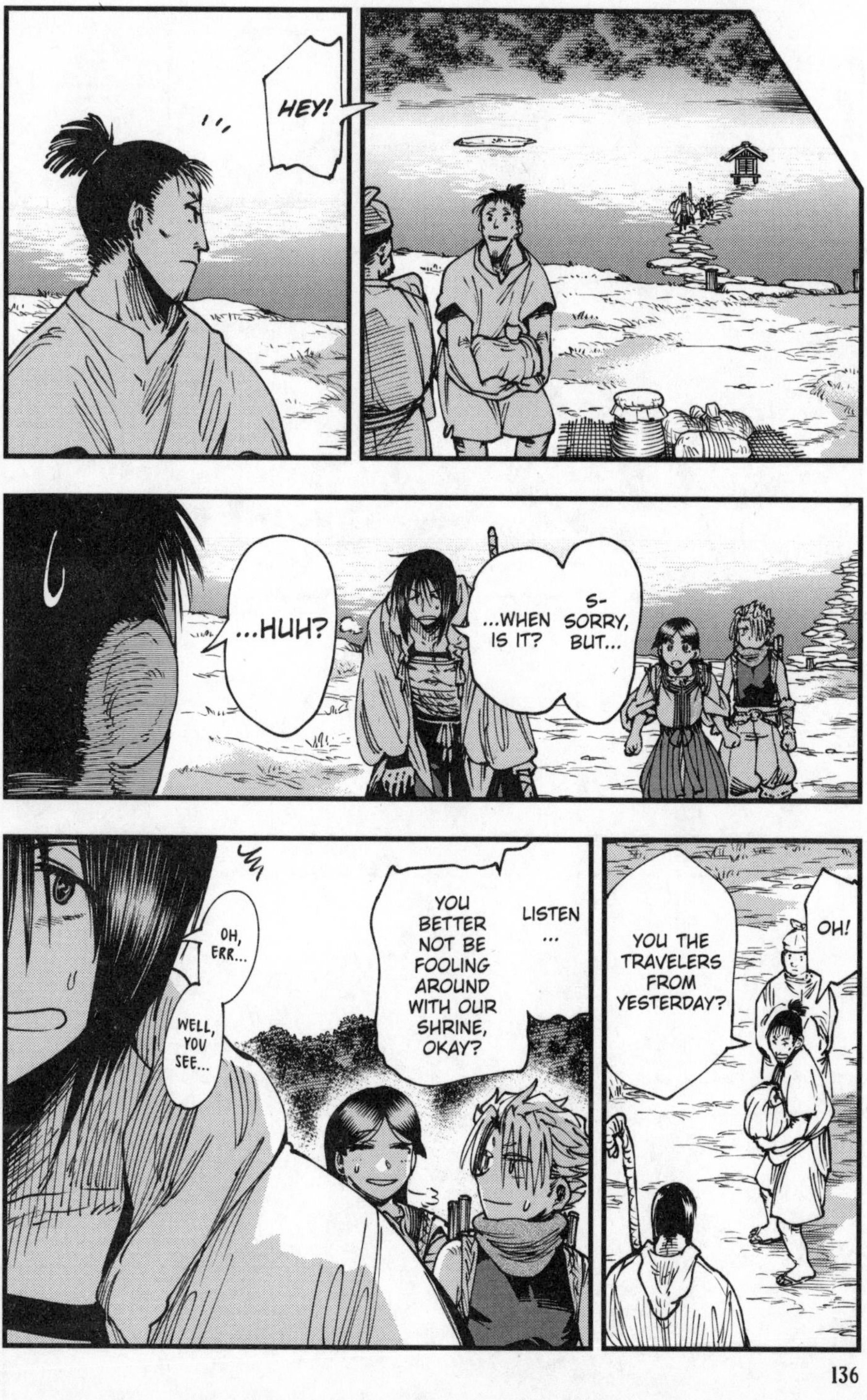
HEY!
S- SORRY, BUT...
...WHEN IS IT?
...HUH?
OH!
YOU THE TRAVELERS FROM YESTERDAY?
LISTEN ...
YOU BETTER NOT BE FOOLING AROUND WITH OUR SHRINE, OKAY?
OH, ERR...
WELL, YOU SEE...

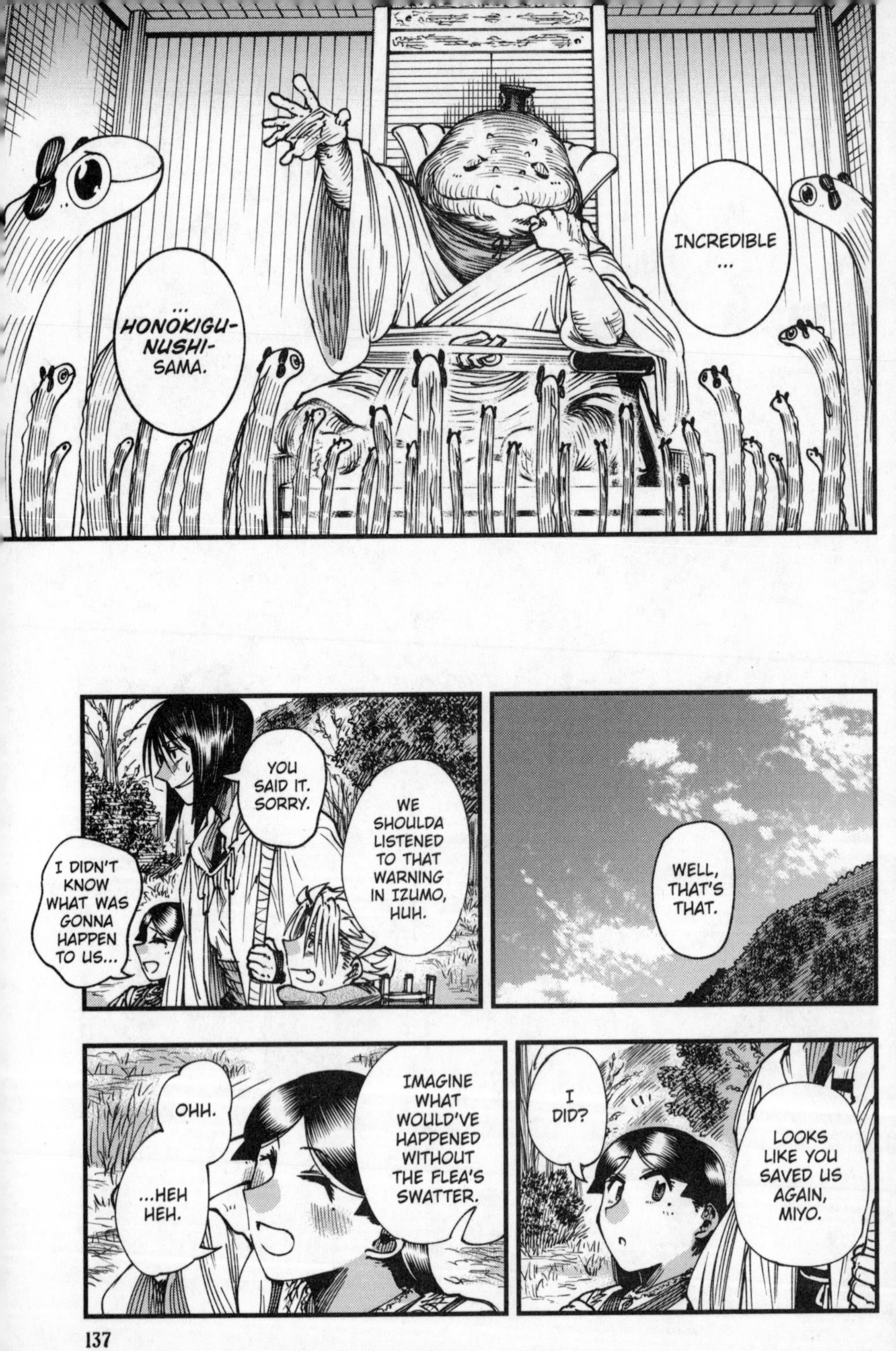
INCREDIBLE ...
... HONOKIGUNUSHI-SAMA.
WELL, THAT'S THAT.
WE SHOULDA LISTENED TO THAT WARNING IN IZUMO, HUH.
YOU SAID IT. SORRY.
I DIDN'T KNOW WHAT WAS GONNA HAPPEN TO US...
LOOKS LIKE YOU SAVED US AGAIN, MIYO.
I DID?
IMAGINE WHAT WOULD'VE HAPPENED WITHOUT THE FLEA'S SWATTER.
OHH.
...HEH HEH.

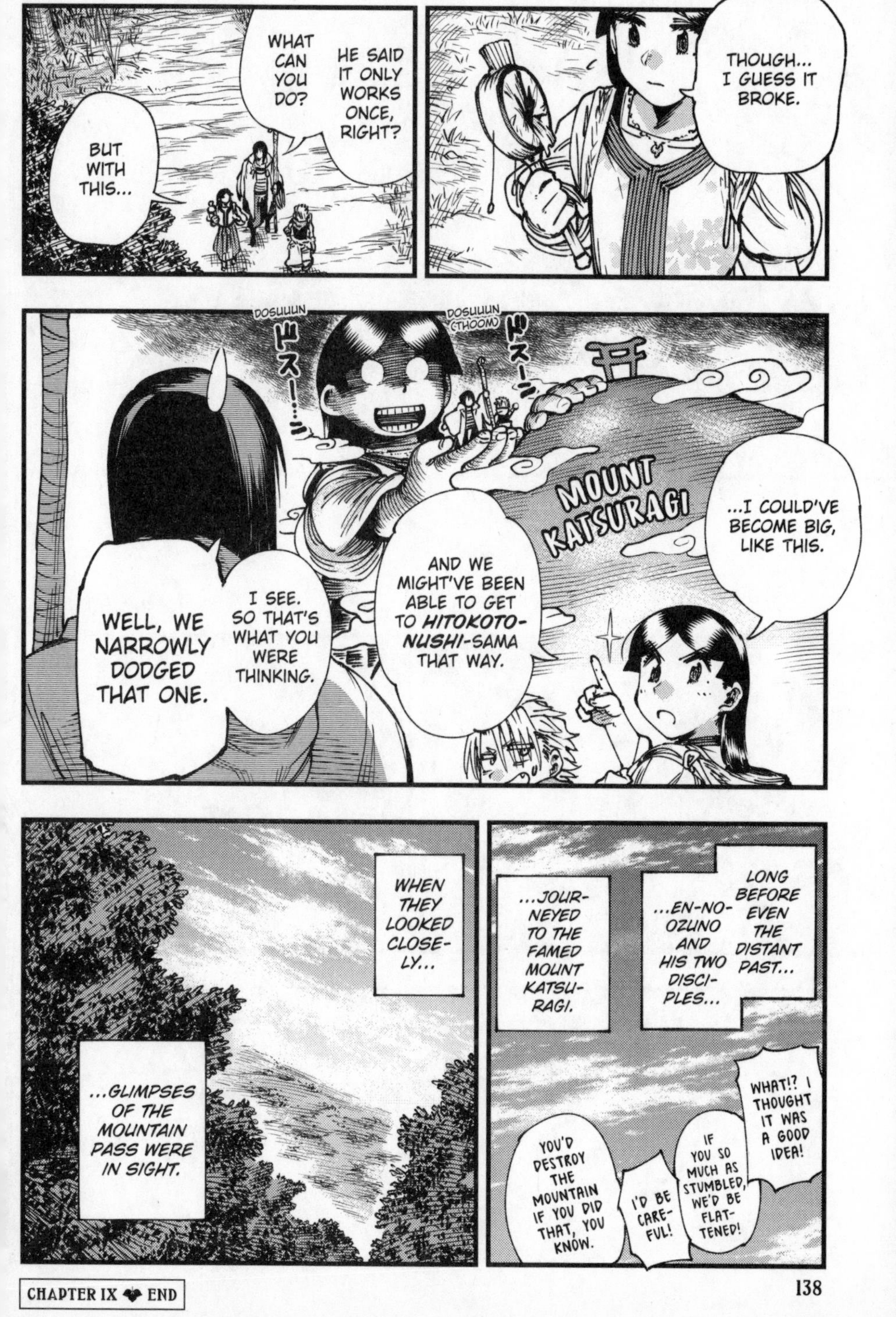
THOUGH... I GUESS IT BROKE.
HE SAID IT ONLY WORKS ONCE, RIGHT?
WHAT CAN YOU DO?
BUT WITH THIS...
DOSUUUN (THOOM) ドスーン
DOSUUUN ドスー…ン
...I COULD'VE BECOME BIG, LIKE THIS.
MOUNT KATSURAGI
AND WE MIGHT'VE BEEN ABLE TO GET TO *HITOKOTO-NUSHI*-SAMA THAT WAY.
I SEE. SO THAT'S WHAT YOU WERE THINKING.
WELL, WE NARROWLY DODGED THAT ONE.
LONG BEFORE EVEN THE DISTANT PAST...
...EN-NO-OZUNO AND HIS TWO DISCIPLES...
...JOURNEYED TO THE FAMED MOUNT KATSURAGI.
WHAT!? I THOUGHT IT WAS A GOOD IDEA!
IF YOU SO MUCH AS STUMBLED, WE'D BE FLATTENED!
I'D BE CAREFUL!
YOU'D DESTROY THE MOUNTAIN IF YOU DID THAT, YOU KNOW.
WHEN THEY LOOKED CLOSELY...
...GLIMPSES OF THE MOUNTAIN PASS WERE IN SIGHT.

CHAPTER IX END

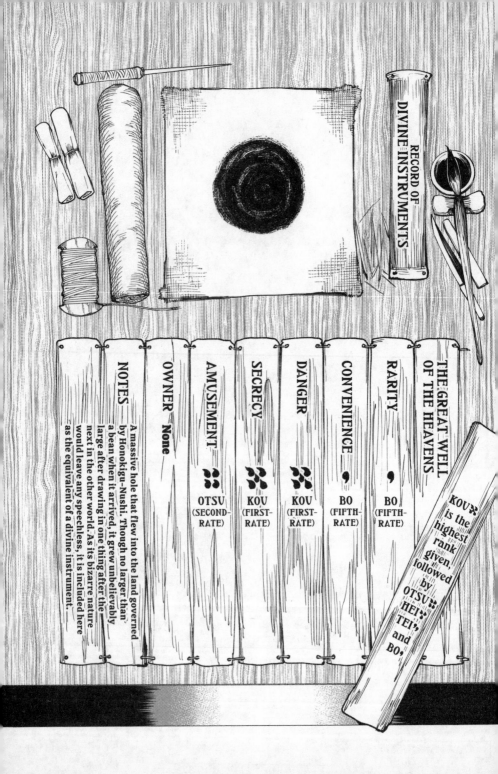

RECORD OF DIVINE INSTRUMENTS

THE GREAT WELL OF THE HEAVENS

RARITY
BO
(FIFTH-RATE)

CONVENIENCE
BO
(FIFTH-RATE)

DANGER
KOU
(FIRST-RATE)

SECRECY
KOU
(FIRST-RATE)

AMUSEMENT
OTSU
(SECOND-RATE)

OWNER None

NOTES
A massive hole that flew into the land governed by Honokigu-Nushi. Though no larger than a bean when it arrived, it grew unbelievably large after drawing in one thing after the next in the other world. As its bizarre nature would leave any speechless, it is included here as the equivalent of a divine instrument.

KOU is the highest rank given, followed by OTSU, HEI, TEI, and BO.

Touge Oni

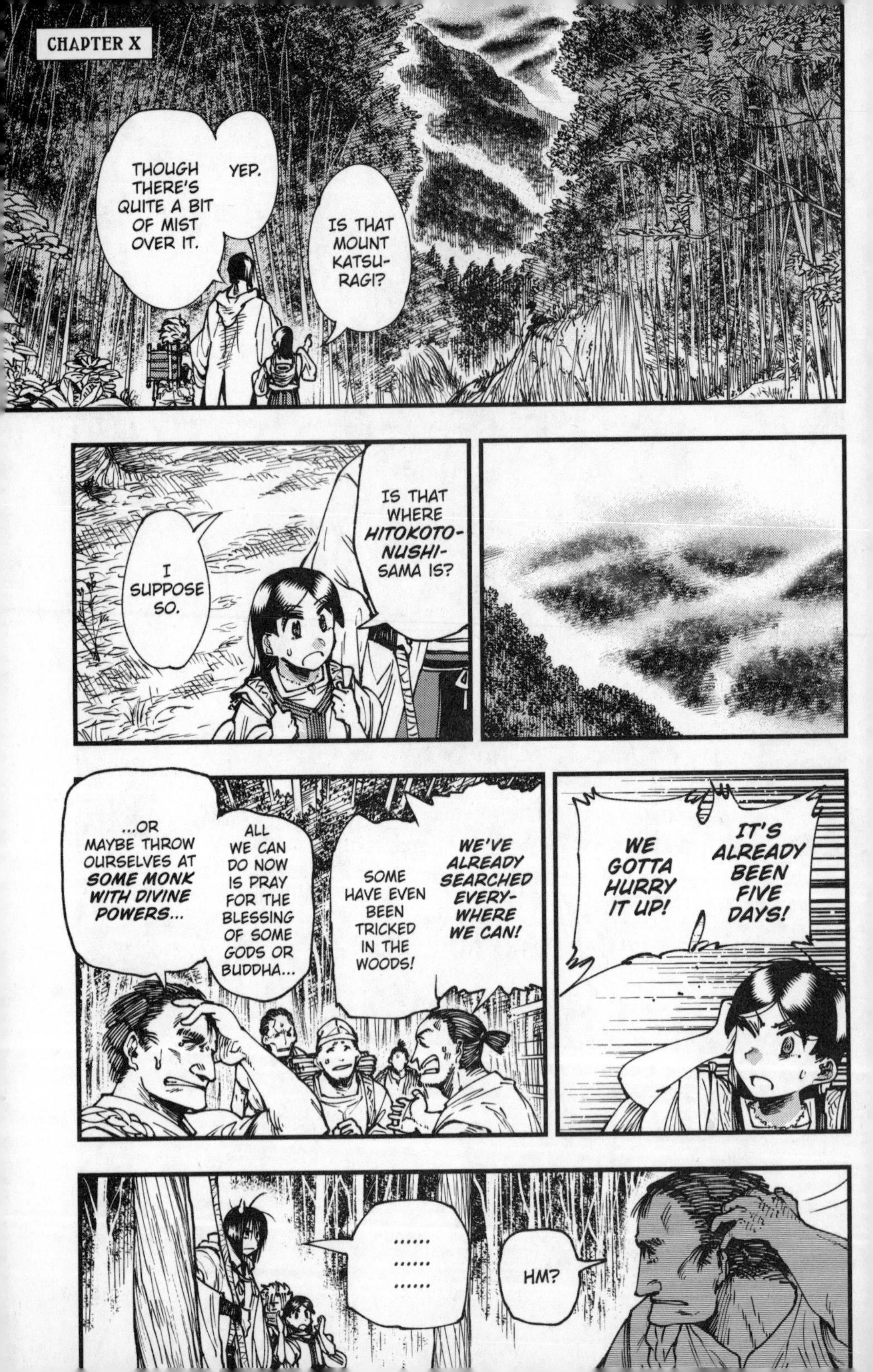
IS THAT MOUNT KATSURAGI?
YEP. THOUGH THERE'S QUITE A BIT OF MIST OVER IT.
IS THAT WHERE HITOKOTONUSHI-SAMA IS?
I SUPPOSE SO.
IT'S ALREADY BEEN FIVE DAYS!
WE GOTTA HURRY IT UP!
WE'VE ALREADY SEARCHED EVERYWHERE WE CAN!
SOME HAVE EVEN BEEN TRICKED IN THE WOODS!
ALL WE CAN DO NOW IS PRAY FOR THE BLESSING OF SOME GODS OR BUDDHA...
...OR MAYBE THROW OURSELVES AT SOME MONK WITH DIVINE POWERS...
HM?
....

CHAPTER X WITHIN THE FOG

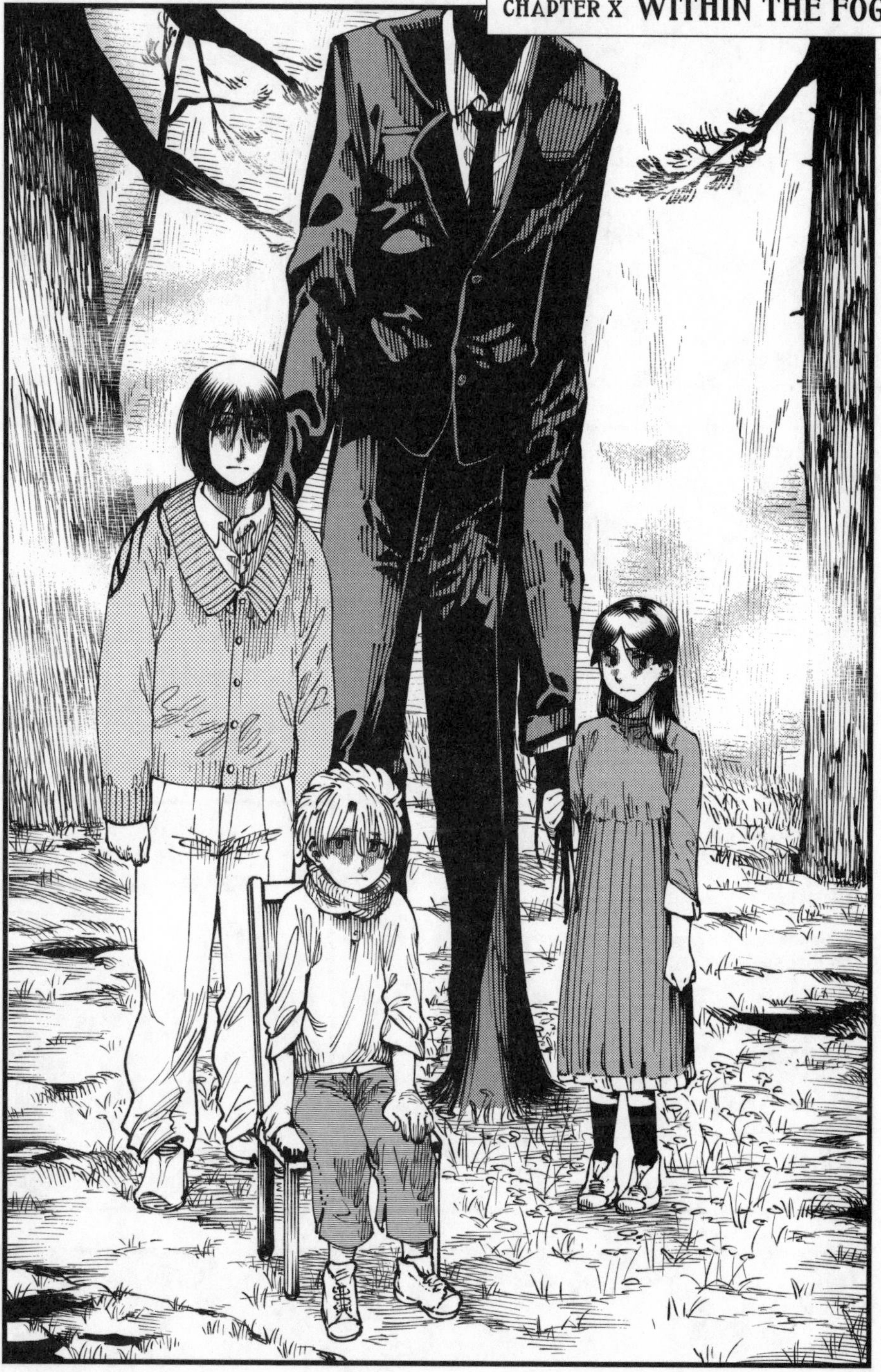

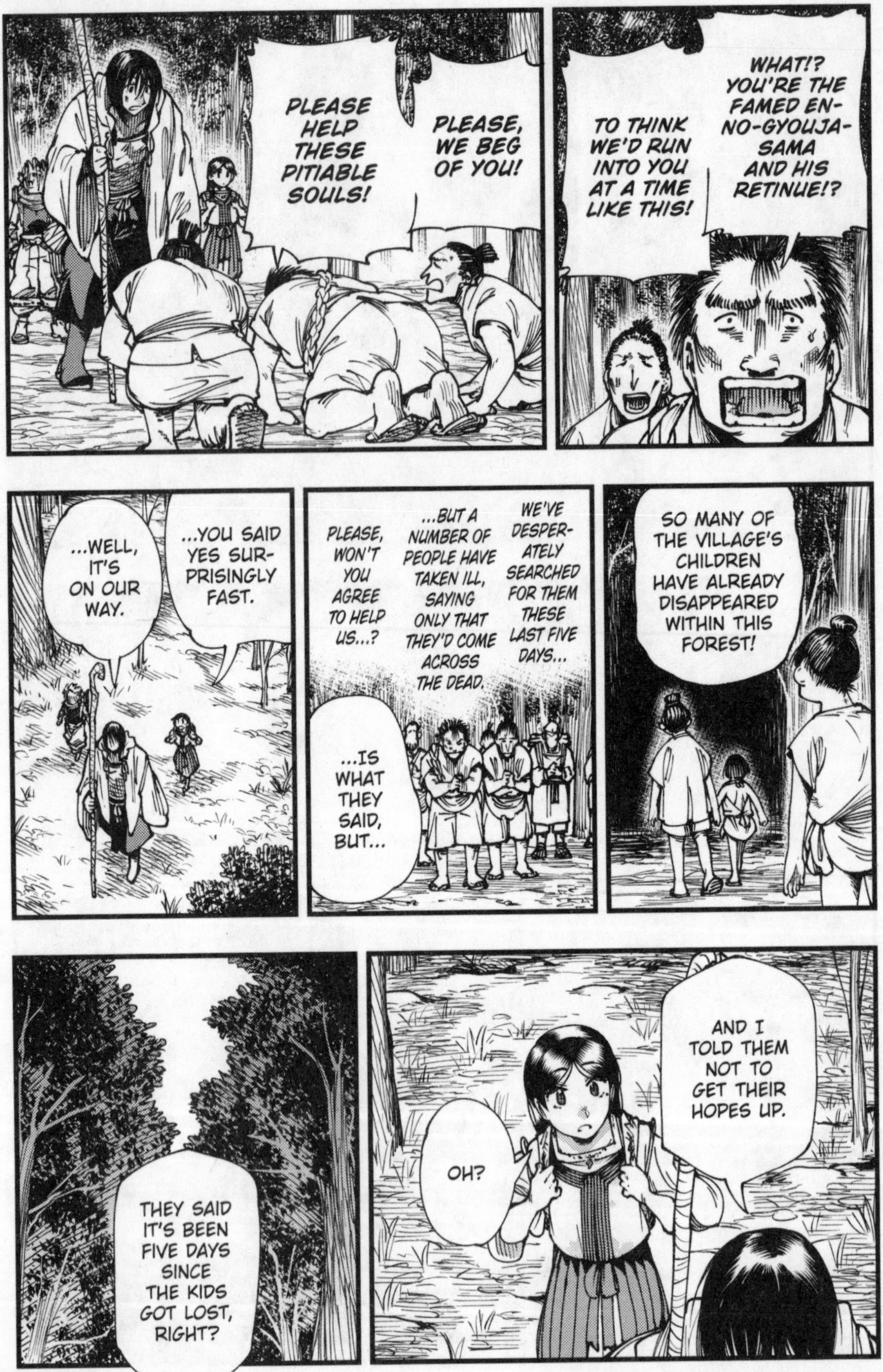
WHAT!? YOU'RE THE FAMED EN-NO-GYOUJA-SAMA AND HIS RETINUE!?
TO THINK WE'D RUN INTO YOU AT A TIME LIKE THIS!
PLEASE, WE BEG OF YOU!
PLEASE HELP THESE PITIABLE SOULS!
SO MANY OF THE VILLAGE'S CHILDREN HAVE ALREADY DISAPPEARED WITHIN THIS FOREST!
WE'VE DESPERATELY SEARCHED FOR THEM THESE LAST FIVE DAYS...
...BUT A NUMBER OF PEOPLE HAVE TAKEN ILL, SAYING ONLY THAT THEY'D COME ACROSS THE DEAD.
PLEASE, WON'T YOU AGREE TO HELP US...?
...IS WHAT THEY SAID, BUT...
...YOU SAID YES SURPRISINGLY FAST.
...WELL, IT'S ON OUR WAY.
AND I TOLD THEM NOT TO GET THEIR HOPES UP.
OH?
THEY SAID IT'S BEEN FIVE DAYS SINCE THE KIDS GOT LOST, RIGHT?

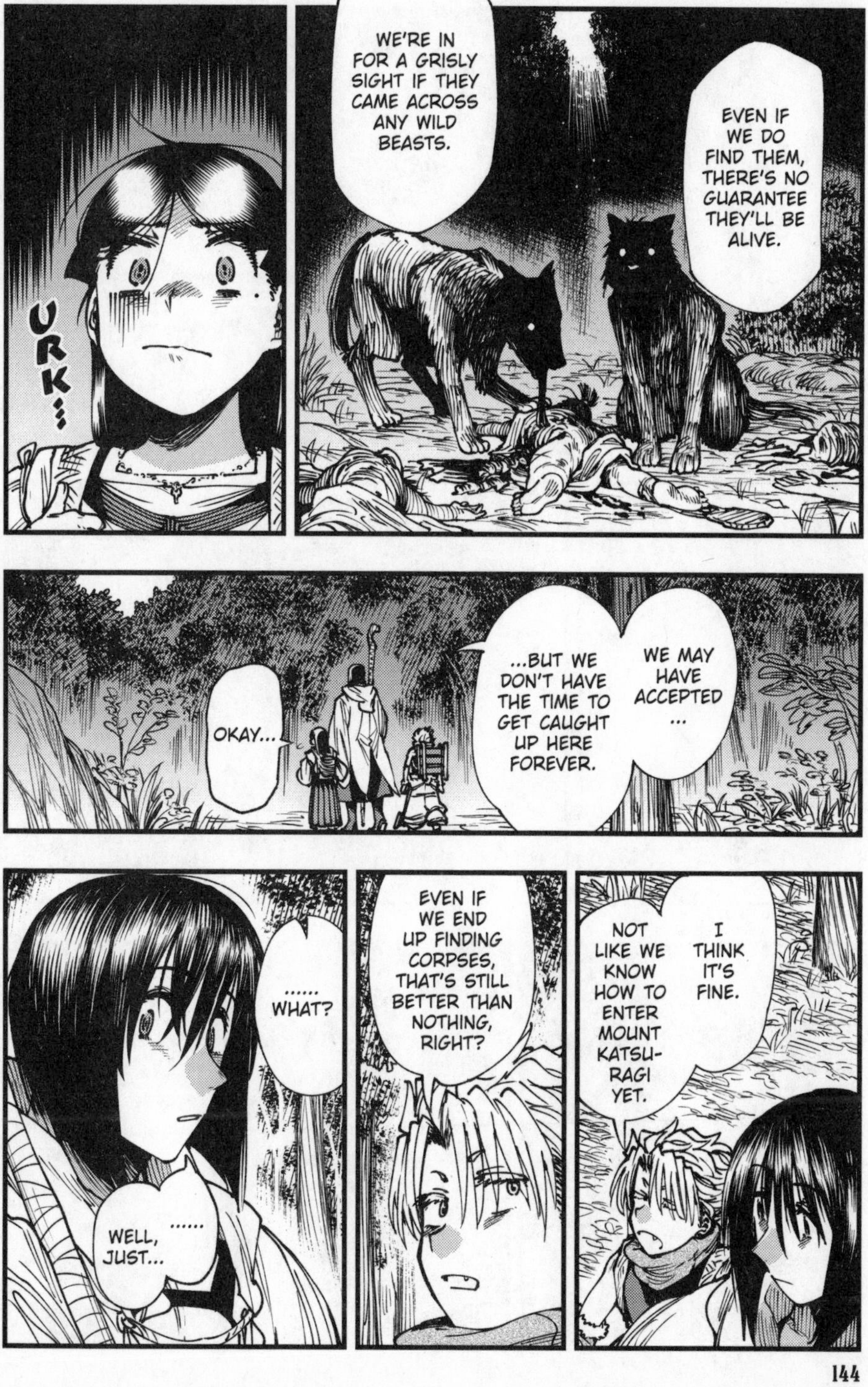
EVEN IF WE DO FIND THEM, THERE'S NO GUARANTEE THEY'LL BE ALIVE.
WE'RE IN FOR A GRISLY SIGHT IF THEY CAME ACROSS ANY WILD BEASTS.
URK...
WE MAY HAVE ACCEPTED ...
...BUT WE DON'T HAVE THE TIME TO GET CAUGHT UP HERE FOREVER.
OKAY...
I THINK IT'S FINE.
NOT LIKE WE KNOW HOW TO ENTER MOUNT KATSURAGI YET.
EVEN IF WE END UP FINDING CORPSES, THAT'S STILL BETTER THAN NOTHING, RIGHT?
...... WHAT?
...... WELL, JUST...

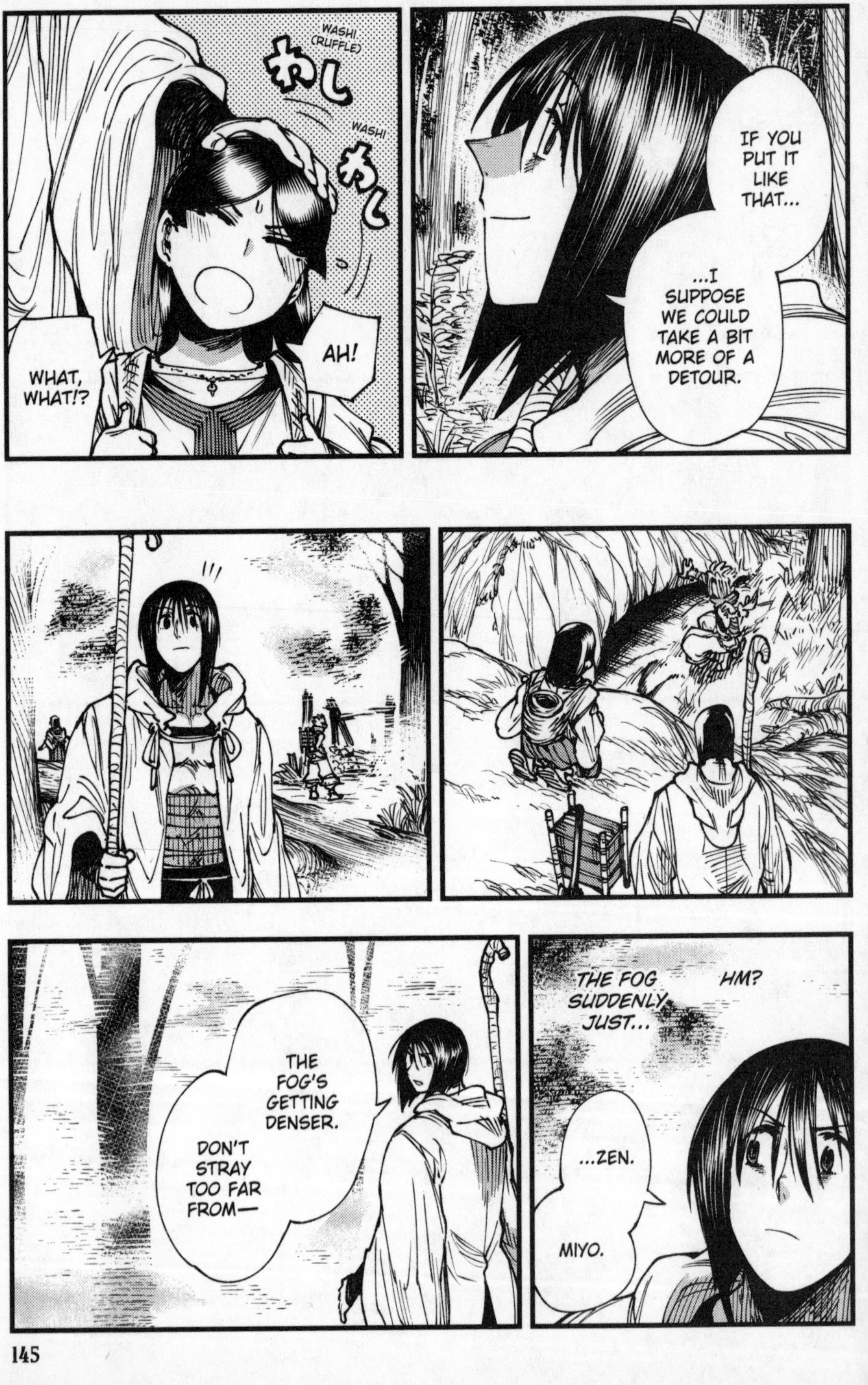
IF YOU PUT IT LIKE THAT...
...I SUPPOSE WE COULD TAKE A BIT MORE OF A DETOUR.
WASHI (RUFFLE)
わし
WASHI
わし
AH!
WHAT, WHAT!?
HM?
THE FOG SUDDENLY JUST...
...ZEN.
MIYO.
THE FOG'S GETTING DENSER.
DON'T STRAY TOO FAR FROM—

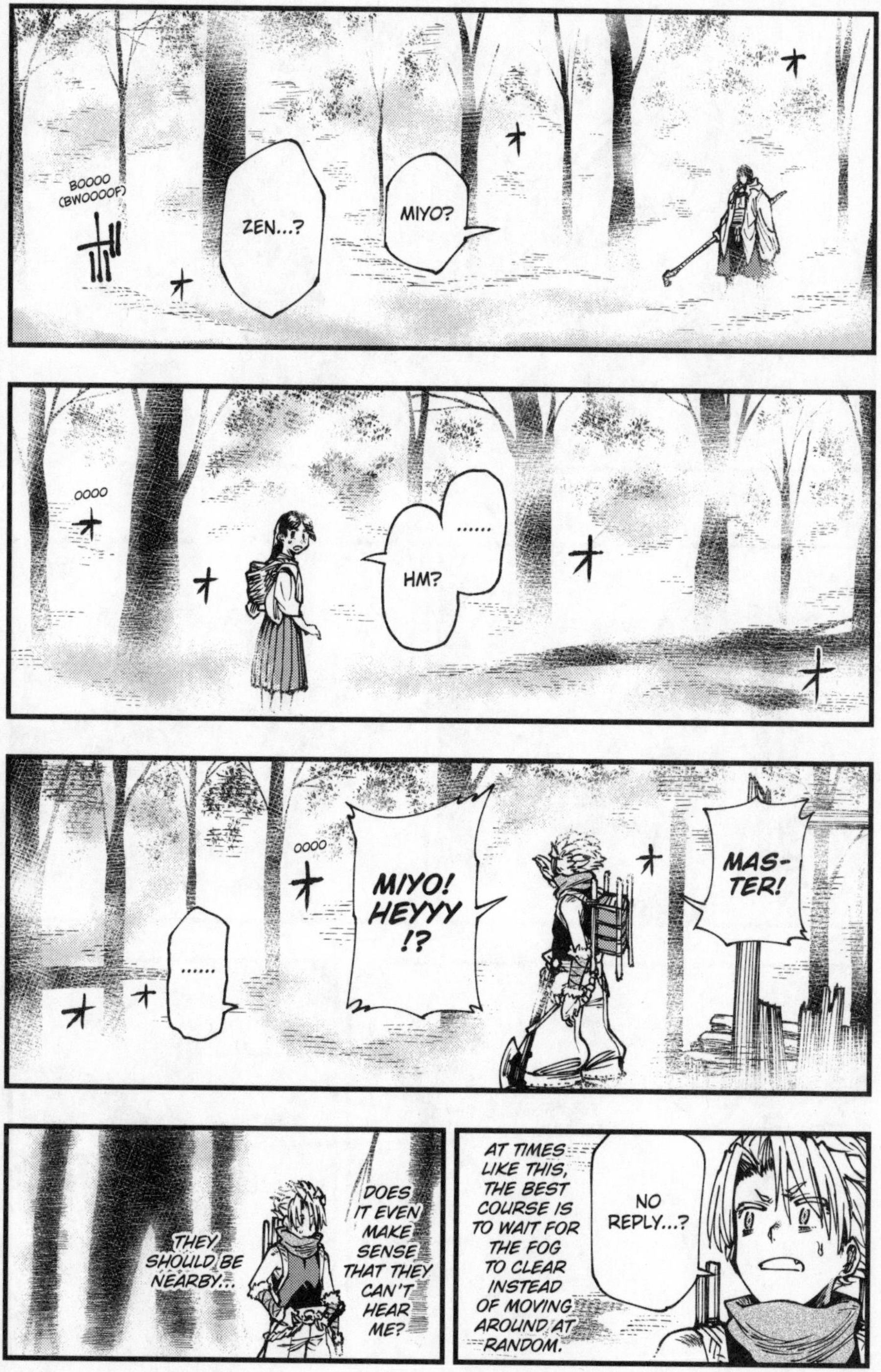
MIYO?
ZEN...?
BOOOO (BWOOOOF)
......
HM?
OOOO
MAS-TER!
MIYO! HEYYY!?
OOOO
......
NO REPLY...?
AT TIMES LIKE THIS, THE BEST COURSE IS TO WAIT FOR THE FOG TO CLEAR INSTEAD OF MOVING AROUND AT RANDOM.
DOES IT EVEN MAKE SENSE THAT THEY CAN'T HEAR ME?
THEY SHOULD BE NEARBY...

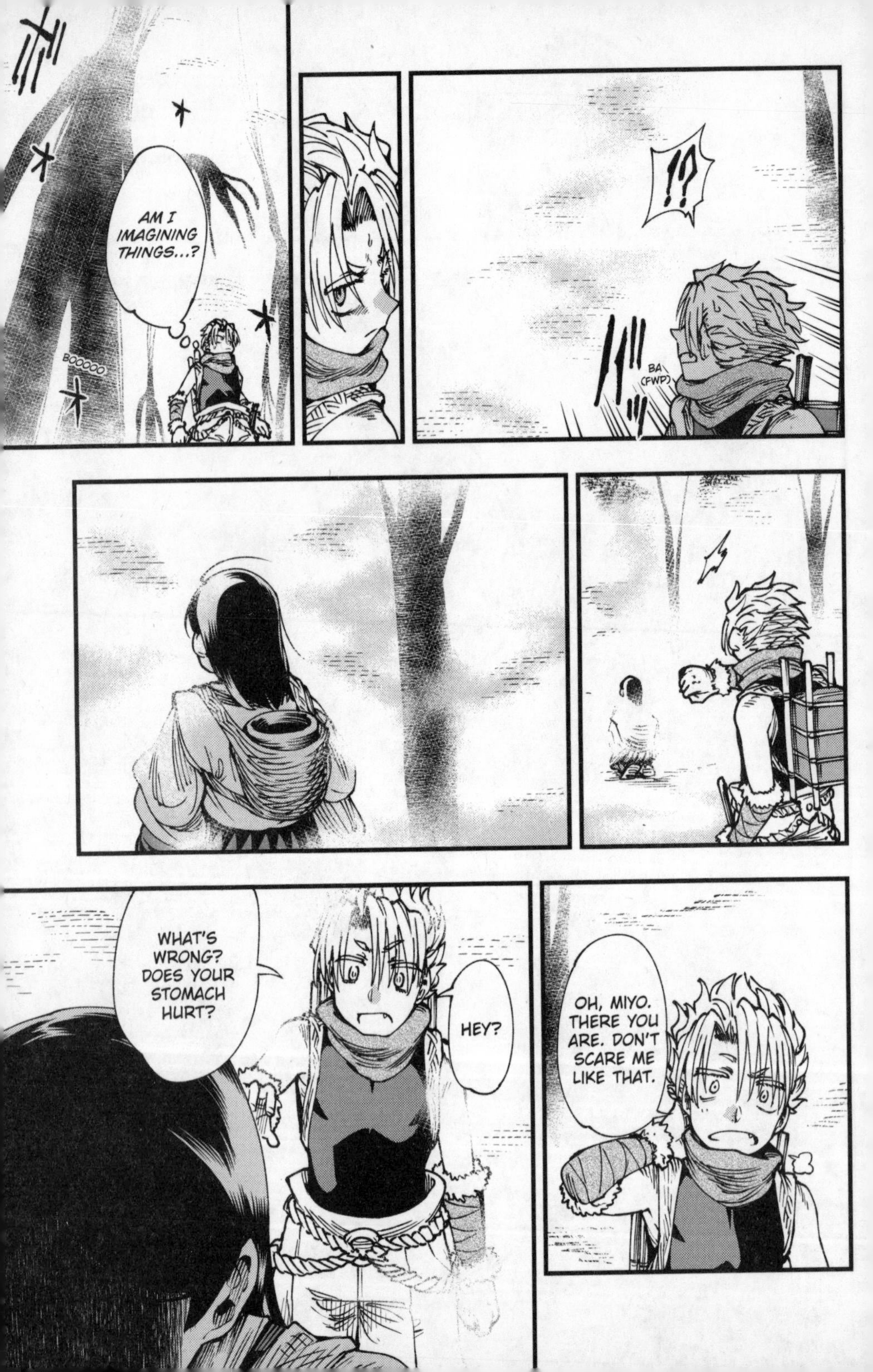
!?
BA
(FWP)
AM I IMAGINING THINGS...?
BOOOOO
OH, MIYO. THERE YOU ARE. DON'T SCARE ME LIKE THAT.
HEY?
WHAT'S WRONG? DOES YOUR STOMACH HURT?

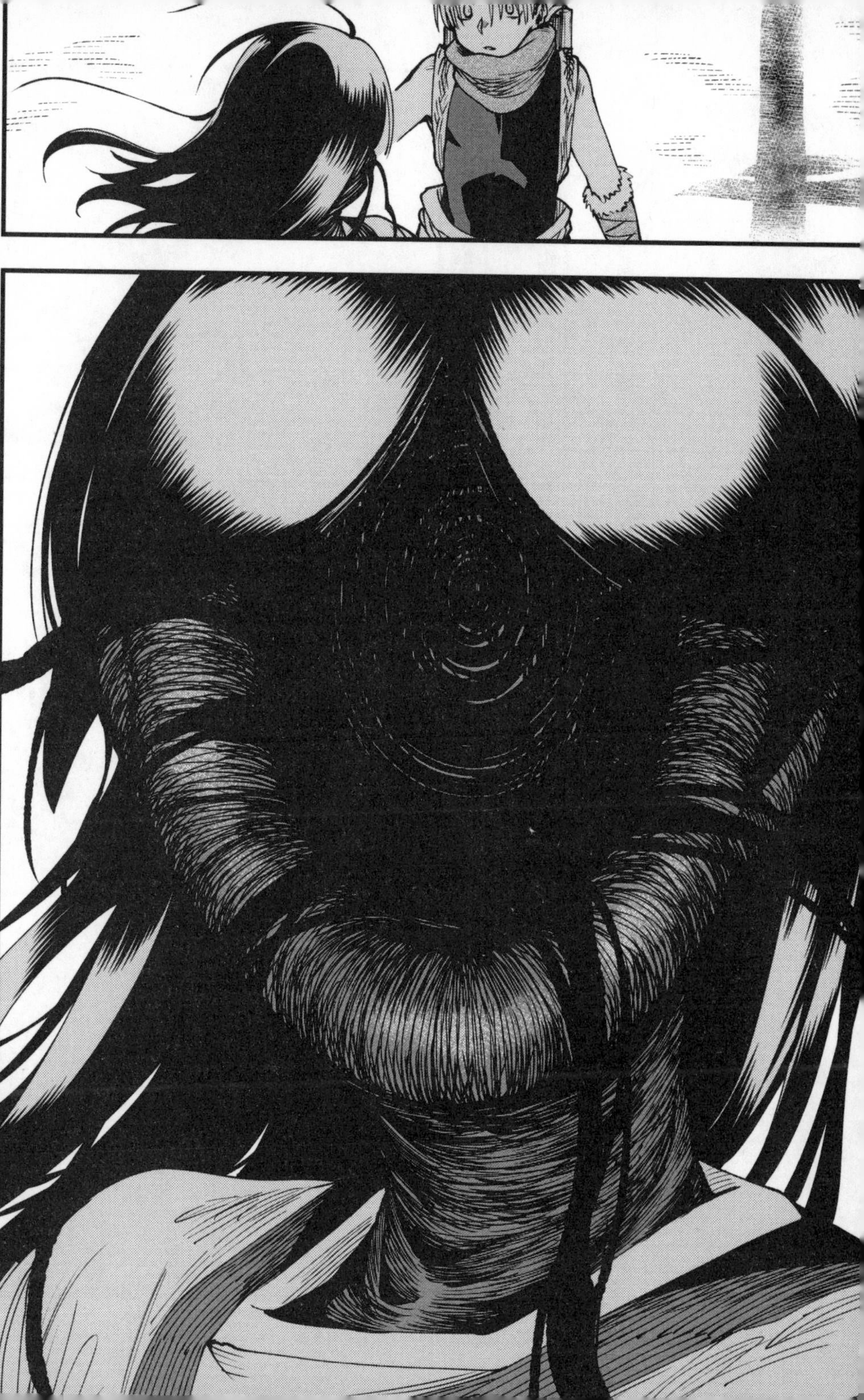

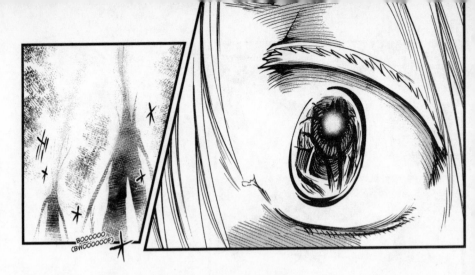

BOOOOOOO
(BWOOOOOOOF)

......
.....

FATHER
...?

!

ZA
(SHHK)

149

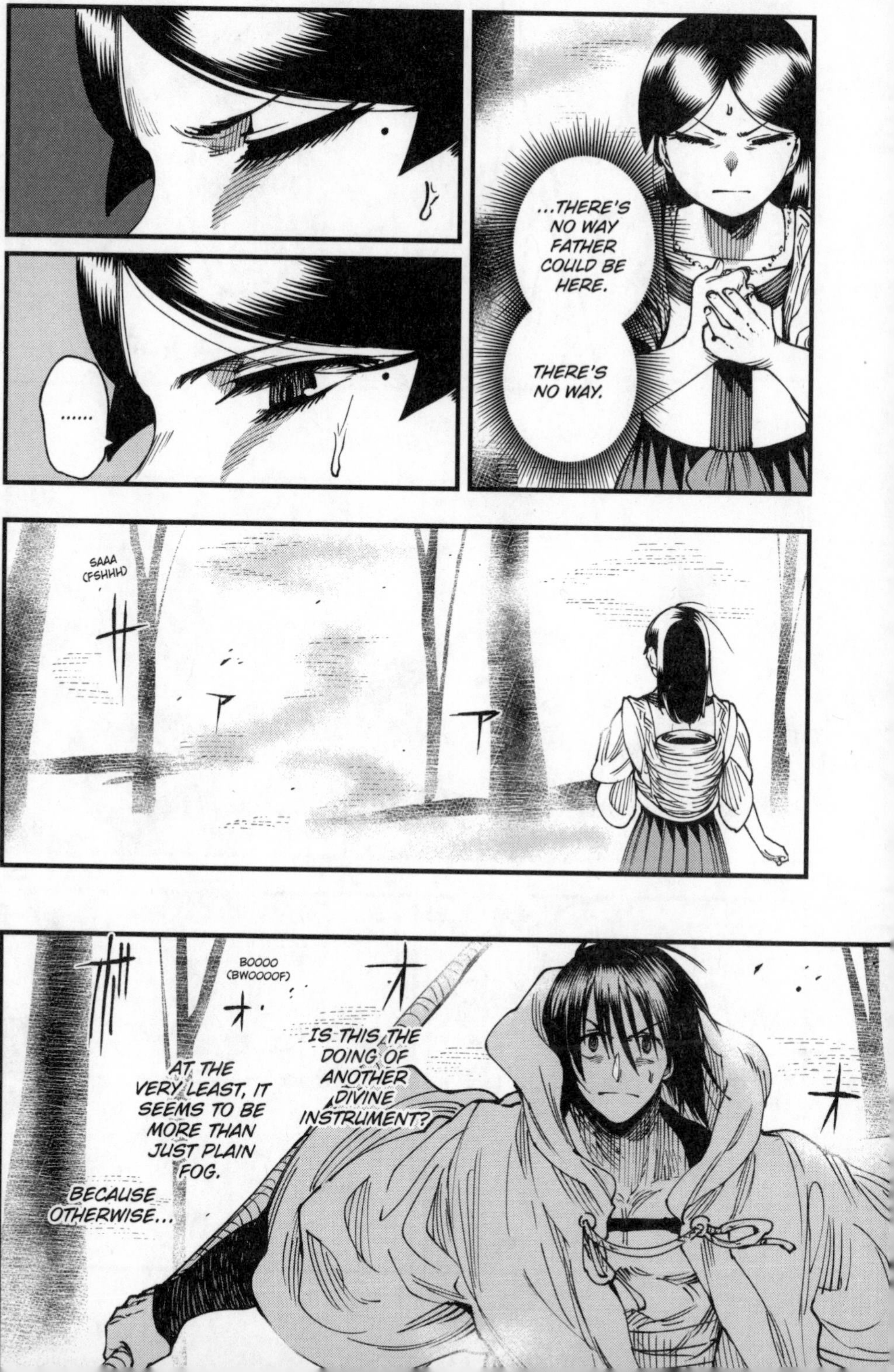
...THERE'S NO WAY FATHER COULD BE HERE.
THERE'S NO WAY.
......
SAAA (FSHHH)
BOOOO (BWOOOOF)
IS THIS THE DOING OF ANOTHER DIVINE INSTRUMENT?
AT THE VERY LEAST, IT SEEMS TO BE MORE THAN JUST PLAIN FOG.
BECAUSE OTHERWISE...

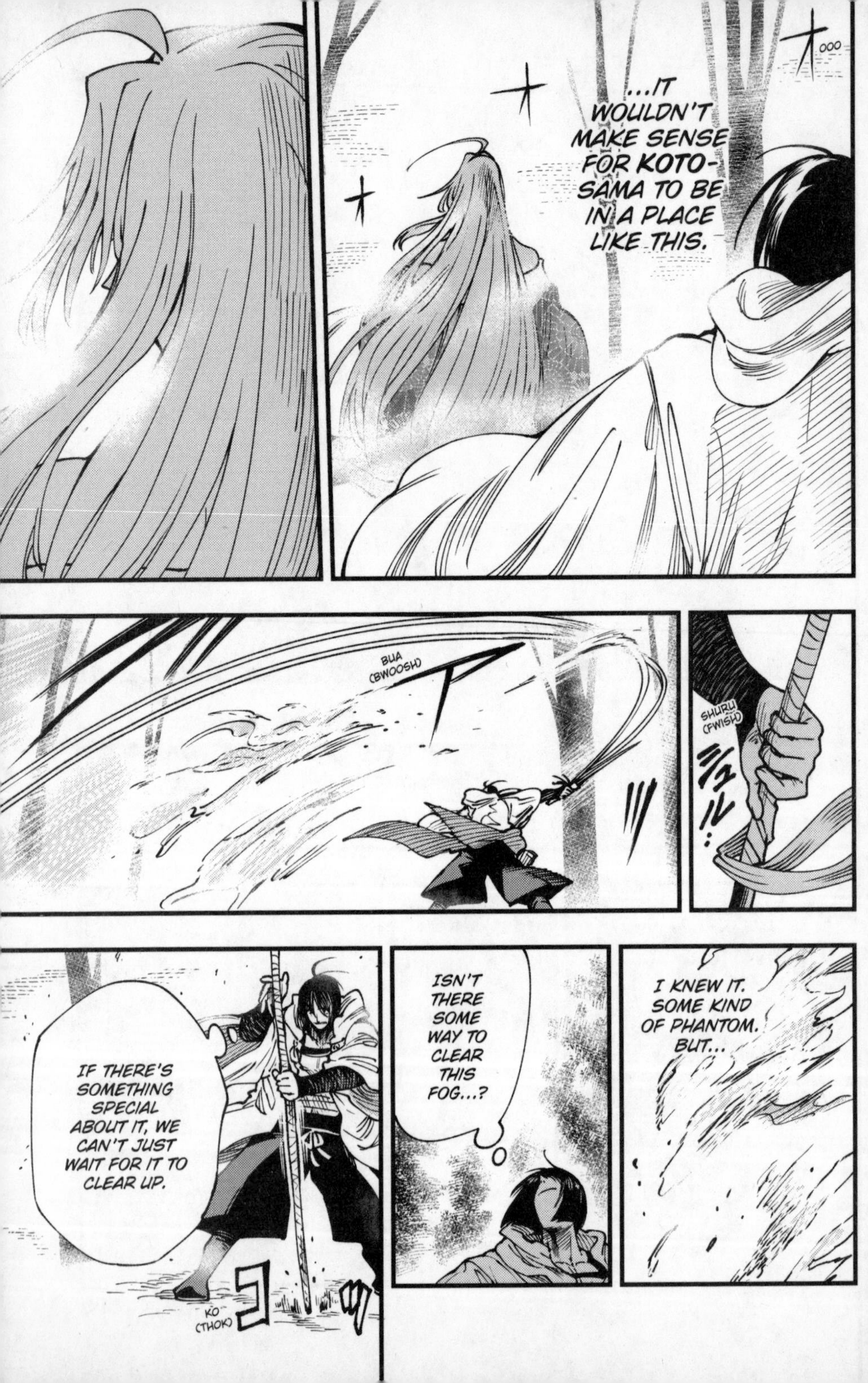
OOO
...IT WOULDN'T MAKE SENSE FOR KOTO-SAMA TO BE IN A PLACE LIKE THIS.
SHURU (FWISH)
BUA (BWOOSH)
I KNEW IT. SOME KIND OF PHANTOM. BUT...
ISN'T THERE SOME WAY TO CLEAR THIS FOG...?
IF THERE'S SOMETHING SPECIAL ABOUT IT, WE CAN'T JUST WAIT FOR IT TO CLEAR UP.
KO (THOK)

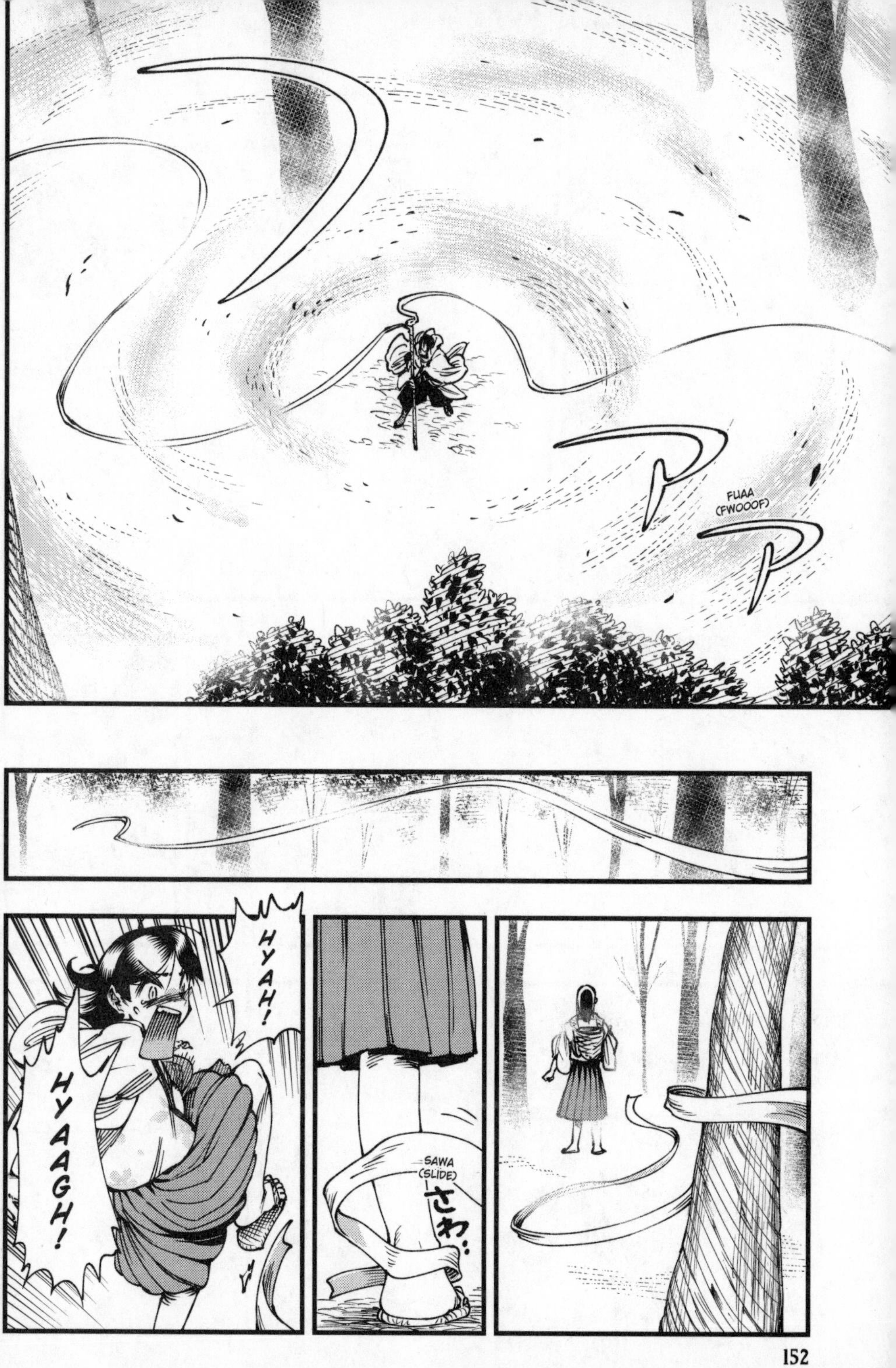
FUAA
(FWOOOF)
SAWA
(SLIDE)
さわ
HYAH!
HYAAAGH!

...THAT FLAPPY THING ON MASTER'S SWORD...!

WAIT— THAT'S...

HM?

......

EE—

FUWA (FWOOF)

FUWA

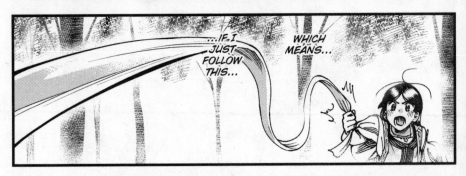

...IF I JUST FOLLOW THIS...

WHICH MEANS...

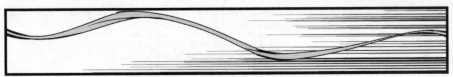

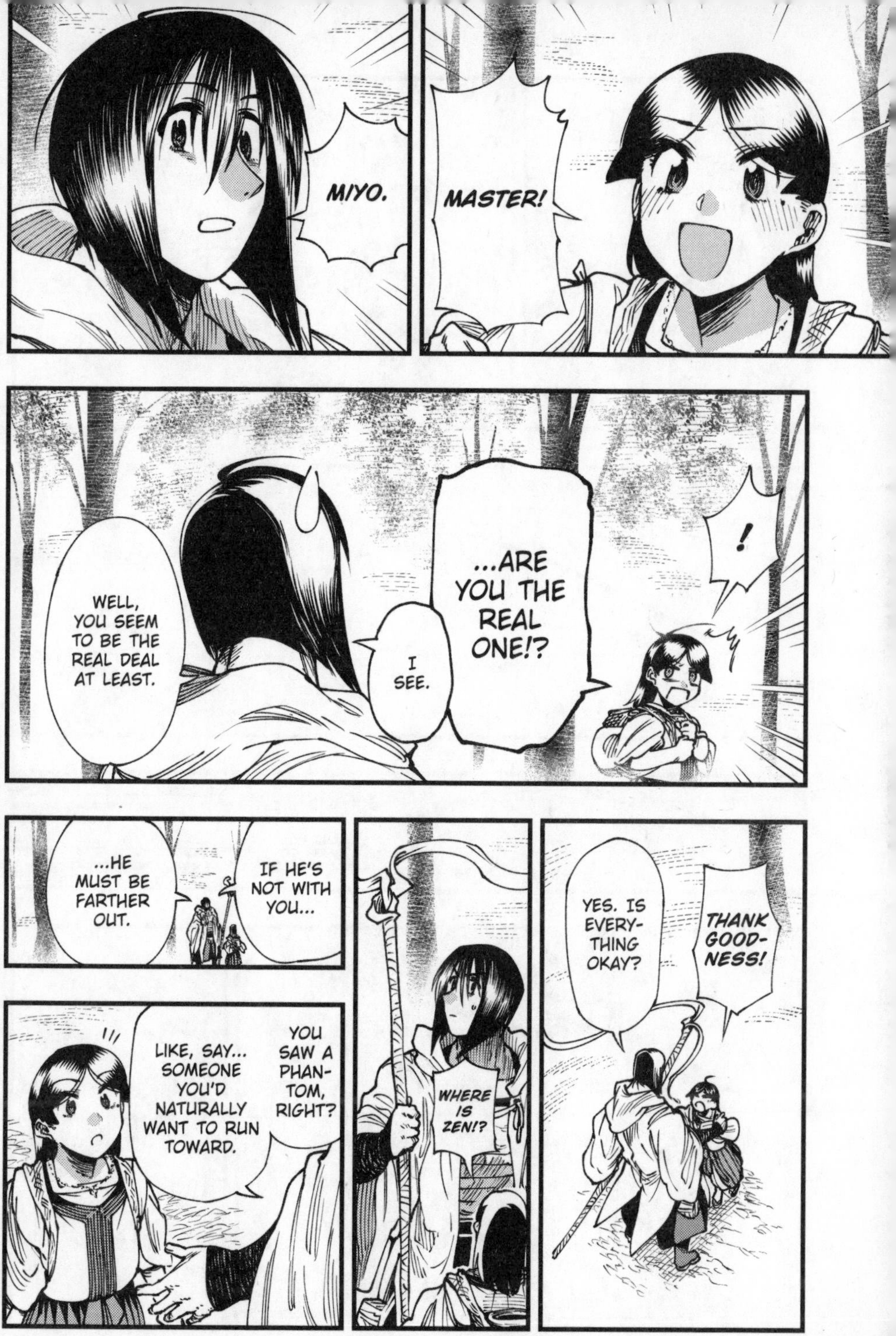
MASTER!
MIYO.
!
...ARE YOU THE REAL ONE!?
I SEE.
WELL, YOU SEEM TO BE THE REAL DEAL AT LEAST.
THANK GOOD-NESS!
YES. IS EVERY-THING OKAY?
WHERE IS ZEN!?
IF HE'S NOT WITH YOU...
...HE MUST BE FARTHER OUT.
YOU SAW A PHAN-TOM, RIGHT?
LIKE, SAY... SOMEONE YOU'D NATURALLY WANT TO RUN TOWARD.

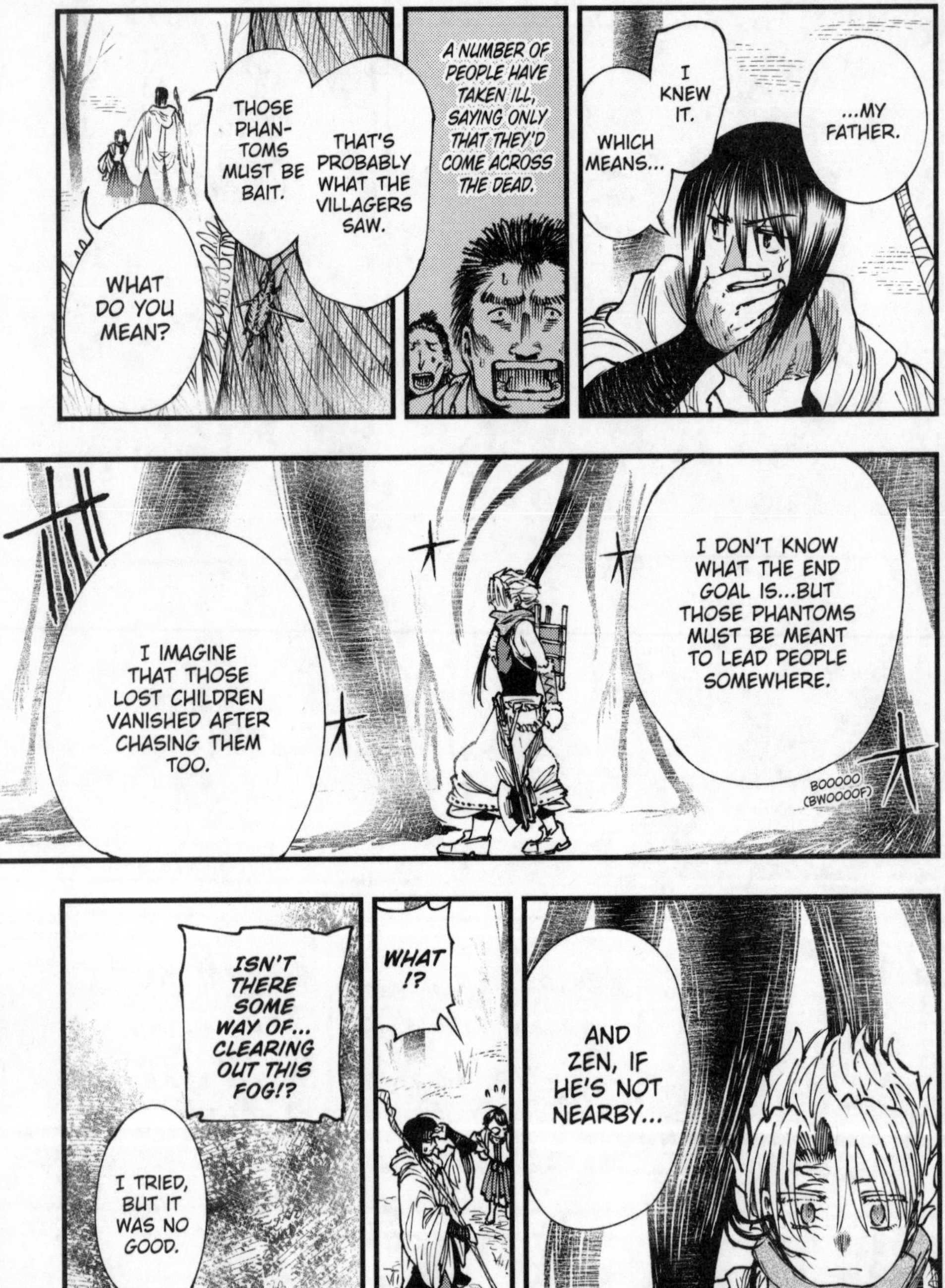
...MY FATHER.
I KNEW IT.
WHICH MEANS...
A NUMBER OF PEOPLE HAVE TAKEN ILL, SAYING ONLY THAT THEY'D COME ACROSS THE DEAD.
THAT'S PROBABLY WHAT THE VILLAGERS SAW.
THOSE PHAN-TOMS MUST BE BAIT.
WHAT DO YOU MEAN?
I DON'T KNOW WHAT THE END GOAL IS...BUT THOSE PHANTOMS MUST BE MEANT TO LEAD PEOPLE SOMEWHERE.
BOOOOO (BWOOOOF)
I IMAGINE THAT THOSE LOST CHILDREN VANISHED AFTER CHASING THEM TOO.
AND ZEN, IF HE'S NOT NEARBY...
WHAT !?
ISN'T THERE SOME WAY OF... CLEARING OUT THIS FOG!?
I TRIED, BUT IT WAS NO GOOD.

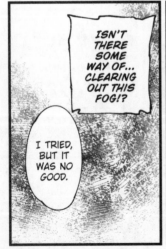

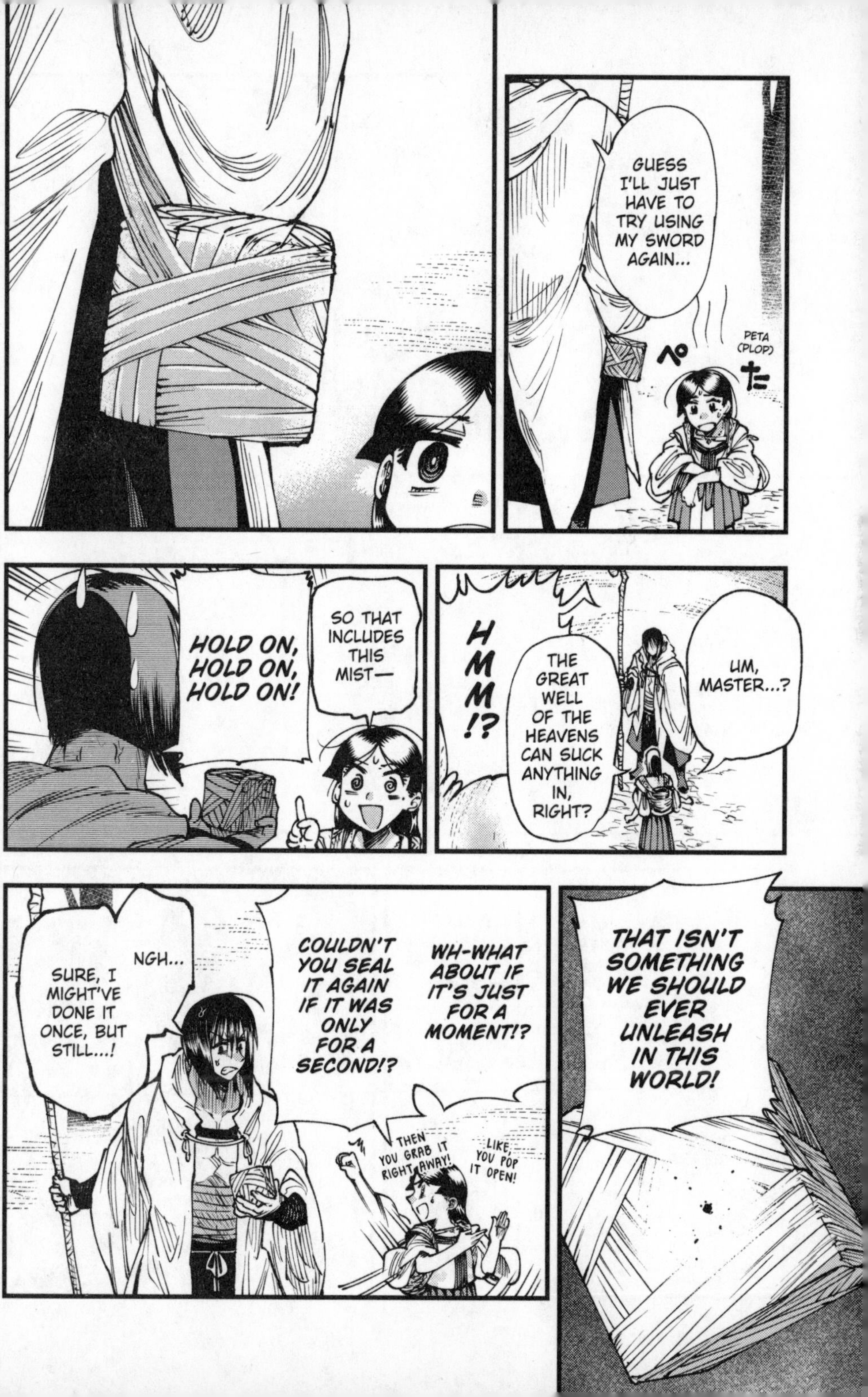
GUESS I'LL JUST HAVE TO TRY USING MY SWORD AGAIN...
PETA (PLOP)
へ
た
UM, MASTER...?
THE GREAT WELL OF THE HEAVENS CAN SUCK ANYTHING IN, RIGHT?
HMM!?
SO THAT INCLUDES THIS MIST—
HOLD ON, HOLD ON, HOLD ON!
THAT ISN'T SOMETHING WE SHOULD EVER UNLEASH IN THIS WORLD!
WH-WHAT ABOUT IF IT'S JUST FOR A MOMENT!?
COULDN'T YOU SEAL IT AGAIN IF IT WAS ONLY FOR A SECOND!?
NGH...
SURE, I MIGHT'VE DONE IT ONCE, BUT STILL...!
LIKE, YOU POP IT OPEN!
THEN YOU GRAB IT RIGHT AWAY!

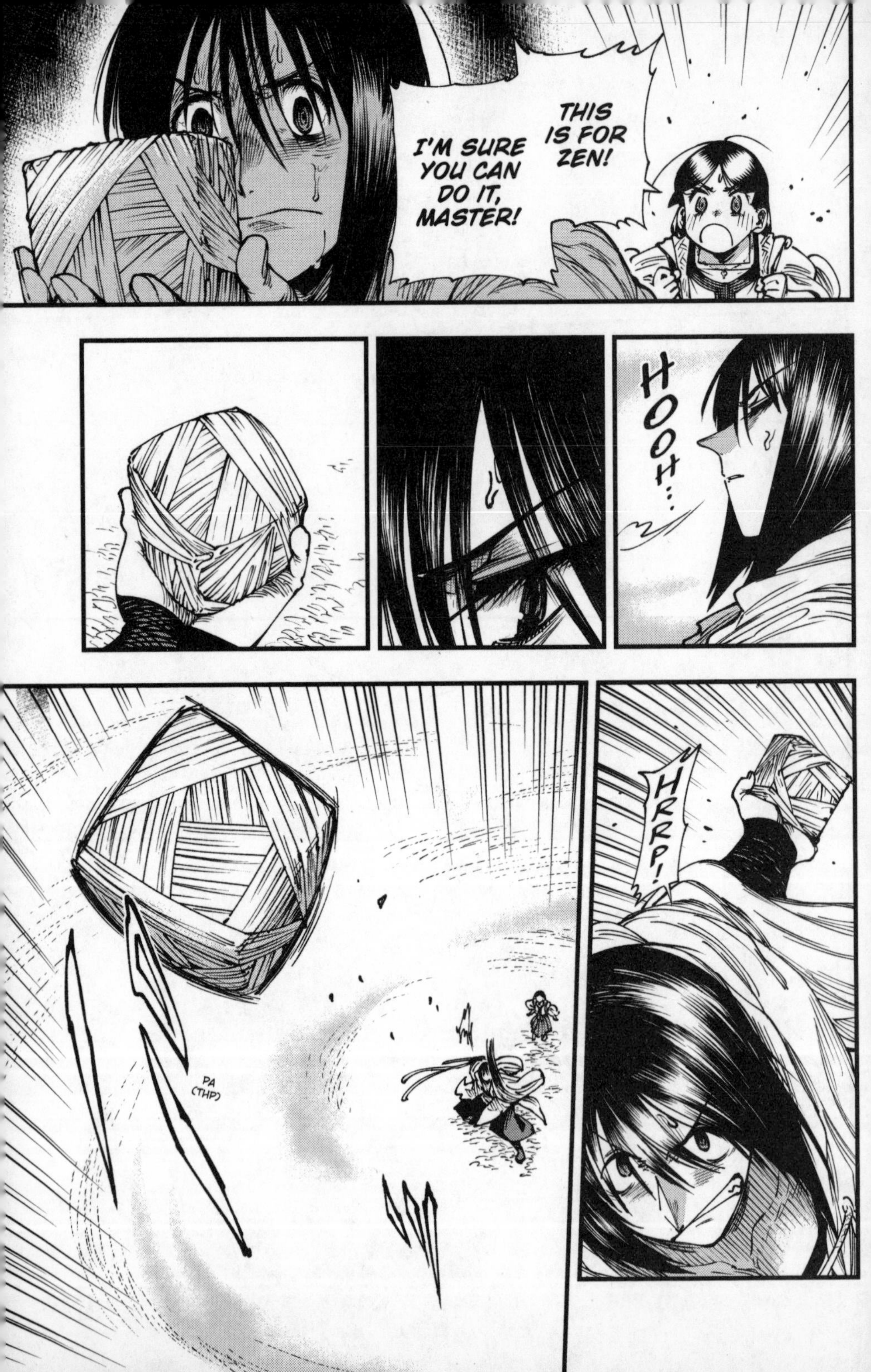
THIS IS FOR ZEN!
I'M SURE YOU CAN DO IT, MASTER!
HOOOH...
HRRP!
PA (THP)

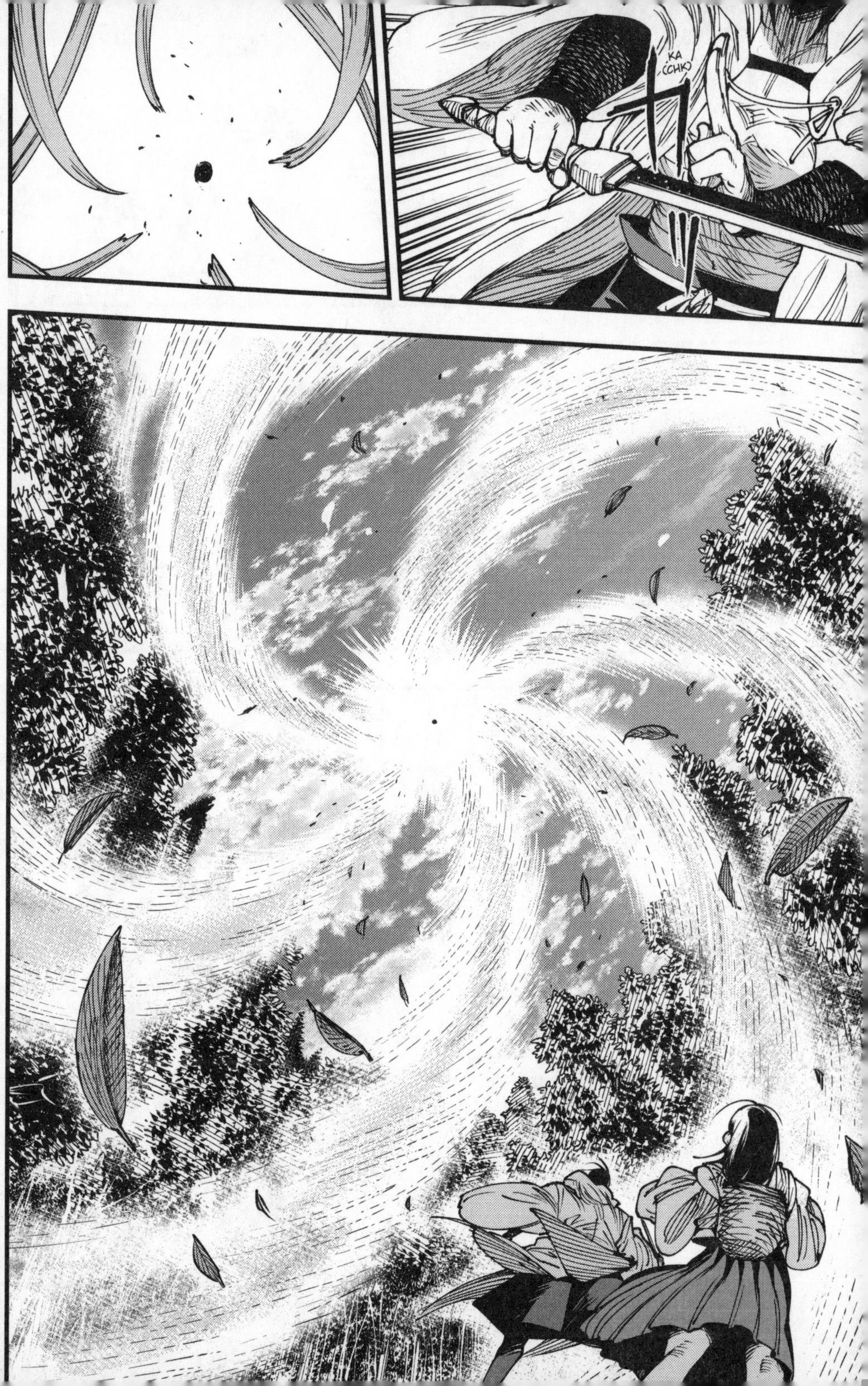
KA (CHK)

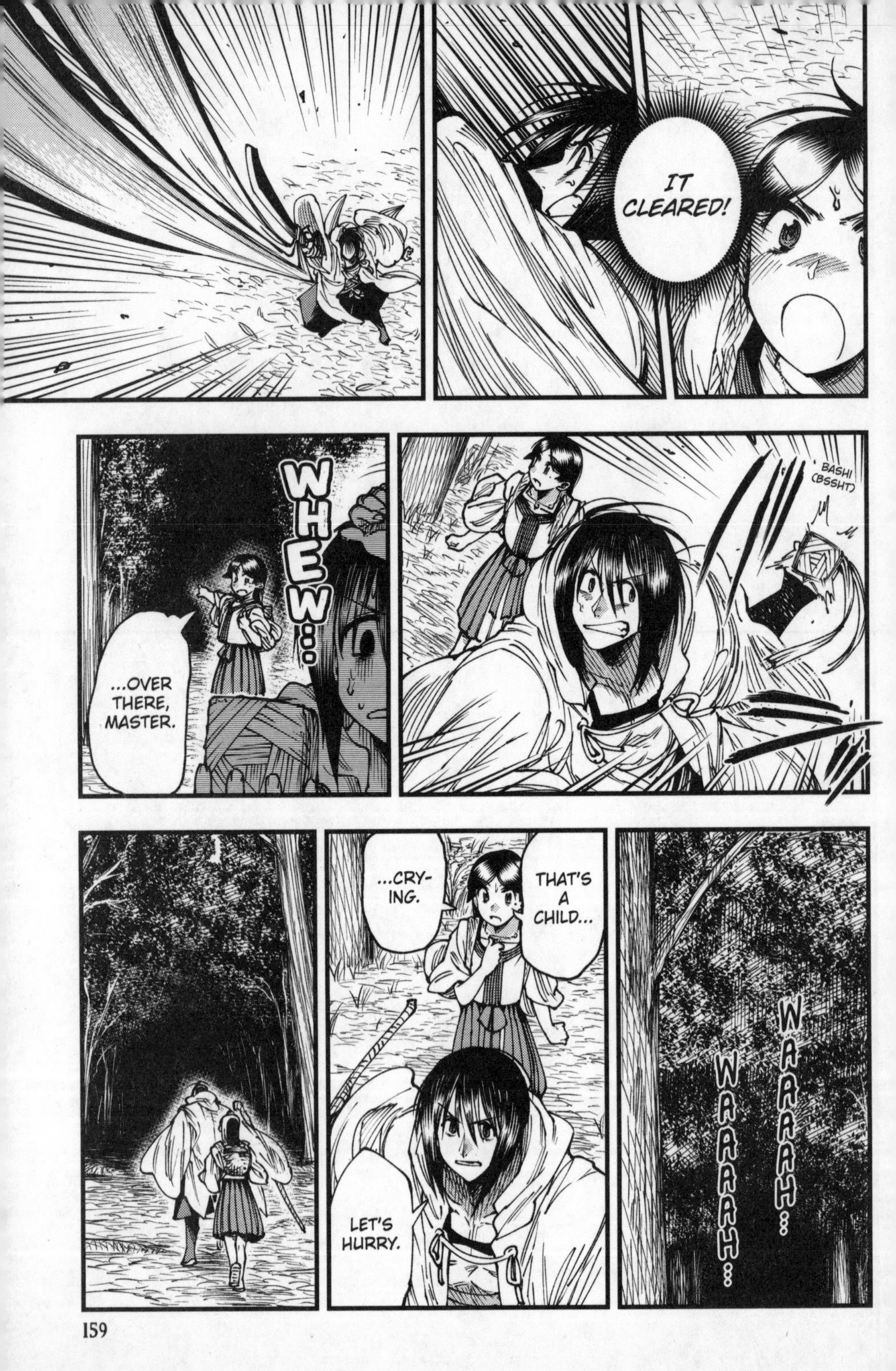
IT CLEARED!
BASHI (BSSHT)
WHEW...
...OVER THERE, MASTER.
WAAAAH...
WAAAAH...
THAT'S A CHILD...
...CRY-ING.
LET'S HURRY.

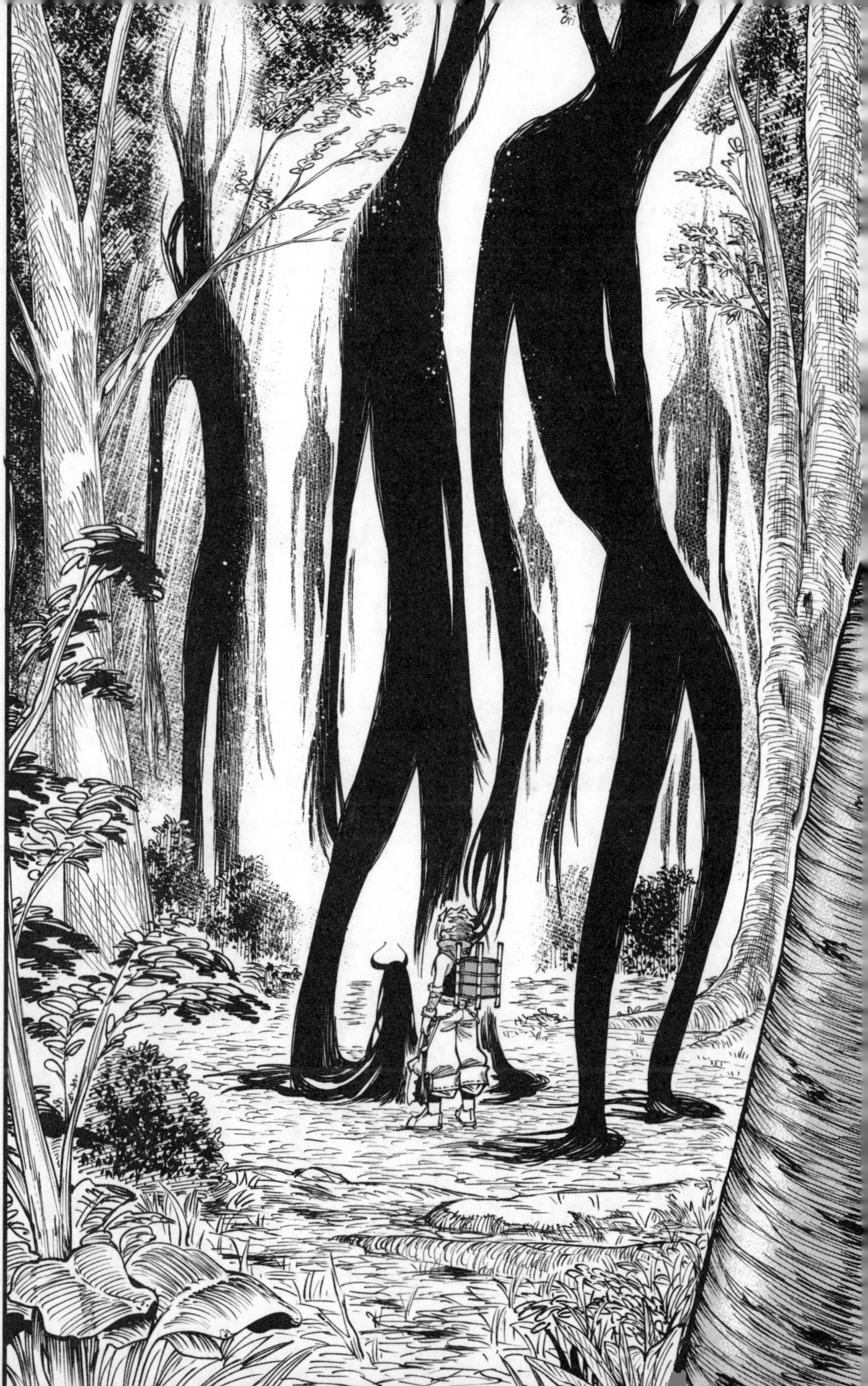

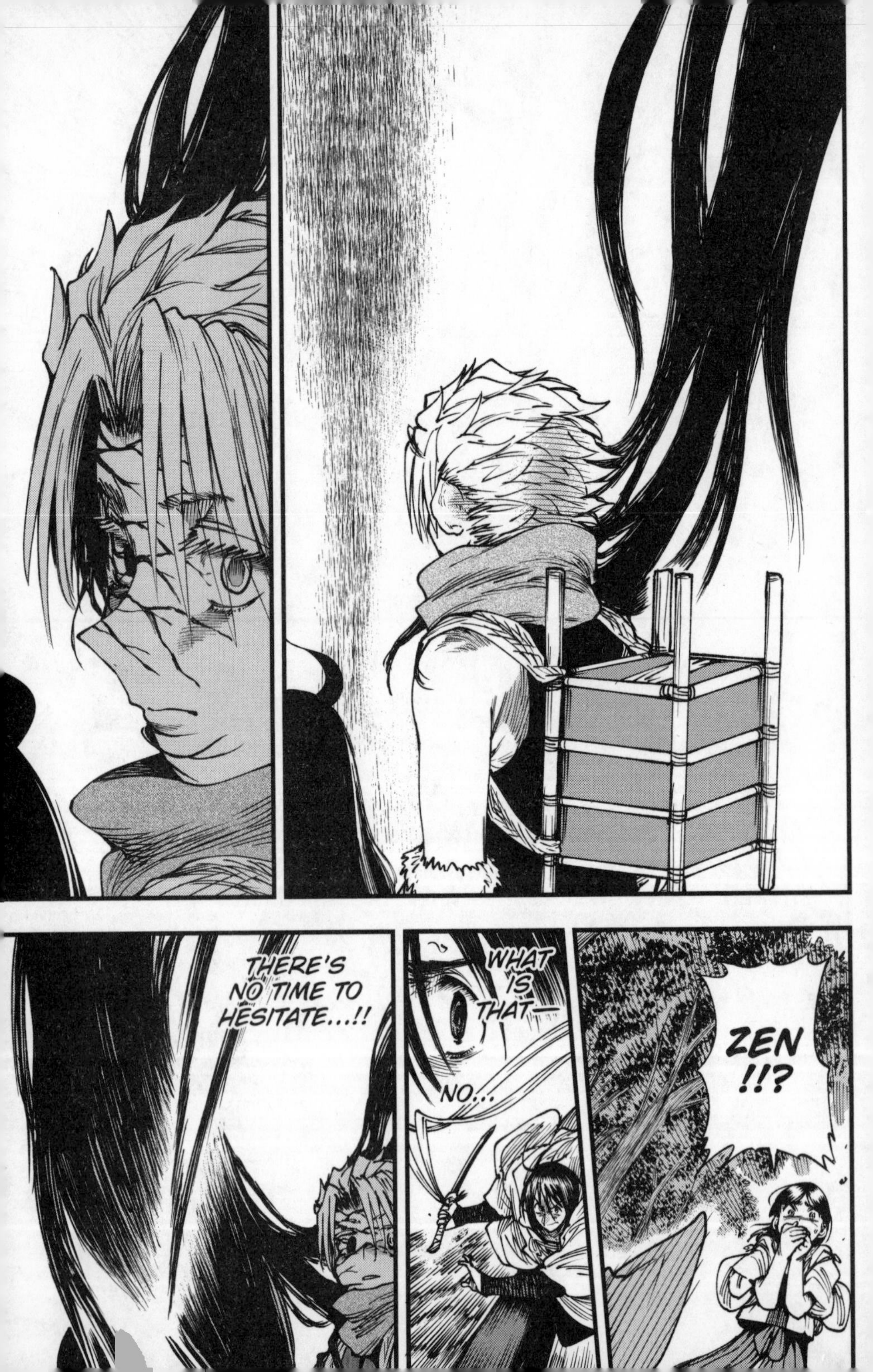
ZEN !!?
WHAT IS THAT—
NO...
THERE'S NO TIME TO HESITATE...!!

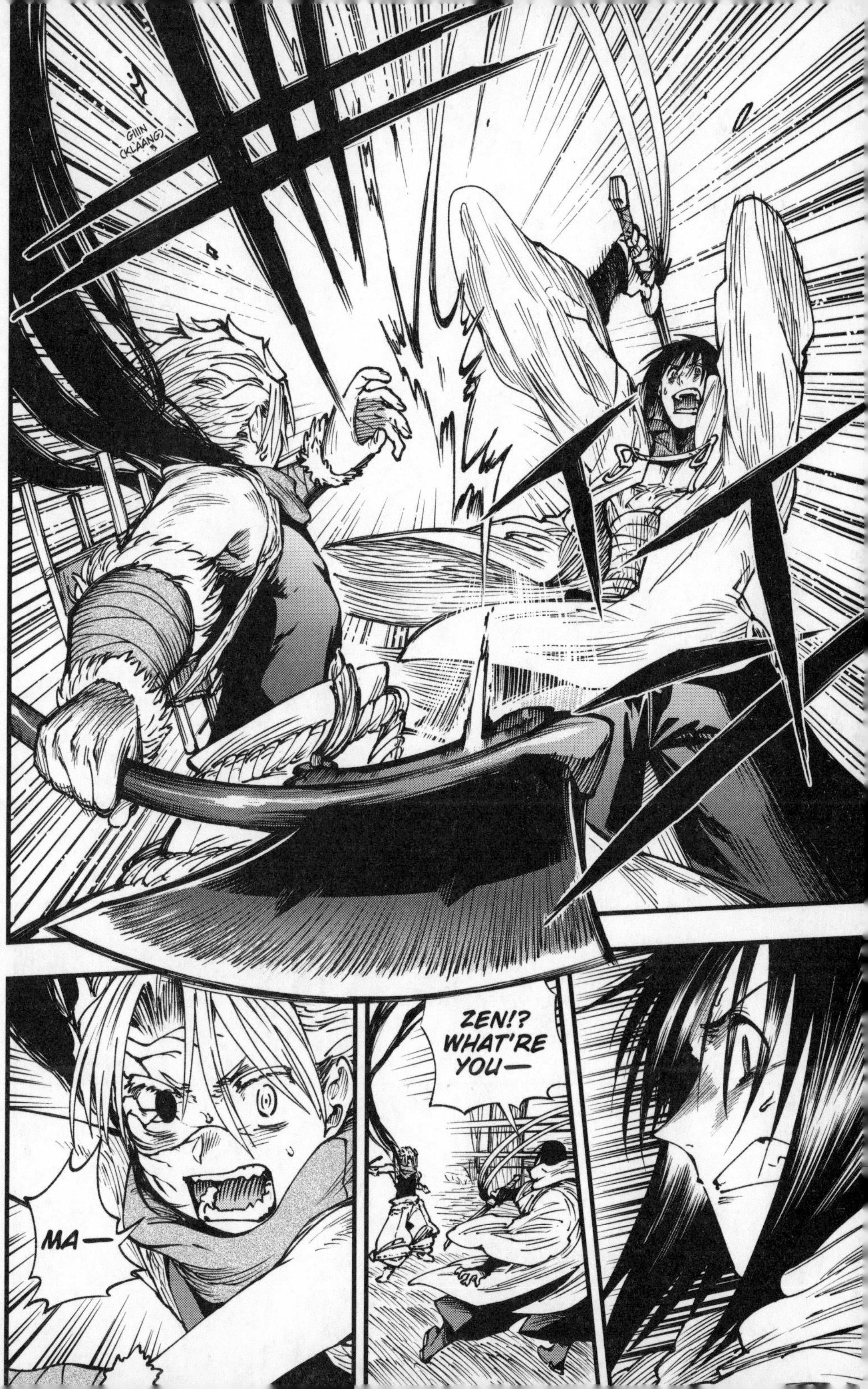
GIIIN
(KLÀÀNG)
ZEN!? WHAT'RE YOU—
MA—

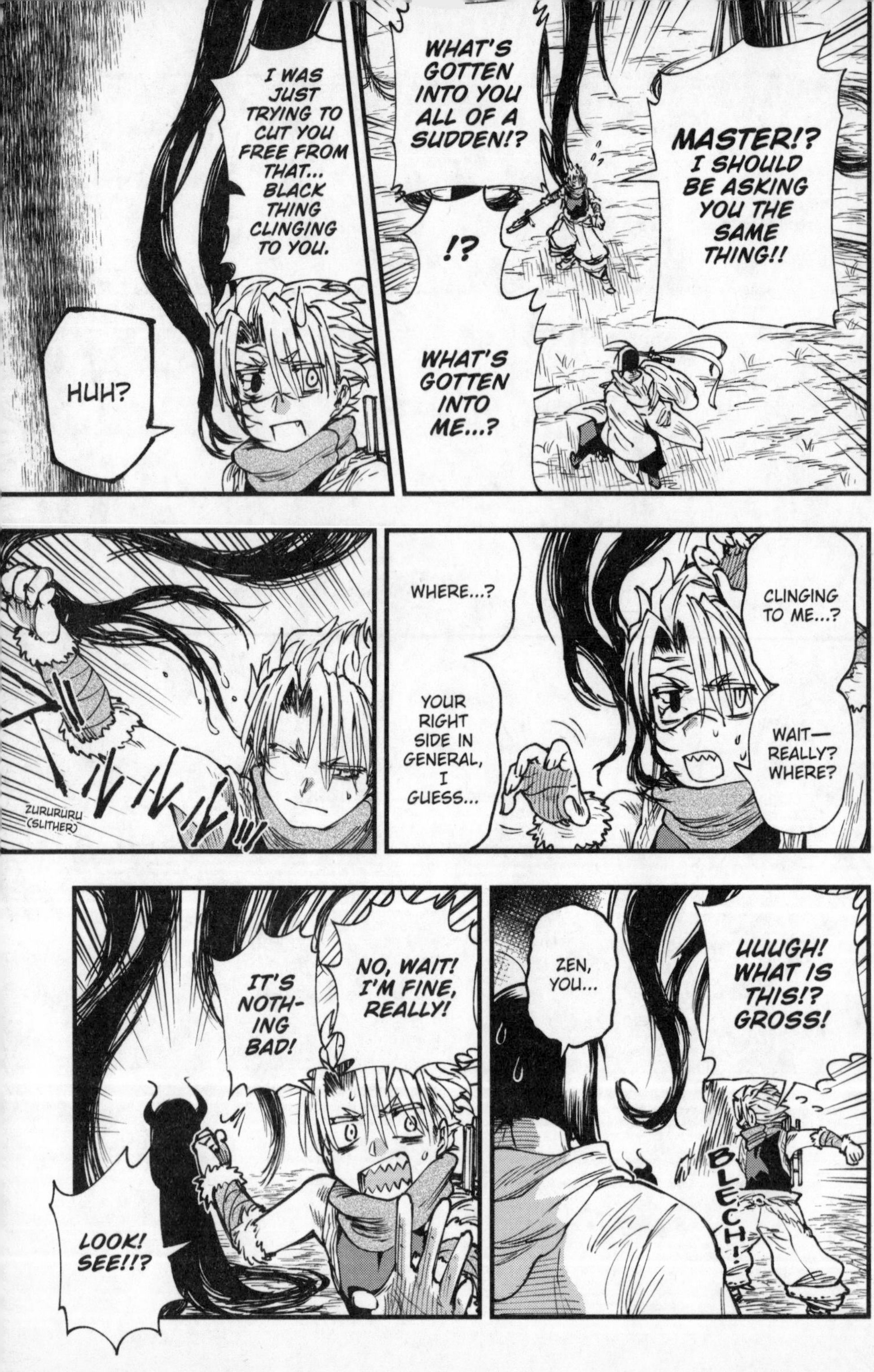
MASTER!? I SHOULD BE ASKING YOU THE SAME THING!!
WHAT'S GOTTEN INTO YOU ALL OF A SUDDEN!?
!?
WHAT'S GOTTEN INTO ME...?
I WAS JUST TRYING TO CUT YOU FREE FROM THAT... BLACK THING CLINGING TO YOU.
HUH?
CLINGING TO ME...?
WHERE...?
WAIT—REALLY? WHERE?
YOUR RIGHT SIDE IN GENERAL, I GUESS...
ZURURURU (SLITHER)
UUUGH! WHAT IS THIS!? GROSS!
ZEN, YOU...
BLECH!
NO, WAIT! I'M FINE, REALLY!
IT'S NOTHING BAD!
LOOK! SEE!!?

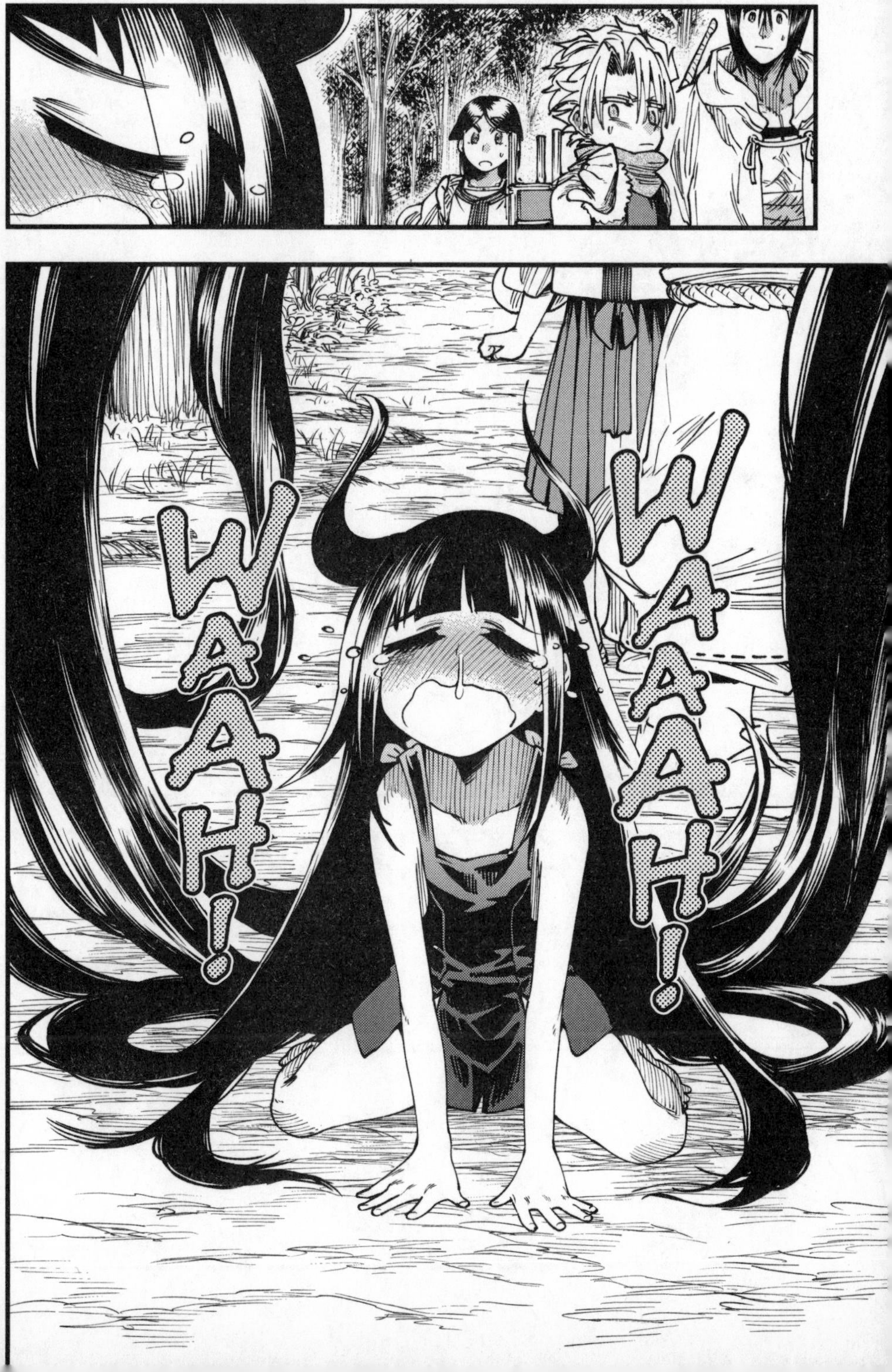
WAAAH!
WAAAH!

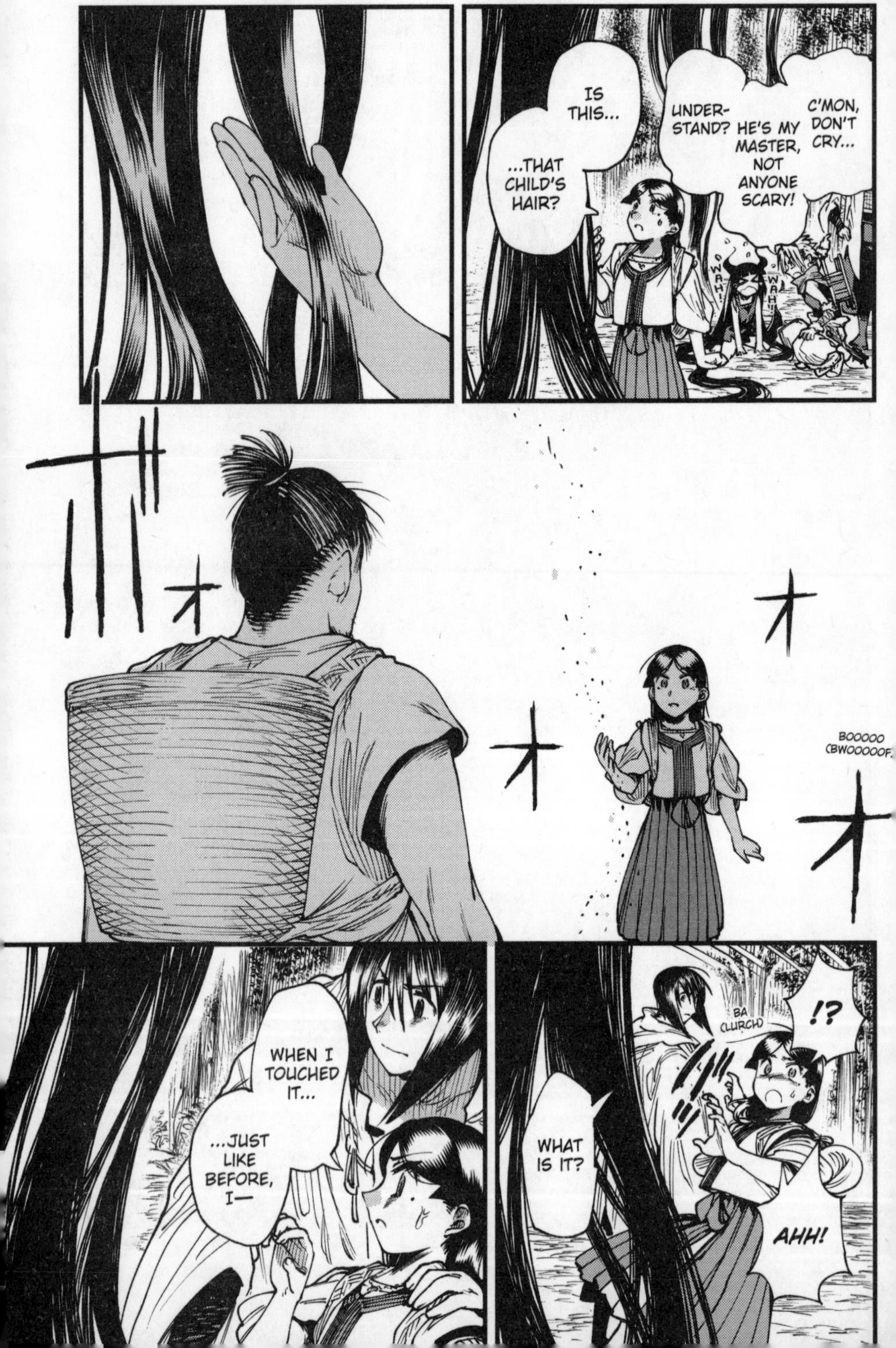
C'MON, DON'T CRY...
UNDER-STAND? HE'S MY MASTER, NOT ANYONE SCARY!
WAH!
WAH!
IS THIS...
...THAT CHILD'S HAIR?
BOOOOO (BWOOOOOF)
!?
BA (LURCH)
WHAT IS IT?
AHH!
WHEN I TOUCHED IT...
...JUST LIKE BEFORE, I—

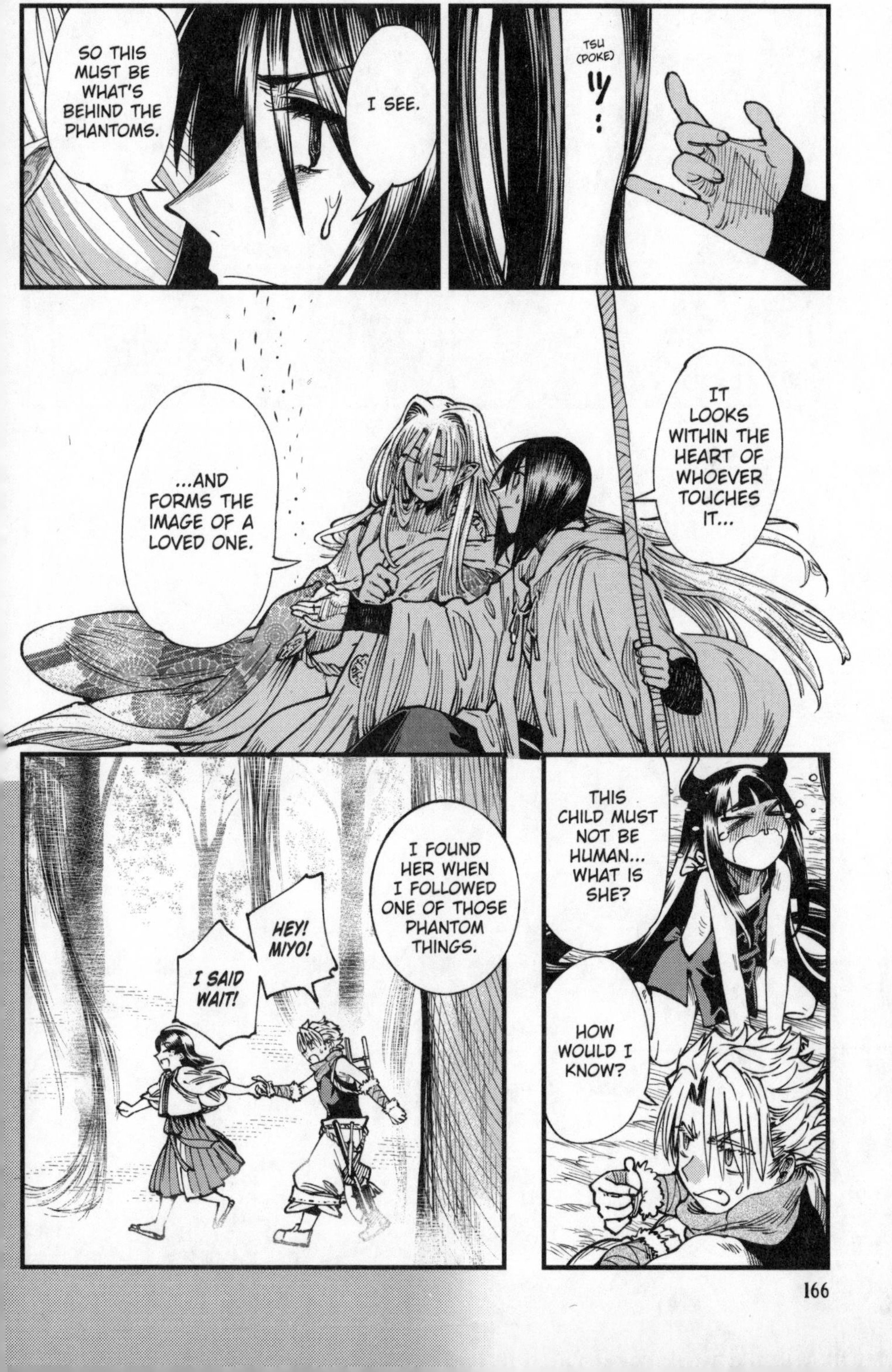
TSU (POKE)
ツ
I SEE.
SO THIS MUST BE WHAT'S BEHIND THE PHANTOMS.
IT LOOKS WITHIN THE HEART OF WHOEVER TOUCHES IT...
...AND FORMS THE IMAGE OF A LOVED ONE.
THIS CHILD MUST NOT BE HUMAN... WHAT IS SHE?
HOW WOULD I KNOW?
I FOUND HER WHEN I FOLLOWED ONE OF THOSE PHANTOM THINGS.
HEY! MIYO!
I SAID WAIT!

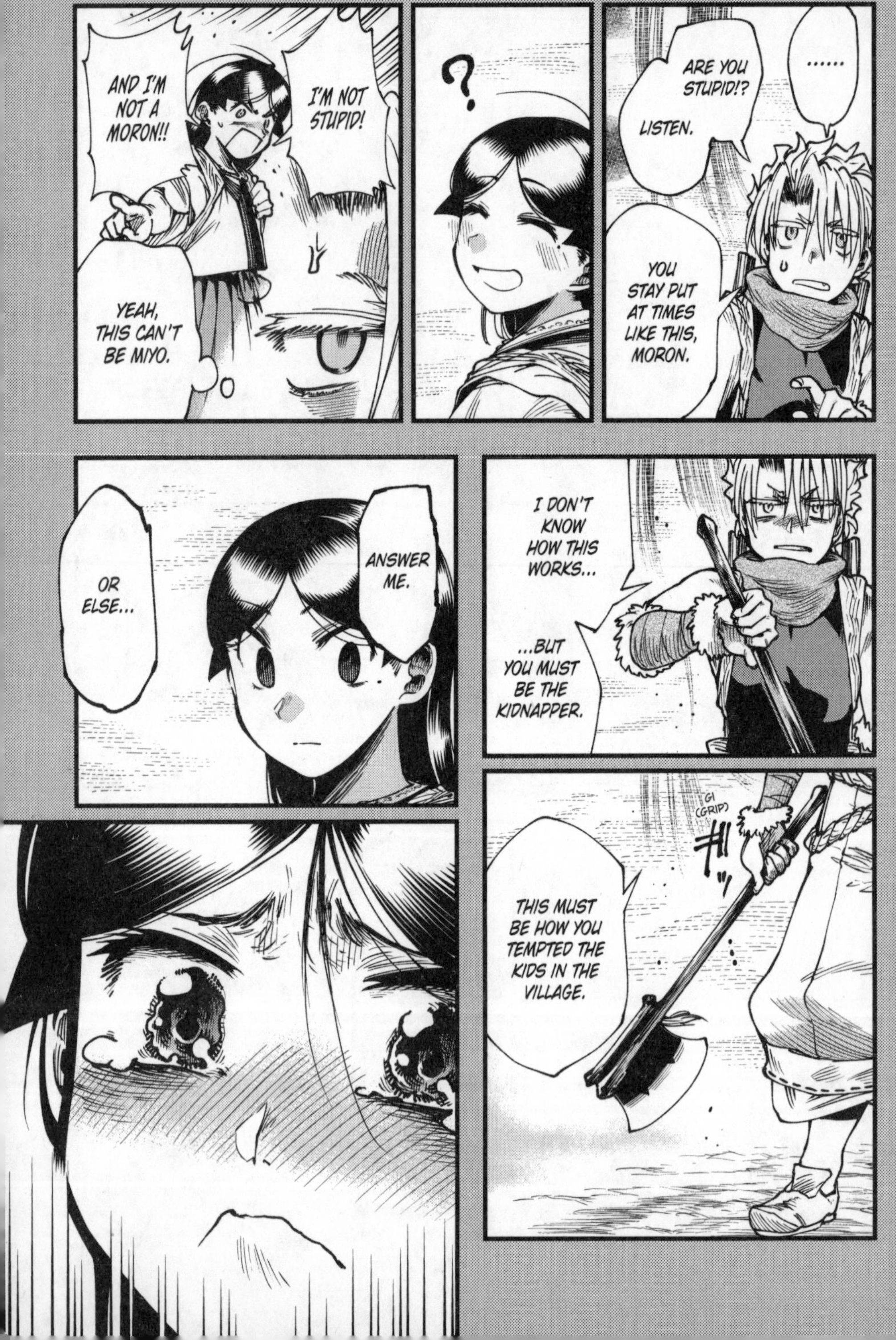
......
ARE YOU STUPID!?
LISTEN.
YOU STAY PUT AT TIMES LIKE THIS, MORON.
?
I'M NOT STUPID!
AND I'M NOT A MORON!!
YEAH, THIS CAN'T BE MIYO.
I DON'T KNOW HOW THIS WORKS...
...BUT YOU MUST BE THE KIDNAPPER.
ANSWER ME.
OR ELSE...
GI (GRIP)
THIS MUST BE HOW YOU TEMPTED THE KIDS IN THE VILLAGE.

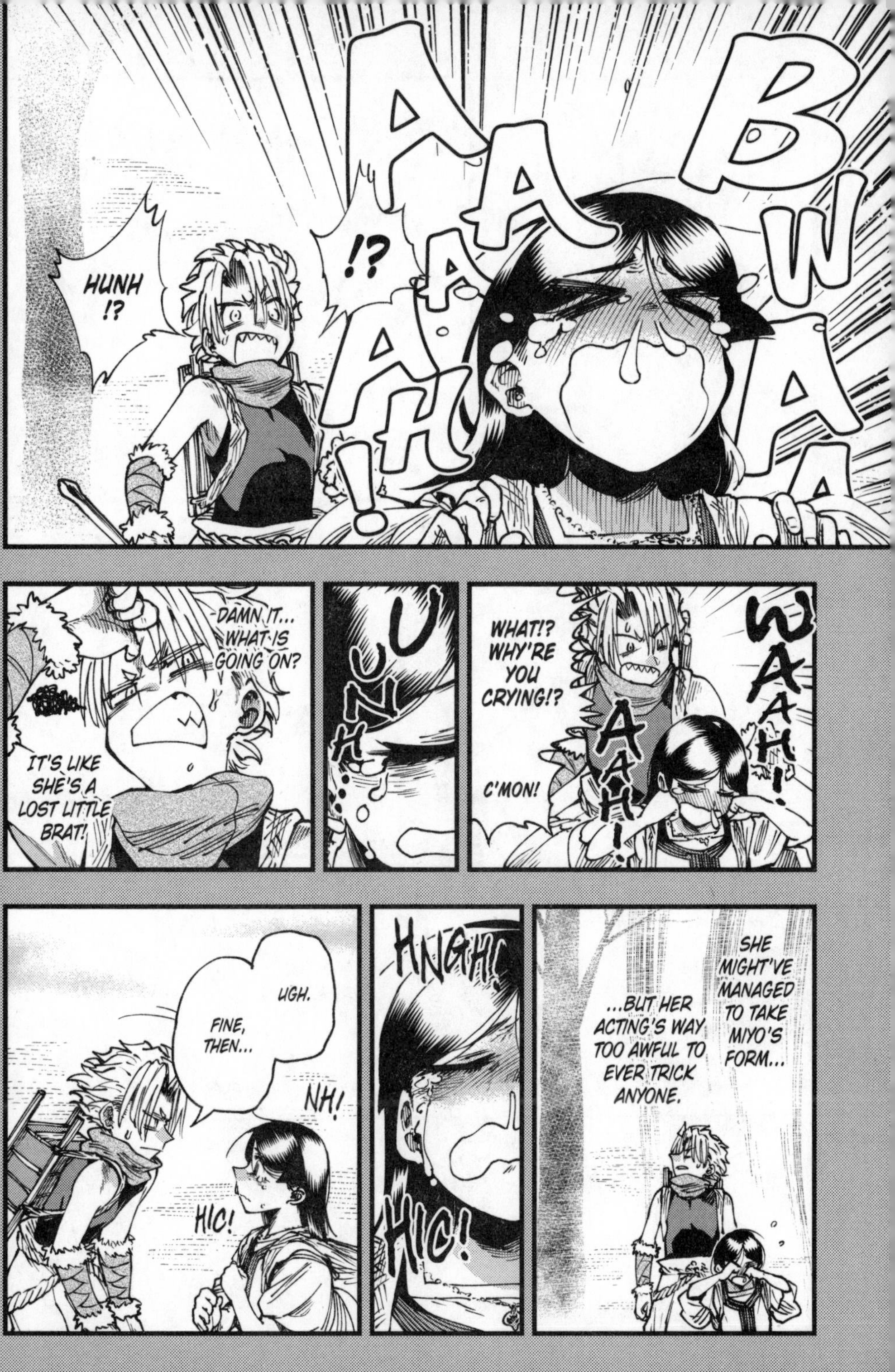
BWAA
AAAAH!
!?
HUNH !?
WAAH!
WHAT!? WHY'RE YOU CRYING!?
AAH!
C'MON!
UUNH...
DAMN IT... WHAT IS GOING ON?
IT'S LIKE SHE'S A LOST LITTLE BRAT!
SHE MIGHT'VE MANAGED TO TAKE MIYO'S FORM...
...BUT HER ACTING'S WAY TOO AWFUL TO EVER TRICK ANYONE.
HNGH!
HIC!
UGH.
FINE, THEN...
NH!
HIC!

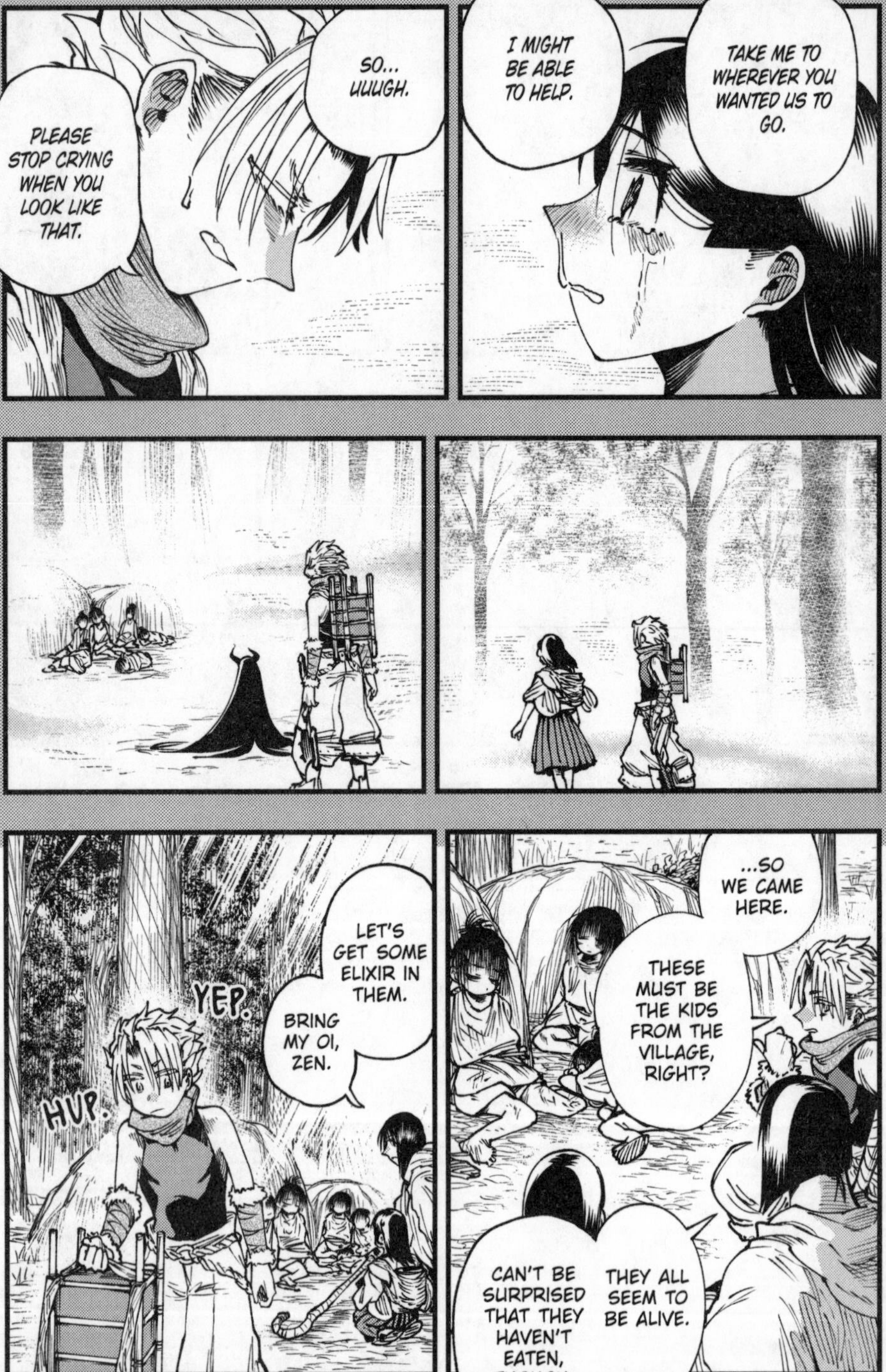
TAKE ME TO WHEREVER YOU WANTED US TO GO.
I MIGHT BE ABLE TO HELP.
SO... UUUGH.
PLEASE STOP CRYING WHEN YOU LOOK LIKE THAT.
...SO WE CAME HERE.
THESE MUST BE THE KIDS FROM THE VILLAGE, RIGHT?
THEY ALL SEEM TO BE ALIVE.
CAN'T BE SURPRISED THAT THEY HAVEN'T EATEN, THOUGH.
LET'S GET SOME ELIXIR IN THEM.
BRING MY OI, ZEN.
YEP.
HUP.

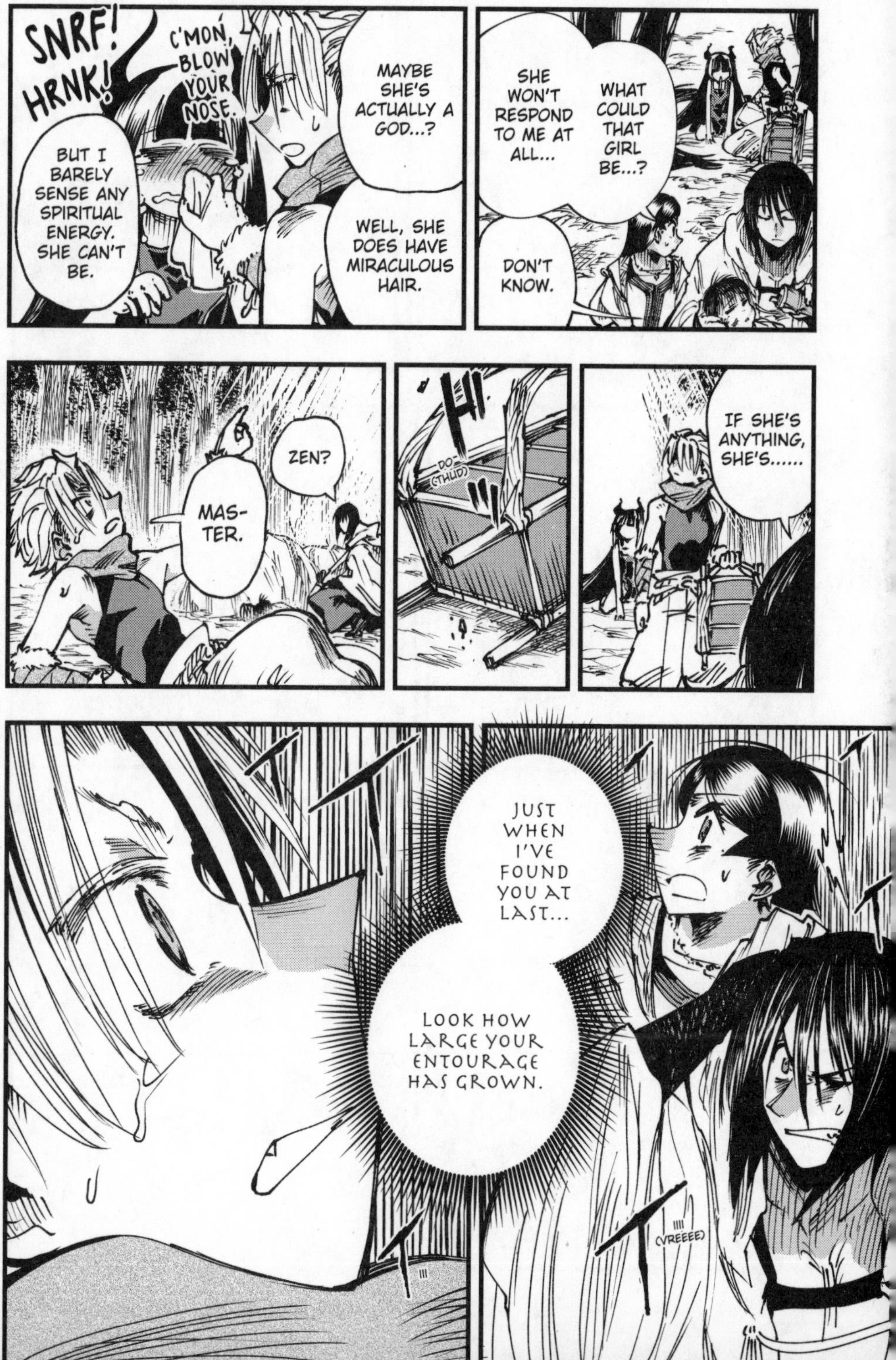
WHAT COULD THAT GIRL BE...?
SHE WON'T RESPOND TO ME AT ALL...
DON'T KNOW.
MAYBE SHE'S ACTUALLY A GOD...?
C'MON, BLOW YOUR NOSE.
SNRF! HRNK!
WELL, SHE DOES HAVE MIRACULOUS HAIR.
BUT I BARELY SENSE ANY SPIRITUAL ENERGY. SHE CAN'T BE.
IF SHE'S ANYTHING, SHE'S......
DO- (THUD)
ZEN?
MAS-TER.
JUST WHEN I'VE FOUND YOU AT LAST...
LOOK HOW LARGE YOUR ENTOURAGE HAS GROWN.
(VREEEE)

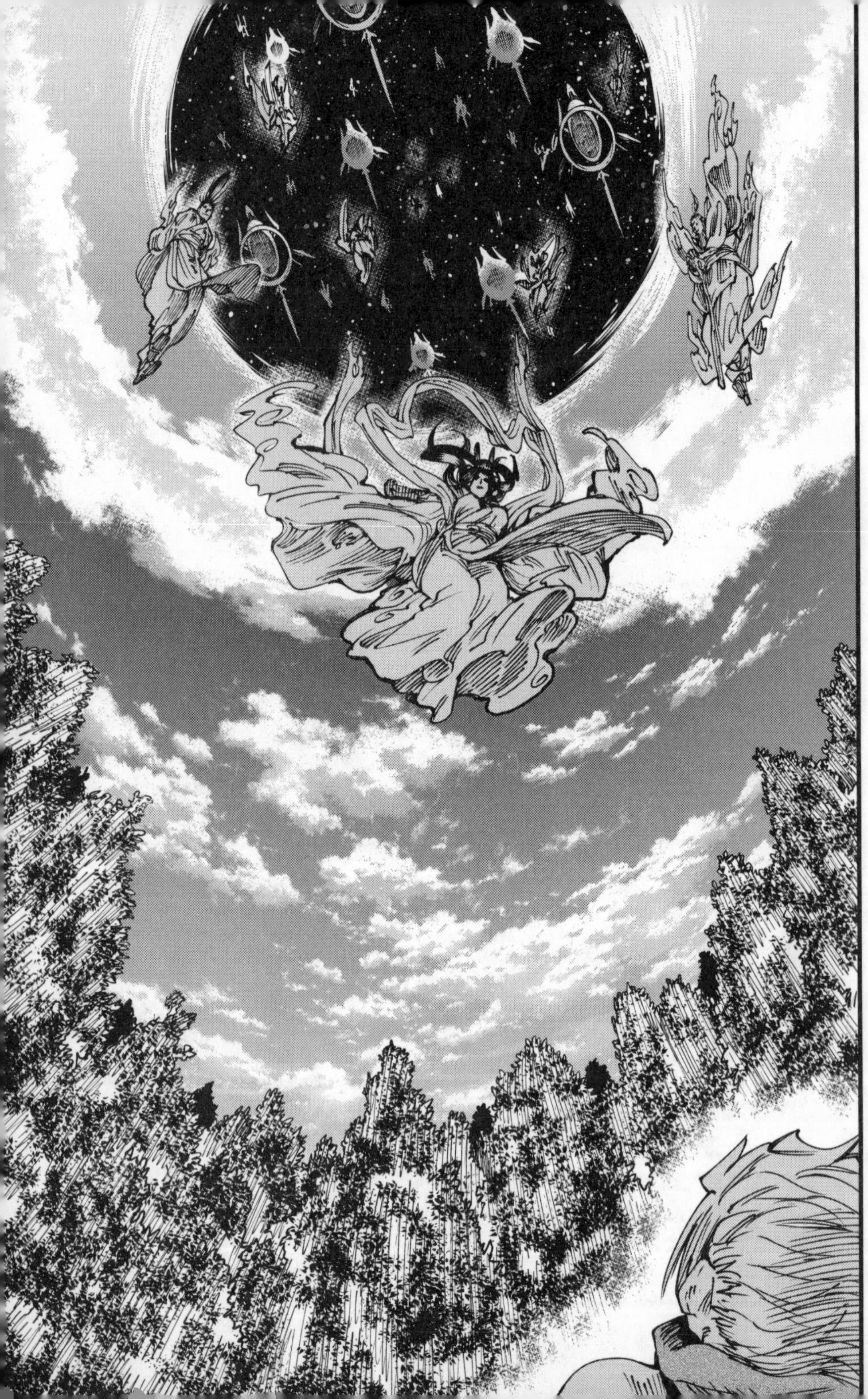

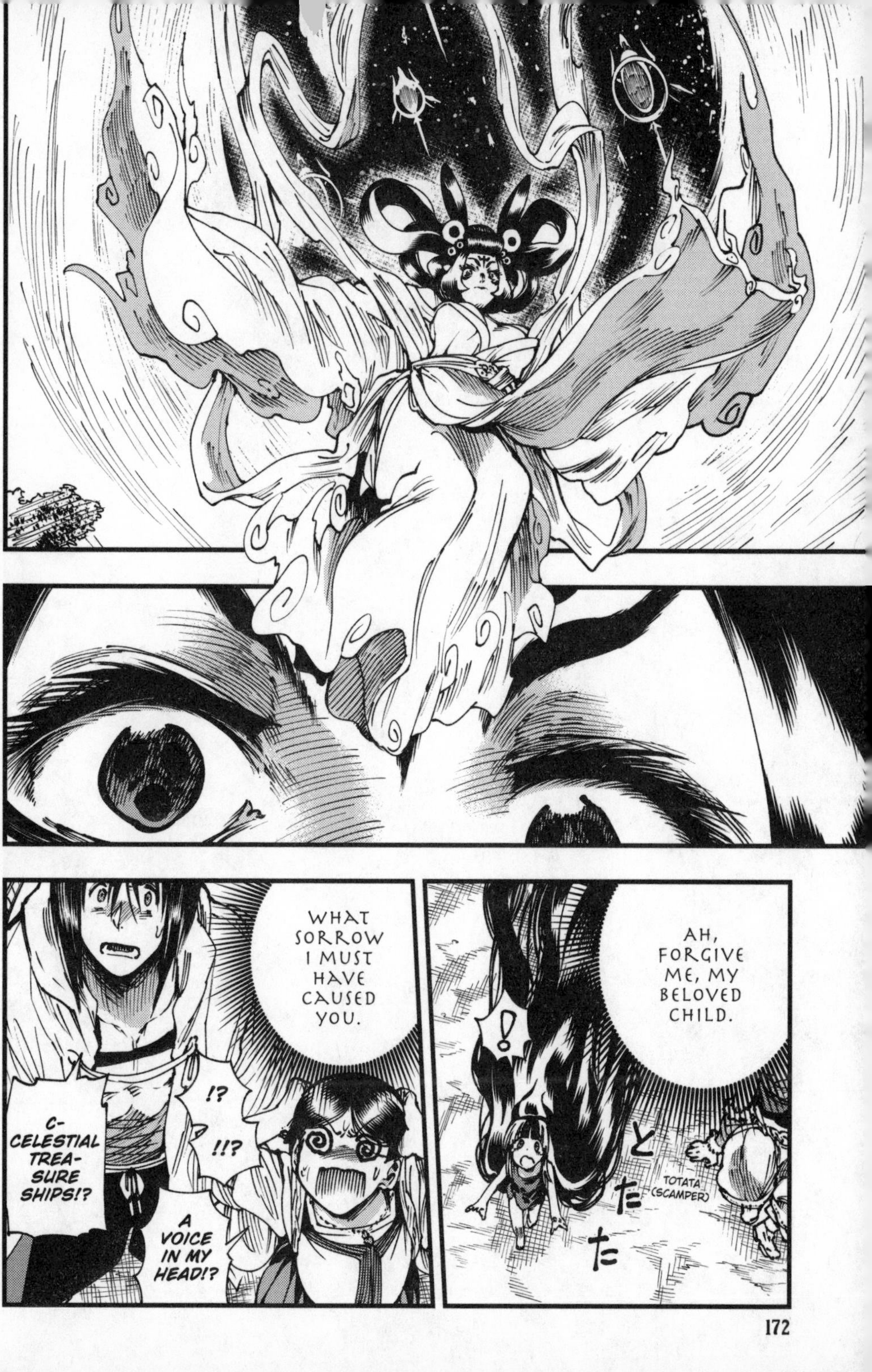
AH, FORGIVE ME, MY BELOVED CHILD.
!
とたた
TOTATA (SCAMPER)
WHAT SORROW I MUST HAVE CAUSED YOU.
!?
!!?
C-CELESTIAL TREA-SURE SHIPS!?
A VOICE IN MY HEAD!?

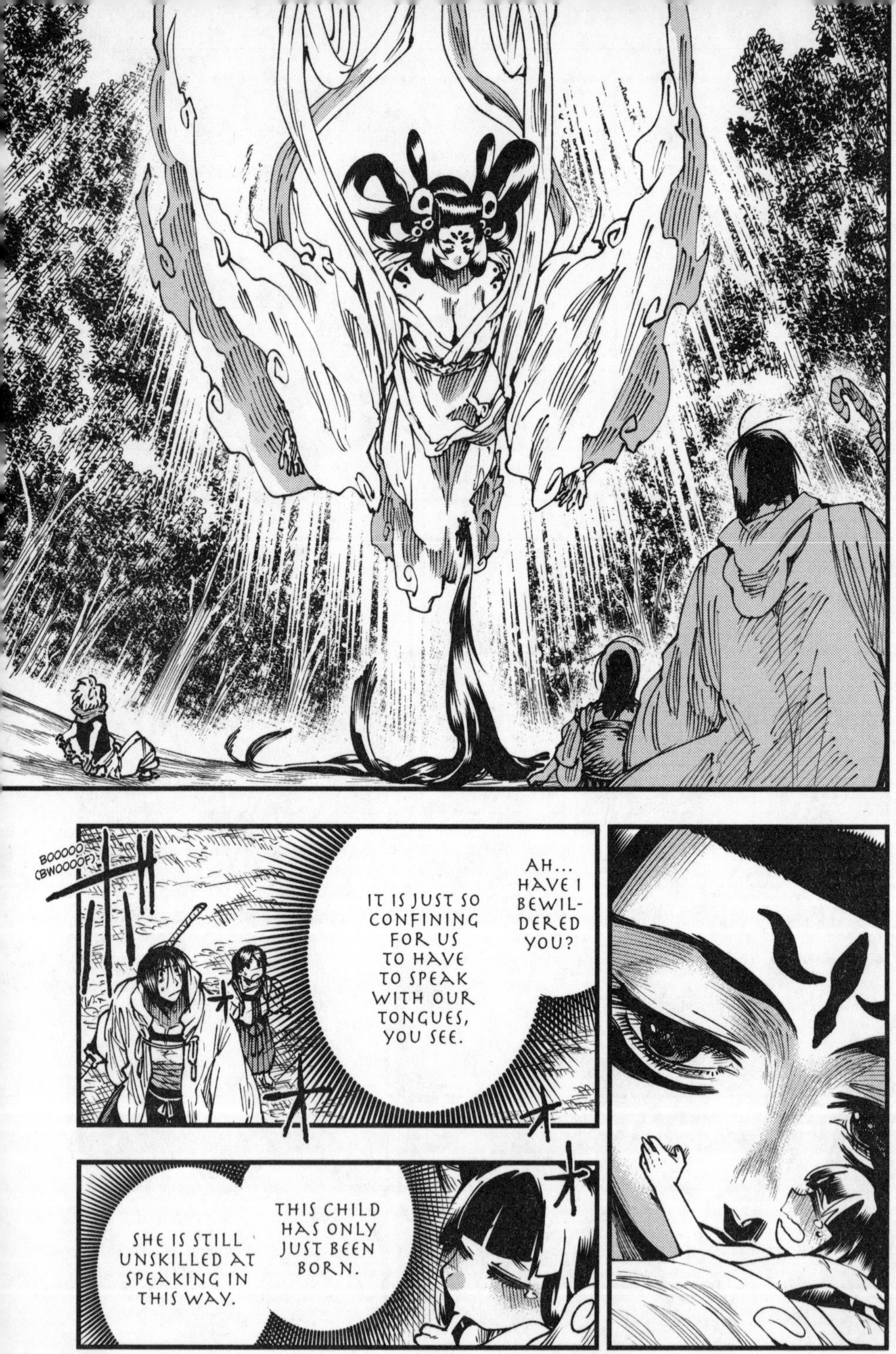
AH... HAVE I BEWIL-DERED YOU?
IT IS JUST SO CONFINING FOR US TO HAVE TO SPEAK WITH OUR TONGUES, YOU SEE.
BOOOOO (BWOOOOP)
THIS CHILD HAS ONLY JUST BEEN BORN.
SHE IS STILL UNSKILLED AT SPEAKING IN THIS WAY.

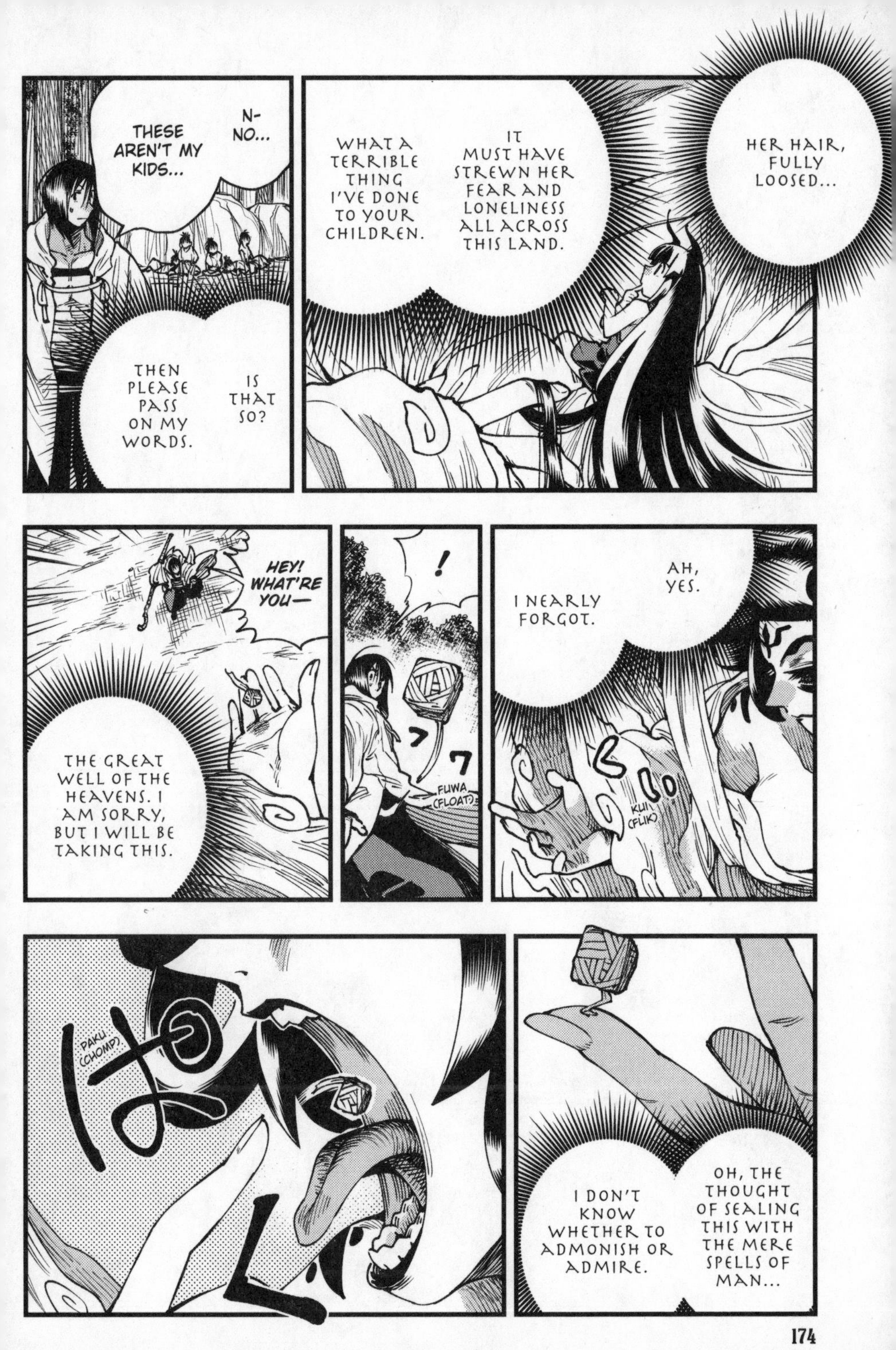
HER HAIR, FULLY LOOSED...
IT MUST HAVE STREWN HER FEAR AND LONELINESS ALL ACROSS THIS LAND.
WHAT A TERRIBLE THING I'VE DONE TO YOUR CHILDREN.
N-NO...
THESE AREN'T MY KIDS...
IS THAT SO?
THEN PLEASE PASS ON MY WORDS.
AH, YES.
I NEARLY FORGOT.
KUI (FLIK)
!
FUWA (FLOAT)
HEY! WHAT'RE YOU—
THE GREAT WELL OF THE HEAVENS. I AM SORRY, BUT I WILL BE TAKING THIS.
OH, THE THOUGHT OF SEALING THIS WITH THE MERE SPELLS OF MAN...
I DON'T KNOW WHETHER TO ADMONISH OR ADMIRE.
PAKU (CHOMP)

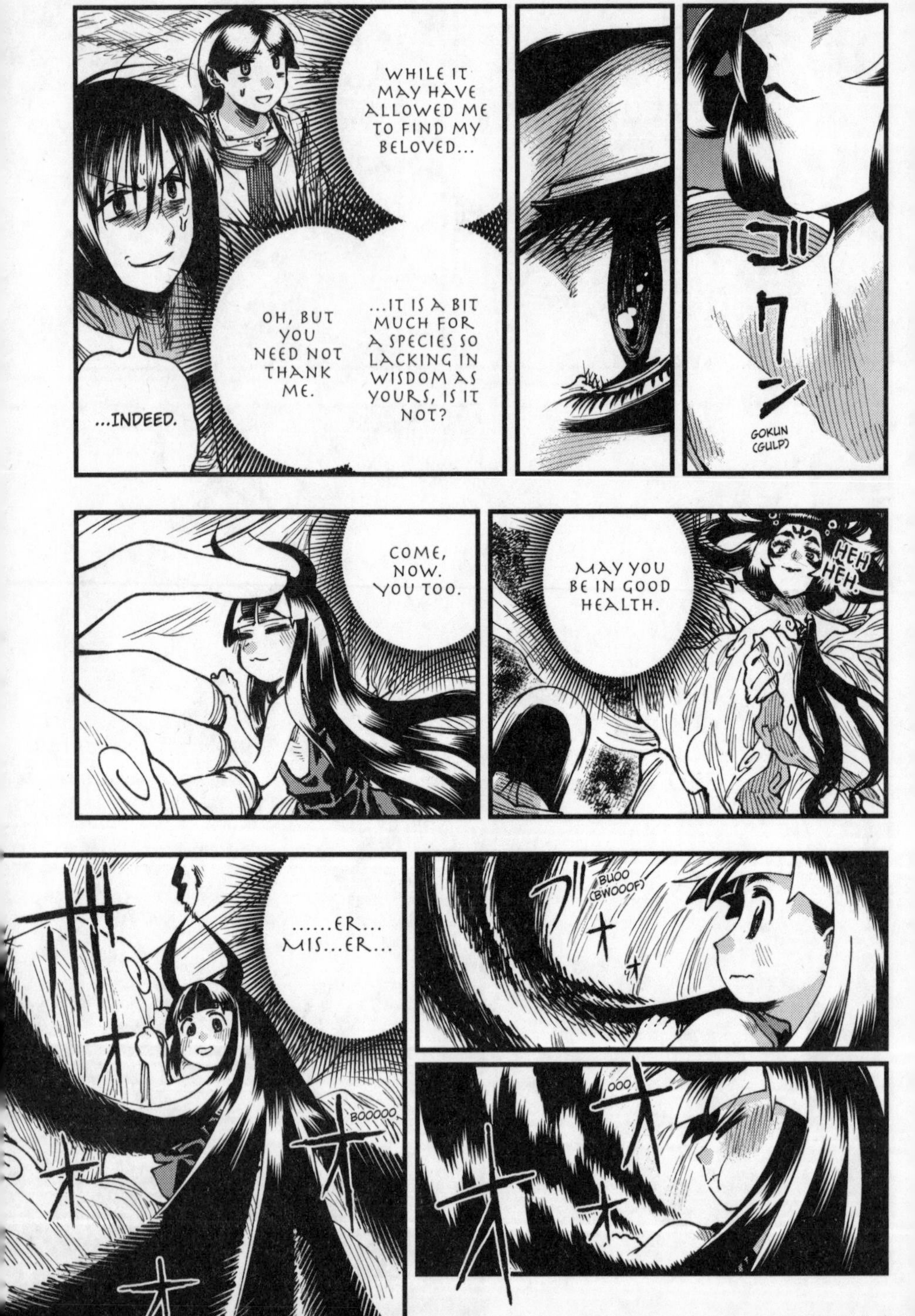
ゴクン
GOKUN (GULP)
WHILE IT MAY HAVE ALLOWED ME TO FIND MY BELOVED...
...IT IS A BIT MUCH FOR A SPECIES SO LACKING IN WISDOM AS YOURS, IS IT NOT?
OH, BUT YOU NEED NOT THANK ME.
...INDEED.
MAY YOU BE IN GOOD HEALTH.
HEH HEH.
COME, NOW. YOU TOO.
BUOO (BWOOOF)
OOO
......ER... MIS...ER...
BOOOOO

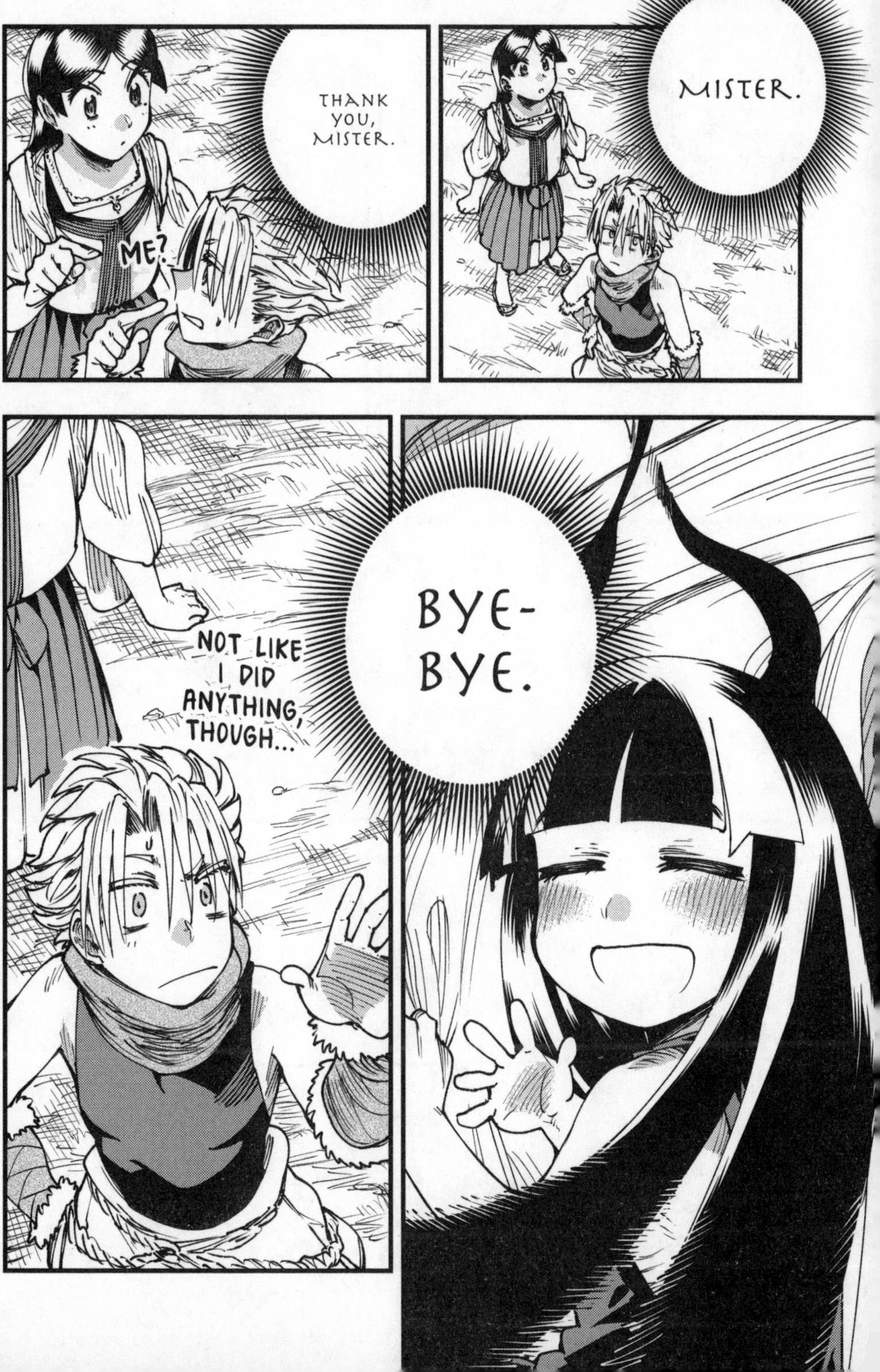
MISTER.
THANK YOU, MISTER.
ME?
BYE-BYE.
NOT LIKE I DID ANYTHING, THOUGH...

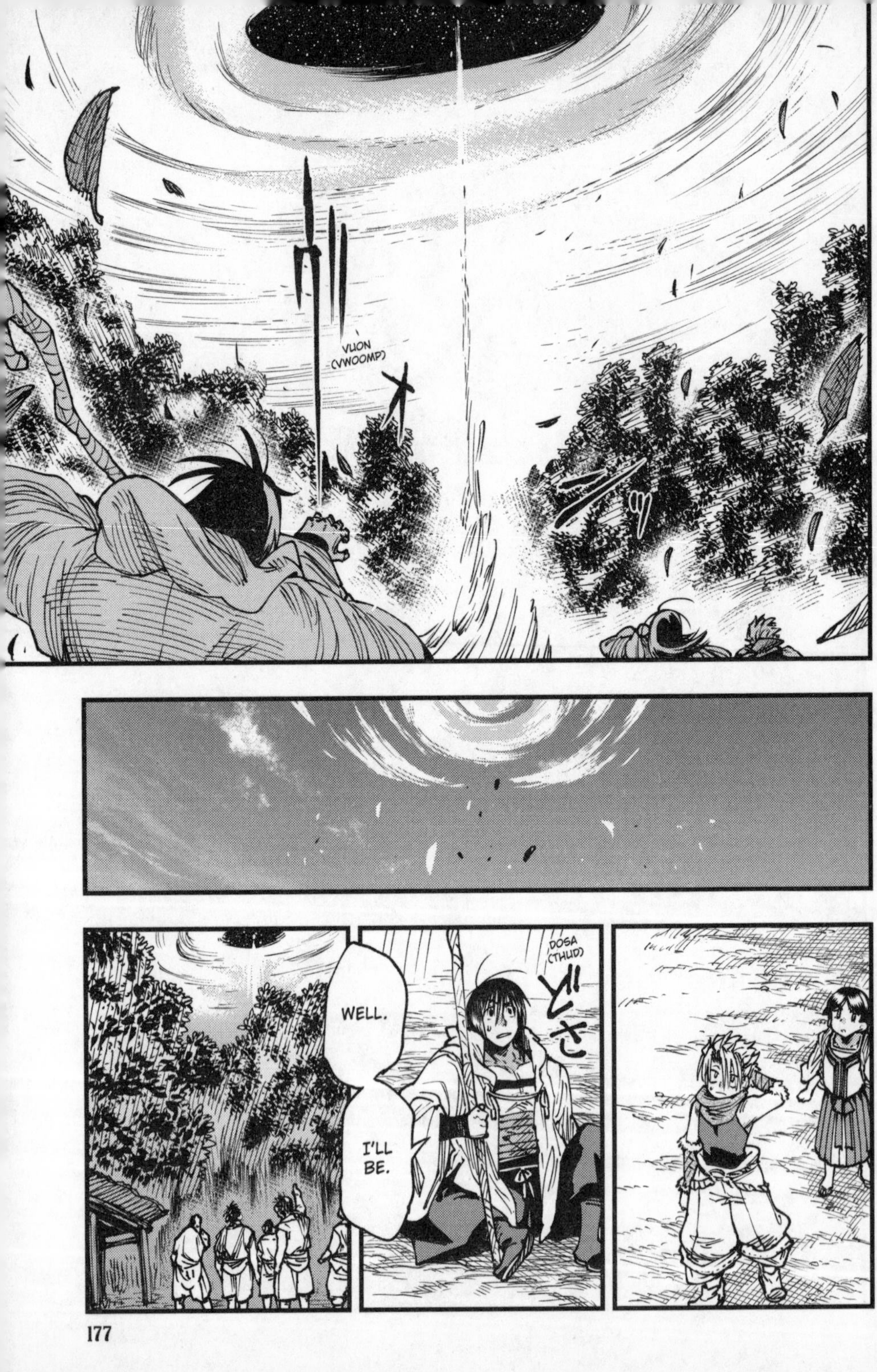
VUON
(VWOOMP)
DOSA
(THUD)
どさ
WELL.
I'LL BE.

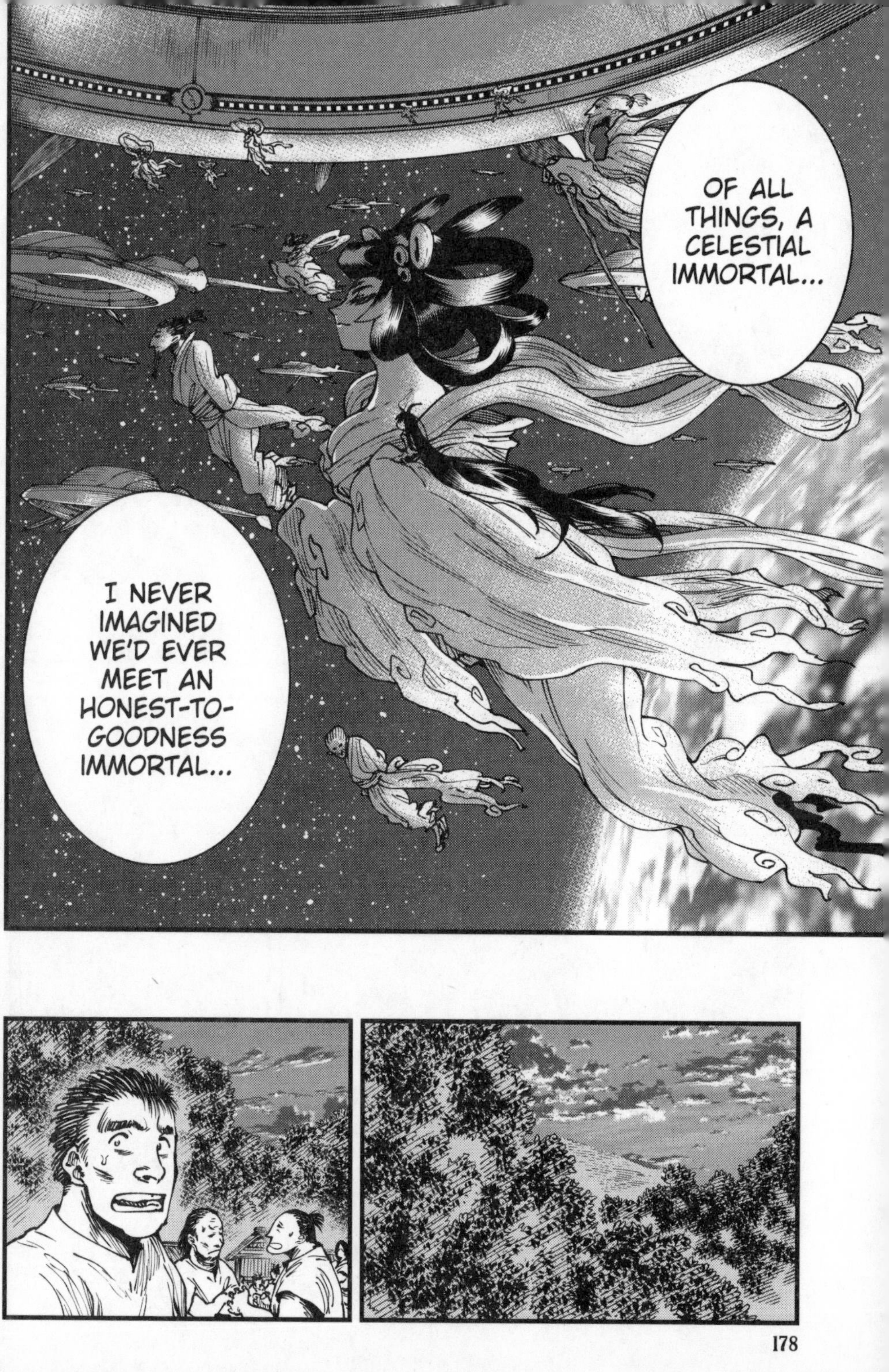
OF ALL THINGS, A CELESTIAL IMMORTAL...
I NEVER IMAGINED WE'D EVER MEET AN HONEST-TO-GOODNESS IMMORTAL...

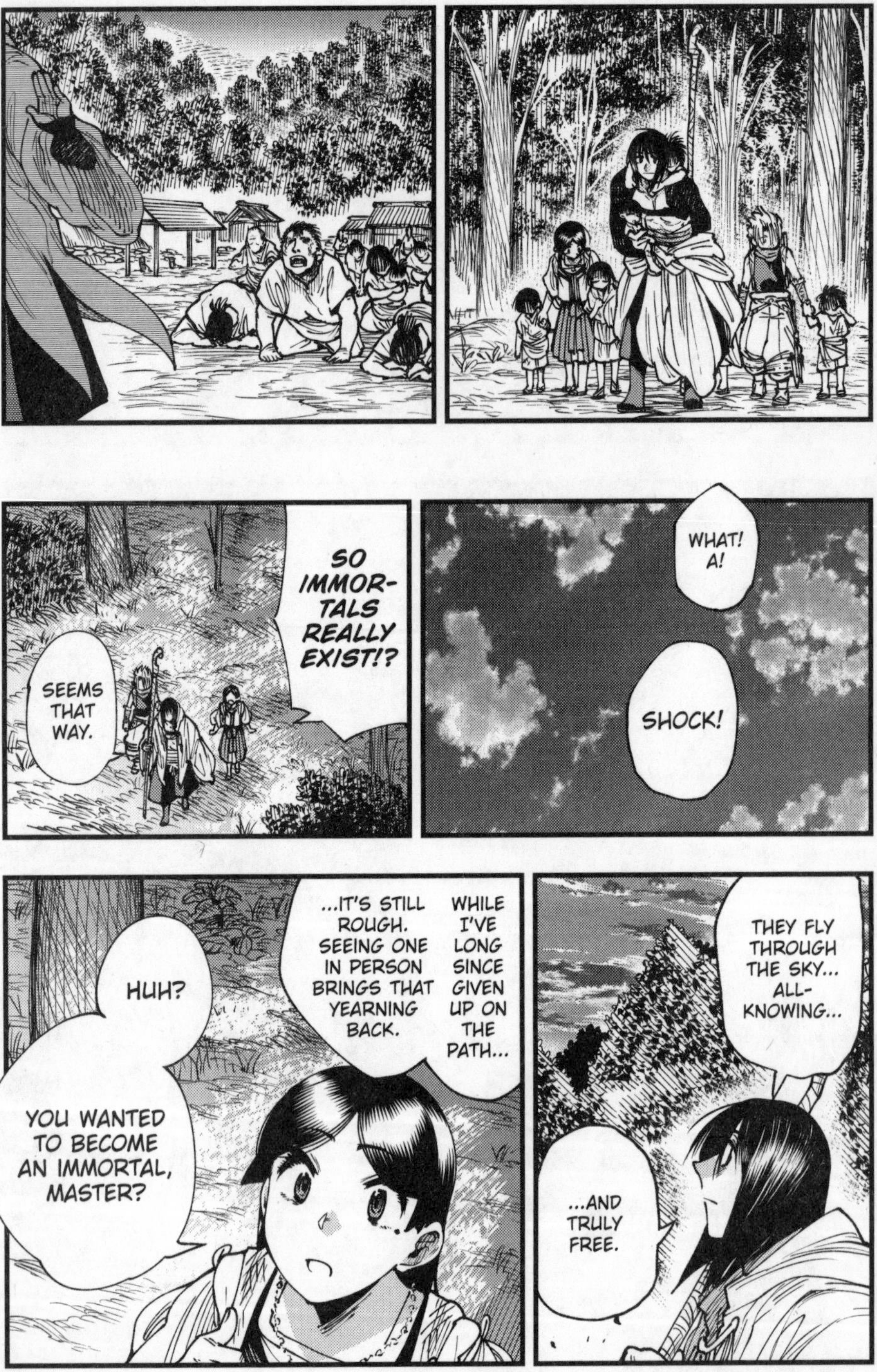
WHAT! A!
SHOCK!
SO IMMORTALS REALLY EXIST!?
SEEMS THAT WAY.
THEY FLY THROUGH THE SKY... ALL-KNOWING...
...AND TRULY FREE.
WHILE I'VE LONG SINCE GIVEN UP ON THE PATH...
...IT'S STILL ROUGH. SEEING ONE IN PERSON BRINGS THAT YEARNING BACK.
HUH?
YOU WANTED TO BECOME AN IMMORTAL, MASTER?

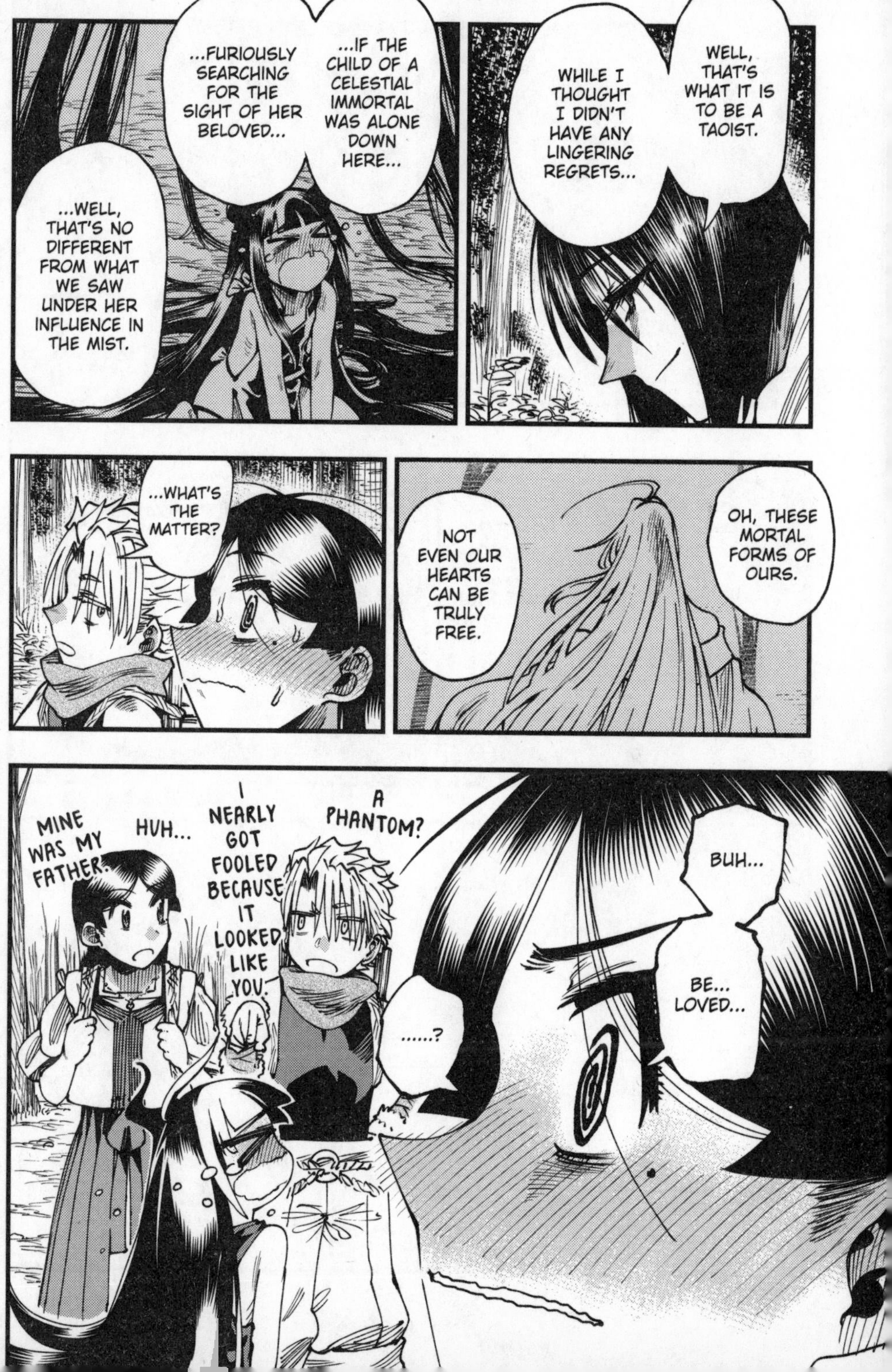
WELL, THAT'S WHAT IT IS TO BE A TAOIST.
WHILE I THOUGHT I DIDN'T HAVE ANY LINGERING REGRETS...
...IF THE CHILD OF A CELESTIAL IMMORTAL WAS ALONE DOWN HERE...
...FURIOUSLY SEARCHING FOR THE SIGHT OF HER BELOVED...
...WELL, THAT'S NO DIFFERENT FROM WHAT WE SAW UNDER HER INFLUENCE IN THE MIST.
OH, THESE MORTAL FORMS OF OURS.
NOT EVEN OUR HEARTS CAN BE TRULY FREE.
...WHAT'S THE MATTER?
BUH...
BE... LOVED...
......?
A PHANTOM?
I NEARLY GOT FOOLED BECAUSE IT LOOKED LIKE YOU.
HUH...
MINE WAS MY FATHER.

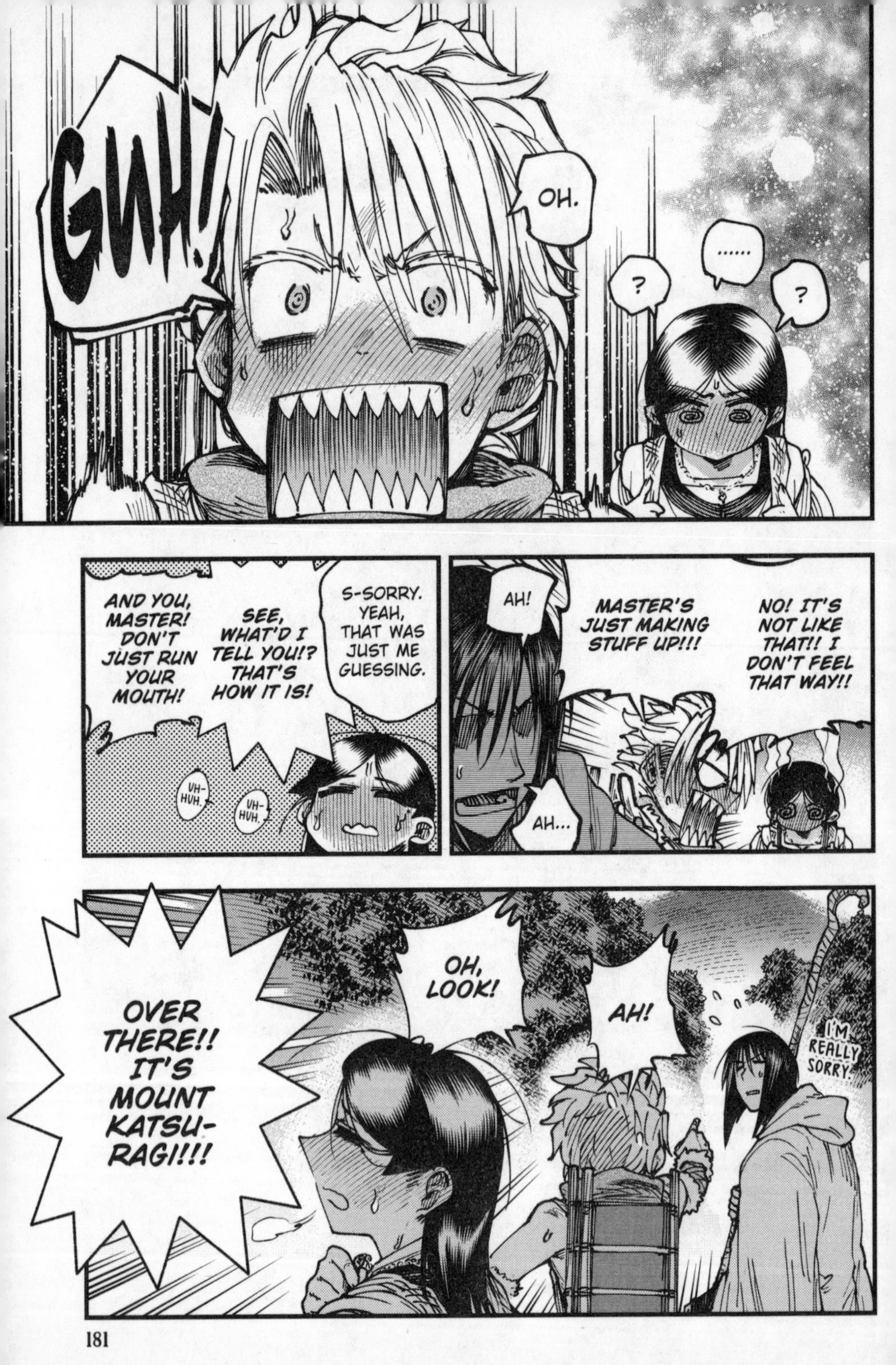
?
......
?
OH.
GUH!!
NO! IT'S NOT LIKE THAT!! I DON'T FEEL THAT WAY!!
MASTER'S JUST MAKING STUFF UP!!!
AH!
AH...
S-SORRY. YEAH, THAT WAS JUST ME GUESSING.
SEE, WHAT'D I TELL YOU!? THAT'S HOW IT IS!
AND YOU, MASTER! DON'T JUST RUN YOUR MOUTH!
UH-HUH.
UH-HUH.
I'M REALLY SORRY.
AH!
OH, LOOK!
OVER THERE!! IT'S MOUNT KATSURAGI!!!

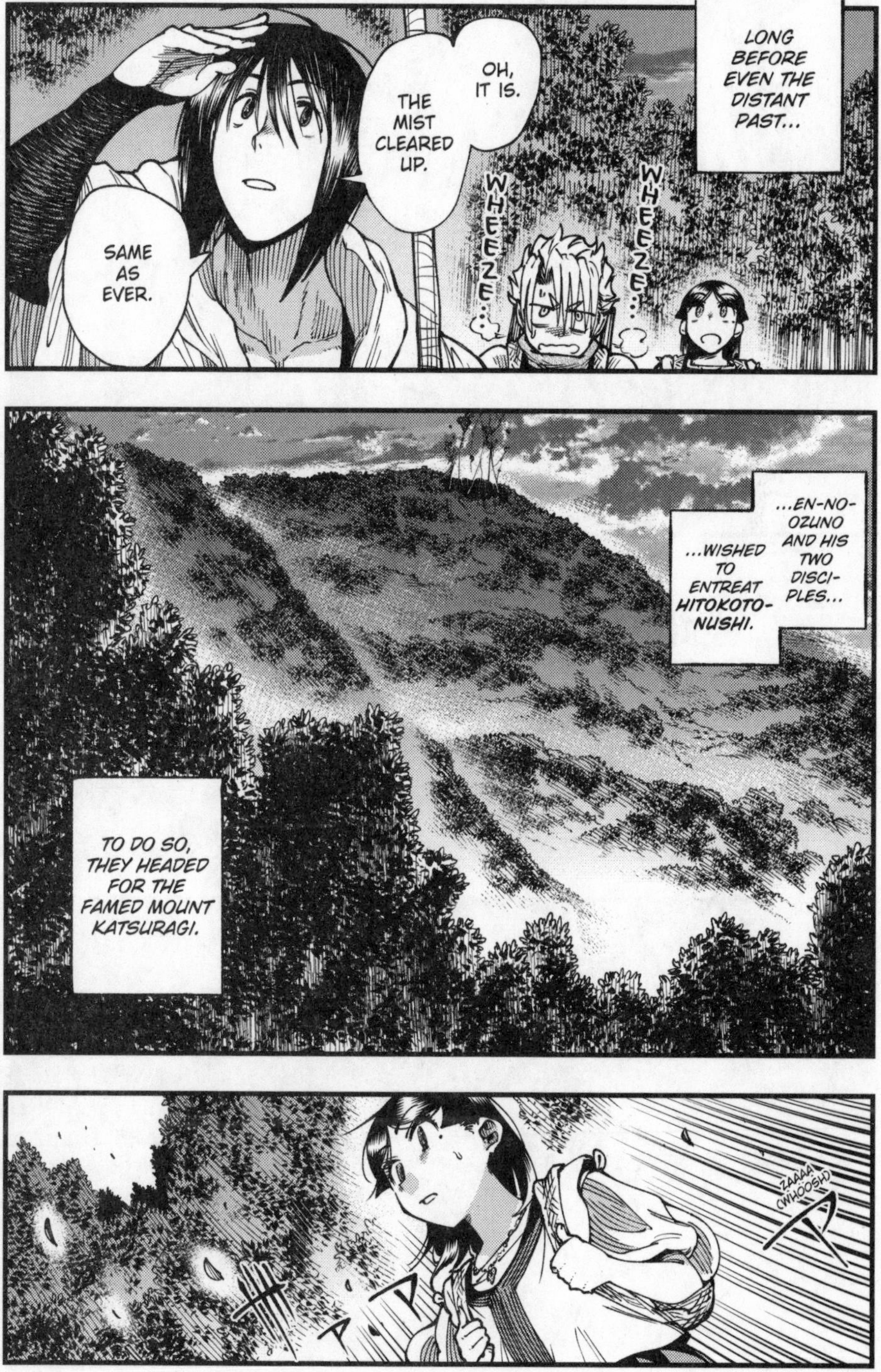
LONG BEFORE EVEN THE DISTANT PAST...
WHEEZE...
WHEEZE...
OH, IT IS.
THE MIST CLEARED UP.
SAME AS EVER.
...EN-NO-OZUNO AND HIS TWO DISCI-PLES...
...WISHED TO ENTREAT HITOKOTO-NUSHI.
TO DO SO, THEY HEADED FOR THE FAMED MOUNT KATSURAGI.
ZAAAA (WHOOSH)

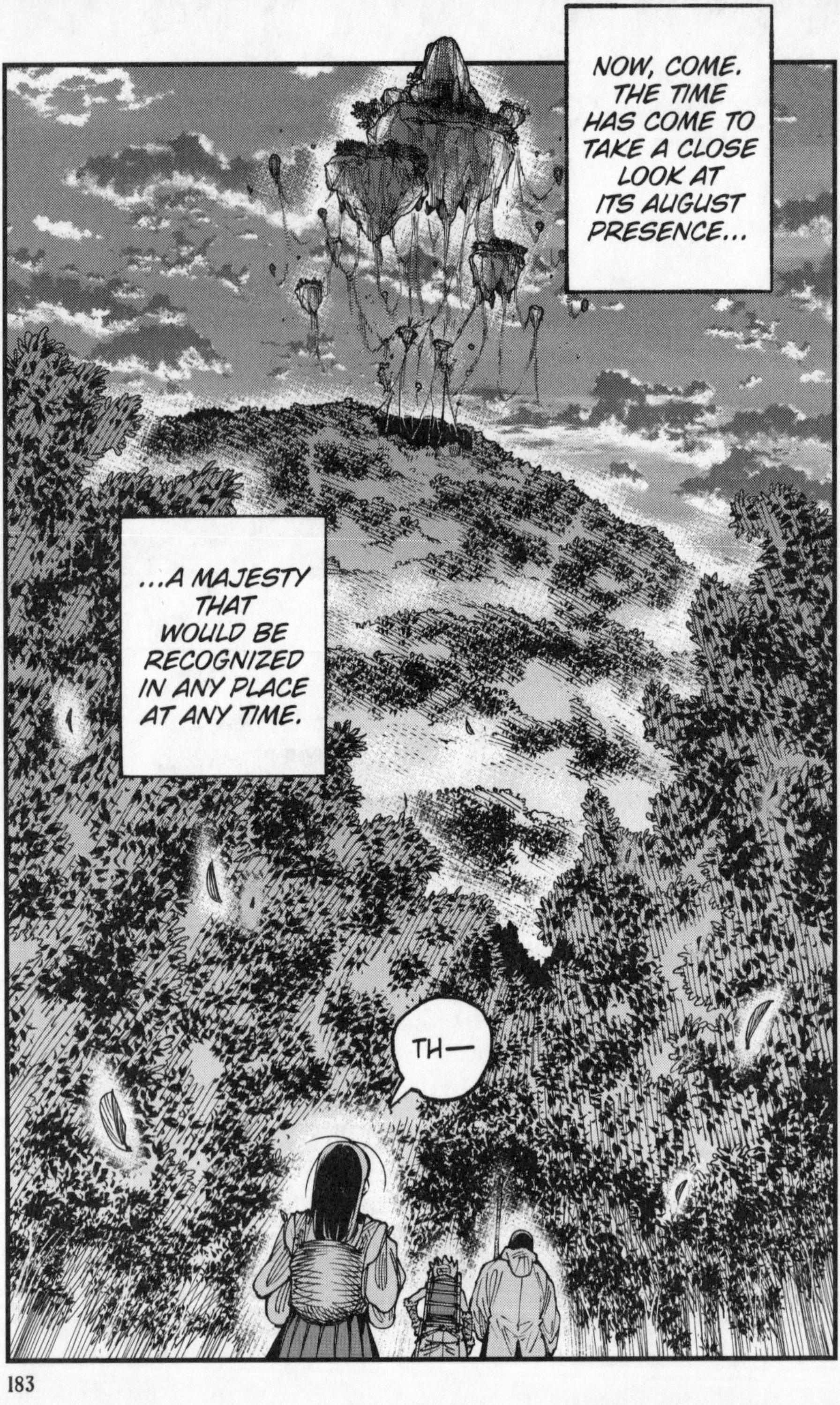
NOW, COME. THE TIME HAS COME TO TAKE A CLOSE LOOK AT ITS AUGUST PRESENCE...
...A MAJESTY THAT WOULD BE RECOGNIZED IN ANY PLACE AT ANY TIME.
TH—

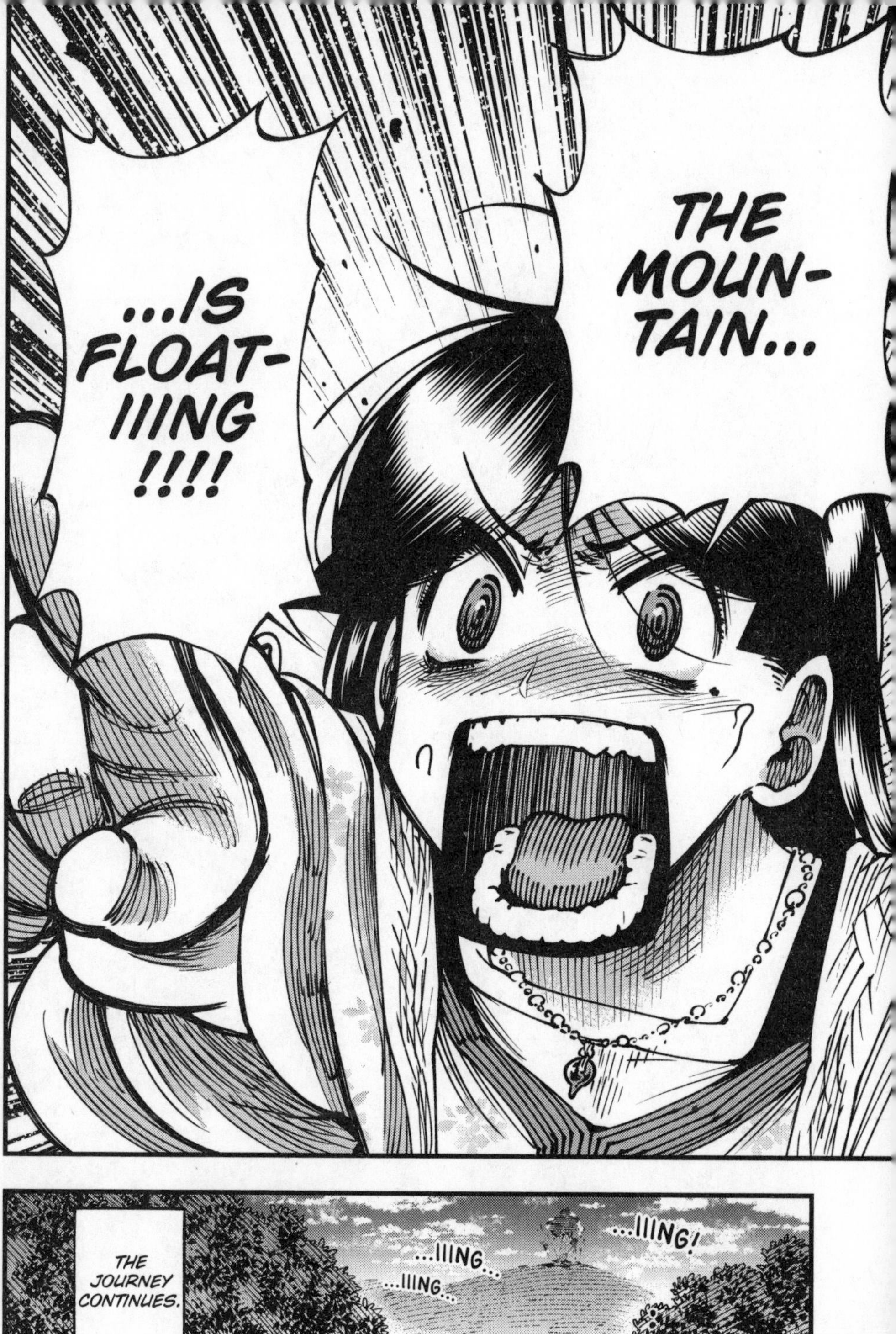
THE MOUN-
TAIN...
...IS
FLOAT-
IIING
!!!!
...IIING!
...IIING...
...IIING...
THE JOURNEY CONTINUES.

CHAPTER X ♥ END

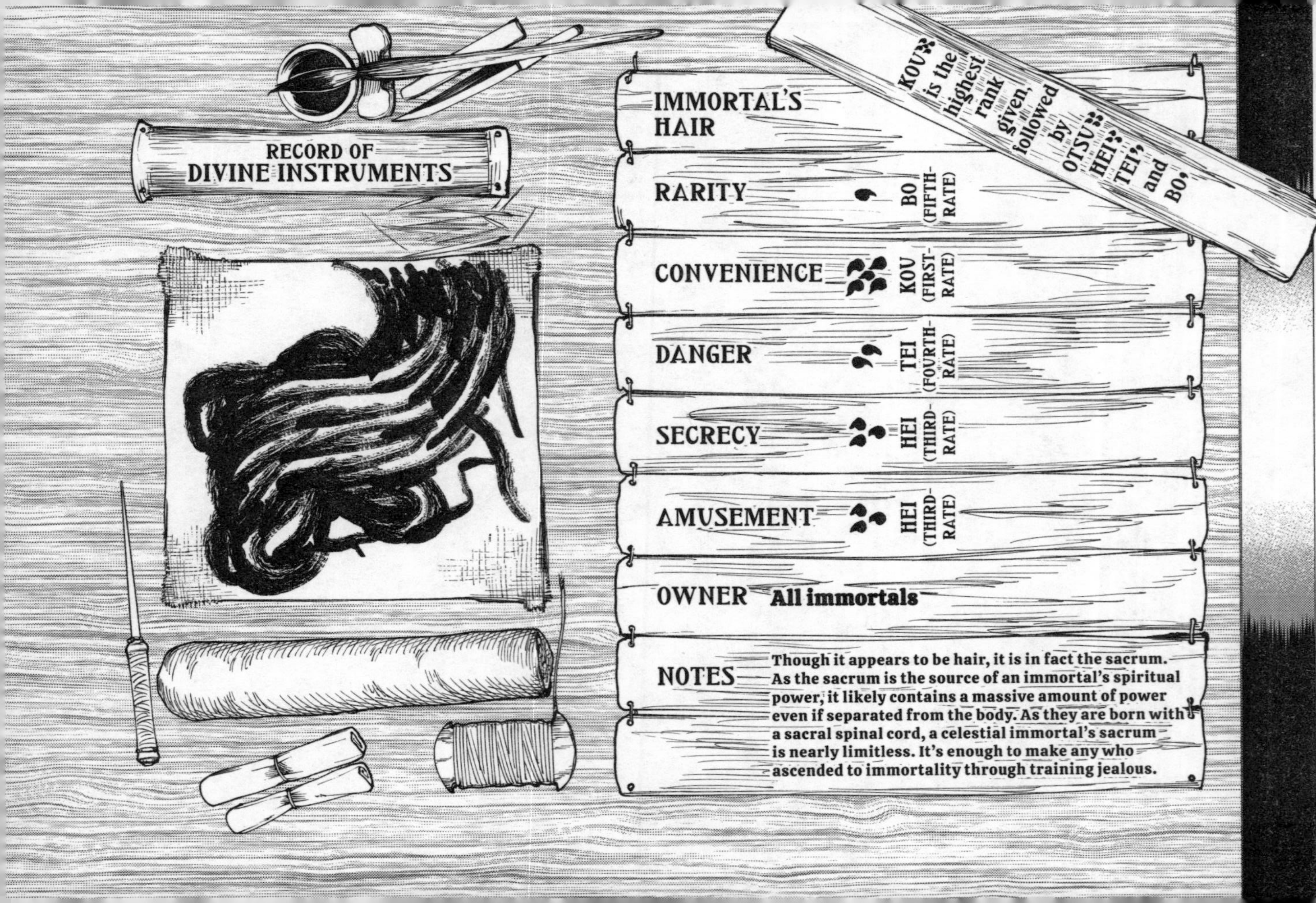
RECORD OF
DIVINE INSTRUMENTS
IMMORTAL'S HAIR
KOU is the highest rank given, followed by OTSU, HEI, TEI, and BO.
RARITY BO (FIFTH-RATE)
CONVENIENCE KOU (FIRST-RATE)
DANGER TEI (FOURTH-RATE)
SECRECY HEI (THIRD-RATE)
AMUSEMENT HEI (THIRD-RATE)
OWNER All immortals
NOTES Though it appears to be hair, it is in fact the sacrum. As the sacrum is the source of an immortal's spiritual power, it likely contains a massive amount of power even if separated from the body. As they are born with a sacral spinal cord, a celestial immortal's sacrum is nearly limitless. It's enough to make any who ascended to immortality through training jealous.

Touge Oni

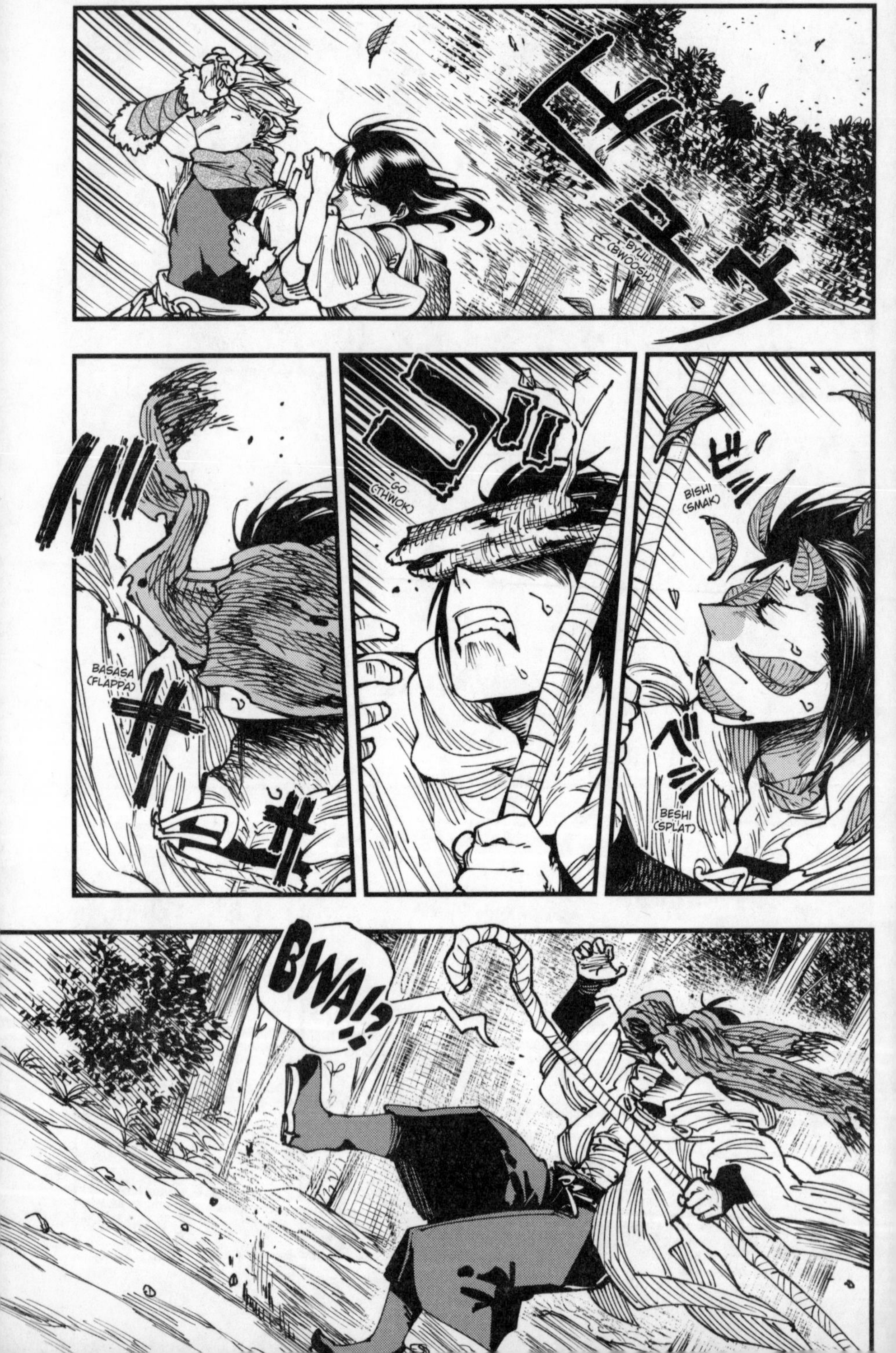
BYUU
(BWOOSH)
BISHI
(SMAK)
BESHI
(SPLAT)
GO
(THWOK)
BASASA
(FLAPPA)
BWA!?

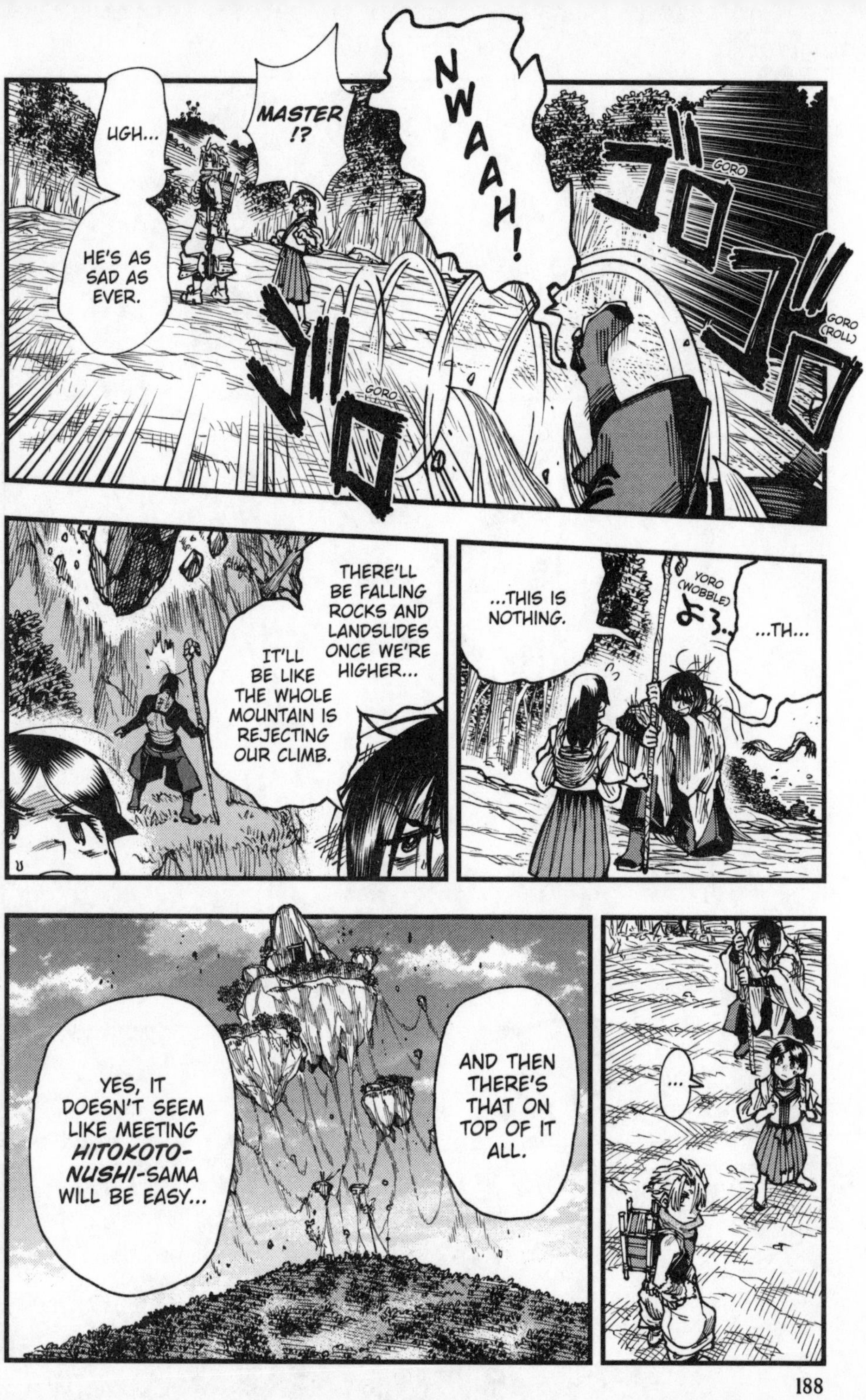
GORO
NWAAH!
GORO (ROLL)
GORO
MASTER !?
UGH...
HE'S AS SAD AS EVER.
...TH...
YORO (WOBBLE)
よろ..
...THIS IS NOTHING.
THERE'LL BE FALLING ROCKS AND LANDSLIDES ONCE WE'RE HIGHER...
IT'LL BE LIKE THE WHOLE MOUNTAIN IS REJECTING OUR CLIMB.
...
AND THEN THERE'S THAT ON TOP OF IT ALL.
YES, IT DOESN'T SEEM LIKE MEETING *HITOKOTO-NUSHI*-SAMA WILL BE EASY...

CHAPTER XI THE TALE OF MOUNT KATSURAGI, ACCORDING TO EN-NO-KIMI

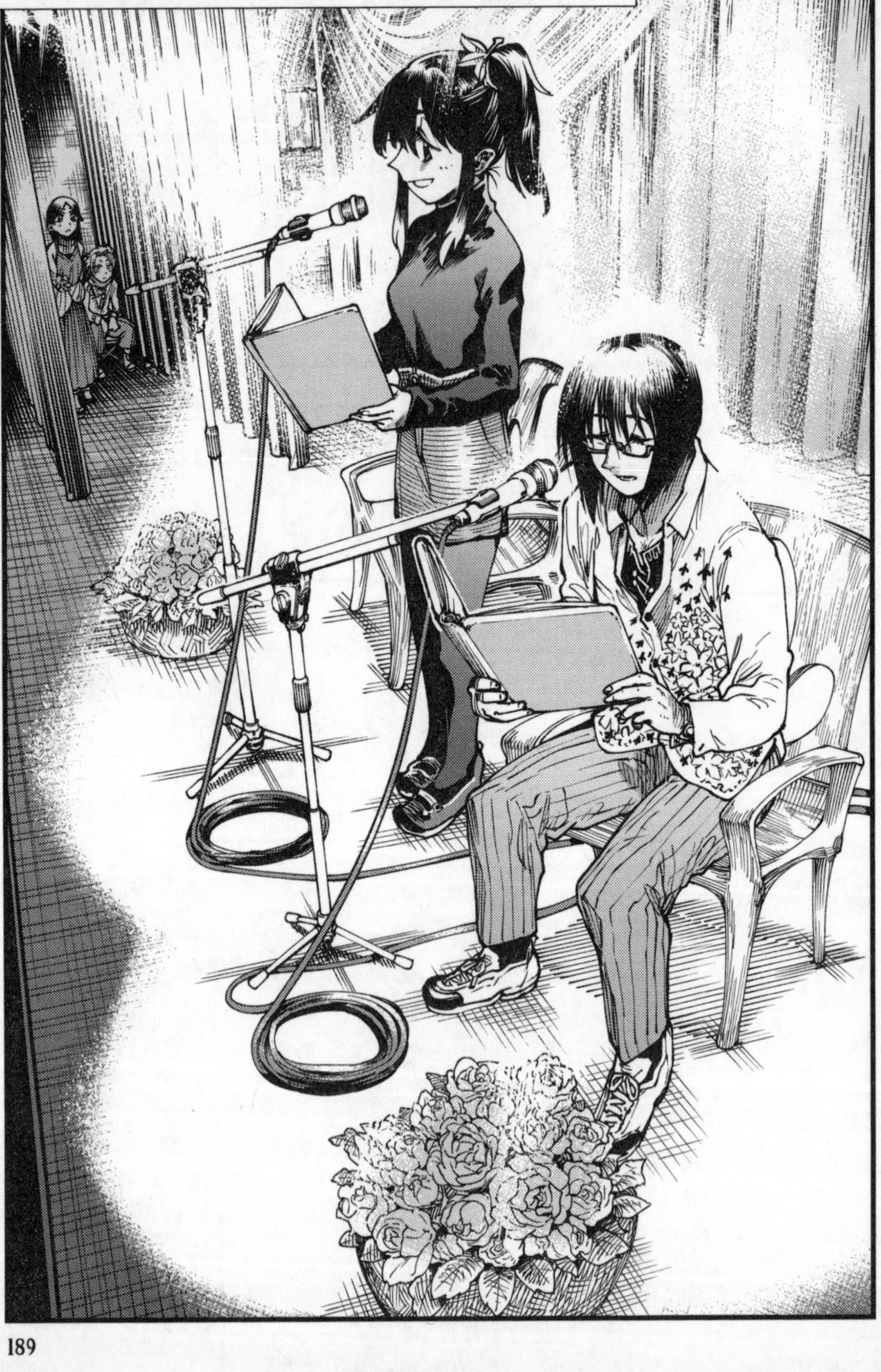

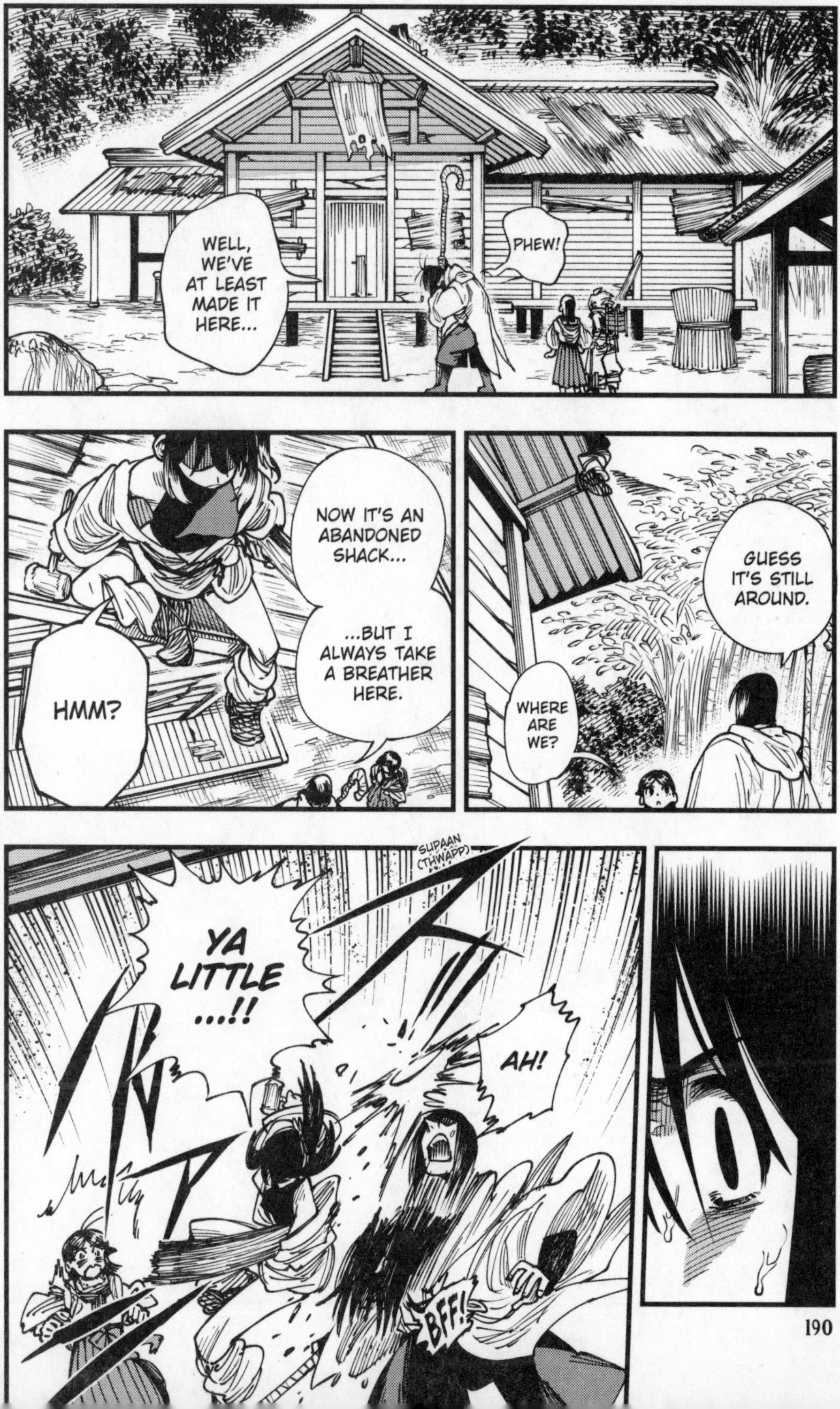
PHEW!
WELL, WE'VE AT LEAST MADE IT HERE...
GUESS IT'S STILL AROUND.
WHERE ARE WE?
NOW IT'S AN ABANDONED SHACK...
...BUT I ALWAYS TAKE A BREATHER HERE.
HMM?
SUPAAN (THWAPP)
YA LITTLE ...!!
AH!
BFF!

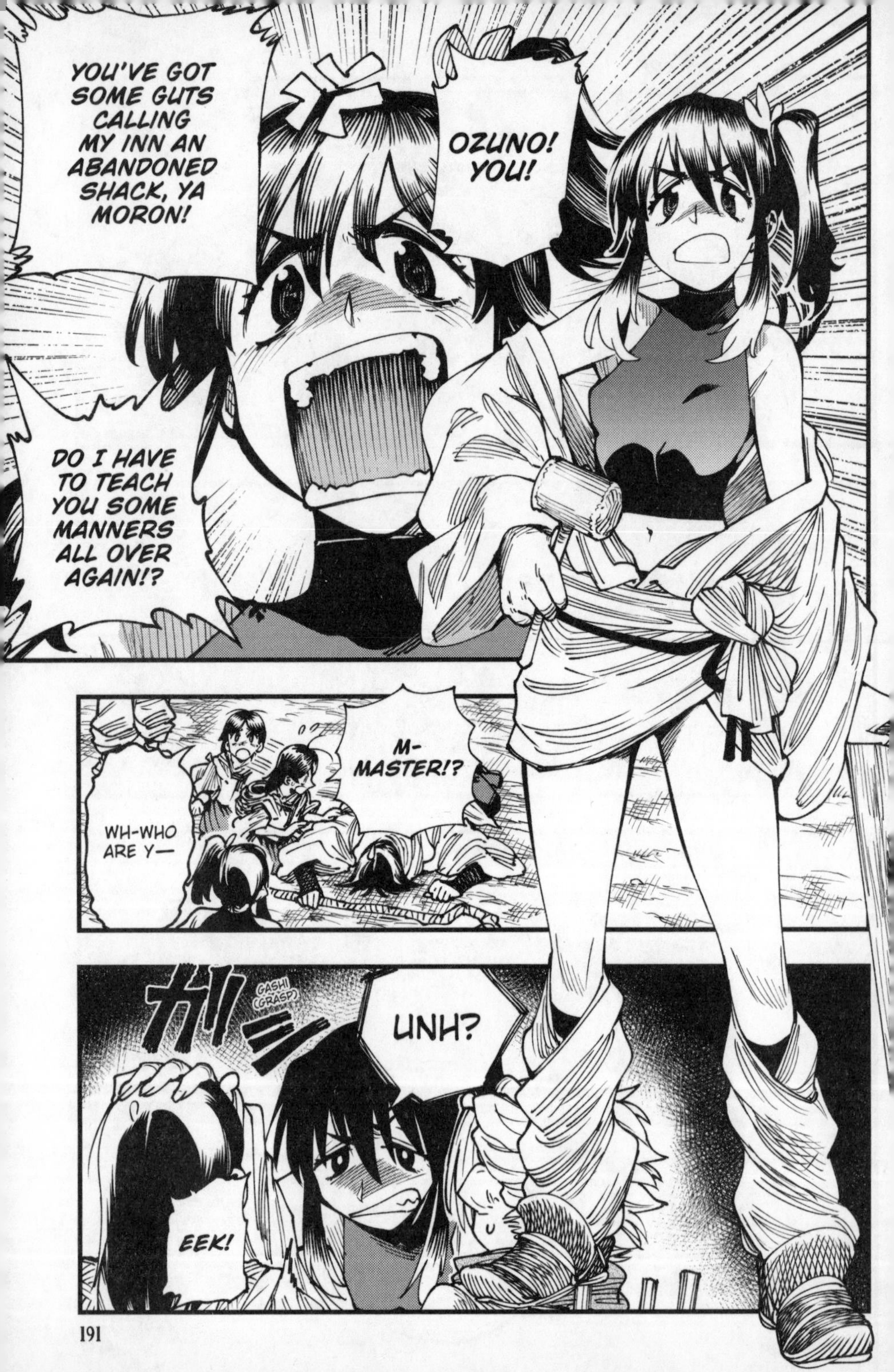
OZUNO! YOU!
YOU'VE GOT SOME GUTS CALLING MY INN AN ABANDONED SHACK, YA MORON!
DO I HAVE TO TEACH YOU SOME MANNERS ALL OVER AGAIN!?
M-MASTER!?
WH-WHO ARE Y—
UNH?
GASHI (GRASP)
EEK!

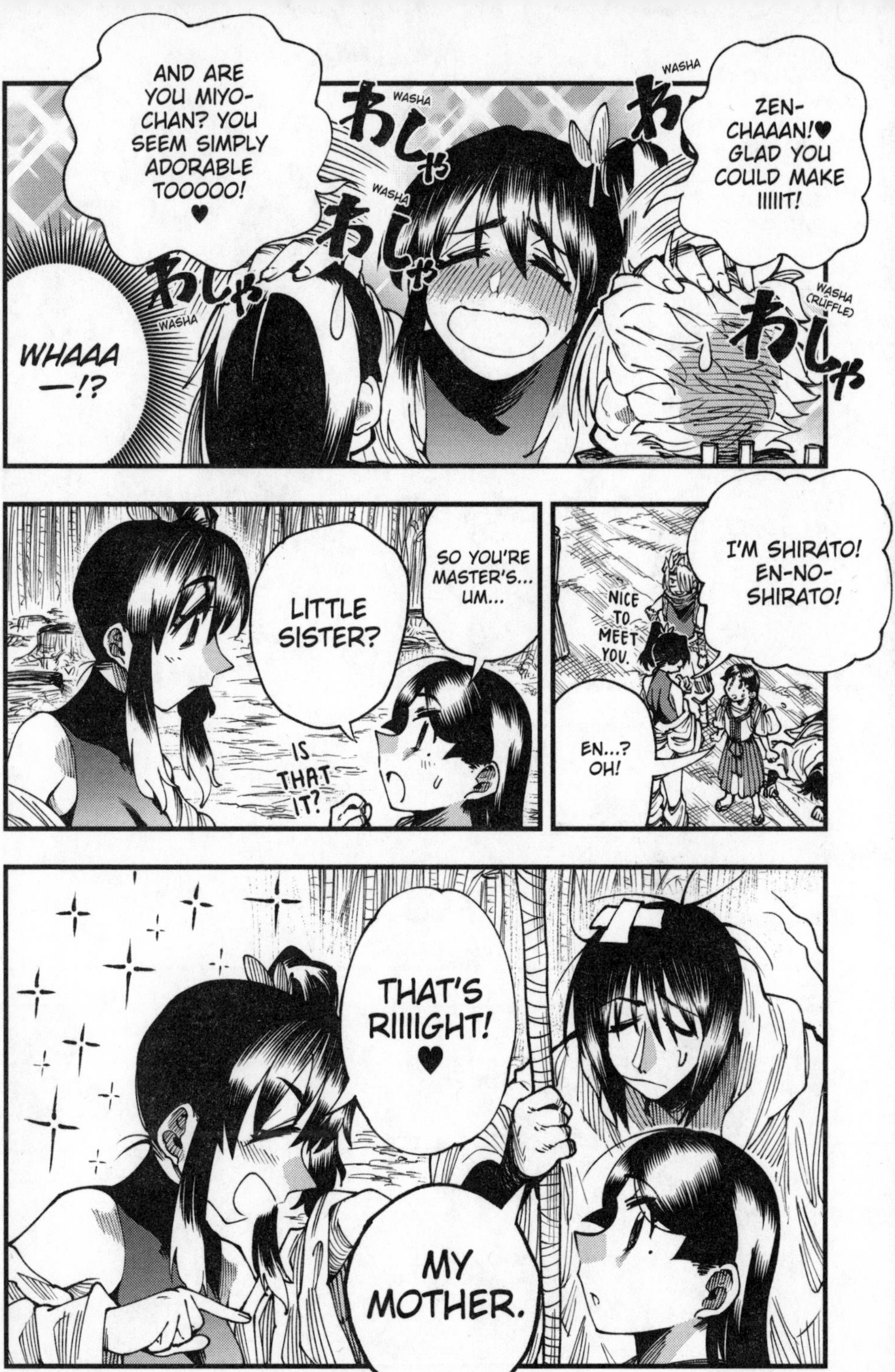
WASHA
ZEN-CHAAAN!♥ GLAD YOU COULD MAKE IIIIIT!
わしゃ
WASHA
WASHA (RUFFLE)
わしゃ
わしゃ
WASHA
AND ARE YOU MIYO-CHAN? YOU SEEM SIMPLY ADORABLE TOOOOO! ♥
わしゃ
WASHA
わしゃ
WASHA
WHAAA—!?
I'M SHIRATO! EN-NO-SHIRATO!
NICE TO MEET YOU.
EN...? OH!
SO YOU'RE MASTER'S... UM...
LITTLE SISTER?
IS THAT IT?
THAT'S RIIIIGHT! ♥
MY MOTHER.

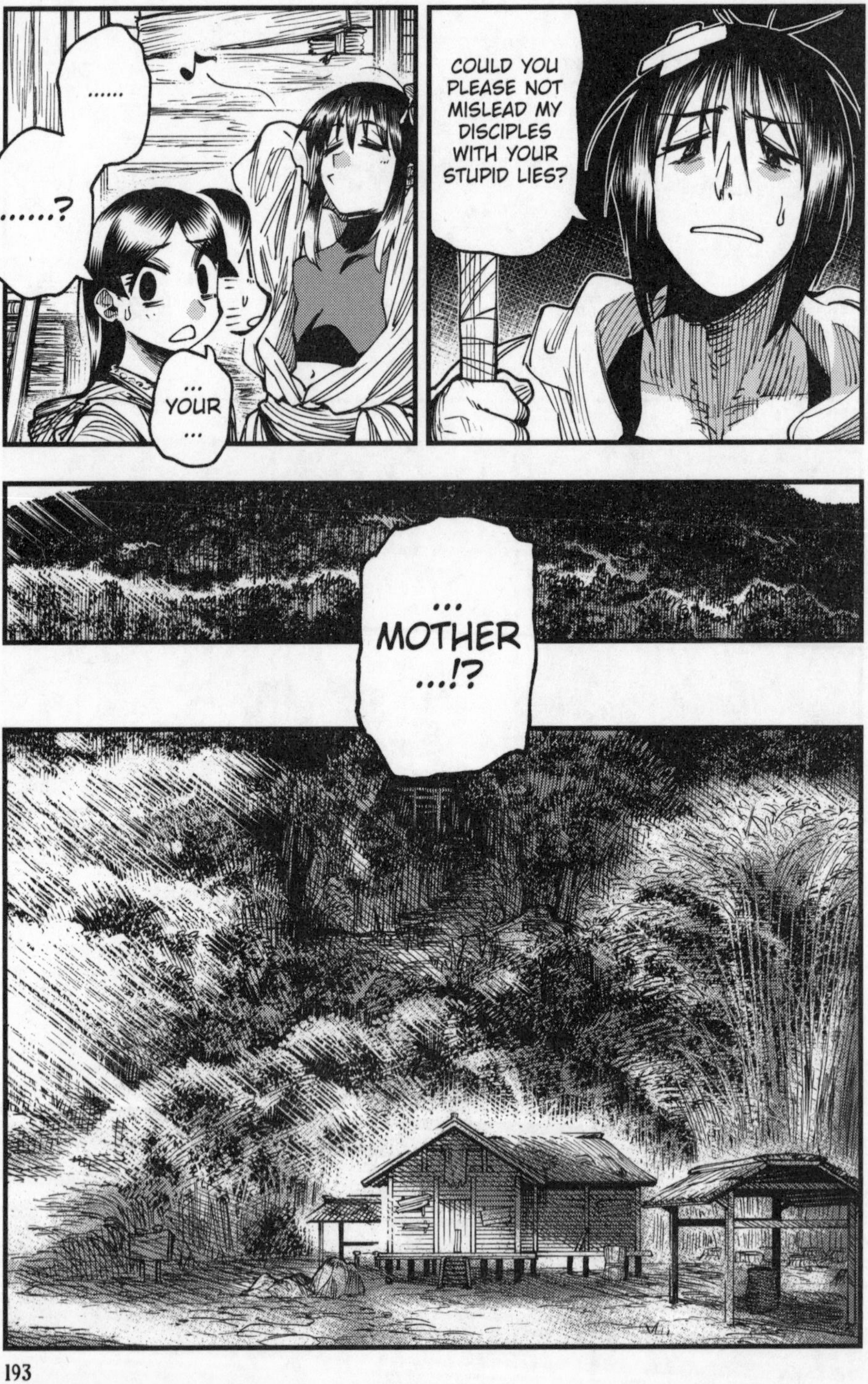
COULD YOU PLEASE NOT MISLEAD MY DISCIPLES WITH YOUR STUPID LIES?
......
......?
... YOUR ...
... MOTHER ...!?

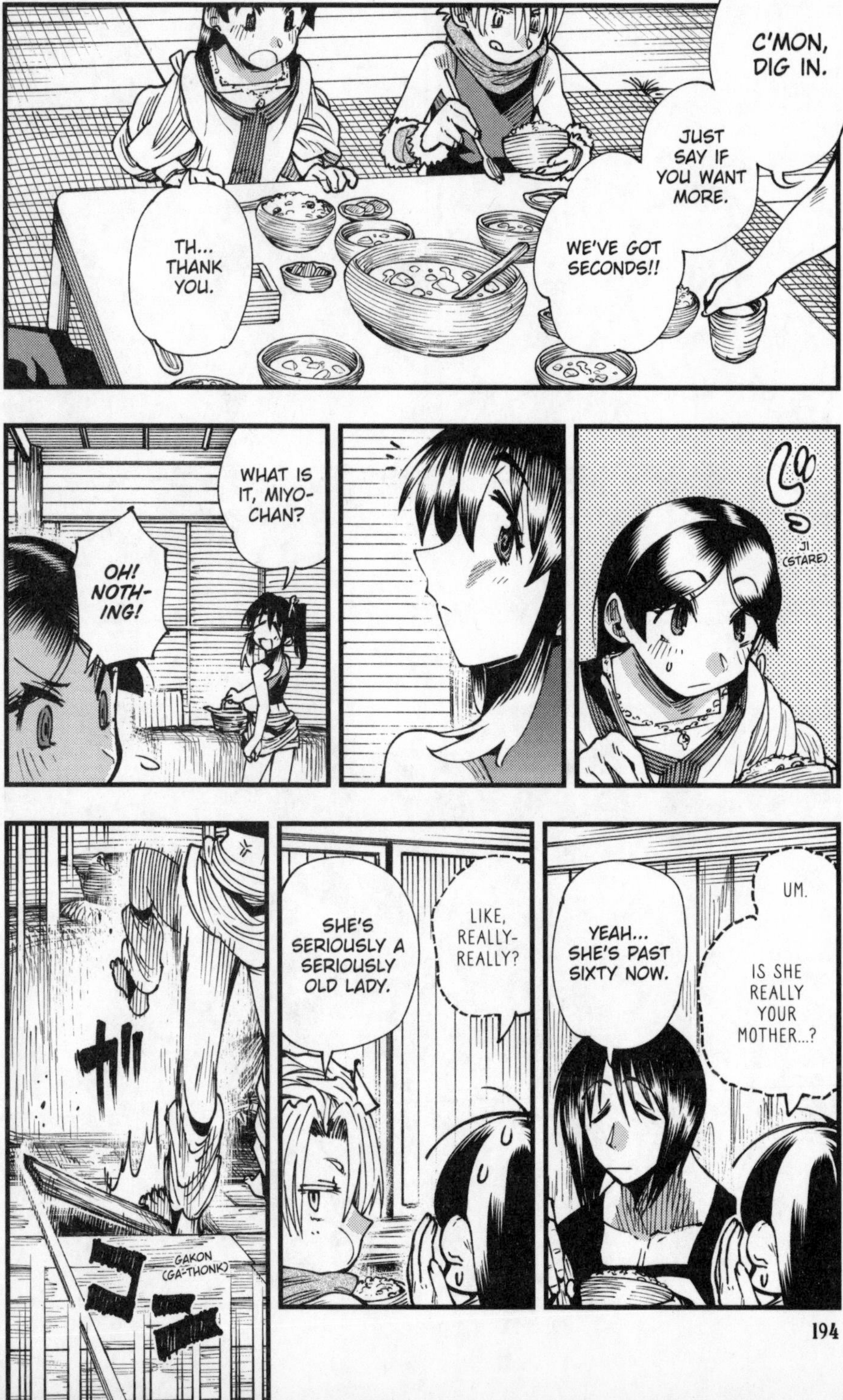
C'MON, DIG IN.
JUST SAY IF YOU WANT MORE.
WE'VE GOT SECONDS!!
TH... THANK YOU.
JI (STARE)
WHAT IS IT, MIYO-CHAN?
OH! NOTHING!
UM.
IS SHE REALLY YOUR MOTHER...?
YEAH... SHE'S PAST SIXTY NOW.
LIKE, REALLY-REALLY?
SHE'S SERIOUSLY A SERIOUSLY OLD LADY.
GAKON (GA-THONK)

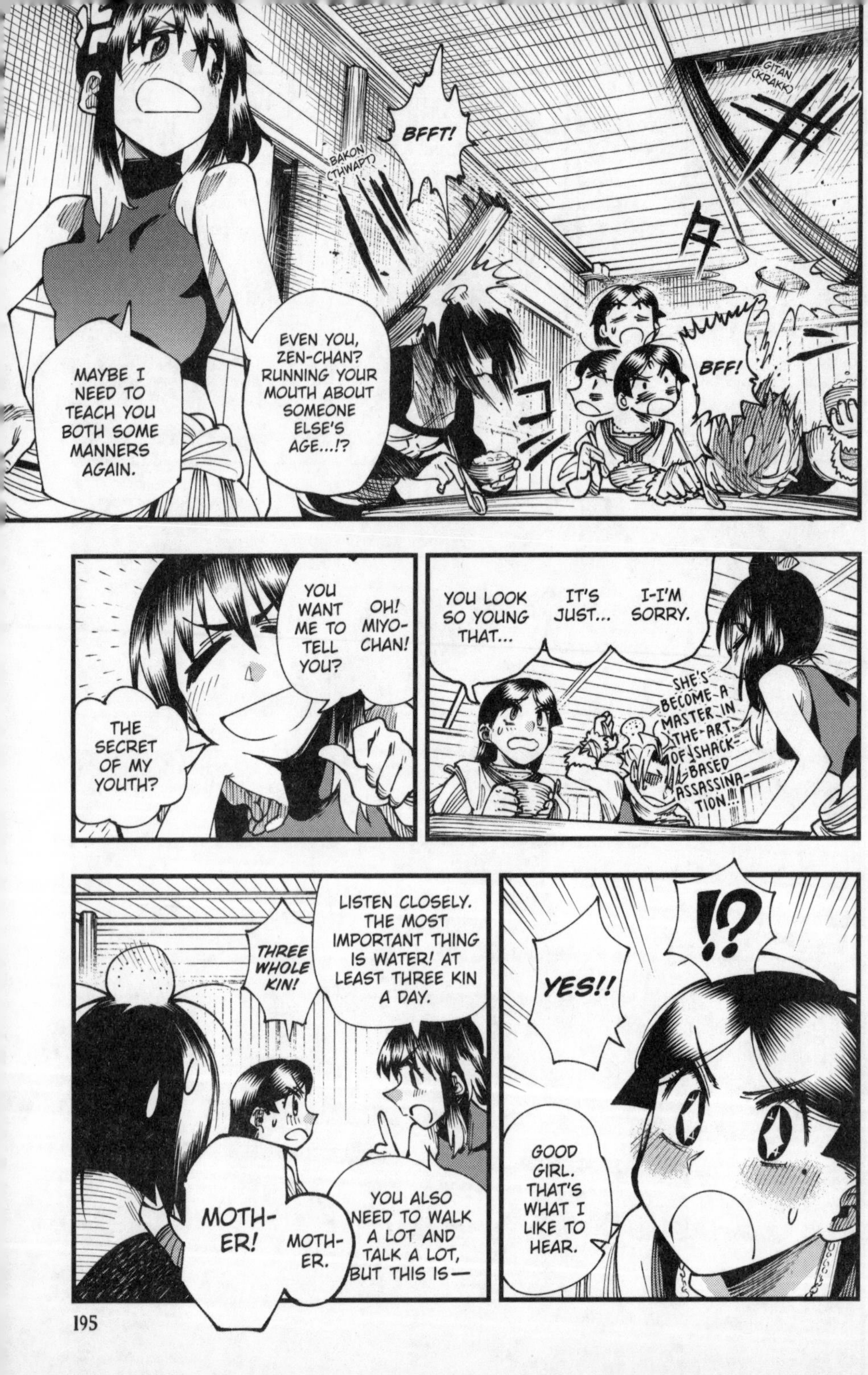
GITAN (KRAKK)
BFFT!
BAKON (THWAPT)
BFF!
EVEN YOU, ZEN-CHAN? RUNNING YOUR MOUTH ABOUT SOMEONE ELSE'S AGE...!?
MAYBE I NEED TO TEACH YOU BOTH SOME MANNERS AGAIN.
I-I'M SORRY.
IT'S JUST...
YOU LOOK SO YOUNG THAT...
SHE'S BECOME A MASTER IN THE ART OF SHACK-BASED ASSASSINATION!!!
OH! MIYO-CHAN!
YOU WANT ME TO TELL YOU?
THE SECRET OF MY YOUTH?
!?
YES!!
GOOD GIRL. THAT'S WHAT I LIKE TO HEAR.
LISTEN CLOSELY. THE MOST IMPORTANT THING IS WATER! AT LEAST THREE KIN A DAY.
THREE WHOLE KIN!
YOU ALSO NEED TO WALK A LOT AND TALK A LOT, BUT THIS IS—
MOTH-ER.
MOTH-ER!

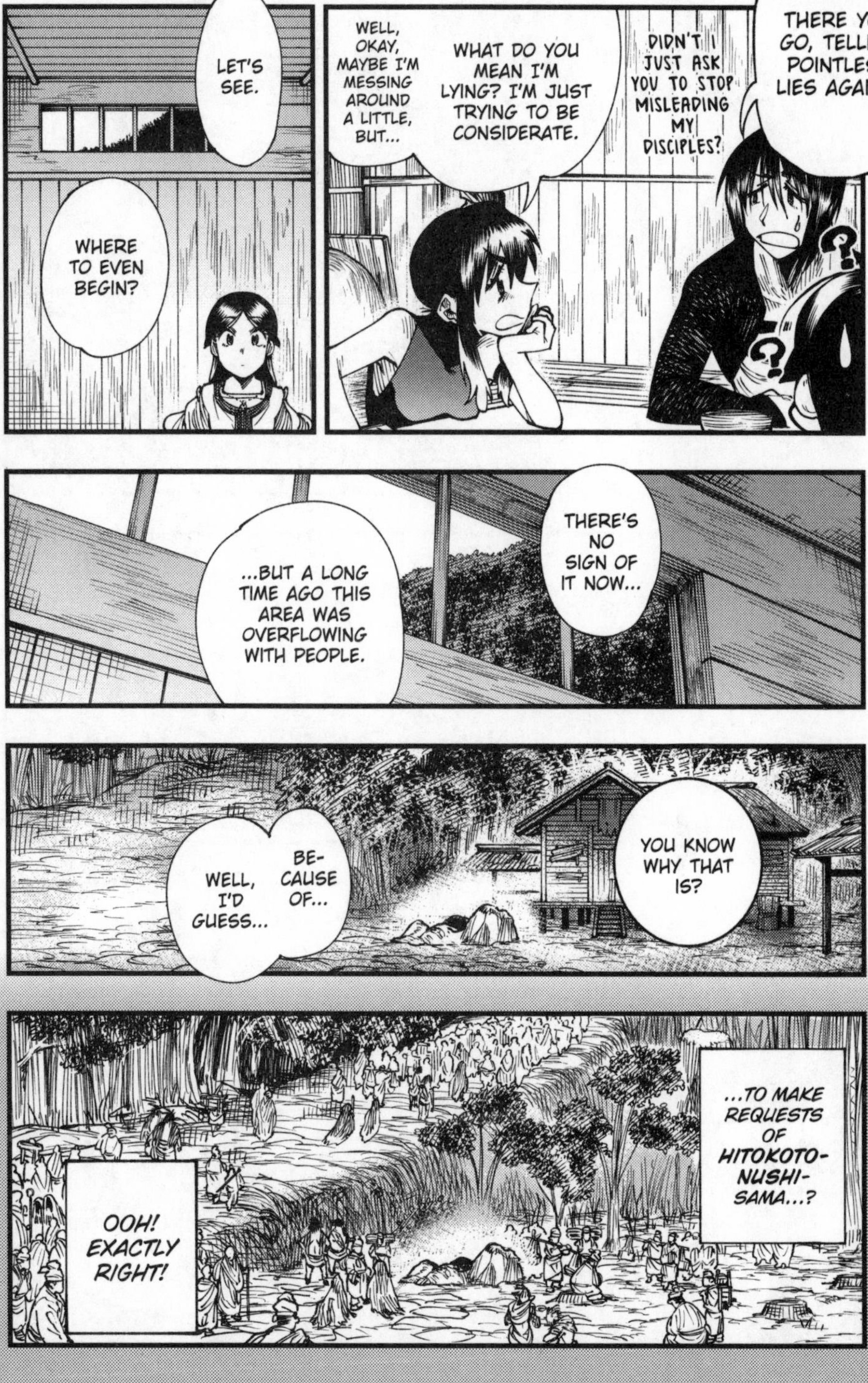
THERE YOU GO, TELLING POINTLESS LIES AGAIN...
DIDN'T I JUST ASK YOU TO STOP MISLEADING MY DISCIPLES?
WHAT DO YOU MEAN I'M LYING? I'M JUST TRYING TO BE CONSIDERATE.
WELL, OKAY, MAYBE I'M MESSING AROUND A LITTLE, BUT...
LET'S SEE.
WHERE TO EVEN BEGIN?
THERE'S NO SIGN OF IT NOW...
...BUT A LONG TIME AGO THIS AREA WAS OVERFLOWING WITH PEOPLE.
YOU KNOW WHY THAT IS?
BE-CAUSE OF...
WELL, I'D GUESS...
...TO MAKE REQUESTS OF HITOKOTO-NUSHI-SAMA...?
OOH! EXACTLY RIGHT!

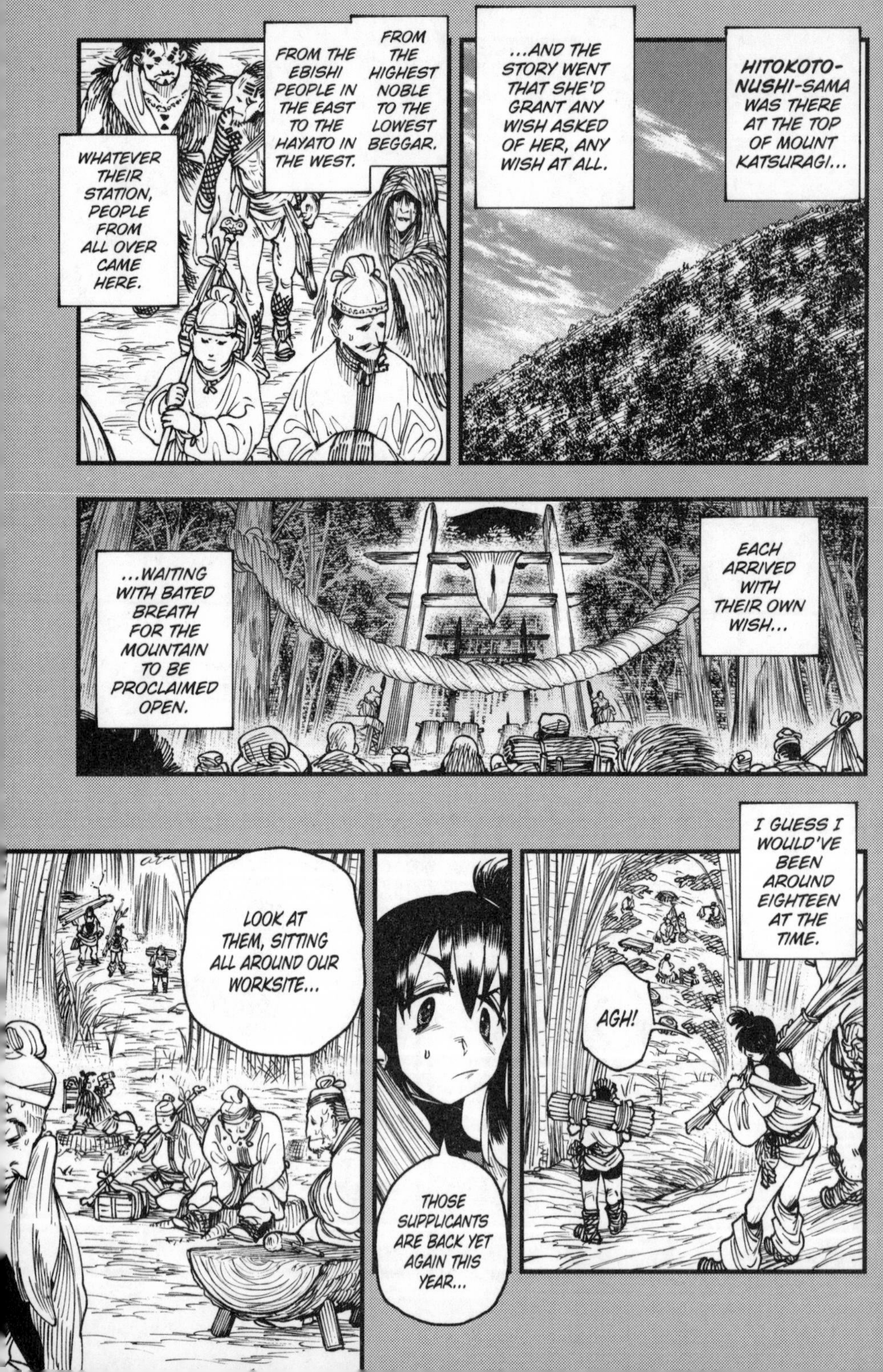
HITOKOTO-NUSHI-SAMA WAS THERE AT THE TOP OF MOUNT KATSURAGI...
...AND THE STORY WENT THAT SHE'D GRANT ANY WISH ASKED OF HER, ANY WISH AT ALL.
FROM THE HIGHEST NOBLE TO THE LOWEST BEGGAR.
FROM THE EBISHI PEOPLE IN THE EAST TO THE HAYATO IN THE WEST.
WHATEVER THEIR STATION, PEOPLE FROM ALL OVER CAME HERE.
EACH ARRIVED WITH THEIR OWN WISH...
...WAITING WITH BATED BREATH FOR THE MOUNTAIN TO BE PROCLAIMED OPEN.
I GUESS I WOULD'VE BEEN AROUND EIGHTEEN AT THE TIME.
AGH!
THOSE SUPPLICANTS ARE BACK YET AGAIN THIS YEAR...
LOOK AT THEM, SITTING ALL AROUND OUR WORKSITE...

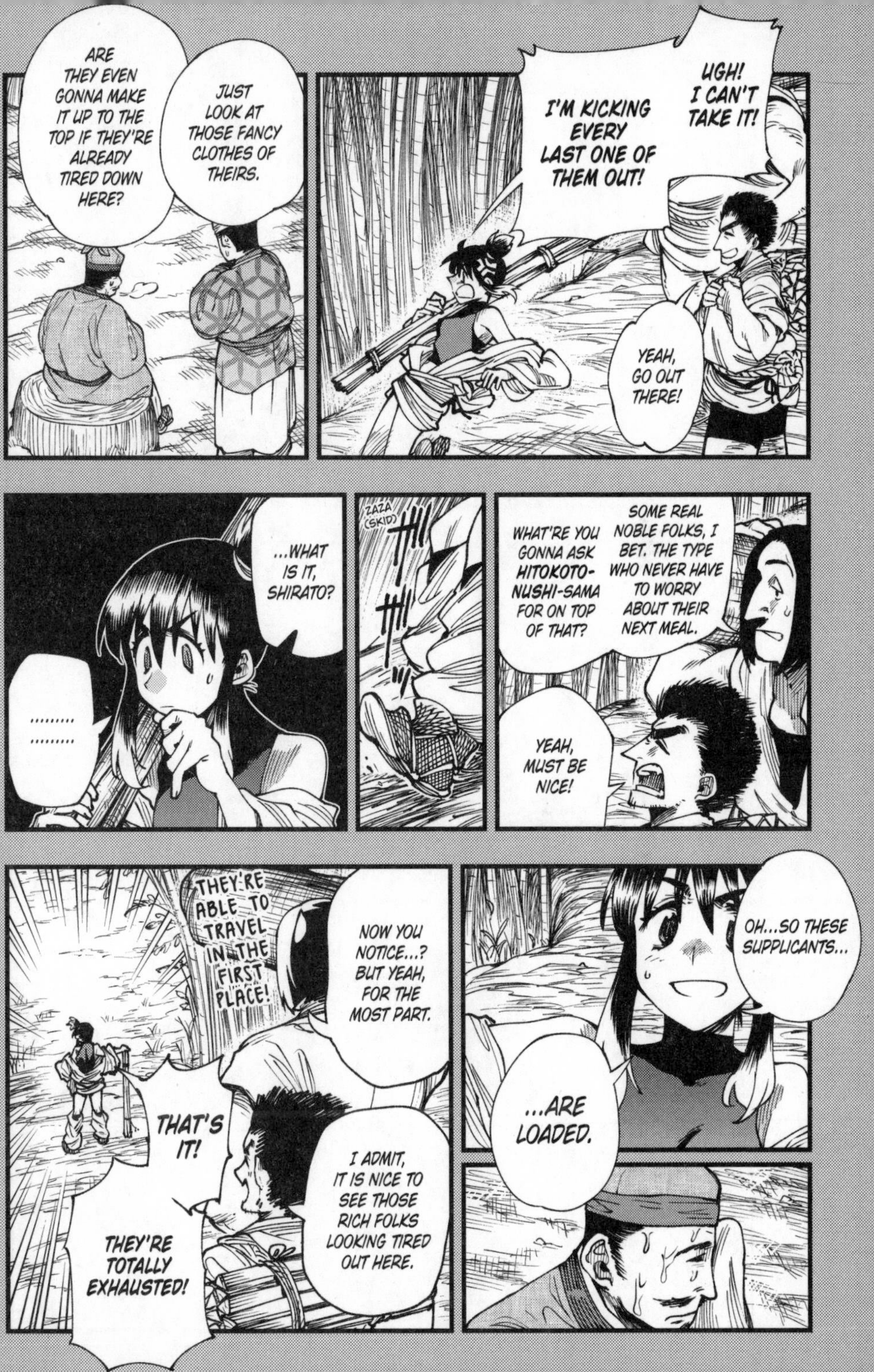
UGH! I CAN'T TAKE IT!
I'M KICKING EVERY LAST ONE OF THEM OUT!
YEAH, GO OUT THERE!
JUST LOOK AT THOSE FANCY CLOTHES OF THEIRS.
ARE THEY EVEN GONNA MAKE IT UP TO THE TOP IF THEY'RE ALREADY TIRED DOWN HERE?
SOME REAL NOBLE FOLKS, I BET. THE TYPE WHO NEVER HAVE TO WORRY ABOUT THEIR NEXT MEAL.
WHAT'RE YOU GONNA ASK HITOKOTO-NUSHI-SAMA FOR ON TOP OF THAT?
YEAH, MUST BE NICE!
ZAZA (SKID)
...WHAT IS IT, SHIRATO?
....
OH...SO THESE SUPPLICANTS...
...ARE LOADED.
NOW YOU NOTICE...? BUT YEAH, FOR THE MOST PART.
THEY'RE ABLE TO TRAVEL IN THE FIRST PLACE!
I ADMIT, IT IS NICE TO SEE THOSE RICH FOLKS LOOKING TIRED OUT HERE.
THAT'S IT! THEY'RE TOTALLY EXHAUSTED!

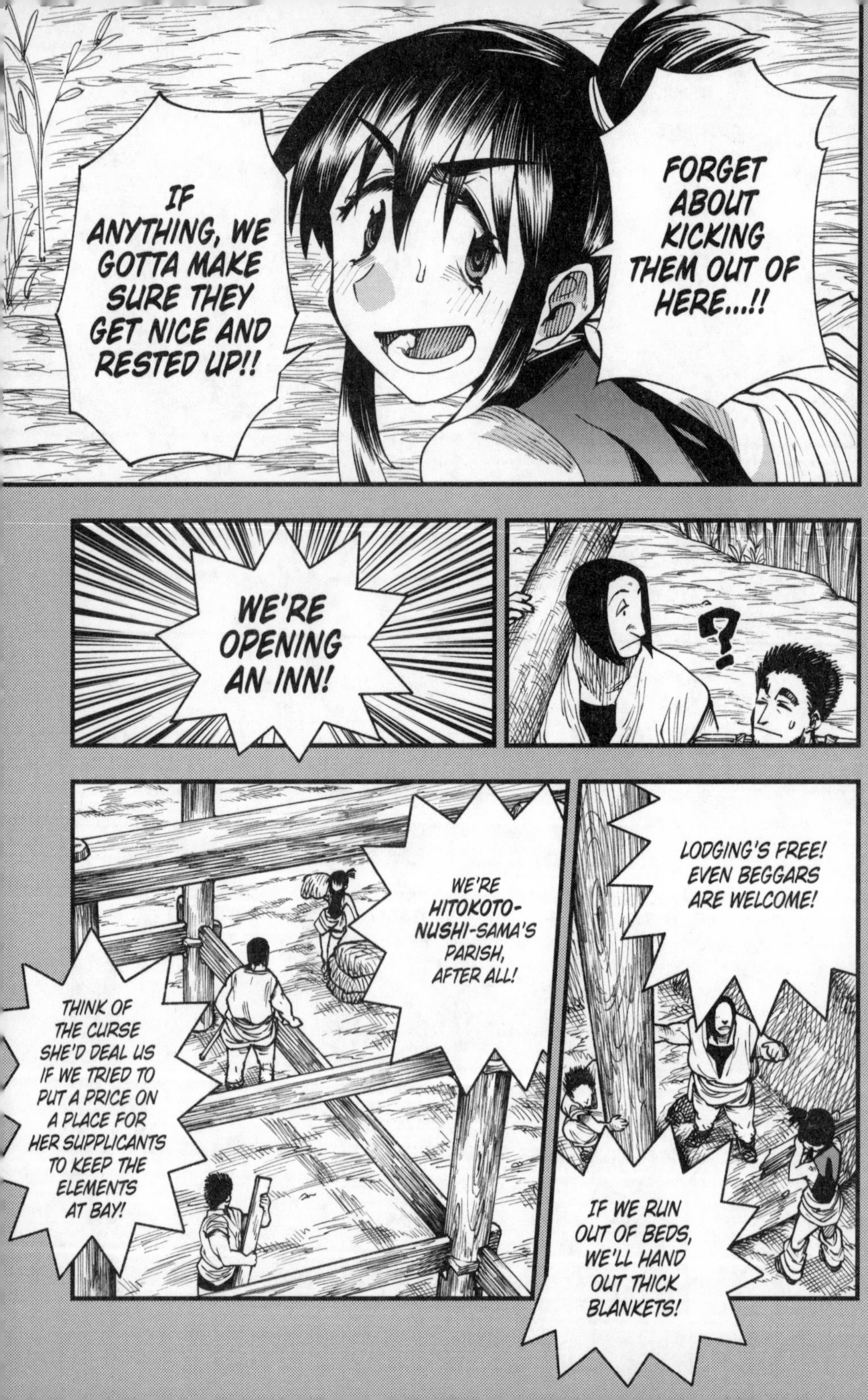
FORGET ABOUT KICKING THEM OUT OF HERE...!!
IF ANYTHING, WE GOTTA MAKE SURE THEY GET NICE AND RESTED UP!!
?
WE'RE OPENING AN INN!
LODGING'S FREE! EVEN BEGGARS ARE WELCOME!
IF WE RUN OUT OF BEDS, WE'LL HAND OUT THICK BLANKETS!
WE'RE HITOKOTO-NUSHI-SAMA'S PARISH, AFTER ALL!
THINK OF THE CURSE SHE'D DEAL US IF WE TRIED TO PUT A PRICE ON A PLACE FOR HER SUPPLICANTS TO KEEP THE ELEMENTS AT BAY!

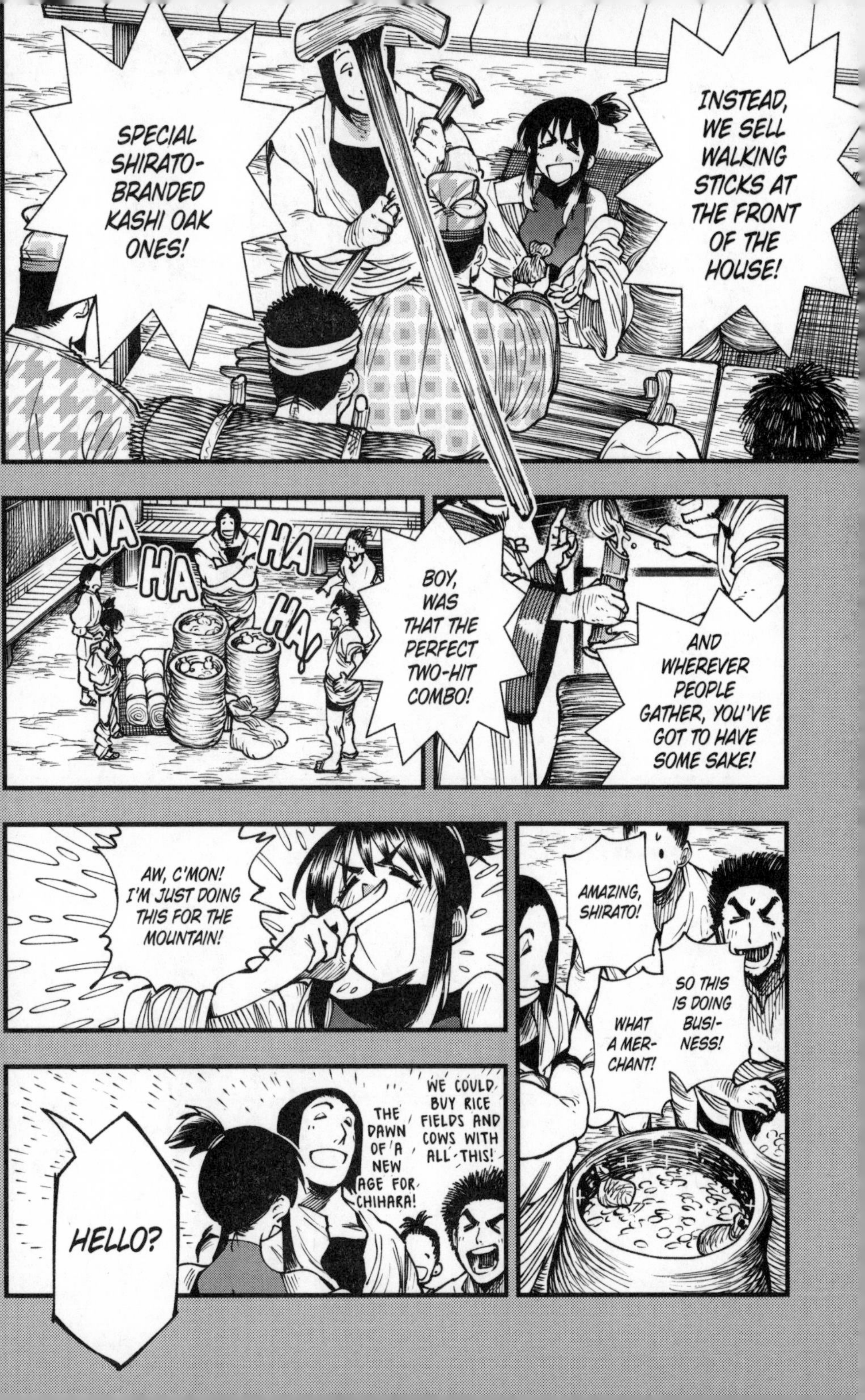
INSTEAD, WE SELL WALKING STICKS AT THE FRONT OF THE HOUSE!
SPECIAL SHIRATO-BRANDED KASHI OAK ONES!
AND WHEREVER PEOPLE GATHER, YOU'VE GOT TO HAVE SOME SAKE!
BOY, WAS THAT THE PERFECT TWO-HIT COMBO!
WA HA HA HA!
AMAZING, SHIRATO!
SO THIS IS DOING BUSI-NESS!
WHAT A MER-CHANT!
AW, C'MON! I'M JUST DOING THIS FOR THE MOUNTAIN!
WE COULD BUY RICE FIELDS AND COWS WITH ALL THIS!
THE DAWN OF A NEW AGE FOR CHIHARA!
HELLO?

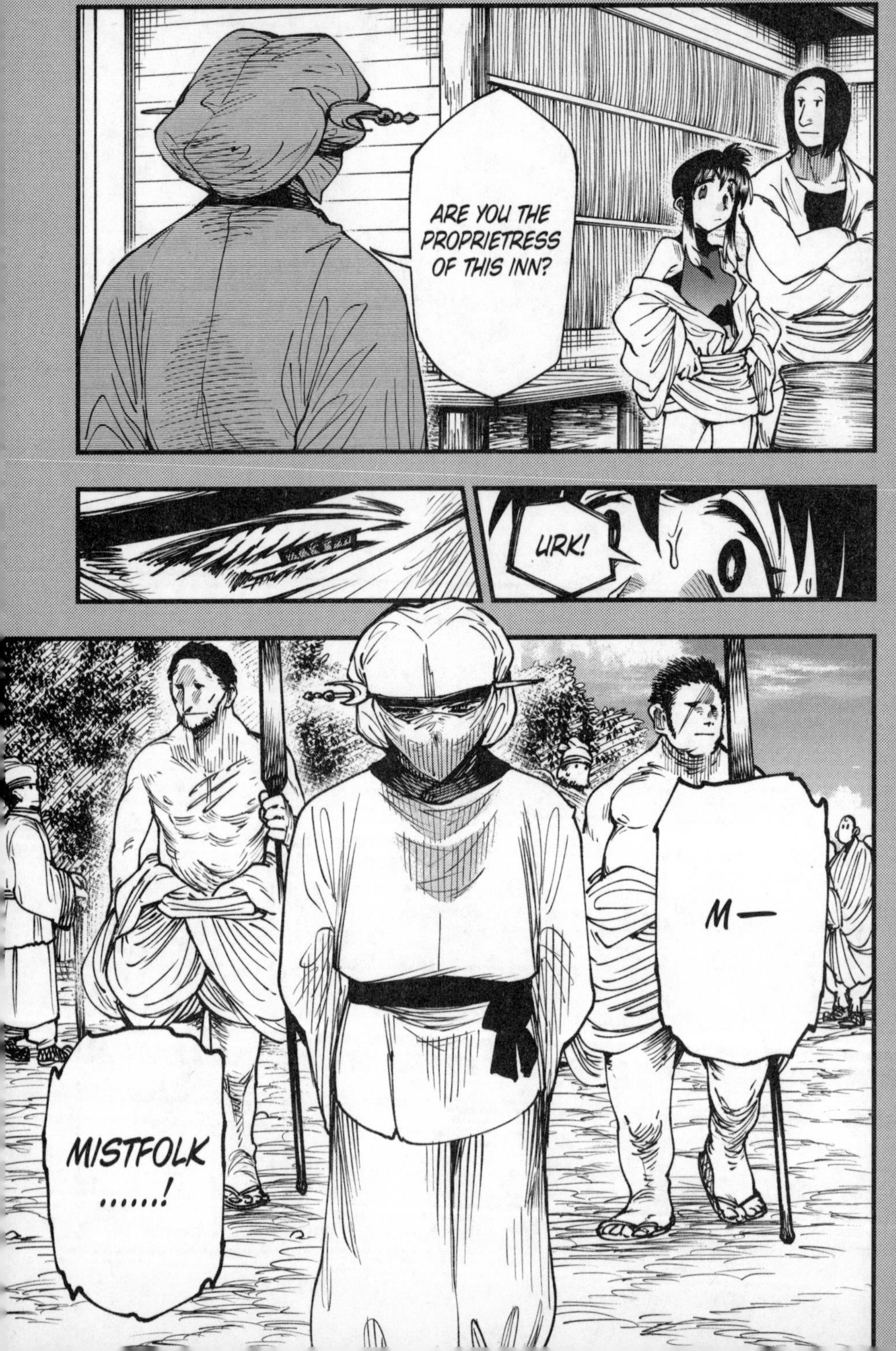
ARE YOU THE PROPRIETRESS OF THIS INN?
URK!
M—
MISTFOLK ......!

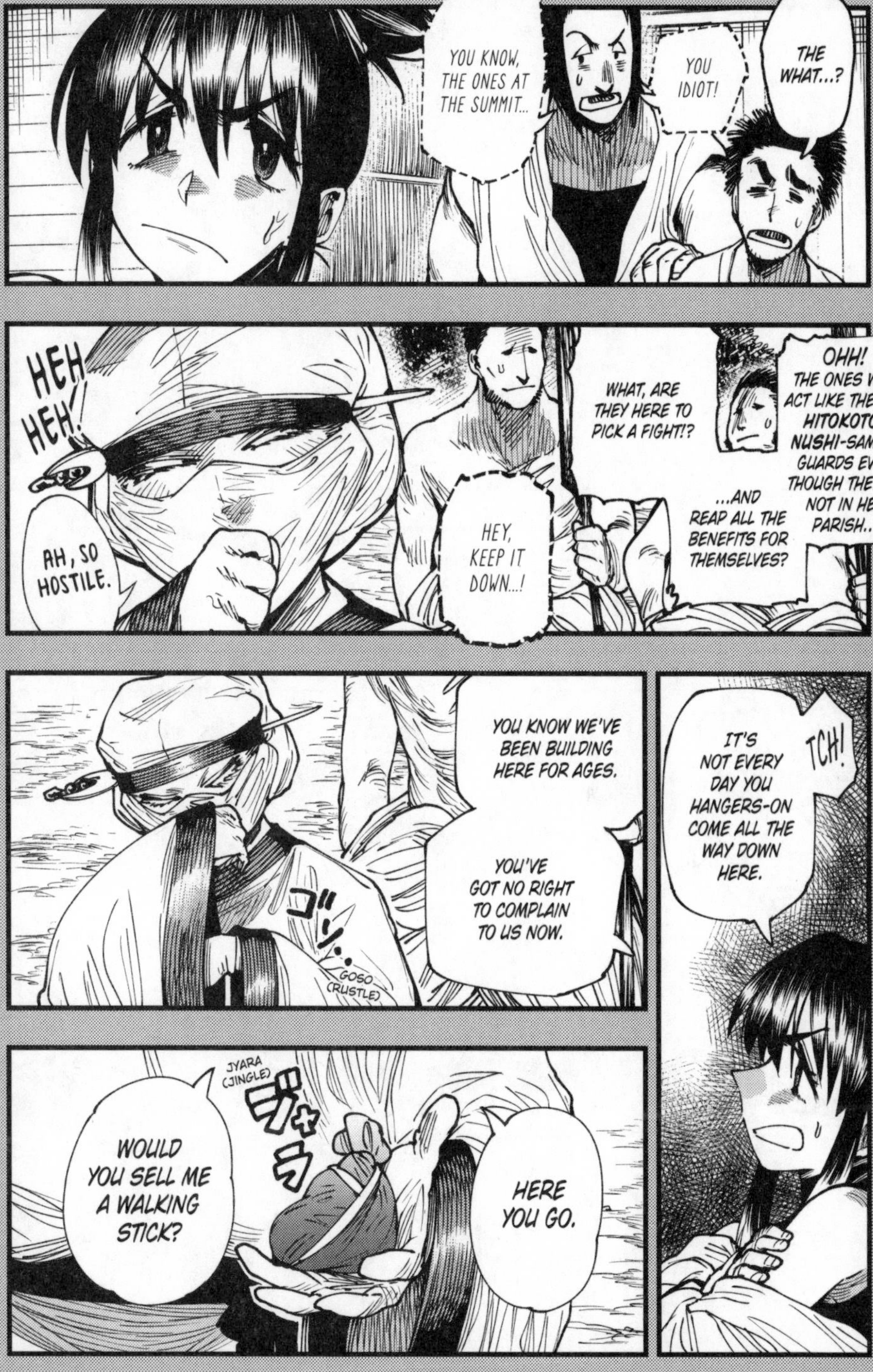
THE WHAT...?
YOU IDIOT!
YOU KNOW, THE ONES AT THE SUMMIT...
OHH! THE ONES WHO ACT LIKE THEY'RE HITOKOTO-NUSHI-SAMA'S GUARDS EVEN THOUGH THEY'RE NOT IN HER PARISH...
...AND REAP ALL THE BENEFITS FOR THEMSELVES?
WHAT, ARE THEY HERE TO PICK A FIGHT!?
HEY, KEEP IT DOWN...!
HEH HEH!
AH, SO HOSTILE.
TCH!
IT'S NOT EVERY DAY YOU HANGERS-ON COME ALL THE WAY DOWN HERE.
YOU KNOW WE'VE BEEN BUILDING HERE FOR AGES.
YOU'VE GOT NO RIGHT TO COMPLAIN TO US NOW.
ゴソ…
GOSO (RUSTLE)
HERE YOU GO.
ジャラ
JYARA (JINGLE)
WOULD YOU SELL ME A WALKING STICK?

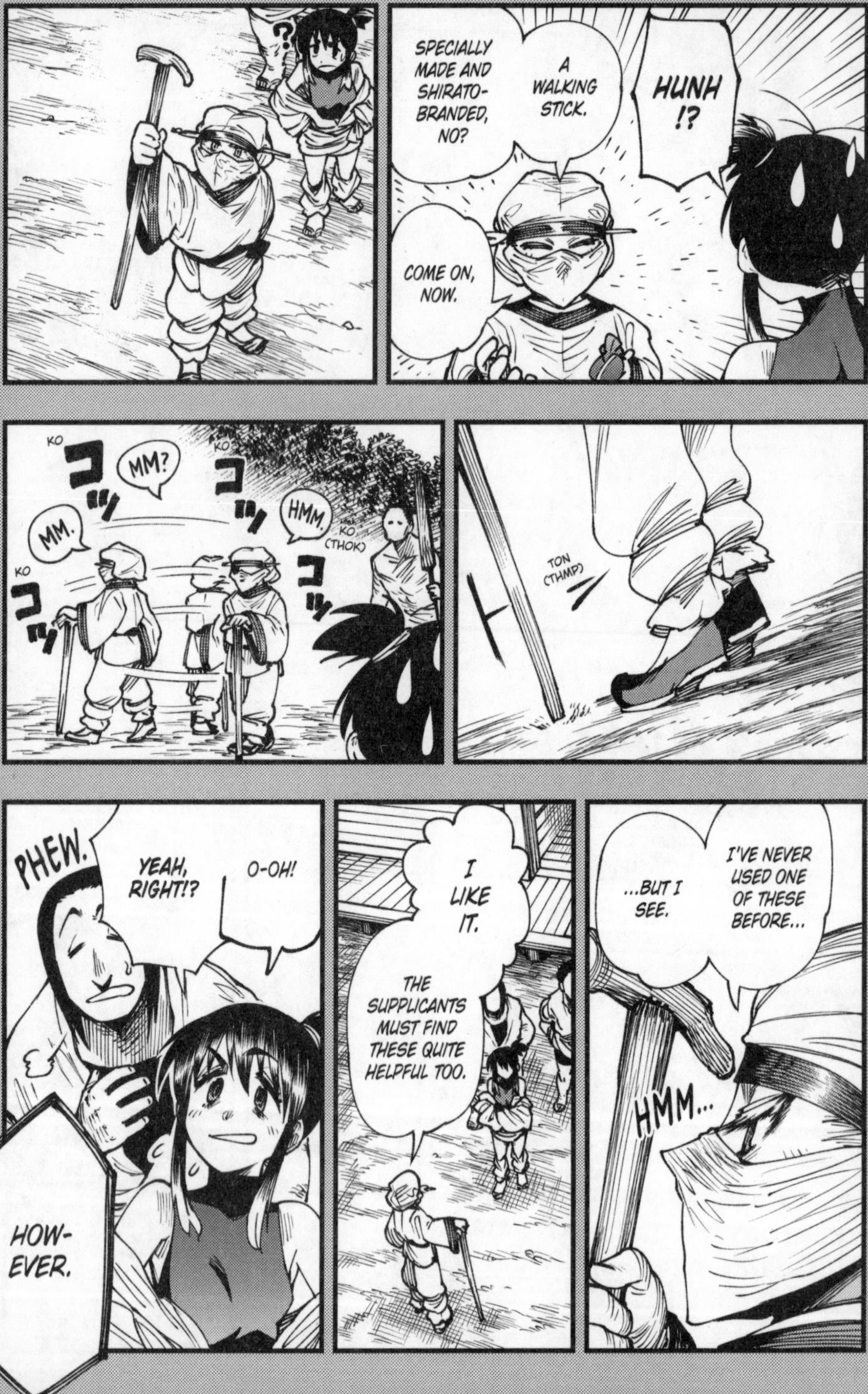
HUNH !?
A WALKING STICK.
SPECIALLY MADE AND SHIRATO-BRANDED, NO?
COME ON, NOW.
?
TON (THMP)
KO
コッ
HMM.
KO (THOK)
コッ
KO
コッ
MM?
MM.
KO
コッ
I'VE NEVER USED ONE OF THESE BEFORE...
...BUT I SEE.
HMM...
I LIKE IT.
THE SUPPLICANTS MUST FIND THESE QUITE HELPFUL TOO.
O-OH!
YEAH, RIGHT!?
PHEW.
HOW-EVER.

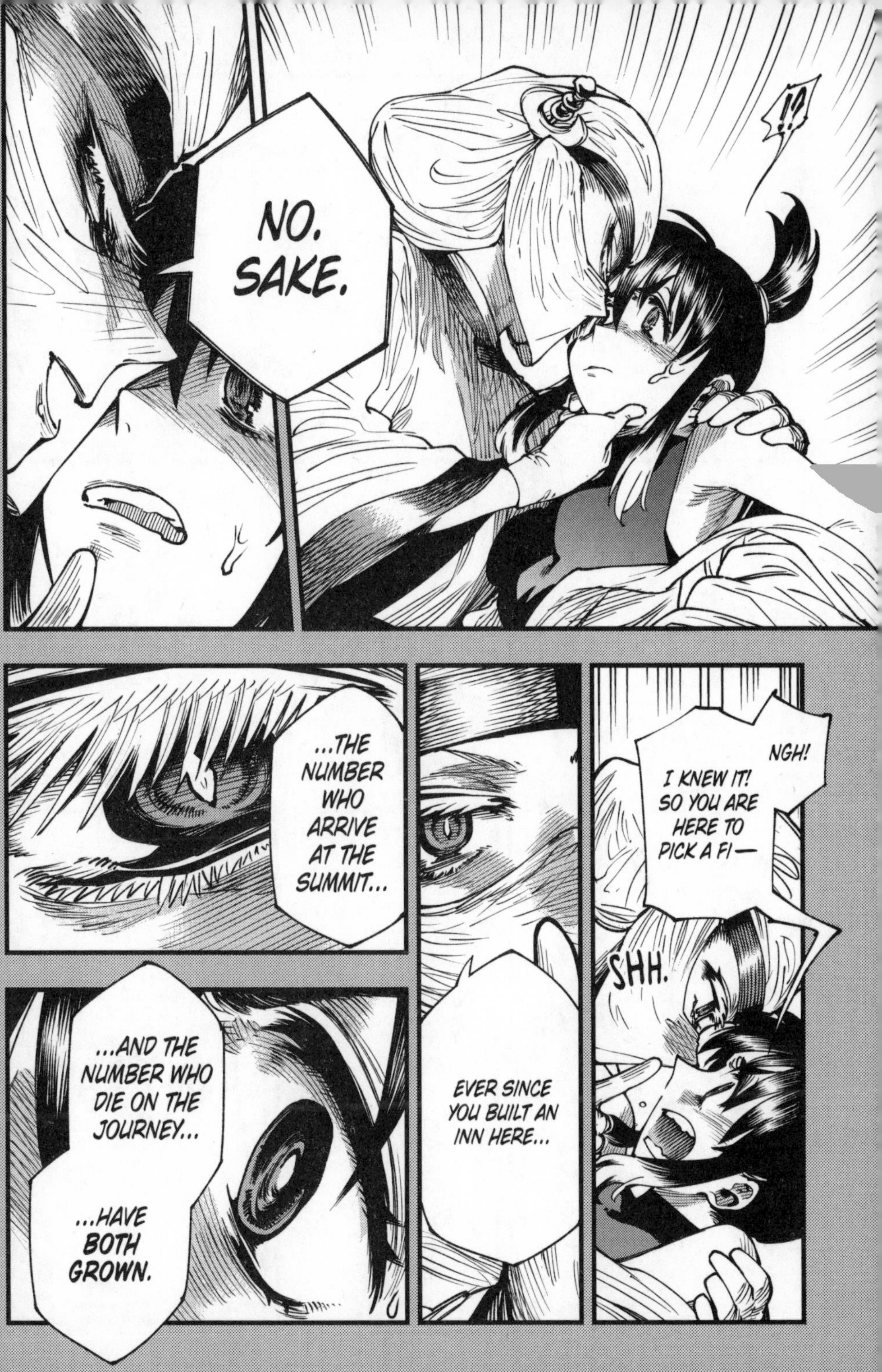
!?
NO. SAKE.
NGH!
I KNEW IT! SO YOU ARE HERE TO PICK A FI—
SHH.
EVER SINCE YOU BUILT AN INN HERE...
...THE NUMBER WHO ARRIVE AT THE SUMMIT...
...AND THE NUMBER WHO DIE ON THE JOURNEY...
...HAVE BOTH GROWN.

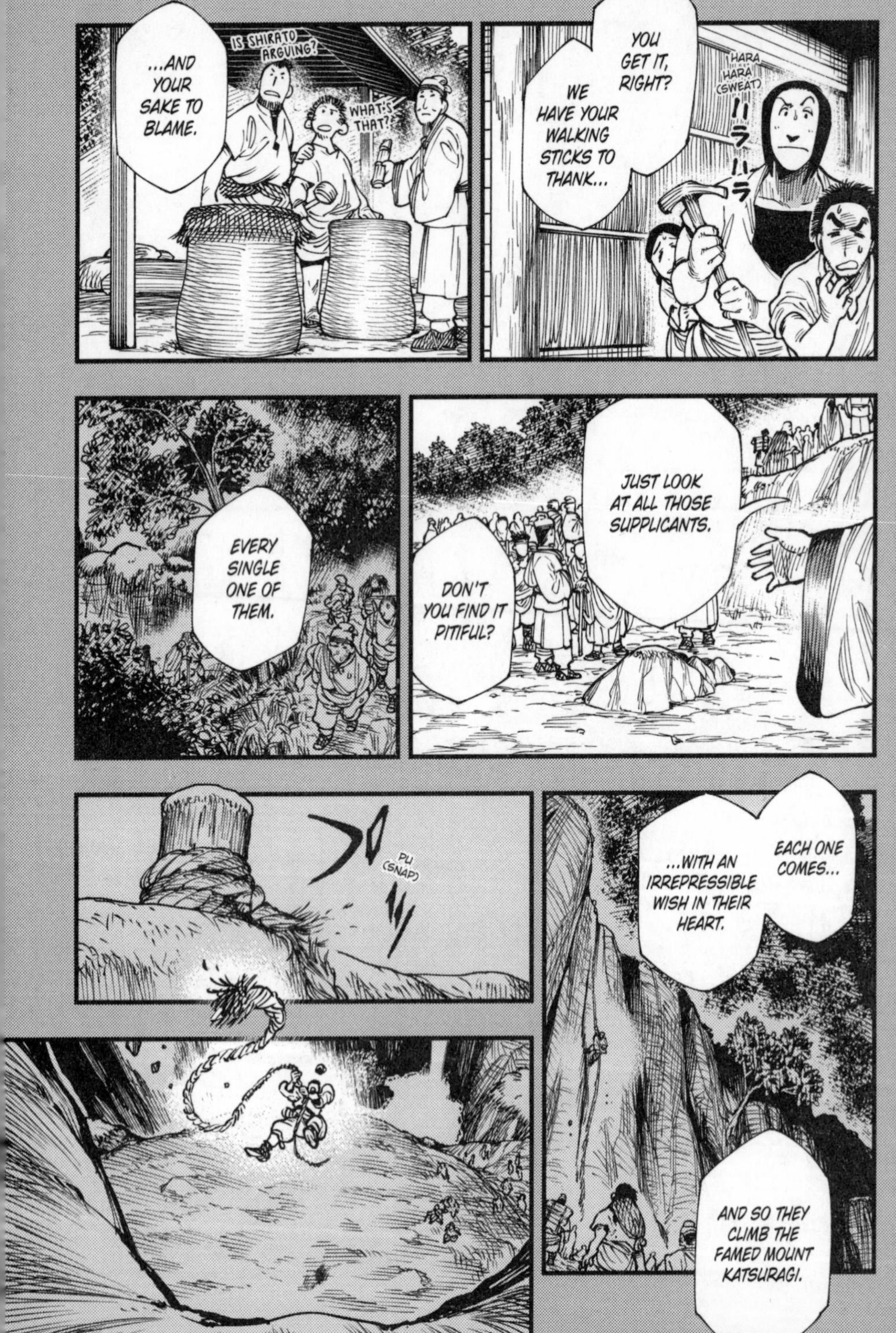
YOU GET IT, RIGHT?
WE HAVE YOUR WALKING STICKS TO THANK...
HARA HARA (SWEAT)
ハラハラ
...AND YOUR SAKE TO BLAME.
IS SHIRATO ARGUING?
WHAT'S THAT?
JUST LOOK AT ALL THOSE SUPPLICANTS.
DON'T YOU FIND IT PITIFUL?
EVERY SINGLE ONE OF THEM.
EACH ONE COMES...
...WITH AN IRREPRESSIBLE WISH IN THEIR HEART.
AND SO THEY CLIMB THE FAMED MOUNT KATSURAGI.
PU (SNAP)

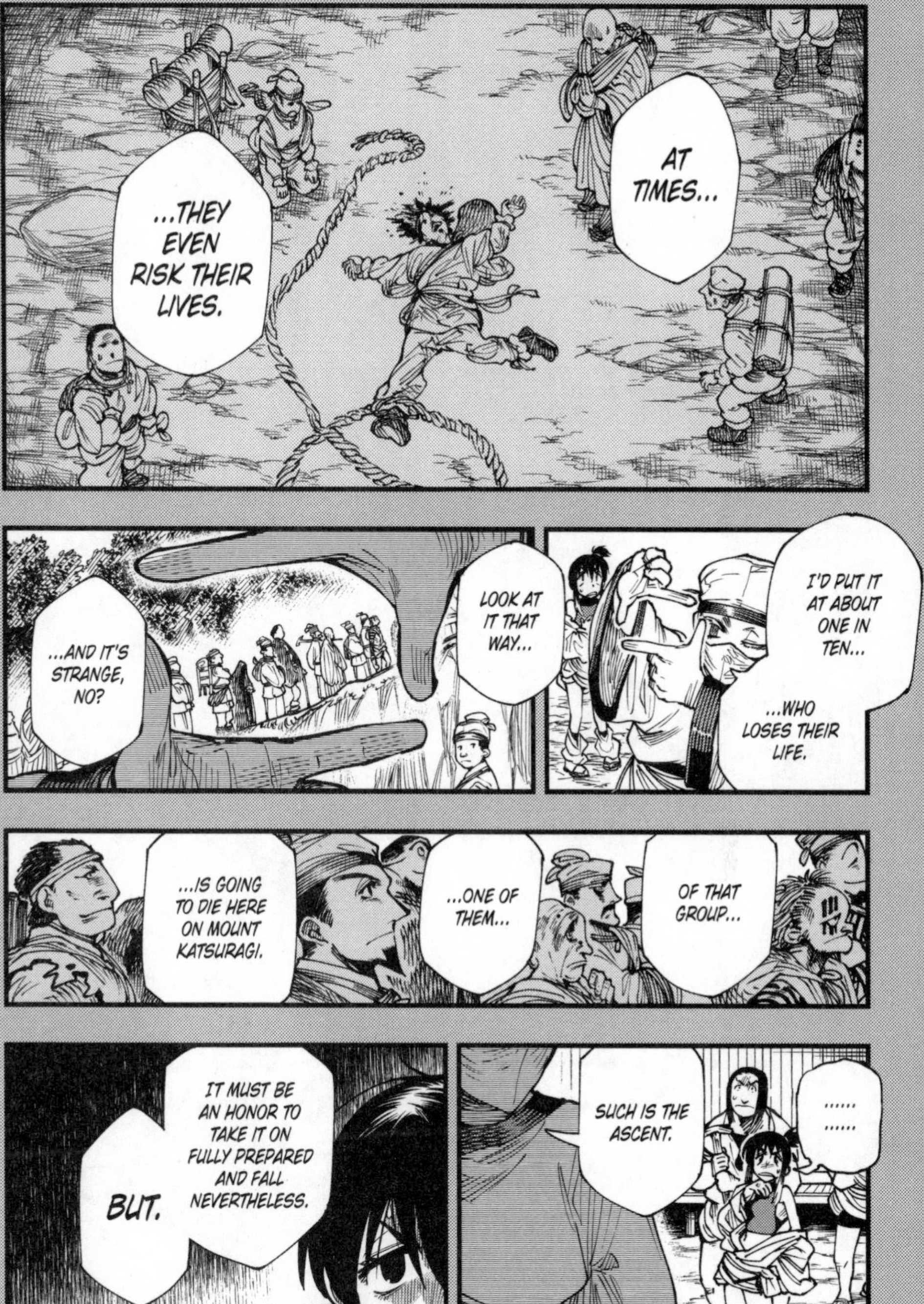
AT TIMES...
...THEY EVEN RISK THEIR LIVES.
I'D PUT IT AT ABOUT ONE IN TEN...
...WHO LOSES THEIR LIFE.
LOOK AT IT THAT WAY...
...AND IT'S STRANGE, NO?
OF THAT GROUP...
...ONE OF THEM...
...IS GOING TO DIE HERE ON MOUNT KATSURAGI.
......
......
SUCH IS THE ASCENT.
IT MUST BE AN HONOR TO TAKE IT ON FULLY PREPARED AND FALL NEVERTHELESS.
BUT.

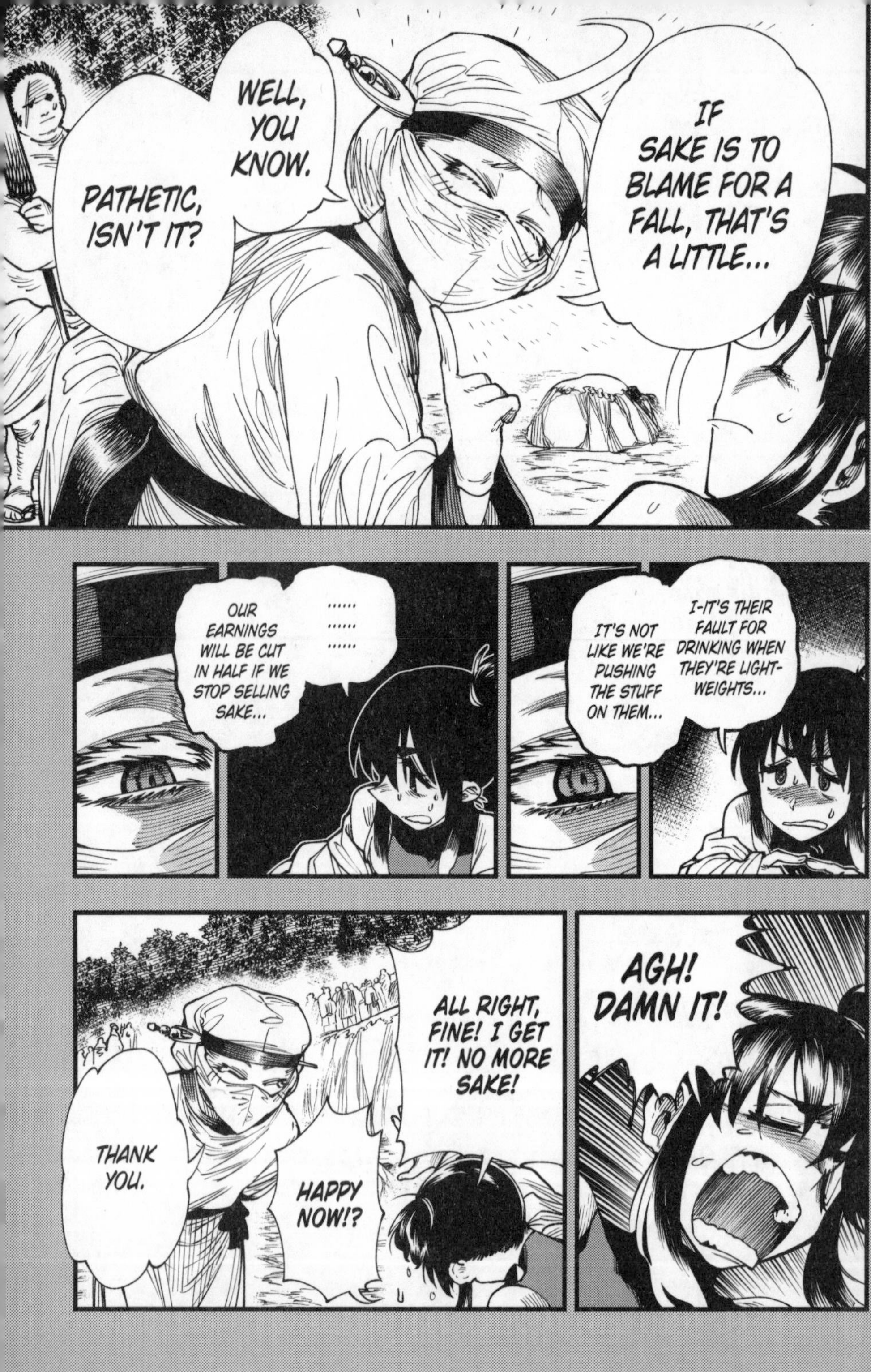
IF SAKE IS TO BLAME FOR A FALL, THAT'S A LITTLE...
WELL, YOU KNOW.
PATHETIC, ISN'T IT?
I-IT'S THEIR FAULT FOR DRINKING WHEN THEY'RE LIGHT-WEIGHTS...
IT'S NOT LIKE WE'RE PUSHING THE STUFF ON THEM...
......
......
......
OUR EARNINGS WILL BE CUT IN HALF IF WE STOP SELLING SAKE...
AGH! DAMN IT!
ALL RIGHT, FINE! I GET IT! NO MORE SAKE!
HAPPY NOW!?
THANK YOU.

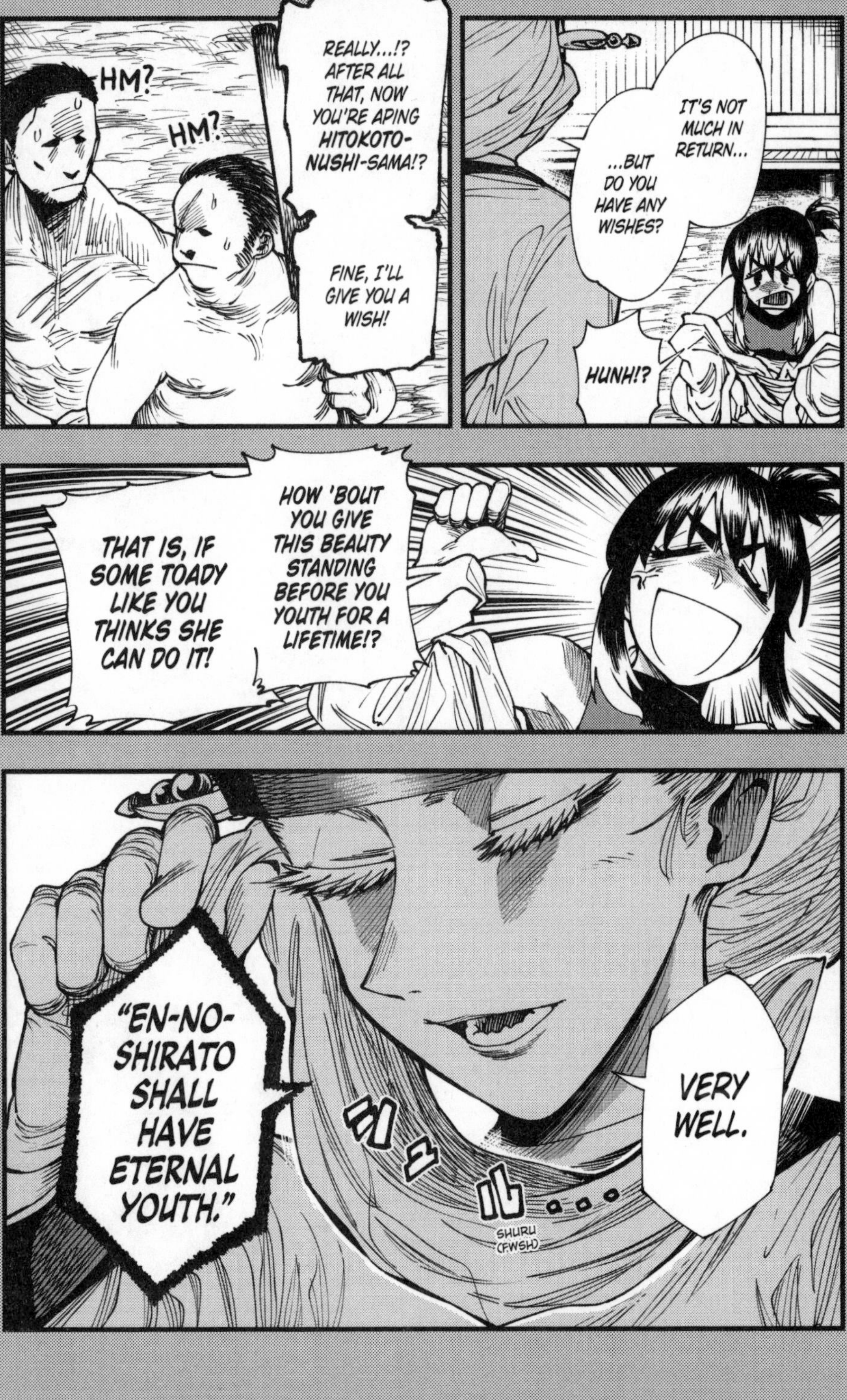
IT'S NOT MUCH IN RETURN...
...BUT DO YOU HAVE ANY WISHES?
HUNH!?
REALLY...!? AFTER ALL THAT, NOW YOU'RE APING HITOKOTO-NUSHI-SAMA!?
FINE, I'LL GIVE YOU A WISH!
HM?
HM?
HOW 'BOUT YOU GIVE THIS BEAUTY STANDING BEFORE YOU YOUTH FOR A LIFETIME!?
THAT IS, IF SOME TOADY LIKE YOU THINKS SHE CAN DO IT!
VERY WELL.
SHURU (FWSH)
"EN-NO-SHIRATO SHALL HAVE ETERNAL YOUTH."

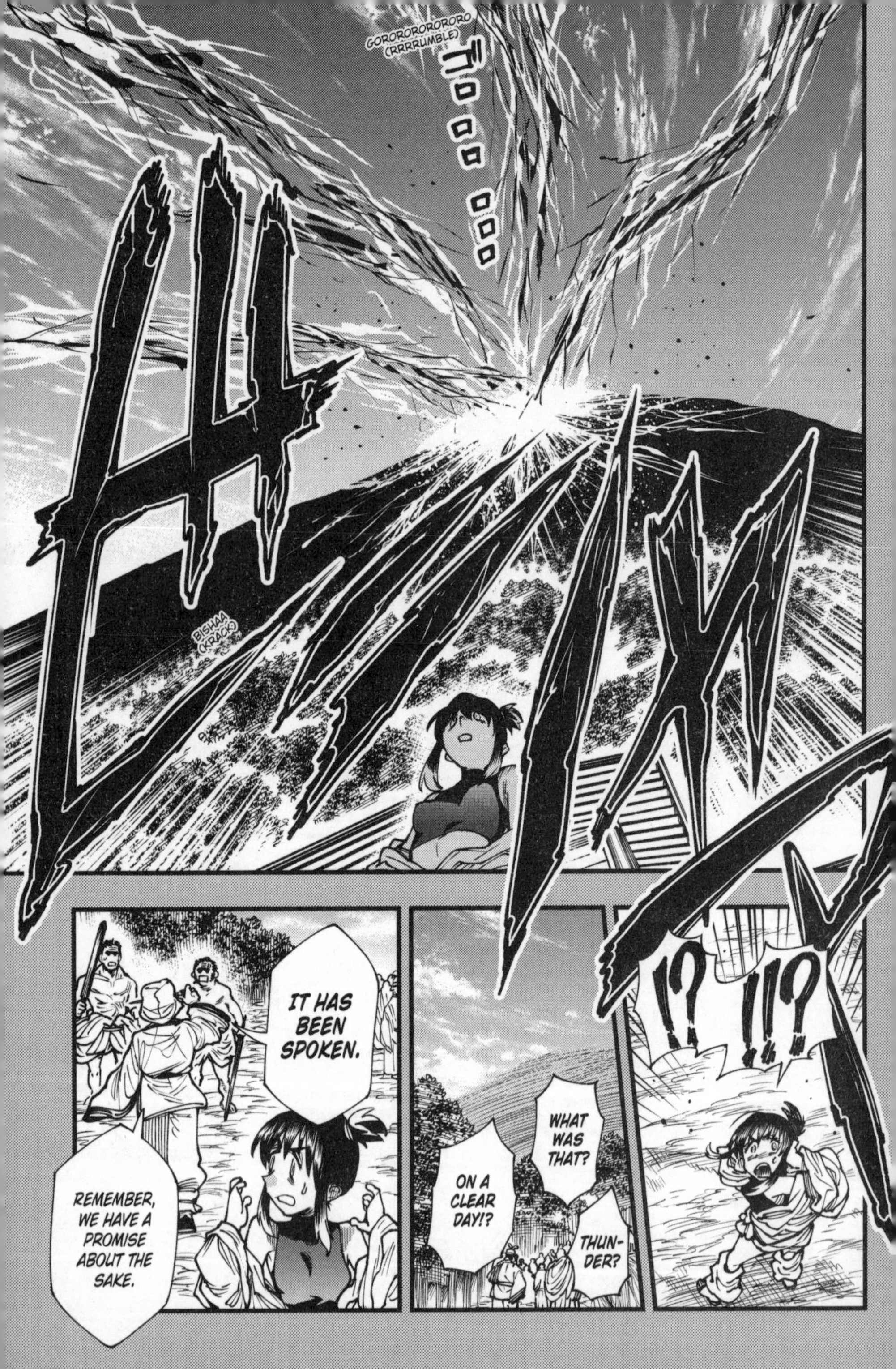
GORORORORORO (RRRRUMBLE)
BISHAA (KRACK)
!?
!!?
WHAT WAS THAT?
THUN-DER?
ON A CLEAR DAY!?
IT HAS BEEN SPOKEN.
REMEMBER, WE HAVE A PROMISE ABOUT THE SAKE.

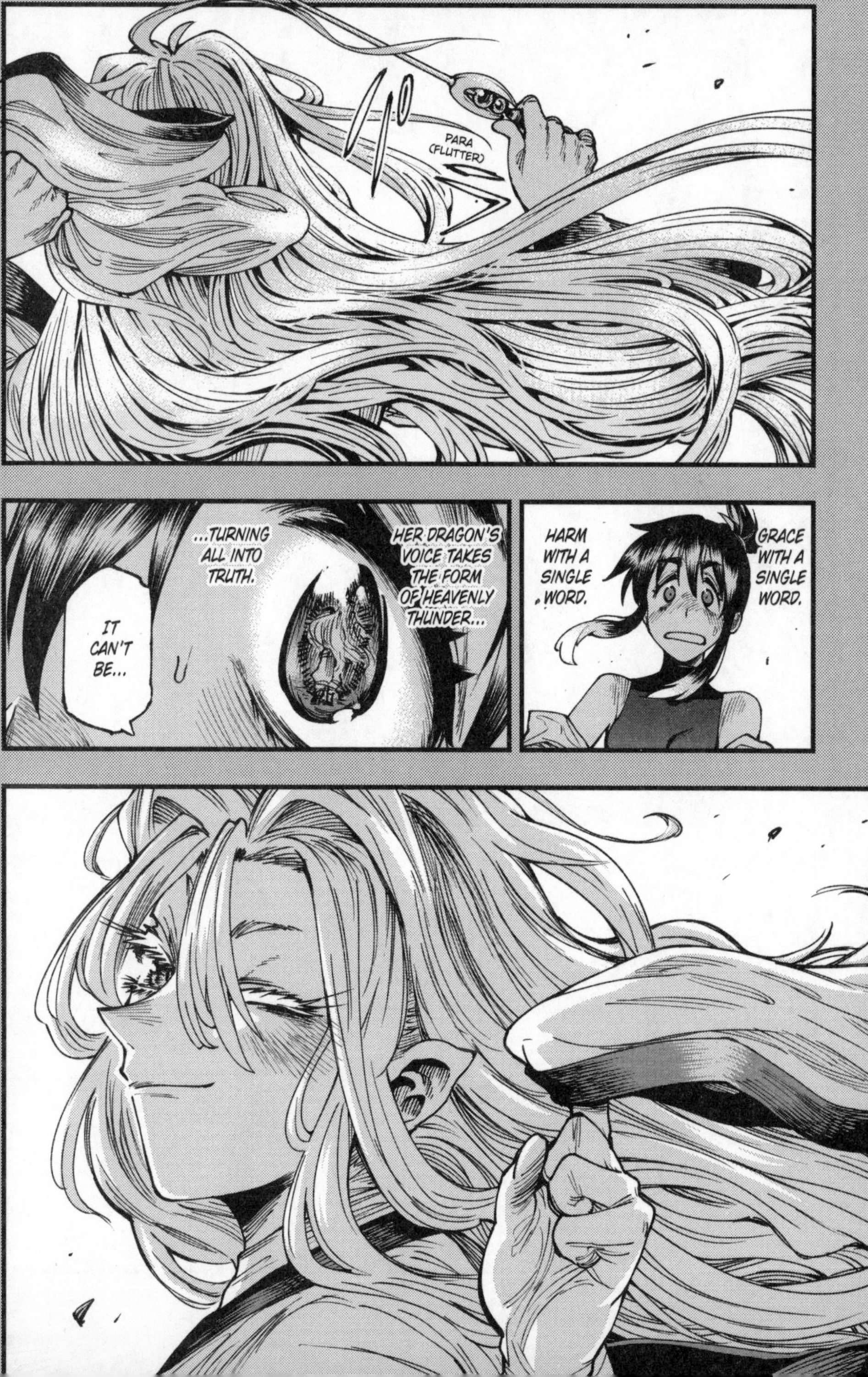
PARA (FLUTTER)
GRACE WITH A SINGLE WORD.
HARM WITH A SINGLE WORD.
HER DRAGON'S VOICE TAKES THE FORM OF HEAVENLY THUNDER...
...TURNING ALL INTO TRUTH.
IT CAN'T BE...

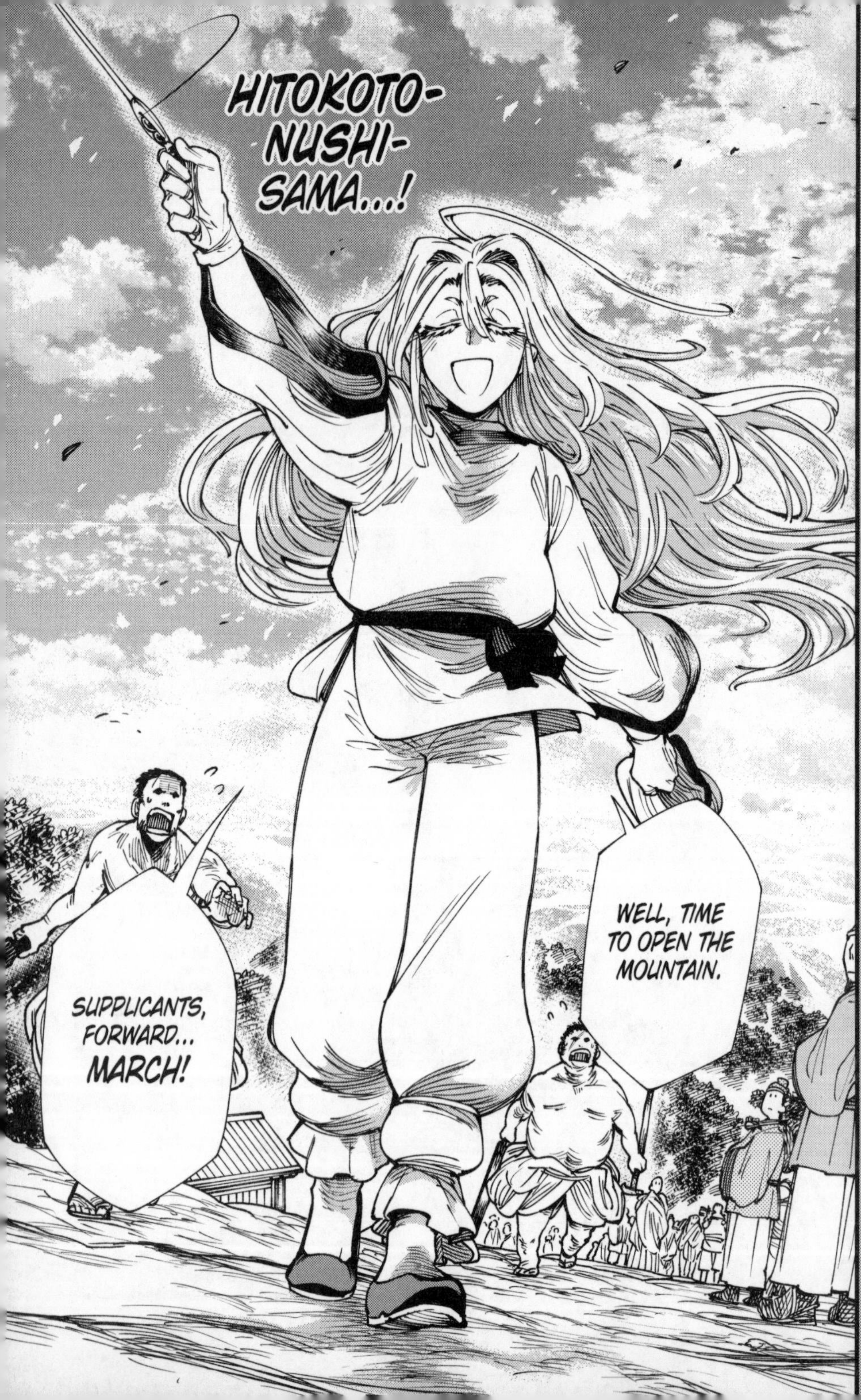
HITOKOTO-NUSHI-SAMA...!
WELL, TIME TO OPEN THE MOUNTAIN.
SUPPLICANTS, FORWARD... MARCH!

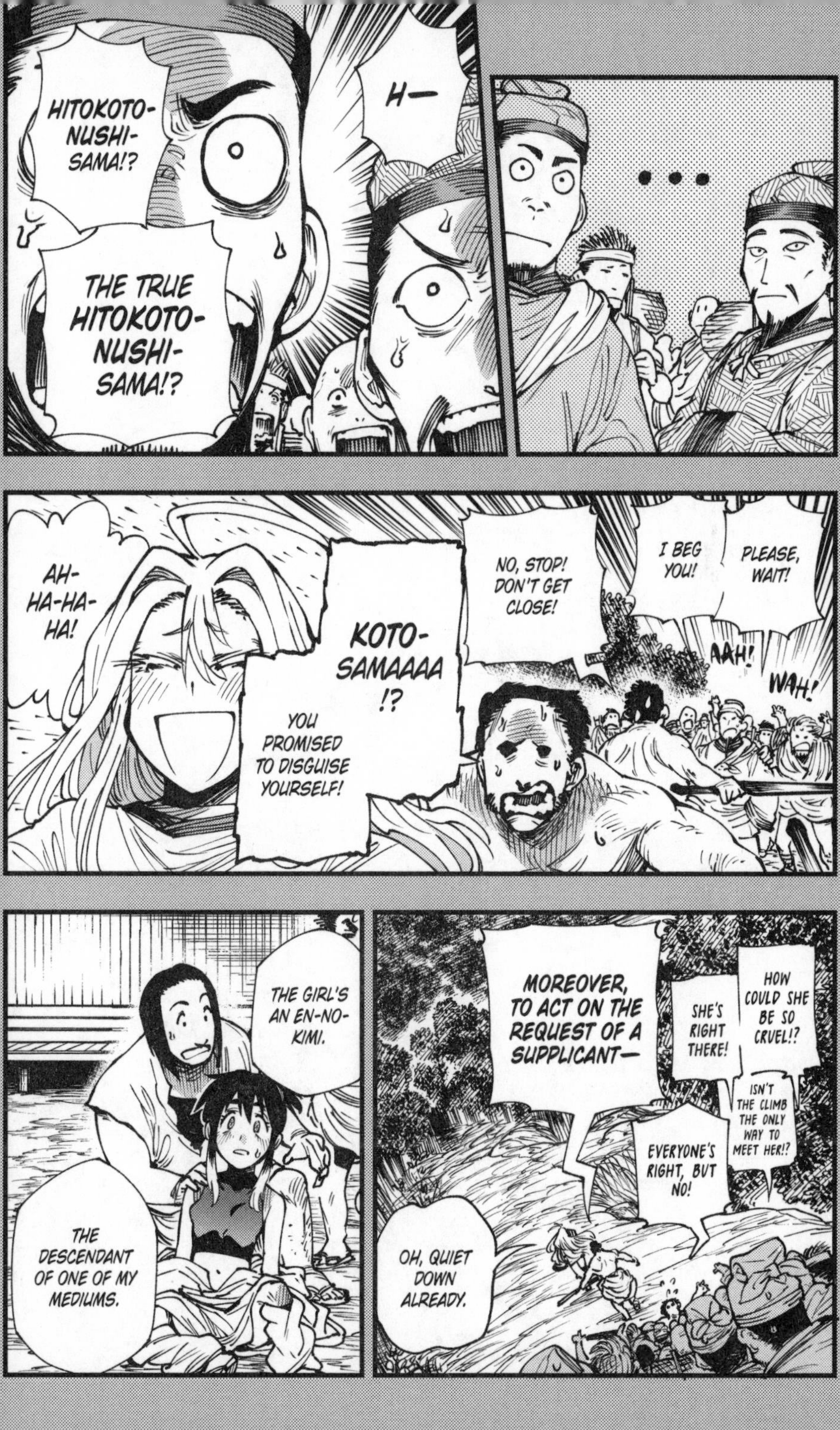
. . .
H—
HITOKOTO-NUSHI-SAMA!?
THE TRUE HITOKOTO-NUSHI-SAMA!?
PLEASE, WAIT!
I BEG YOU!
AAH!
WAH!
NO, STOP! DON'T GET CLOSE!
KOTO-SAMAAAA!?
YOU PROMISED TO DISGUISE YOURSELF!
AH-HA-HA-HA!
HOW COULD SHE BE SO CRUEL!?
SHE'S RIGHT THERE!
MOREOVER, TO ACT ON THE REQUEST OF A SUPPLICANT—
ISN'T THE CLIMB THE ONLY WAY TO MEET HER!?
EVERYONE'S RIGHT, BUT NO!
OH, QUIET DOWN ALREADY.
THE GIRL'S AN EN-NO-KIMI.
THE DESCENDANT OF ONE OF MY MEDIUMS.

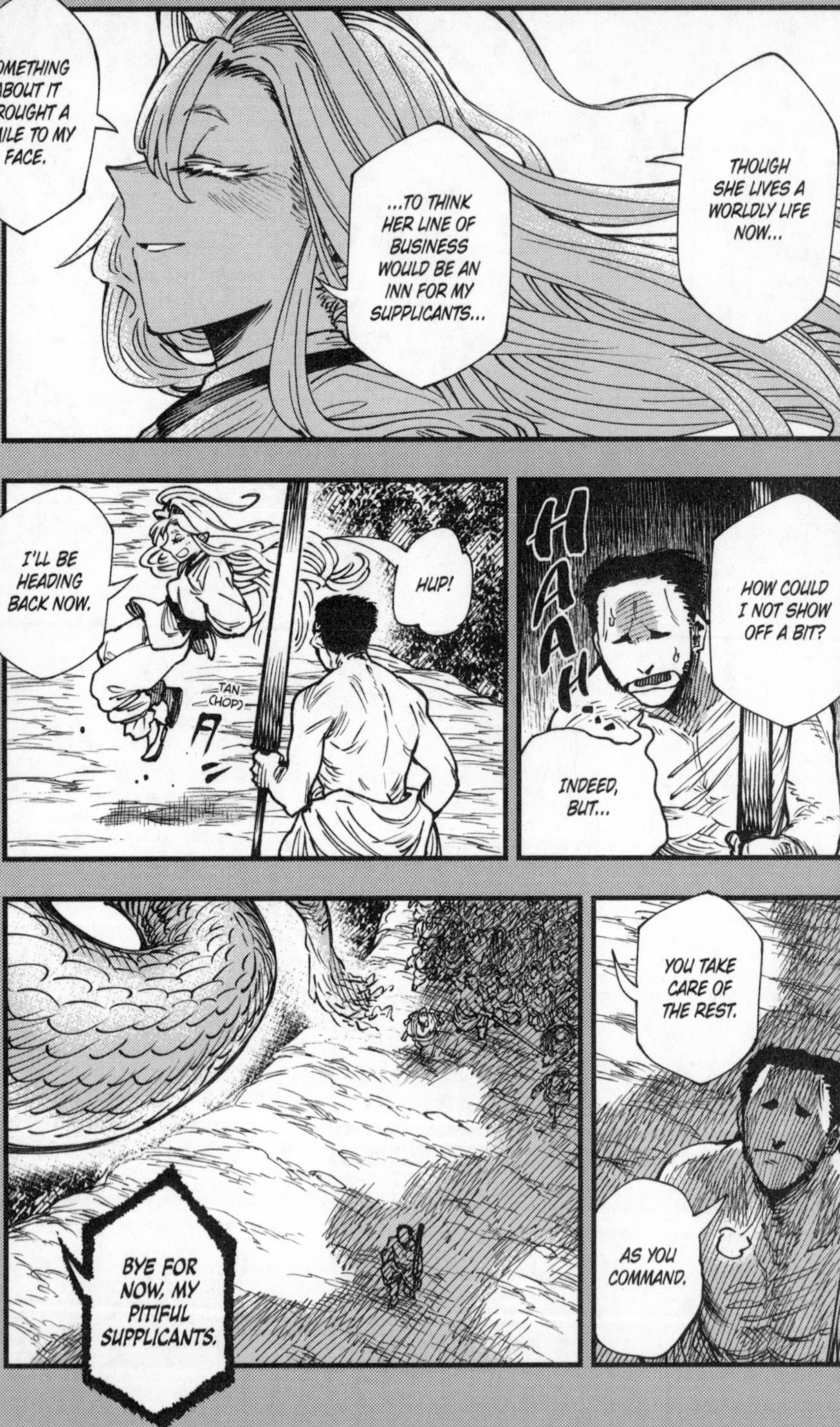
THOUGH SHE LIVES A WORLDLY LIFE NOW...
...TO THINK HER LINE OF BUSINESS WOULD BE AN INN FOR MY SUPPLICANTS...
SOMETHING ABOUT IT BROUGHT A SMILE TO MY FACE.
HAAAH
HOW COULD I NOT SHOW OFF A BIT?
INDEED, BUT...
HUP!
I'LL BE HEADING BACK NOW.
TAN (HOP)
YOU TAKE CARE OF THE REST.
AS YOU COMMAND.
BYE FOR NOW, MY PITIFUL SUPPLICANTS.

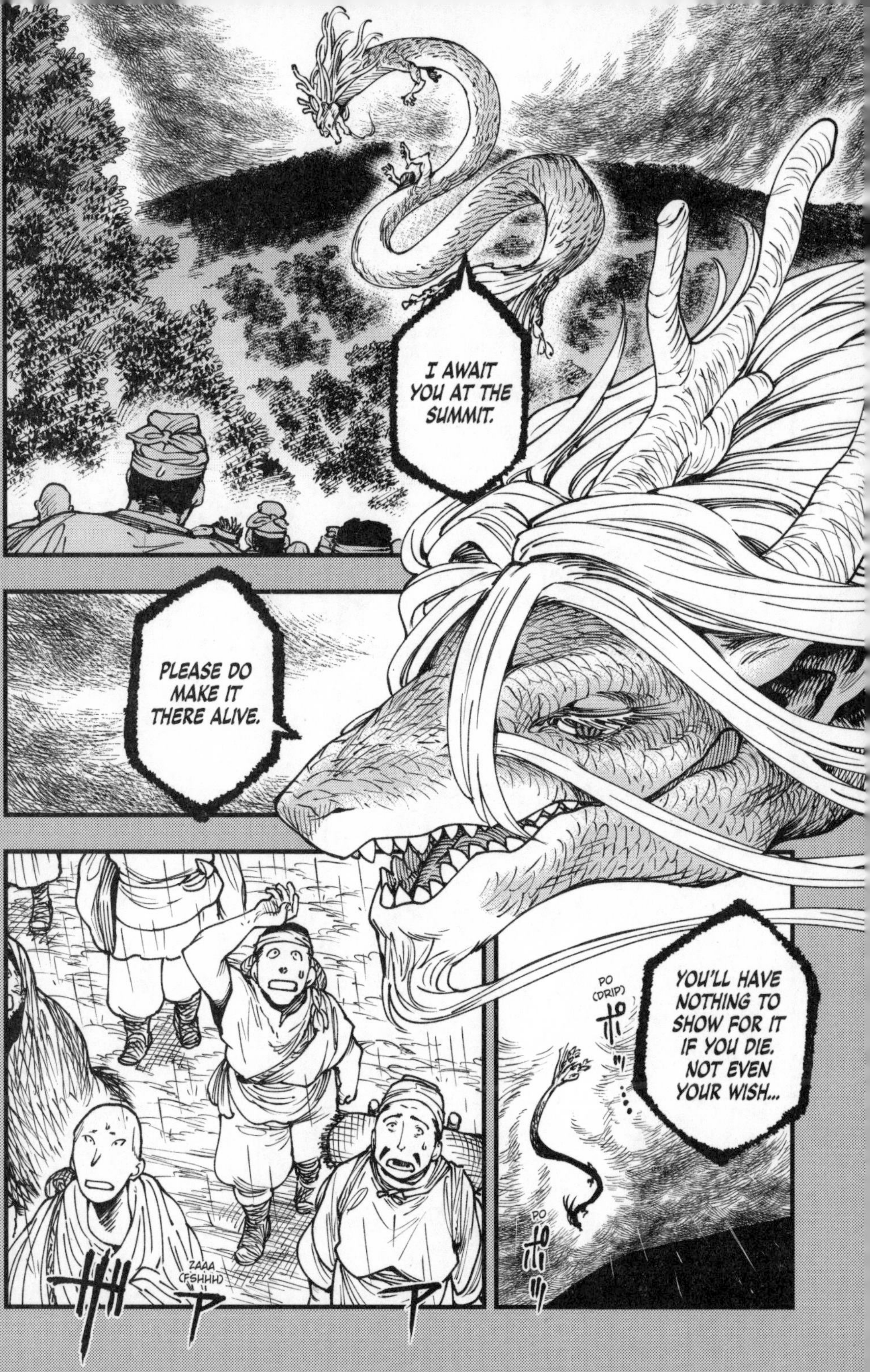
I AWAIT YOU AT THE SUMMIT.
PLEASE DO MAKE IT THERE ALIVE.
PO (DRIP)
YOU'LL HAVE NOTHING TO SHOW FOR IT IF YOU DIE. NOT EVEN YOUR WISH...
PO
ZAAA (FSHHH)

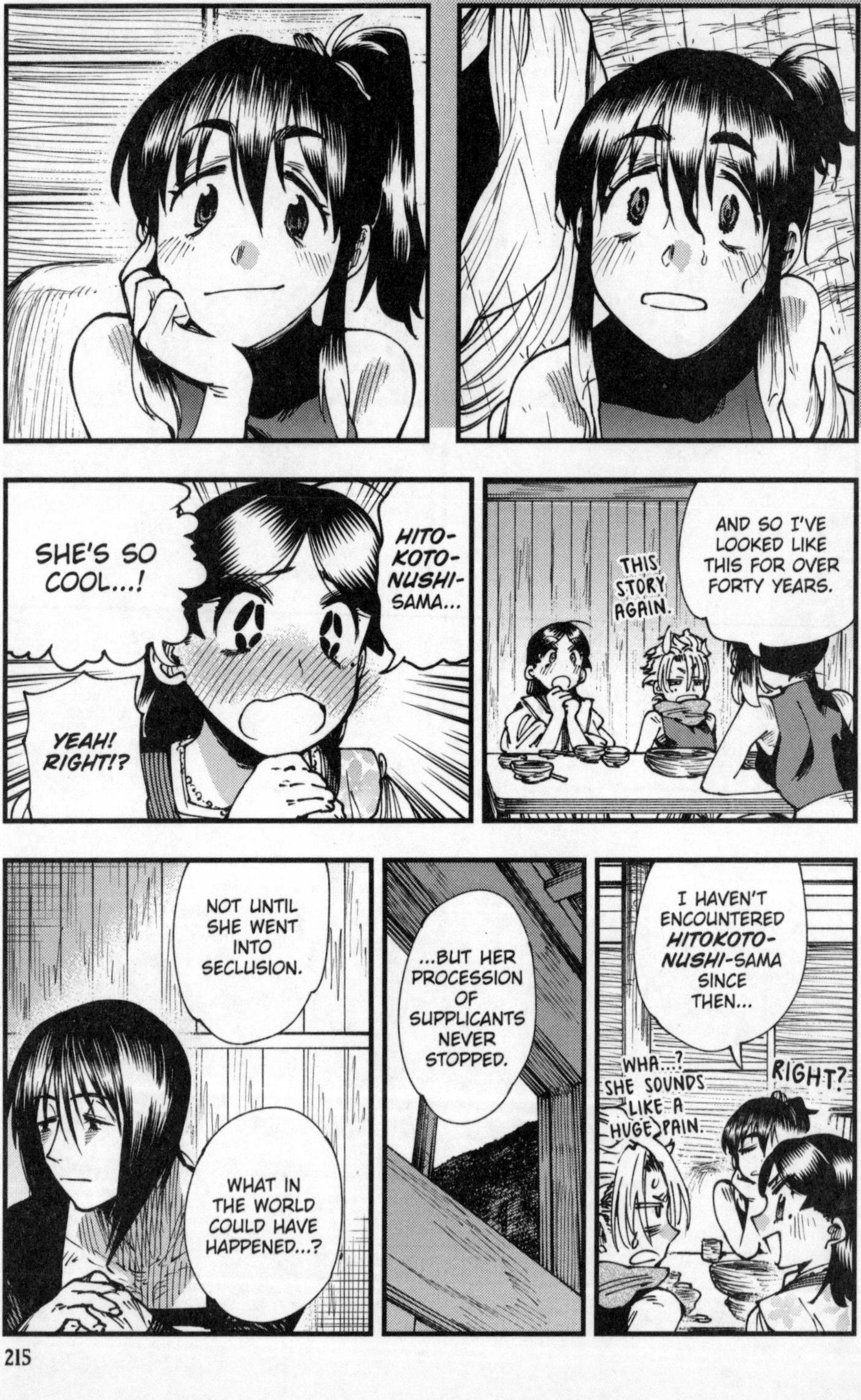
AND SO I'VE LOOKED LIKE THIS FOR OVER FORTY YEARS.
THIS STORY AGAIN.
HITO-KOTO-NUSHI-SAMA...
SHE'S SO COOL...!
YEAH! RIGHT!?
I HAVEN'T ENCOUNTERED HITOKOTO-NUSHI-SAMA SINCE THEN...
RIGHT?
WHA...? SHE SOUNDS LIKE A HUGE PAIN.
...BUT HER PROCESSION OF SUPPLICANTS NEVER STOPPED.
NOT UNTIL SHE WENT INTO SECLUSION.
WHAT IN THE WORLD COULD HAVE HAPPENED...?

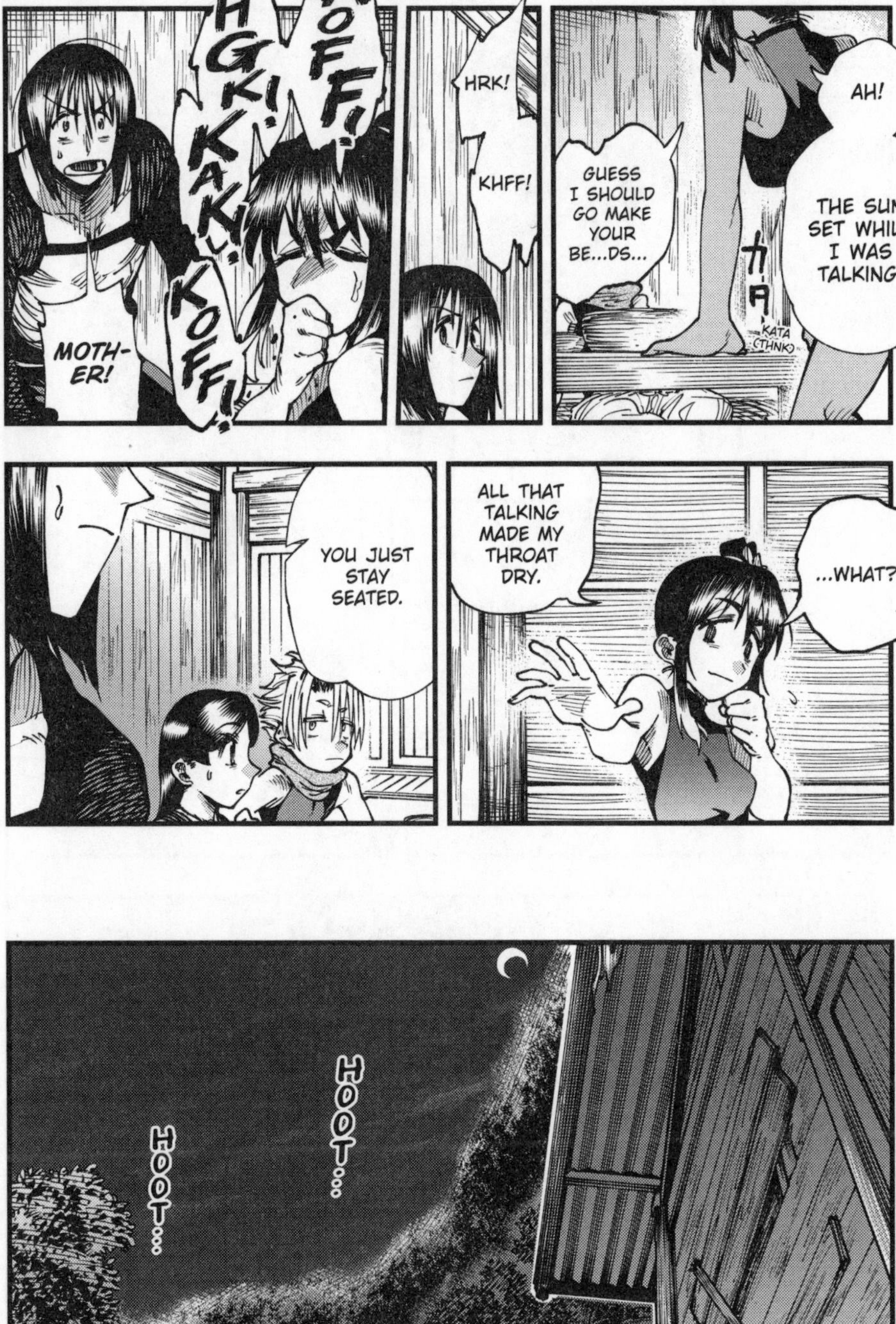
AH!
THE SUN SET WHILE I WAS TALKING.
GUESS I SHOULD GO MAKE YOUR BE...DS...
ガタ
KATA (THNK)
HRK!
KHFF!
KOFF!
HGK!
KAK!
KOFF!
MOTH-ER!
...WHAT?
ALL THAT TALKING MADE MY THROAT DRY.
YOU JUST STAY SEATED.
HOOT...
HOOT...

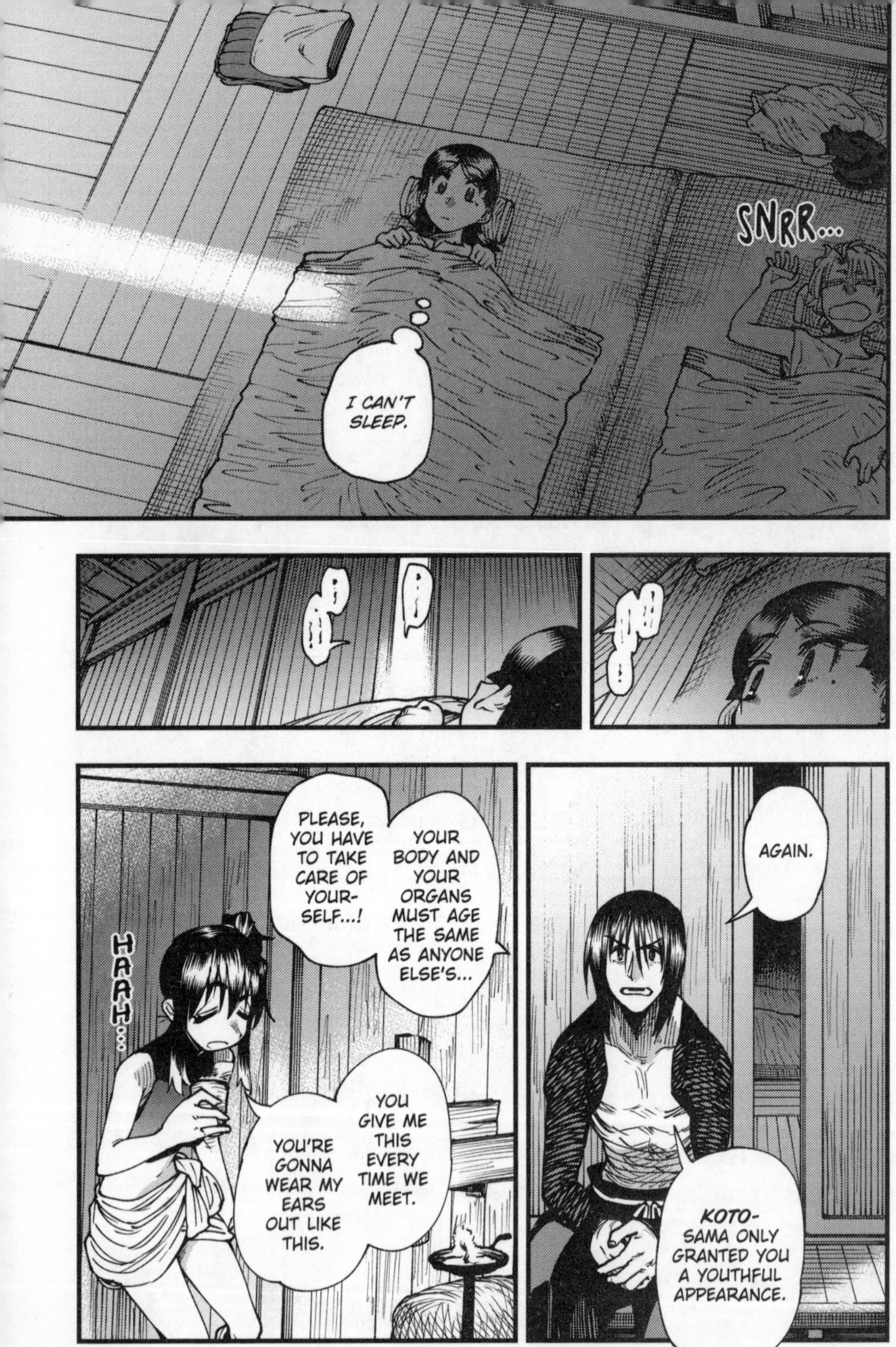
SNRR...
I CAN'T SLEEP.
AGAIN.
KOTO-SAMA ONLY GRANTED YOU A YOUTHFUL APPEARANCE.
YOUR BODY AND YOUR ORGANS MUST AGE THE SAME AS ANYONE ELSE'S...
PLEASE, YOU HAVE TO TAKE CARE OF YOUR-SELF...!
HAAAH...
YOU GIVE ME THIS EVERY TIME WE MEET.
YOU'RE GONNA WEAR MY EARS OUT LIKE THIS.

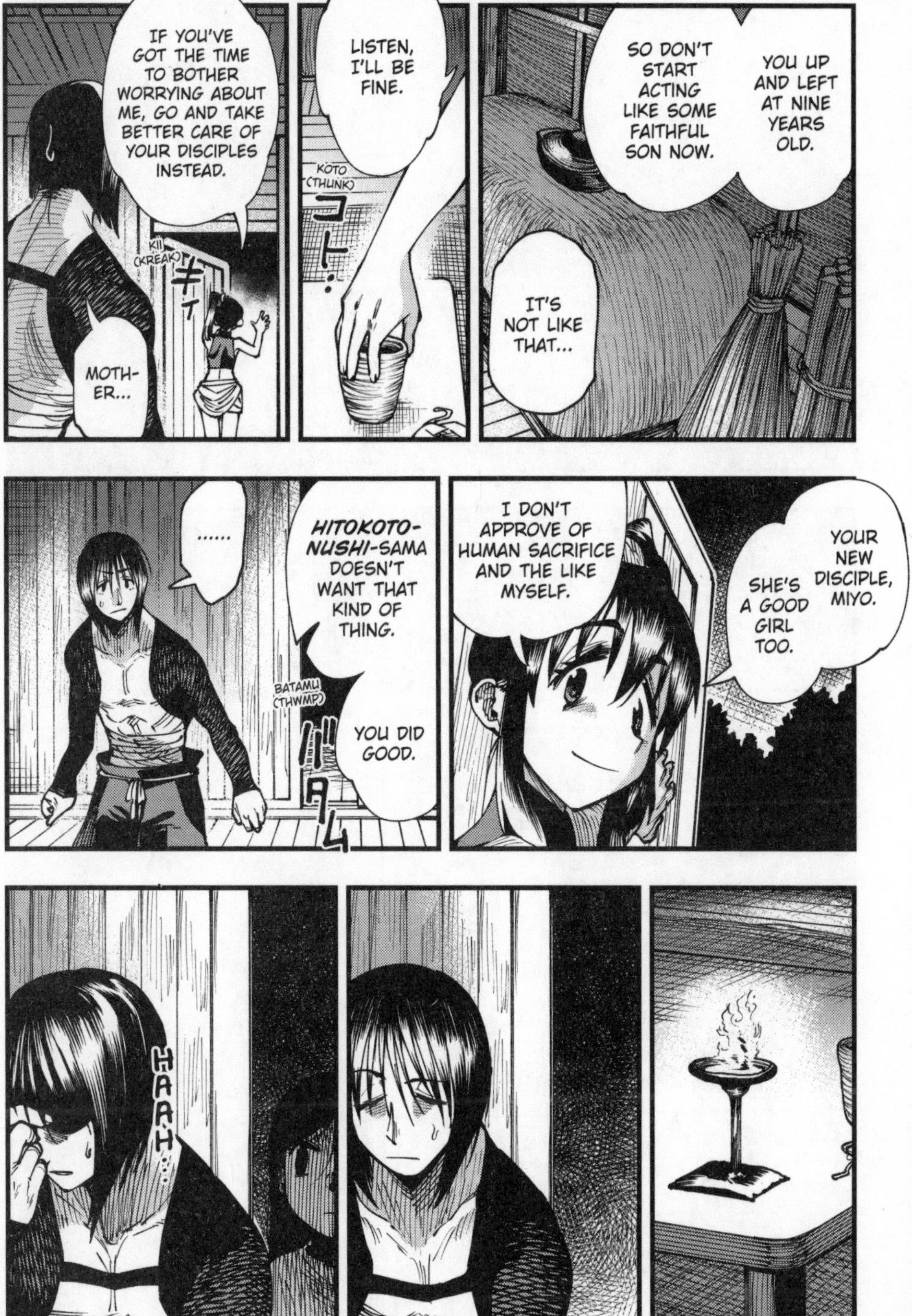
YOU UP AND LEFT AT NINE YEARS OLD.
SO DON'T START ACTING LIKE SOME FAITHFUL SON NOW.
IT'S NOT LIKE THAT...
LISTEN, I'LL BE FINE.
KOTO (THUNK)
IF YOU'VE GOT THE TIME TO BOTHER WORRYING ABOUT ME, GO AND TAKE BETTER CARE OF YOUR DISCIPLES INSTEAD.
KII (KREAK)
MOTH-ER...
YOUR NEW DISCIPLE, MIYO.
SHE'S A GOOD GIRL TOO.
I DON'T APPROVE OF HUMAN SACRIFICE AND THE LIKE MYSELF.
HITOKOTO-NUSHI-SAMA DOESN'T WANT THAT KIND OF THING.
YOU DID GOOD.
BATAMU (THWMP)
......
HAAAH...

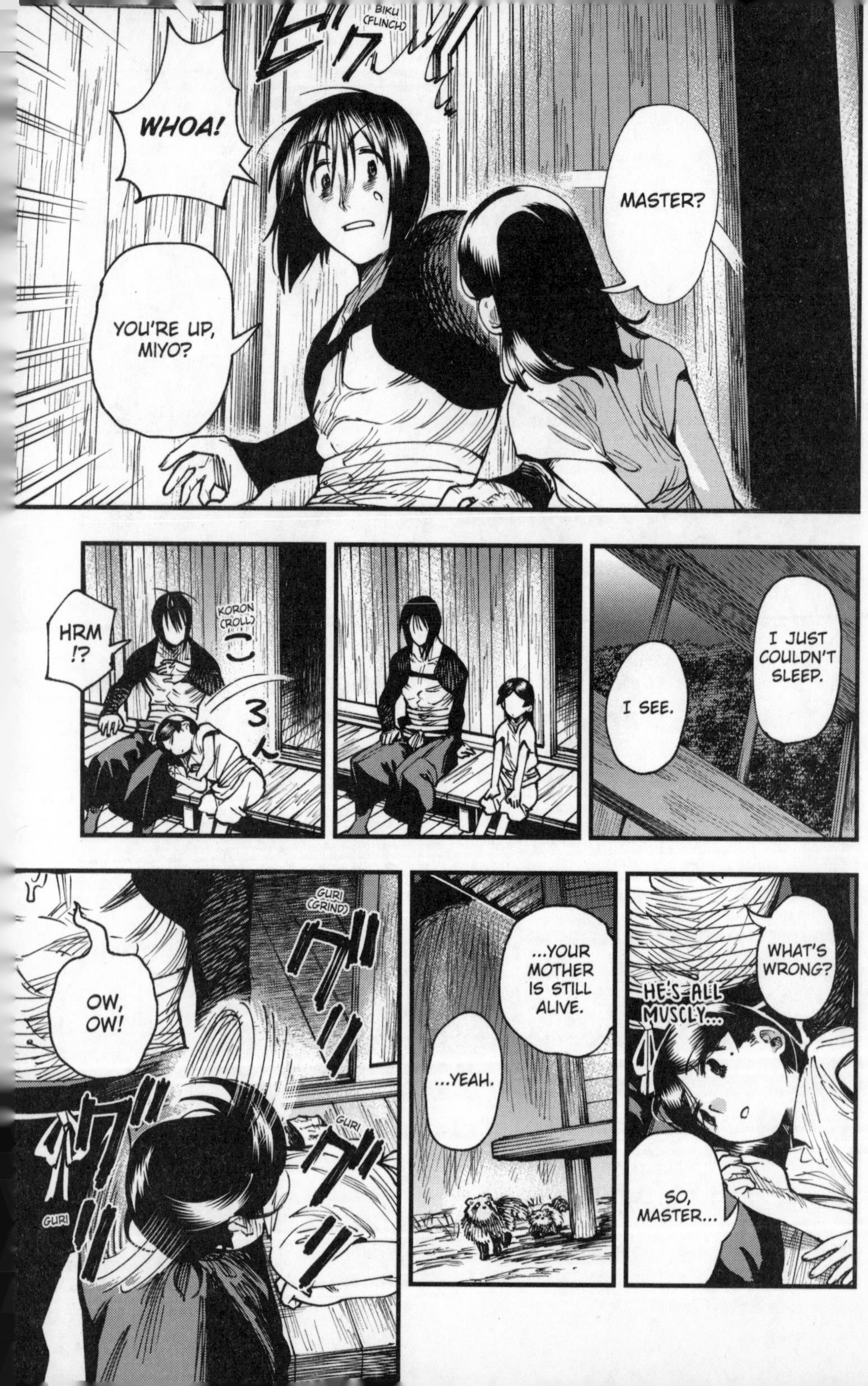
BIKU (FLINCH)
MASTER?
WHOA!
YOU'RE UP, MIYO?
I JUST COULDN'T SLEEP.
I SEE.
KORON (ROLL)
HRM !?
WHAT'S WRONG?
HE'S ALL MUSCLY...
SO, MASTER...
...YOUR MOTHER IS STILL ALIVE.
...YEAH.
GURI (GRIND)
OW, OW!
GURI
GURI

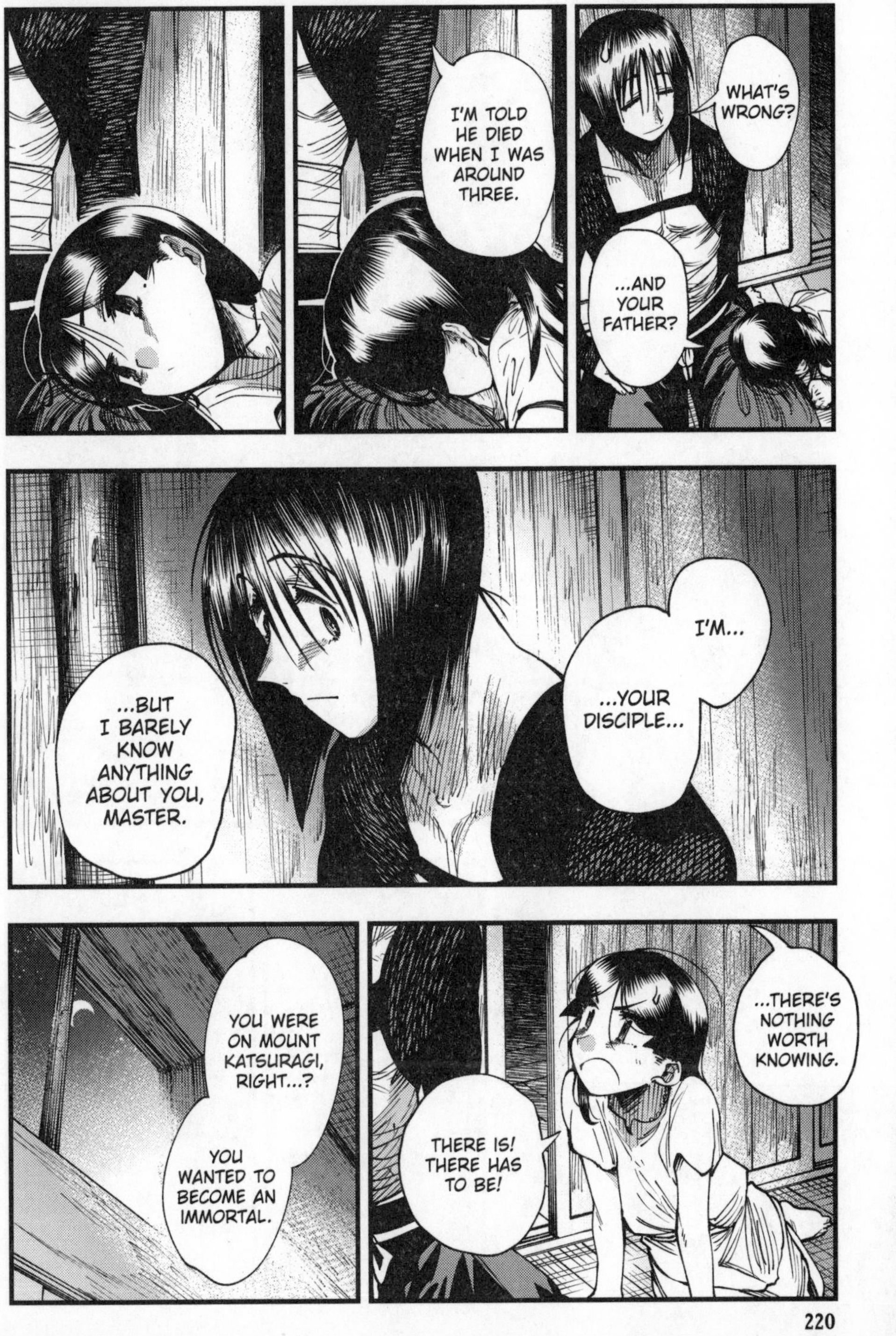
WHAT'S WRONG?
...AND YOUR FATHER?
I'M TOLD HE DIED WHEN I WAS AROUND THREE.
I'M...
...YOUR DISCIPLE...
...BUT I BARELY KNOW ANYTHING ABOUT YOU, MASTER.
...THERE'S NOTHING WORTH KNOWING.
THERE IS! THERE HAS TO BE!
YOU WERE ON MOUNT KATSURAGI, RIGHT...?
YOU WANTED TO BECOME AN IMMORTAL.

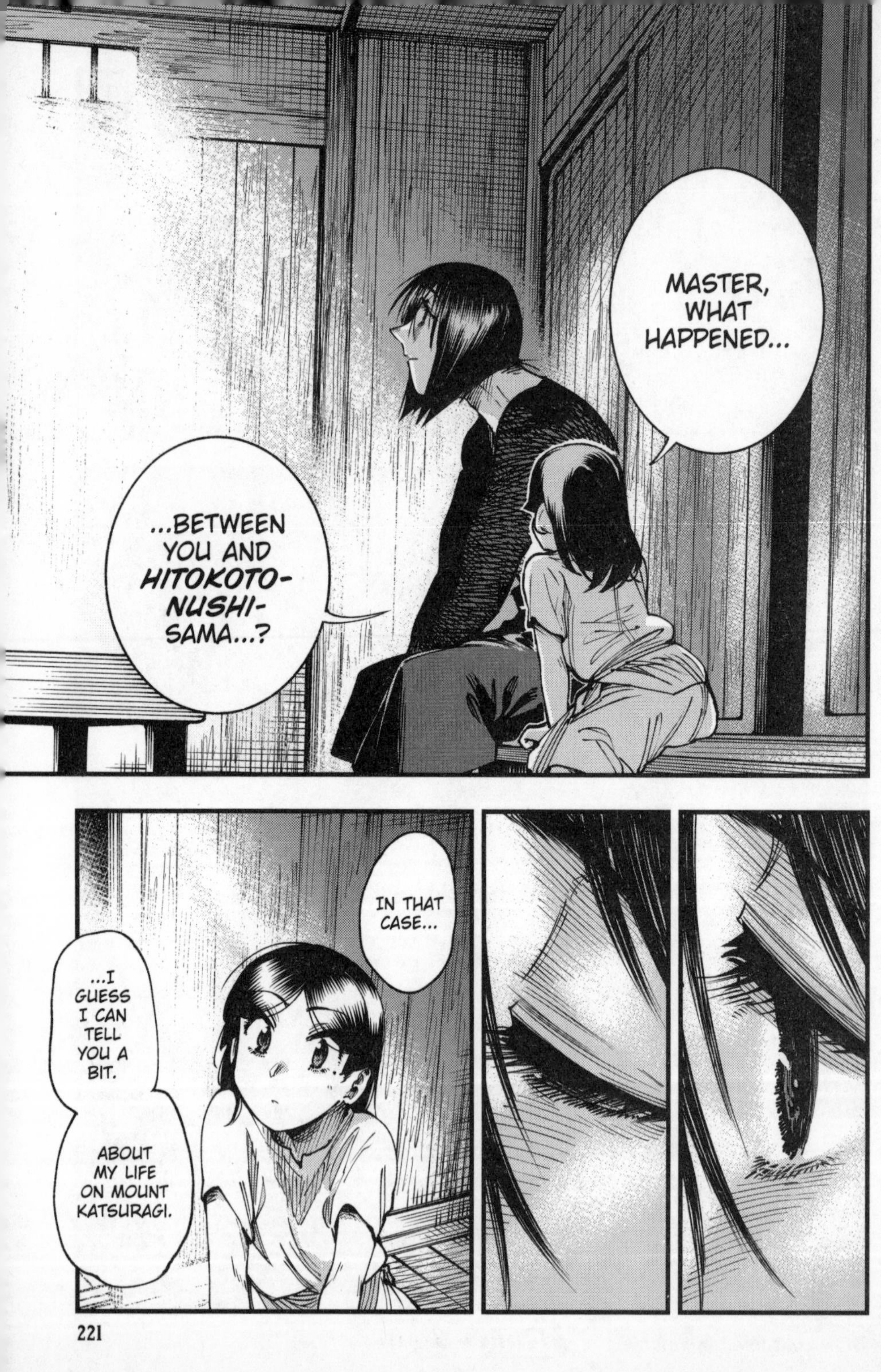
MASTER, WHAT HAPPENED...
...BETWEEN YOU AND *HITOKOTO-NUSHI-*SAMA...?
IN THAT CASE...
...I GUESS I CAN TELL YOU A BIT.
ABOUT MY LIFE ON MOUNT KATSURAGI.

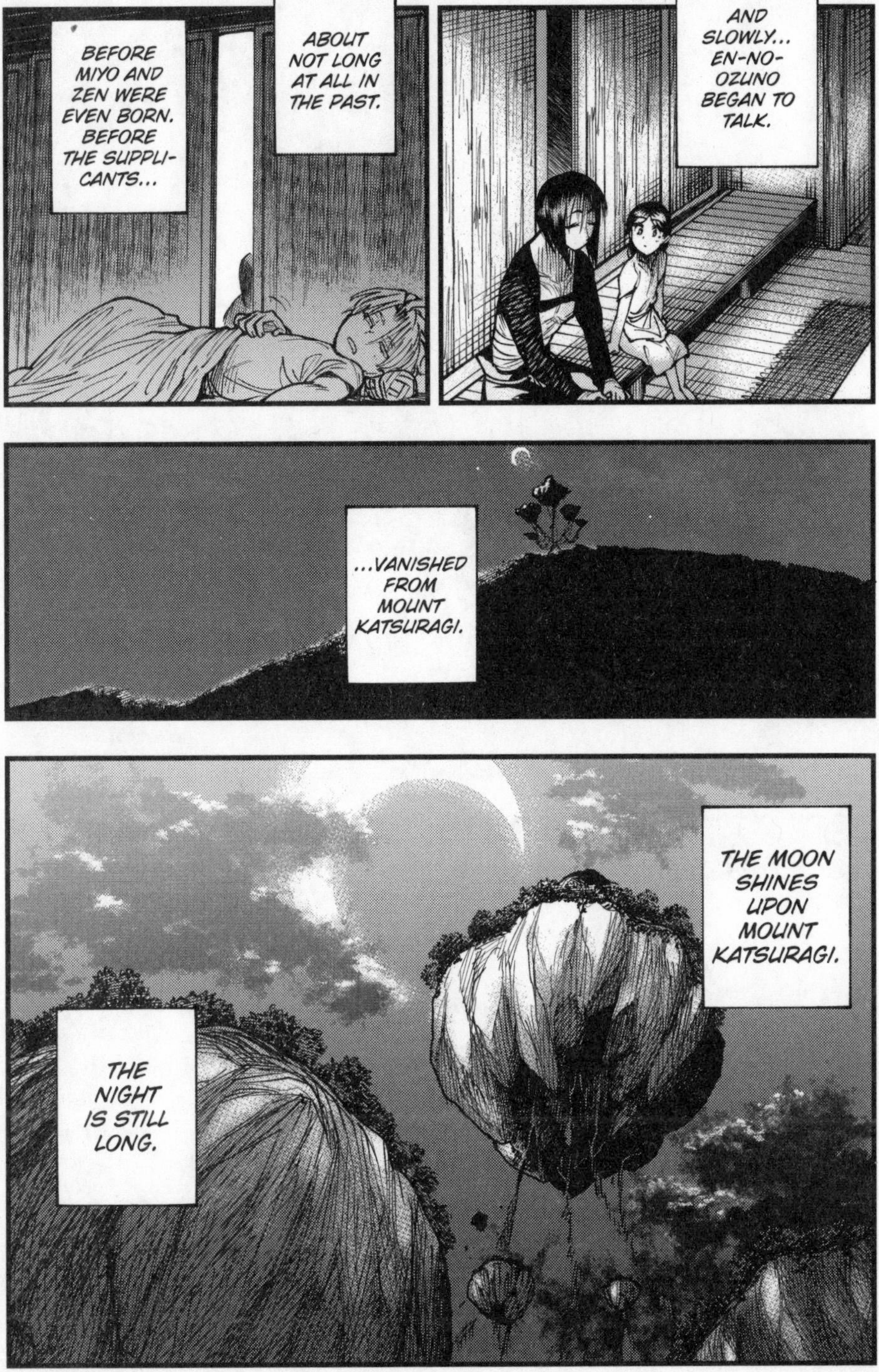
AND SLOWLY... EN-NO-OZUNO BEGAN TO TALK.
ABOUT NOT LONG AT ALL IN THE PAST.
BEFORE MIYO AND ZEN WERE EVEN BORN. BEFORE THE SUPPLI-CANTS...
...VANISHED FROM MOUNT KATSURAGI.
THE MOON SHINES UPON MOUNT KATSURAGI.
THE NIGHT IS STILL LONG.

To be continued in Volume 4

CHAPTER XI END

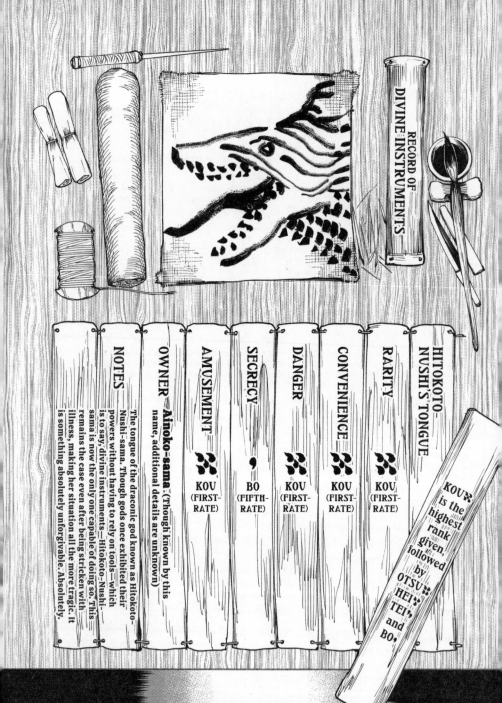

RECORD OF DIVINE INSTRUMENTS

HITOKOTO-NUSHI'S TONGUE

RARITY — KOU (FIRST-RATE)

CONVENIENCE — KOU (FIRST-RATE)

DANGER — KOU (FIRST-RATE)

SECRECY — BO (FIFTH-RATE)

AMUSEMENT — KOU (FIRST-RATE)

OWNER — **Ainoko-sama** (Though known by this name, additional details are unknown)

NOTES — The tongue of the draconic god known as Hitokoto-Nushi-sama. Though gods once exhibited their powers without having to rely on tools—which is to say, divine instruments—Hitokoto-Nushi-sama is now the only one capable of doing so. This remains the case even after being stricken with illness, making her situation all the more tragic. It is something absolutely unforgivable. Absolutely.

KOU is the highest rank given, followed by OTSU, HEI, TEI, and BO.

TOUGE...

PRIMAL GODS IN ANCIEN...

KENJI TSURUBUCHI

Translation: **KO RANSOM** Lettering: **ABIGAIL BLACKMAN**

TOGEONI Vol. 3
©Kenji Tsurubuchi 2020
First published in Japan in 2020 by KADOKAWA CORPORATION, Tokyo.
English translation rights arranged with KADOKAWA CORPORATION, Tokyo through TUTTLE-MORI AGENCY, INC., Tokyo.

English translation © 2024 by Yen Press, LLC

Yen Press
150 West 30th Street, 19th Floor
New York, NY 10001

Visit us at yenpress.com
facebook.com/yenpress • twitter.com/yenpress
yenpress.tumblr.com • instagram.com/yenpress

First Yen Press Edition: April 2024
Edited by Abigail Blackman and Yen Press Editorial: Carl Li
Designed by Yen Press Design: Lilliana Checo, Wendy Chan

Yen Press is an imprint of Yen Press, LLC.
The Yen Press name and logo are trademarks of Yen Press, LLC.

The publisher is not responsible for websites
(or their content) that are not owned by the publisher.

Library of Congress Control Number: 2023938326

ISBNs: 978-1-9753-6261-4 (paperback)
       978-1-9753-6262-1 (ebook)

10 9 8 7 6 5 4 3 2 1

WOR

Printed in the United States of America